WORKING CLASS MOVEMENT IN INDIA IN THE WAKE OF GLOBALIZATION

Working Class Movement in India in the Wake of Globalization

Edited by

JOSE GEORGE

MANOJ KUMAR

DHARMENDRA OJHA

MANOHAR

2012

First published 2012

ISBN 978-81-7304-963-7

Published by

Ajay Kumar Jain *for*
Manohar Publishers & Distributors
4753/23 Ansari Road, Daryaganj
New Delhi 110 002

Typeset at

Digigrafics
New Delhi 110 049

Printed at

Salasar Imaging Systems
Delhi 110 035

To the fond memory of

Dr. Madhukar Kashinath Pandhe

(11 July 1925–20 August 2011)

A Veteran Leader of the Working Class

and a Committed Communist

Contents

Foreword

The Department of Civics and Politics of University of Mumbai had done a remarkable job by organizing a two-day national seminar on 'Working Class Movement in India: Past, Present and Future' on 24-5 September 2009. It was a unique attempt since it dealt with the subject which is grossly neglected in our country at the time being. It needs much more attention in view of its importance. I felt greatly privileged when I got an opportunity to submit the keynote address for the seminar. Several prominent trade union leaders and academicians contributed valuable papers which were followed by lively and thought-provoking discussions. It was one of the well-organized seminars on this subject that I have ever attended. The papers covered almost all the important aspects of the working class movement in India, making the exercise developing into a mini encyclopaedia of the movement.

The national seminar pointed out the achievements as well as shortcomings of the existing trade union movement in the country and valuable suggestions were put forward to strengthen the quality of the level of activities of our trade unions. Some of the speakers underlined the experience of the international trade union movement and tried to apply in the present Indian context. The working class of India is the most organized sector of our contemporary society which can play an important role in developing public opinion in India in favour of a social transformation. Whether this role is played effectively in the present social set-up is a question being debated at a national level and various views are being expressed today in the country.

The trade union movement in the past had to face oppressive measures by the foreign rulers who had considered trade union movement as a conspiracy to throw over the yoke of foreign power. At present, it is facing several challenges by the policies of globalization and structural adjustment programme. It is a matter to be seriously pondered over today that what strategy and approach should be undertaken by the trade union movement so that it can play a crucial role in the coveted objective of social transformation. Some seminar papers succinctly have noted the growing trend of confining only to economism and lack of participation of the working class in political struggles which is adversely affecting the role of trade unions in the present period. The trade union movement is facing several challenges today after the dismantling of socialism in Soviet Union and eastern Europe. The working class people face attacks on their living standards, working conditions and social security. The inability of the working class to fight these challenges due to the disunity in the ranks of the trade union movement has been reflected in these seminar papers as well as in the discussions followed.

Despite difference in the views expressed by various speakers, the level of criticism and dissent was of a higher level which resulted in a meaningful outcome. The 25 papers and 22 abstracts received by the University of Mumbai expressed varied thinking prevailing in the country. However, the common emphasis was always on the significance of the role of working class movement in the present social economic situation in the country. Some of the papers are no doubt critical of the present state of affairs in the trade union movement. However, their approach is to emphasize the need for an improved role of the trade unions to meet the present challenging situation. Though there were occasions during the seminar when participants expressed diametrically opposing views, there was a clarity of thinking which resulted in better understating of each other's views. The persistent differences underlined the need for further debate to arrive at common understanding on issues under discussion. The approaches to the problem by the academicians and trade union representatives were of different trajectories. Even then they could find a common ground in a general manner which contributed to the success of the seminar.

The running thread of the discussion during the seminar was on the multiplicity of trade unions leading to lack of unity in approach which drastically reduced the collective bargaining strength of the working class. The employers have been taking advantage of the situation to their benefit adversely affecting the growth of trade unionism in the country. So to enhance the credibility of the trade union movement, the leadership should rise to the occasion and overcome the present discordant state of affairs in the overall interest of the working class, the speakers emphasized. However, situation has changed since then. Trade union movement in India came together during 2010 on a common platform despite their ideological differences as well as international affiliations. A joint movement of trade unions was organized on some major issues, such as, checking the rising prices of essential commodities; creation of more jobs; ensuring proper and effective implementation of the labour laws; improving the conditions of the unorganized labour and stopping the disinvestment of profit-making public sector undertakings. All the national trade unions, supporters and opponents of the government of India, have joined their hands in the common struggles to protect the interest of the working class. Thus, the idea expressed on future perspective of the trade union movement is already in the process of catching the imagination of the trade union leadership. The trade unions have risen to the occasion and realized that only through their unity they can effectively defend the interest of the working class.

Dr. Jose George and his team of committed organizers deserve congratulations for the painstaking efforts they had undertaken to hold this national seminar. They have done a systematic preparatory work to organize submission of such a large number of papers and meaningful debate despite different contradictory views. The publication of the papers submitted in the seminar will be extremely useful for trade union cadres as well as students of labour economics in understanding the working class movement as it exists today and the perspective it visualizes.

New Delhi M.K. PANDHE
6 June 2011

Preface

Indian economy, society and polity have been undergoing fundamental changes since Independence and particularly during the last three decades. One prominent area of these changes is the structure, consciousness, role and the movements of the significant classes, especially among the Indian working class. This encompasses not only the organized industrial workers, but also the vast majority of the unorganized industrial and non-industrial urban and rural working class.

Decades of the 1950s and 1960s witnessed government investments for the industrialization process of the country through public sector undertakings and organized struggle of the working class for wage rise and trade union rights. End of 1980s and 1990s, witnessed the ushering in of a new phenomenon called 'globalization' in our economy which was accompanied by the fall of Soviet Union and other socialist countries, the erstwhile bastions of the working class. The international 'non-state actors' like the World Trade Organization and other international financial institutions have increasingly started assuming the role of 'quasi-state powers' and have been shaping the developmental as well as the political processes with a special emphasis on 'governance'.

Liberalized markets, globalized trade and marginalization or contraction of the 'state-power' in the area of economic matters and welfare activities have fuelled the immense mobility, flexibility and the capability of capital *vis-à-vis* labour. The global monopoly capital, especially the finance capital, while strengthening its hegemonic hold over not only material, but also intellectual spheres of social life, has also sharpened the contradictions in our society and polity. These techno-commercial changes in the industrial as well as services sector have led to reorganization of the production process and restructuring of the work organization. This in turn has led to diverse effects in developing and developed countries all over the world and to a new international division of labour. Outsourcing, informalization and feminization of labour are becoming the hallmark of this 'new international division of labour'. The major industrial centres or the metropolitan cities in India are undergoing structural changes encompassing the changes in the composition and relations of various classes, particularly the working class. The new lifestyle, consumerism and cultural-ideological changes poured and propagated by the media and entertainment industry have also taken a firm grip over the daily lives and the consciousness of the working masses in India.

How has the Indian working class and its movement responded to these changes? These changes have challenged not only the striking capability of the working class, but also the very survival and legitimacy of the working class movement in countries like India. Earlier the post-Industrial Revolution period and the resultant exploitative capitalist production necessitated mobilization of the most exploited working class section of the society to effect social transformation along the lines of humanist goals at the global level. The nature and pattern of the working class resistance in various countries of the world including India was mainly guided by the ideology of communism, according to which, only working class has the revolutionary potential capable of taking lead in the process of social transformation. In India, the development of class consciousness among workers, especially in industrial sector and their mobilization against the capitalist exploitative forces began in the early twentieth century which continued despite ups and downs at various stages of its historical development.

Various political parties tried to channellize the discontent and anger of urban and rural working class to bring about changes in the character of the socio-economic order of the Indian society. The working class movement played its vital role in adding content of socio-economic goals to the Indian national movement. The movements of the workers (industrial and non-industrial) achieved success not only in compelling state to make policies and implement them in the interest of workers, but also contributed to strengthen the secular democratic and federal character of Indian polity and society. But the post-1990 phase, especially after the collapse of Soviet Union and the weakening of progressive and socialist forces at global scale, saw the onslaught of liberal economic policies in the name of development and economic growth. The new economic policies create illusions of economic betterment of society, but in reality, they are proved to be detrimental to the interests of the working class. The agenda of globalization has changed the process of capitalist production with effective use of the tools of revolution in information and communication technology and proved exploitative and oppressive in more subtle and sophisticated forms. Sufferings of the working class have increased and the identification of the contradiction remains elusive that leads to the decline of workers' movement as well as the revival of the medieval tendencies of communalism, casteism and linguistic chauvinism. It necessitates the identification of evils of this capitalist mode of production and changing economic order with an aim to mitigate the eruption of sufferings of workers and to find out a sustainable solution.

Against the backdrop of all these developments, the Department of Civics and Politics, University of Mumbai organized a national seminar on the theme 'Working Class Movement in India' during 24–5 September 2009. The objectives of the seminar was to bring together a multidisciplinary group of researchers, academicians, trade unions leaders and political activists to have a dialogue between various groups to arrive at an understanding on the role of trade union in shaping the Indian society, polity and economy; to see how far the trade union succeeded to protect the interest of the working class in raising their economic conditions and political consciousness and to assess the efforts made by the trade union movements to combat the onslaught of neo-liberalism and globalization on Indian working class in recent years.

The seminar commenced with the keynote address by M.K. Pandhe, an eminent scholar and then president of the Centre of Indian Trade Unions. The presentation by him located the working class movement in India and mapped out their contemporary relevance in the era of globalization. The sessions of the seminar covered themes on working class movements in India—emergence and growth; working class movement—aspects of ideology, programme and strategy; working class movements in the industrial sector; the emergence and struggles of the modern rural working class and its problems; working class movements in the era of liberalization, globalization and privatization and the working class movement in India *vis-à-vis* the various political streams, state responses and the challenges ahead. The seminar concluded with a brilliant presentation by Professor Prabhat Patnaik, an eminent economist from Jawaharlal Nehru University, New Delhi.

A number of scholars, college and university teachers, trade union activists, political leaders, representatives of non-governmental organizations and policy makers participated and made presentations in the seminar on different aspects of working class movements in

India. The selected papers presented in the seminar and some of the papers submitted later are included in this book. We wish to record our debt to many scholars and friends who helped to publish this book. Since a number of people were involved to carry out the present work, it is impossible to thank them all by name. Nevertheless, some at least must be mentioned. The success of the seminar and publication of this book has become a reality with the committed involvement of the colleagues and students of the Department of Civics and Politics of Mumbai University. We are thankful to all contributors, especially M.K. Pandhe, who inspired us by delivering the keynote address and writing a foreword to this book. Unfortunately, Dr. M.K. Pandhe (11.7.1925–20.8.2011), a veteran trade Unionist and senior Polit Bureau member of the CPI(M), passed away before the publication of this book. The country has lost one of its foremost leaders who actively involved himself in organizing and mobilizing the working classes for more than seven decades. The working class and progressive sections of the society will always cherish the contributions and sacrifices that he made and as a mark of respect, we are dedicating this book to him. We are deeply indebted to Leela P.S. for going through the papers thoroughly and making valuable suggestions. We are really indebted to Avinash Khandare, research scholar with the Department of Civics and Politics for taking all the pain, including preparing and printing the abstracts of the papers presented in the seminar. We are obliged to P.R. Krishnan, a well-known trade union leader and columnist for helping in organizing the seminar and persuading trade union leaders to contribute papers for the seminar and for this book.

Special thanks are due to our colleagues from academic fraternity including Anuradha Kalhan, P.G. Jogdand, Arvind Ganacharya and Kanchana Mahadevan for helping the publication of this important work in very many ways. We are deeply indebted to the concerned persons of Mumbai University's administration department, especially the General Administration and Finance for providing financial assistance toward the publication of this book. Finally, we are thankful to Ramesh Jain and his team at Manohar Publishers & Distributors, New Delhi for an excellent designing and printing job.

We hope that the present volume will not only help the scholars, academics, activists and policy makers in understanding the complex dynamics of capital-labour relationship and its impact on working class life in India, but also generate hope among the toiling masses that as value creators, they have the right to perform for general transformation and welfare of the society.

JOSE GEORGE
MANOJ KUMAR
DHARMENDRA OJHA

Contributors

V.B. ATHREYA (venkatesh.athreya@gmail.com) is currently a Visiting Professor with the Tata Institute of Social Sciences, Mumbai and an advisor to M.S. Swaminathan Research Foundation, Chennai.

ASHOK BANERJI (nwucitu@dataone.in) is the President of the General Employees Union, Mumbai.

JOSE GEORGE (josegeorgem@hotmail.com) is a Professor and former Head of the Department of Civics and Politics, University of Mumbai.

M.A. HUSSAIN (prof.m.a.hussain@gmail.com) is a former Professor with the Department of Political Science and Public Administration, S.V. University, Tirupati, Andhra Pradesh.

SRINATH JAGANNATHAN (srinath.jayanti@gmail.com) is a Fellow with the Indian Institute of Management, Ahmedabad.

B. KRISHANAMURTHY (bkris53@gmail.com) is an Associate Professor with the Department of Politics and International Studies, Pondicherry University, Pondicherry.

P.R. KRISHNAN (comprkrishnan@hotmail.com) is the Secretary of the Centre of Indian Trade Unions, Maharashtra State Committee.

MANOJ KUMAR (manoj.harmony@gmail.com) is an Assistant Professor with the Department of Political Science and International Relations, Faculty of Social Sciences, Wollega University, Nekemte, Oromia State, Ethiopia.

M.M. LAWRENCE (citukerala@yahoo.com) is the national Secretary of the Centre of Indian Trade Unions (CITU).

B.N. MEHRISH (brijesh.mehrish@gmail.com) is the former Professor of the Department of Civics and Politics, University of Mumbai.

VIVEK MONTEIRO (vivekmonteiro@yahoo.com) is the Secretary of the Centre of Indian Trade Unions, Maharashtra State and the Convener of Asanghatit Kamgar Sanghatana, Mumbai.

UDAY NARKAR (udaynarkar@gmail.com) is a freelance writer and lecturer.

DHARMENDRA KUMAR OJHA (dksem2000@yahoo.com) was with the Oil & Natural Gas Corporation Ltd. as a Scientist and is a regular contributor to various literary and cultural periodicals and news magazines.

M.K. PANDHE was the President of the Centre of Indian Trade Unions (CITU) and a senior Polit Bureau member of the Communist Party of India (Marxist).

SANGEETA N. PAWAR (sangeetanp@gmail.com) is an Associate Professor, Department of Commerce, University of Mumbai.

C. NAGARAJA RAO (c_n_rao@yahoo.com) is the former Additional Director, Department of Municipal Administration, Government of Andhra Pradesh.

R. RAMAKUMAR (ramakumarr@gmail.com) is an Associate Professor at the Centre for Development Studies, School of Social Sciences, Tata Institute of Social Sciences, Mumbai.

P.N. SAMANT (dadasamant@indiatimes.com) is the President of the Kamghar Aghadi, Mumbai.

KUMAR SHIRALKAR (kumarshiralkar@gmail.com) is the Vice-President of the All India Agricultural Workers' Union (AIAWU) and a Central Committee member of the Communist Party of India (Marxist).

ANURADHA KALHAN SIDDIQUI (anuradhakalhan@yahoo.com) is an Associate Professor and the Head of the Department of Economics, Jaihind College, Mumbai.

ASHOK KUMAR SINGH (ashokksdc@rediffmail.com) is an Associate Professor with the Department of Political Science, Kunwar Singh P.G. College, Ballia, Uttar Pradesh.

RAKHI SINGH (rakhibhu2@gmail.com) is an Assistant Professor, Department of Political Science, DAV Postgraduate College, Varanasi, Uttar Pradesh.

K. SRINIVASULU (srinivasulukarli@gmail.com) is a Professor in the Department of Political Science, Osmania University, Hyderabad.

P.C. RETHI THAMPATTY (rethithampatty@yahoo.com) is an Associate Professor of Commerce in the Zamorin's Guruvayurappan College, Kozhikode, Kerala.

KISHORE KUMAR THECKEDATH (djay25@rediffmail.com) is the former President of the All India Federation of College and University Teachers Organizations (AIFUCTO) and is, currently, the Editor of the *Teachers of the World*.

B. VENUGOPAL (venugopal2snc@yahoo.com) is an Associate Professor at the Postgraduate and Research Department of Political Science, Sree Narayana College, Kollam, Kerala.

ABDULRAHIM VIJAPUR (vijapur_rahim@rediffmail.com) is a Professor and the Chairman, Department of Political Science, Aligarh Muslim University, Aligarh.

CHAPTER 1

Introduction

Neoliberalism and Working Class Interests: Need for Revitalizing the Movement

JOSE GEORGE AND MANOJ KUMAR

The working class movement emerged and started growing during the nineteenth century as a product of the socio-economic circumstances created by the industrial revolution. In the process of industrial development, there were two distinct classes, which were extremely opposite to each other from the point of view of privileges and positions in the social system. One, the rich or bourgeois class who possessed the ownership of means and forces of production and they held a hegemonic position in the society and also the capability to oppress and exploit the workers. Second, innumerable workers were the victims of constant and unbridled exploitation and oppression by the bourgeois class. Their life was of subhuman standard condemned to a position of vulnerability, while the bourgeoisie lived a life of luxury and domination, controlling all facets of social order.

The process of domination and oppression did not remain confined to the territory of nation states, but it was spread across the boundaries of countries making this phenomenon global in nature. This had given birth to a new era in the history of human civilization—the period of imperialism with direct and specific characteristics of colonizing and exploiting various parts of the world. The continuous process of exploitation was not limited to the industrial workers in the urban region, but also to the rural-based agricultural labourers and landless peasants where the feudal forces worsened the living conditions of poor and subjected them to inhuman conditions. The realization of the need of saving workers from further deterioration and for protecting their interests and improving their life sowed the seed of the working class movement which, in the course of time, pervaded various sectors—almost all. However, the workers in the formal sector were better organized than in the informal sectors.

The ideology of communism, a philosophy aiming at creating an exploitation-free, just, secular and humanist social order came to rescue the workers from the vicious circle of exploitation and suffering. There were several streams of organizations functioning for the alleviation of workers' pitiable conditions; most of them operating under the guidance of communism and communist parties. The working class movement grew in intensity and strength in different countries with the rise and growth of the communist movement at an international scale.

When the world was witnessing the intense workers' agitations and resistance against the tsarist regime in Russia in the beginning of the twentieth century, mill workers of Mumbai (then Bombay) registered a historic demonstration of their strength and will to fight against imperialistic forces by observing a mass strike in 1908 in protest against the arrest of a firebrand nationalist leader, Bal Gangadhar Tilak. The movement of workers in India continued progressing with the encouragement provided by the international communist movement, especially after the victory of the working class in the Bolshevik Revolution in October 1917. However, after securing a number of laurels to its credit from 1920s to 1980s, the movement, particularly the trade union movement started getting weakened during the 1990s. This process continued under the impact of global onslaught of the process of globalization pursuing the agenda of neoliberal economic policies with the help of neo-imperialist tools, such as the World Trade Organization (WTO), the International Monetary Fund (IMF) and the World Bank.[1]

The history of the working class movement in India began with the process of industrialization in the country. The regions near the ports like Bombay were more affected by industrialization during the period of British rule. They started industries related to railways and factories of jute, sugar and cement in different parts of India, drawing a substantial portion of workforce from rural areas. Due to the land-related exploitative colonial policy making, the life of peasantry was miserable in their native places and as a consequence the process of de-peasantization had begun. Industrial workers were working for extremely low wages in poor conditions. They even worked for unlimited hours around 14-15 hours without any safeguards at the time of accidents, injuries or illness. Besides, apart from class domination and exploitation, working class people were suffering caste prejudices and oppression in rural India.[2] Despite the multiplicity of workers' identities, such as caste, religion, region and language that impeded the development of class and political consciousness among workers, solidarity was developed among them and the All India Trade Union Congress (AITUC) as a national level umbrella organization of workers was formed. It raised the demands of workers belonging to various sectors.[3] The communist leaders were closely associated with the AITUC unions. Later, the union leaders like, N.M. Joshi, Deewan Chamanlal and others opposed the domination of unions by communists and formed a new trade union, the Indian Trade Union Federation. The working class movement suffered setbacks during 1930s because of repressive measures of the British regime against trade unions and communist leaders, besides the global economic meltdown. However, the trade union movement managed to not only survive, but also strengthened itself. During the final phase of the freedom movement, i.e. 1945-6, the workers' movements and their industrial actions made remarkable contributions to India's Independence.

Independent India adopted a policy of mixed economy keeping in view of the principles of social democracy and developmental efforts which were made by the governments and Indian bourgeois class in industrial and agricultural sectors. The Indian National Trade Union Congress (INTUC) was organized by the non-communist leadership and was controlled and dominated by the Congress party, whereas the AITUC was identified with the Communist Party of India (CPI). The Hind Mazdoor Sabha (HMS) was formed by the Socialist Party. When socialists developed cracks within their organization, the Rammanohar Lohia group formed their own union, the Hind Mazdoor Kisan Panchayat. The small factions of Leftists with allegiance to Revolutionay Socialist Party formed the United Trade Union Congress (UTUC). Other trade unions that emerged on the scene were: Bharatiya Mazdoor Sangh (BMS) that was connected with Jan Sangh (now BJP); Centre of Indian Trade Union (CITU) which emerged in 1970 and was identified with the Communist Party of India (Marxist) [CPI(M)]; Punjab Mazdoor Dal organized by the Akali Dal; Hind Mazdoor Panchayat; the All India Red Trade Union Congress, the National Labour Organization and National Federation of Indian Trade Union.

In 1982, the mill workers in Bombay went on a strike in huge numbers under the leadership of Datta Samant. It was a historical event in the trade union movement in India. This new development in working class movement disturbed all political parties, especially the Congress leaders and the latter started manipulating to break the union of the workers. Realizing this, Datta Samant, formed a political wing of the workers' union, the Kamgar Aghadi to counter the manipulation of trade unions by other political parties for political gains. Meanwhile, Shiv Sena, a regional party in Maharashtra, formed Bhartiya Kamgar Sena (BKS) which emerged as a powerful trade union in the state.

Workers' movements and trade union activities in urban regions and the movements of poor peasantry in rural areas of the country continued growing despite the manipulation of bourgeois elements to weaken such movements by causing a split in their organizations. The ideological difference within the communist movement itself finally led to the split in the CPI in 1964 and the economic crisis during the period of 1960s.[4]

Rural poor struggled against feudal oppression aiming to destroy the structures and processes of the class/caste domination and exploitation. The inefficient implementation of land reform measures except in Kerala and West Bengal proved to be another cause of agrarian unrest in various parts of the country in which poor and landless peasants actively participated. Whenever the working class movement and peasants' agitations accelerated, the government created illusions of fulfilling the demands and improving the conditions of peasants and workers, by making some provisions and claiming to implement them effectively.

The working class movement which grew stronger and remained substantially assertive in the 1960s and 1970s began losing its vigour after the 1980s in the fast changing situations characterized by lay off, retrenchment, closure of the industrial units, strategy of volunteer retirement scheme (VRS), contractual labour, recruitment of workers for fixed terms and with designations, like, officers and executives, so as to keep them away from union activities, declining role and power of labour welfare section in the industry and domination of human resource department catering to the needs and concerns of officials, etc. The condition of workers worsened in the context of new manipulative policies and tactics of corporate sector with the support of government, media and even judiciary. At the global level liberal economic policies are dominating the international economy against the backdrop of the collapse of socialist economics in eastern Europe and former Soviet Union. In post-1991, the problems of peasantry have also increased due to the special economic zones (SEZ) and acquisition of cultivable land in the name of development. Contractual farming and unfinished agenda of land reform measures aggravated the situation. As the industrial workers' occasional outbursts were witnessed in urban regions, peasants' resentment and frustration were finding expressions in the form of demonstrations and other ways in a scattered manner yielding no substantial results. The present scenario necessitates reorganization and sharpening of working class movements acquainted with its historical mission of proletarian revolution making it a vanguard agent[5] for transformation of prevailing socio-economic order.

The significant changes in the *modus operandi* of the global capitalism with its new ways of extracting surplus, characteristics of multinational and transnational corporations and the changing roles of nation states resulting from the change in internal dynamics of the capitalist mode of production would have its impact on various aspects of the society across the globe, particularly on the working class. The parasitic and predatory character of capital was manifested in different forms making it difficult for the labour to posit effective challenge to the capital.[6] The process of production, in the globalized period, appears to be decentralized but the decision-making and the process of accumulation of wealth are centralized benefitting the owners of the firms controlling from thousands of miles away from the site of operation of industrial units and business firms. One of the major reasons for the income and growth of the economy of the industrialists, business firms, especially of the multinationals is the availability of cheap labour. Absence of the scope of trade union activities and virtually non-existent labour laws also helped the present crisis. Long working hours, poor living conditions, no protective measures and cheap labour rate remind one of the conditions of workers during nineteenth century when the production activities and market mechanism were characterized by the free competition between and among the monopolistic capitalist forces with the involvement of the imperialistic countries in such phenomena at global scale that had made the lives of workers below human and pathetic. The achievements made by the sacrifices and struggle of the workers for their better life and living seem to be undone and reversed. Therefore, there is an urgent need to analyse the newly-emergent situation, understand the *modus operandi* of capital, its economic policy, politics and new ways of establishing ideological, political and cultural hegemony while identifying the challenges of the working class movement, its foes and friends, and determine the strategy and tactics so as to wage struggle to revive and revitalize the workers' movement to bring about a humanist change in the present socio-economic structures and processes. The realization of the need to initiate a new wave of workers' struggle for a better social order is reflected in various ways through the articles of this book which are revised versions of the papers presented during a national seminar on the theme 'Working Class Movement in India: Past, Present and Future' by the Department of Political Science and Civics, University of Mumbai.

This book is divided into five parts. The first part of the book comes under the title 'Emergence and Growth of Working Class Movement in India' deals with a general idea of the evolution of trade unionism among the working class people of India as well as the peasant movement. It reveals the role of the Left parties in making the movement widespread. It also highlights the challenges facing by the movement today. There are six papers under this part.

M.K. Pandhe in his paper 'Trade Union Movement in India at a Glance' discusses the challenges faced by the trade union movement. It describes the historical evolution and development of the movement that had been undergoing through various phases with its distinct features and trends. He also points out that the trade union movement faces a number of problems in the globalized period, besides serious division, dissentions and aberrations within the movement which have reduced its bargaining power. In the pre-Independence period, unbearable working and living conditions left the working class with no choice but to resist the practices of oppression and exploitation.

The demands of the workers in the British regime were; limitation of the duration of work to eight hours a day, weekly off, increase in wage rate, compensation for injuries during accidents, etc. Thus began the resistance movement of the workers leading to the consequences, such as, destruction of machines by the workers, instances of workers beating their supervisors, resorting to protest methods, such as, strikes including occasional clashes inside the factory. The formation of the AITUC in 1920 was a milestone in the history of the trade union movement and indicated the growth of workers' consciousness and their movement. In post-Independent

India, legislations were enacted to improve the conditions of the workers but many of the provisions remained unimplemented. The globalization process proved to be highly detrimental to the workers' interests as the major focus of the industrial and business activities was confined to profit-making objectives at the cost of labourers' interests in organized as well as unorganized sectors. Insecurity of job and low wage rates without any protective measures in the time of difficulties and adversities, loss of employment and downsizing of manpower as a cost-cutting measure have become the major characteristics of the process of production and development. The public sector firms started getting closed down and the idea of economic development with social justice became a part of history.

The author highlights the challenges encountered by the movement while focusing on its prospects. He presents a number of causes for the internal weaknesses of the trade unionism, such as, multiplicity of trade union organizations, the phenomenon of undemocratic functioning of trade unions and divisions within trade unions, etc. Individual interests, ambiguity in legislations, virtual non-implementation of the labour laws, corruption in labour administrative departments, inefficient and biased labour-related judicial system, biased method of verification of membership to the trade unions, subordination of labour ministry, decline of tripartism for resolution of industrial disputes, ignoring the rights of women workers and their declining membership to the trade unions, marginalization and harassment of women in workplaces as well as within the trade unions, increasing incidences of child labour, worsening conditions of workers in information technology sector and denial of benefits of labour laws to the workers of the SEZs are the main reasons for the weakness of trade unionism. He makes some remedial suggestions for the success of the trade union movement and improvement in the life of workers. In his opinion, the formation of the confederation of trade unions as an interim arrangement is possible to revitalize the movement. The merger of trade unions does not seem to be a possibility in the near future. Trade unions should work for a common cause and should emphasize the practice of democratic functioning of the trade unions.

M.M. Lawrence in 'Working Class Movement in Kerala' describes the emergence, evolution and growth of the working class movement in Kerala, including the current scenario. Also he has given an overview of the cultural-historical background of the social order rooted in caste system. Coir and tile factories and tea plantations heralded the advent of industrial era in the state. Though the large-scale industrial employment in Kerala began in the tea plantation sector, it was the coir factory workers of Alleppy who pioneered to form a trade union. The first labour strike took place in 1907 to protest against the 12-hour work norm prevalent in the Derragh Smail & Company that resulted in reduction in hours of work by one and half hours. Vadapuram B.K. Bava was the main driving force in the formation of a union of workers in Alleppey that was known as the Labour Union. In April 1922, the Travancore Labour Association (TLA) came into existence which was later registered as the Travancore Coir Factory Workers' Union (TCFWU) under the Travancore Trade Union Act of 1937. The major demands of TCFWU were increase in wage rates, improvement in working conditions, guarantee of minimum earnings, abolition of contract labour and prohibition of illegal deductions in workers' wages.

In the plantation sector, trade union emerged in 1930 in Mundakayam. The All Travancore Trade Union Congress was formed as a platform for all Left-oriented trade unions in the state. The difference between radical communists and socialists on the issue of Quit India movement led to a split among the workers' organizations. Alleppey had become the hotbed of the communist movement and even mass armed struggle was considered as an appropriate option to achieve the goal of social change. Later this movement had spread to other parts and inspired the strikes of Kozhikode Commonwealth Cotton Mill labourers, cashew and tile factory workers in Quilon district, etc. The unions and Left parties succeeded in getting some of the cashew factories nationalized.

In 1946, peasants revolted in Punnapra-Vayalar and workers in Alleppey declared a general strike that led to armed conflicts between workers and the police. It was a turning point in the history of working class movements in Kerala. Although the tripartite system was adopted and Industrial Relation Committees (IRCs) were formed, including establishment of labour department, the political orientation of the unions was not accepted which resulted in the imposition of a ban on the Communist Party and pro-communist trade unions. AITUC, a central trade union organization, remained as an umbrella trade union organization for all communist-oriented trade unions until 1970. The ideological difference within the party led to the formation of the CITU later. Generally, workers belonging to different sectors, such as coir and cashew factories, plantations, services such as ports, road transport, shipping, etc., including brick and mortar industries as well as self-employed and artisans are organized and have their own trade unions. However, migrant workers are not organized so far. Ideological leanings amongst new generations of workers are in a decline.

V.B. Athreya in his paper 'Workers' Struggles and Challenges Ahead' narrates various phases and trends, process of emergence, growth and decline, of the working class movements in India facing exploitation and oppression of pre-capitalist, colonial and capitalist elements that were aggravated by the obscurantism because of their different identities and affiliation to caste, religion, region, etc. He also focuses on the challenges that the movement is facing in the post-1980s period due to the process of liberalization, privatization and globalization (LPG).

The workers' movement played an important role during the freedom movement. The country witnessed economic growth for a brief period but entered a phase of crisis from the mid-1960s to the end of the 1970s. However, the working class continued expanding significantly despite major differences within the communist movement. In the decade of 1980s, working class rights and trade unions faced repression from the capitalist forces due to rise of finance capital and liberal economic policies. Trade unions in India could not remain unaffected and encountered constraints as a result of passage of the National Security Act (NSA) and the Essential Services Maintenance Act (ESMA). The pace of weakening of the trade unions increased after the collapse of socialist economics by the end of the 1980s and attack on trade unions by the capitalist-imperialist forces. The process of LPG and the phase of neoliberal reforms posed a great challenge to the working class movement, especially in the wake of collapse of socialism in many countries and a strong ideological offensive launched by the capitalist elements forcing trade unions to wage a defensive struggle when the state began supporting interests of international and domestic capital while ignoring the interests of working class. The United Progressive Alliance government passed two important pro-people Acts; the National Rural Employment Guarantee Act (NREGA) and the Tribal Forest Rights Act (TFRA) which were substantially influenced by the progressive forces but remained committed to the neoliberal economic policies even after witnessing a global economic crisis that made the advanced capitalist economies to seek greater regulation of non-state actors.

The working class movement is facing immense challenges today. A small portion of the workforce has regular employment while the major portion is engaged either in casual/contractual or in self-employed work with a substantial portion of workforce depending on land and pre-capitalist relations. The challenges of the working class are compounded by the forces of obscurantism and identity politics. The divisions of caste, religion, language and ethnicity continue to influence the consciousness of workers making the task of developing the class and political consciousness of the working class a major challenge. The working class movement can advance only through a relentless struggle against both neoliberal policies and obscurantist forces of all hues. The current global economic crisis and the bankruptcy of neoliberalism provide an opportunity for the movement to make a successful advance.

B. Krishnamurthy in his paper 'Movement of Left Trade Unions in French India' discusses the role played by the working class in the freedom movement in French India. The working class movement, first, demanded and secured labour rights, and thereafter, political freedom from the yoke of French colonialists. The workers' condition in French India was pitiable; long hours of work from about 12 to 14 hours, no job security, no compensation in case of accident and injury, forced work without weekly off in poor condition.

The workers' movement began in 1908 with the demand for an increase in their wages and against retrenchment of some of their co-workers. The movement was suppressed because of the bickering within the working class. By 1935, the working class movement grew stronger and forced the mill owners to accept their demand for reduction in working hours and increase in wage rates. The workers succeeded in achieving better labour rights as their movement kept on growing stronger encouraging them to make serious efforts for achieving political right to self-determination and political privileges.

The colonial authorities tried to create dissention within the nationalist movement and temporarily, they succeeded in doing so, but finally, the French India territory was united with the Indian union in November 1954, in which the Leftists, particularly, the French India Communist Party played an important role.

Ashok Kumar Singh in his 'Peasants' Struggle and Freedom Movement' focuses on the role of peasant movements during the freedom struggle of India after the First World War. It also mentions the historical background of the peasant movement during the nineteenth century, before the outbreak of the First World War.

The peasants of India were badly exploited which left them with no choice but to rise against the exploitation of the zamindars, moneylenders and British rule. In the beginning, the movements of peasants were not well-organized but often emerged spontaneously in different parts of the country. The peasant movements grew stronger and became more organized after the First World War.

These movements were guided more effectively by the communist ideology of class-based struggle which was not acceptable to Congress in general, and Mahatma Gandhi in particular, as the latter believed in cooperation and reconciliation between peasants and zamindars. He gave more emphasis on the national movement. Powerful leaders like Swami Sahajanand Saraswati and Rahul Sankrityayan led the movement. During and after the 1940s, the movement came closer to the Marxist ideology and was mostly guided and led by the communists.

The second part is called 'Aspects of Ideology, Programme and Strategy of Working Class Movement', and presents seven papers. Anuradha Kalhan in her paper titled 'Working Class and the Insecurity Hypothesis' focuses on the phenomena of increasing insecurities across sectors, including the ones that have been traditionally considered secured, for example, the public sectors which are empirically measurable. The author argues, on the basis of the empirical studies conducted in the member states of the Organization for Economic Cooperation and Development (OECD), such as, United Kingdom, the United States, including some developing countries, like, India, that this phenomenon is global in nature as even the workforce belonging to the developed countries faces the risk and uncertainty of insecurity. Such recent unstable and uncertain changes in employment relations have become a part of the essential features of the contemporary social life.

Job insecurity leads to social, political, economical and psychological consequences. It is in this context that the phrase 'insecurity hypothesis' is referred to. The central proposition of the insecurity hypothesis is that the economic risk of increased global competition is being passed on from the employer to the employee which is constantly increasing. The long-term consequence affects productivity and economic performance as in times of rapid economic and technological change. The insufficient management of social and human capital can become a limiting factor to growth. The factors that make the workers insecure are measurable, such as, spells of unemployment, number of jobs changed due to organizational decisions, time spent in searching another job, time period of unemployment, decreasing or stagnant real wages, hours of work, contingent employment, etc.

Employment in the developed countries has become insecure in both continuity and the level of remuneration which indicates a clear shift from the earlier pattern in which internal labour markets shielded workers from the affect of market forces. The difficulty of finding replacement work has risen since the early 1980s. The compounded nature of the insecurity has resulted from the heightened global competition for economic growth and dominance, structural and technological changes in the economy, and the national systems of regulation that have created flexible labour markets, adverse changes in benefit systems, pressure to accept flexible terms of employment, attenuation of individual employment rights, increase in the qualifying period for the right, not to be unfairly dismissed (from six months to two years), severe and continuous decline in trade union strength and bargaining power. This trend of insecurity is not confined to a particular section of society or sector of work but involves various sectors and class of workers and professionals.

D.K. Ojha in his paper 'Working Class in Mumbai: A Perspective' describes the social, economic, political and economic aspects of society in Mumbai with a special focus on the life and working conditions of the labourers that constitute almost 75 per cent of the city's population. Mumbai city, that once used to be the centre of working class activism, has been converted into contentious ground of fraternal conflicts on parochial issues of traditional identities like, region, religion, language and caste, especially after the mid-1960s when the Shiv Sena driven by regional aspirations emerged and started expanding at the expanse of the communist base. Mumbai began to witness the continuous decline of Left forces, particularly, working class movement after the emergence of Shiv Sena. The Left influence on workers diminished to great extent creating a space for occupation and intervention by some other effective political force which was occupied by neo-emergent regional political power of Shiv Sena. The emergence of non-economic issues and dominance of the regional, communal and parochial politics suited the scheme of the rule of the capital.

The advent of the phase of the LPG transformed Mumbai into a city of service industry from that of the textile industry. The erstwhile industries in which a large number of workers worked were closed down by declaring them as sick industries, thus escaping from the liabilities that the industrialists-employers owed to the workers, and/ or industrial firms were shifted to new places where labour was available at cheap rates. The face of the city has undergone a process of metamorphosis and it is now alien to its own people. The working class assertion has declined and capitalist design triumphed making the life of working class in the city pitiable. Besides, distortion in their economic, social and cultural life, they encounter the crisis of their political identity and affiliation. Instead of having their own political parties, they find themselves divided into and appendages of various political parties using them and their political privileges for their own class interest. Capitalist forces hide the real issues related to the life of common people preventing them from developing as a political class on the basis of class consciousness and solidarity through media projection and capitalist ideological propaganda with the help of capital-oriented writers and ideologues.

Ashok Banerji in 'Capitalist Labour Process and its Consequences' focuses on the impact of changes on labour process as a result of development of capitalist mode of production and its consequences on forces of labour. In the early period of Industrial Revolution, the power of capital over labour was limited despite of despotic control because the machinery and division of labour were insignificant, as employers relied heavily on handicraft and domestic production. In the course of time, the large-scale workshops replaced domestic work. At this stage, there was more emphasis on reorganizing work than on mechanizing it.

Large-scale production and mechanized factories needed technological and economic change that reached its peak in the mid-nineteenth century which has been described by Marx as a particular stage in the development of the labour process. He argues that in the contemporary period, capitalist labour process has not remained confined to manufacturing of commodities through blue colour labour in the factories, but involved the white colour labour in the office. Changes in labour process and labour markets generated three major changes in economy at the global level: (1) flexible accumulation based on market liberalization, (2) commodification of services by the 1970s and 1980s, and (3) the digital exchange—the exchange of products and labour is increasingly supported by an electronic infrastructure rather than paper documents or paper money.

K.K. Theckedath in 'Teachers' Movement as a Potential Ally of the Working Class Movement' contends that the teachers' movement can be considered as an ally not only of the workers' movement for achievement of welfare measures and improvement in their condition, but also in accomplishment of the historic task of the revolutionary overthrow of the capitalist system and the building of a socialist society. Unlike other sections of the middle classes engaged in trade, banking and credit, advertising, and other such professions, teachers create surplus value, in the sphere of production. Their participation in the transfer of value in the sphere of distribution makes them an ally of the workers in the process of creating surplus value.

In terms of historical evolution and features, the teachers' movement and the working class movement shared commonalities, for instance, in the period of their emergence and methods of strikes. The historical events of the working class movement are evidence to this fact that the teachers' movement had played an important role in the working class movement by participating in a number of agitations and struggles waged by the workers' organizations.

The author emphasizes the need of waging an ideological struggle besides and on par with the economic and political struggles to promote the interest of the workers and also to ensure the successful achievement of the goals of working class movement. The teaching class represents a reserve force and can help working class movements in countering the ideological attacks on socialism.

Vivek Monteiro in his 'Need for Social Scientific Studies for Organizing the Unorganized Sector in India' argues that the neoliberal policies of LPG are on a decline across the globe, including India which is manifested in defeat of the Bharatiya Janata Party (BJP)-led government of National Democratic Alliance (NDA) in 2004.

The struggle of the trade unions and opposition of the Left parties to the expansion of the process of the LPG have succeeded to some extent in checking its growth in India and averting the collapse of the financial, energy and infrastructural sectors. Monteiro criticizes the second National Labour Commission Study for its unscientific methodology and characteristics aimed at complete dilution of labour laws while he emphasizes the need for scientific studies on a number of issues. Such as, relation between development and energy consumption, use of resources for social sector expenditure and social security measures, labour market legislation and the organization of the workers in an unorganized sector, problem of food security and the provision of public distribution system and energy related legislation, particularly to understand the anatomy of the unorganized sector so as to evolve a compatible strategy and programme to organize the workers belonging to the unorganized sector as an essential element for amelioration of the workers' condition.

P.R. Krishnan in 'Broken Pledges of Constitutional Mandates and the Anti-People Role of Judiciary' makes a reference to the constitutional provisions that guarantee the social, political, economical, religious, educational and cultural rights of the people of India. The judiciary organ of the government has set a precedent of delivering judgements in the interest of people and society.

There are a number of instances when the judiciary declared *ultra vires* the legislations by the legislative wing of the government if they were not in the interest of common people and in larger interest of society. The credibility that the judiciary established for itself seems to be diminishing and vanishing. Under the influence of the policy and process of the LPG, the scene in India is changing. The government is undertaking policy and programmes under the direction of the World Trade Organization, International Monetary Fund and the World Bank.

The principles of democracy and the interests of the workers are no longer important for the judicial system. It is unreasonably imposing restrictions on the democratic rights of the workers to voice their dissent and grievance against the governments and officials. Their rights are violated, the interests of the working class are ignored and workers are left to defend for themselves. The character and functioning of the judicial organs have become insensitive to the people's concerns and needs, thus disregarding the constitutional provision of social and economic justice by the very institutions that are expected to honour the principle and provisions of the constitutions in the interest of society and the country.

Srinath Jagannathan in 'Work Processes: Insights from Theatre of the Oppressed' discusses that the labour process creates insecurities and the workers resist against the process of marginalization, oppression and injustices in their own unique ways that have been presented through an imagery of the theatre of the oppressed. This paper focuses on how work processes can become a site for aesthetic introspection for workers. It also finds how the workers conscientize themselves, understand the contradictions and seek creative solutions for the problems that arise in the processes of emancipation.

The involvement of the workers in everyday aesthetics is a programme of theatre of the oppressed. As a victim of insecurity, the workers struggle to transform the oppressive work processes in which they participate and transform them through an aesthetic practice. Work processes are a theatre in which the workers, who are oppressed by insecurity, can creatively discover liberating practices. The author argues that the politics of the theatre of the oppressed is the politics of making the oppressors feel ashamed. The labour process of accessing justice is the politics of shame that seeks to destabilize the legitimacy apparatus of the state, for failing in its responsibility to protect and promote the interests of its citizens. The theatrical practice of shaming the oppressor is the assertion of the humanity of the oppressed and their refusal to be subordinated by hegemonic practices. The theatre of the oppressed critiques the processes of subordination and raises their conscientized voices to transform the work processes of subordination. The conscientized pedagogy of the oppressed is the labour process of learning to perceive social, political and economic contradictions and to take action against the oppressive elements. The resistance that reflects the concepts of the theatre of the oppressed is an important method for regenerating their humanity. This represents post-structural approaches to workers' resistance.

According to the author, the aims of the theatre of the oppressed are a method for reading and enacting workers' actions that seek to humanize the work processes in which they are situated. The stateless workers seek to humanize work processes by protesting against the marginalizations that they are subjected to while the unorganized sector workers refuse to see themselves merely as spectators in the enactment of the city's universalist ideals, which renders them homeless and poor, but see themselves as creative actors who contribute to the city, and therefore, resist domination and injustice. Contract workers challenge the unjust deprivations that they are subjected to. The organized sector workers make efforts to destroy the processes that subordinate them and resort to resistance with an aim to transform the conventional configurations of work processes. From the imagery of the theatre of the oppressed, workers are challenging the oppressive structures by coming on to public stages intending to shame the oppressors and appealing to their conscience while discerning the contradictions embedded in work processes and seek a humanist transformation of these processes. The theatre of the oppressed is thus an attempt to transform society.

The third part of the book is 'Experience of Working Class Movement: Urban Industrial Sector' which comprises six papers. Jose George and Manoj Kumar in their paper 'Democratization of Industrial Management: The Kamani Experience from Mumbai' discuss the idea and process of the democratization of industrial management with special reference to the experiment in Kamani Tubes Limited (KTL) located in Mumbai. The takeover of the management of the KTL in 1988 by the workers' cooperative which was closed down in 1985 has been marked as a unique experiment in the history of the trade union movement in India. The authors focus on the problems faced by the workers' union and leadership during the process of takeover and operation.

The paper, on the basis of examination of the constraining factors that led to the failure of this unique historical experiment, makes an attempt to ascertain the feasibility of workers' takeover and management of the ailing industrial firms, officially, sick industries, while making suggestions for success of management of industries by the workers unions. KTL which was established in 1959 made remarkable progress for more than a decade. Then it started declining and ailing due to ensuing feuds within the family of employer, mismanagement, corruption and financial crunch and finally it was closed in 1885. The process of takeover of this ailing industrial unit under the provision of the Sick Industrial Companies (Special Provisions) Act, 1987, was arduous but after its takeover by the workers' union, it began showing the signs of satisfactory progress which, unfortunately, remained for a short period of about three years and then in early 1990s, began collapsing due to, mainly, uncooperative attitude of the state and its administrative and financial institutions, lack of sufficient working capital, the impact of neoliberal economic policies, disturbed social atmosphere in the aftermath of the demolition and resultant outbreak of religious violence, including the lack of workers' indoctrination and training in cooperative culture and practices.

Workers' union is still struggling for the arrears of its members and against the manipulation of capitalist elements, particularly promoters, however, without a hope of reviving the operation of this industrial unit. The paper argues that the takeover and management of sick industries could be successful if the workers were in a position of receiving cooperation and assistance from the state apparatus, besides training and indoctrination of workers in cooperative culture and their keen interest and efforts in development process.

K. Srinivasulu in his paper 'Handloom Weavers' Struggles in the Context of Liberalization' focuses on the neo-emergent crisis in handloom sector, particularly in Andhra Pradesh as a consequence of liberalized economic policies and reforms, including resultant mobilization of workers engaged in handloom industries to protest against the exploitative economic reforms initiated by the process of liberalization and the lack of protective measures. Handloom sector in India employs a major portion of workforce next only to agriculture. Andhra Pradesh, after Tamil Nadu, has the second largest concentration of handlooms in the country.

Crises in this sector began emerging since the 1980s affecting the survival factors of this sector, mainly due to the increase in the price of inputs, tough competition from the powerloom sector, half-hearted governmental response to the concerns and interests of this sector as well as the lack of effective implementation of the policy safeguards to protect this sector. Ineffective state support to the traditional occupational communities has led to an erosion of livelihoods and loss of employment. The insecurity of the weavers forced them to starve, some of them committed suicides, and some of them, finally, agitated against the policies and system responsible for their sufferings. The political parties too began expressing their solidarity with the agitating weaver-workers but only when the movement expanded with the help of civil society organizations and non-party independent intellectuals.

The author discusses the policy changes in the textile industries in general and the handloom sector in particular along with the impact of the policies in this sector with special focus on the policies of liberalized economic reform measures, the main factor responsible for the crises in this sector and the weavers' grassroot mobilization as a response to the current situation of crisis.

P.N. Samant in 'Working Class Movement in Individual Sector' focuses on the problems and challenges that the working class movement faces in the current era with a historical background of the working class movement in India. The author argues that the movement has undergone various phases of ups and downs and today the situation is entirely different that has posed a big threat to the interests of the workers.

In the post-Independent India, the trade union movement was

politicized and trade unions were largely used as instruments to serve the interests of political parties. This phenomenon of politicization of the trade union movement gained political benefits at the expense of workers' interests. A situation for a strong trade union movement having its own political wing was realized at the time of the formation of Kamgar Aghadi under the leadership of Datta Samant in the 1980s. Two and half lakh workers of the Bombay textile mills went on a strike which was the longest and strongest in the history of the trade union movement in India.

In the post-1990 period, the labour scene saw an oceanic change. Policies and mechanisms were adopted by the employers-industrialists not only to curtail the scope of trade unionism, but also to completely destroy the scope and activism of trade unions. As a result, the permanent employees are offered VRSs. Meanwhile, the process of appointing employees on contractual basis or for a fixed period of one or two years has become more and more common. This necessitates a rethinking on the nature, method and strategy for developing an effective working class movement.

M.A. Hussain and C. Nagaraja Rao in their paper 'Municipal Working Class Movement in Andhra Pradesh' reveal the struggle of the municipal workers, especially those who were engaged in menial works, such as, sweeping roads, cleaning drains, and manual scavenging. They had been struggling for amelioration of their condition and to lead a life with dignity but without much success because of the manipulation and manoeuvring of local politicians.

Besides, facing professional hazards, the workers' plight was aggravated because of non-payment of wages for several months forcing them to borrow money from private moneylenders at exorbitant high rates, thus getting caught in debt trap and leading a miserable life. The condition of workers was deteriorating after 1986 when the expenditure of municipalities began exceeding their income as a consequence of the stoppage of general revision of taxes on some pretext and their collection. The municipal workers went on strikes in 1986 demanding immediate payment of wages which they called off after getting assurance from the government which was not fulfilled. In 1991, the workers went on an indefinite fast demanding provincialization of municipal services. Again in 1993, the workers went on strikes with the same demand.

However, in 2009 after a long struggle, the state government decided to pay their monthly salary and allowances from the consolidated funds of the government. The Government of Andhra Pradesh issued an order of payment to the regular municipal health workers' salaries directly from the consolidated funds of the state which provided much needed solace to them. The government adopted a new measure of not filling the vacancies created due to retirement or death of municipal health workers and instead started to outsource contract workers. It also generated crisis among the workers. The contractor or supplying agency began exploiting workers by taking away half of the wage payable to the workers. These workers started agitation for payment of minimum wages with provisions for insurance coverage and provident fund which made the government direct all the urban local bodies to pay minimum prescribed wages to the workers with provident fund and insurance facilities that provided great relief to the outsourced public health workers.

P.C. Rethi Thampatty in 'Employment and Existence *vs* Ethics and Social Responsibility: A Case Study' focuses on people's struggle for environmental protection and healthy atmosphere, and the workers' struggle to re-open Grasim Industries, while discussing the causative factors that led to the closure of the factory. It gives in detail the issues related to environmentalists, society and working class. Besides this the author also includes the outcome of the struggle and situation pertaining to employment and health.

The author finds many reasons for the closure of the factory. Workers were socially less responsible, and therefore, deprived of public support. The inter- and intra-organizational, ideological differences among trade unions as well as personality clashes were very high. The lack of awareness of workers about self-employment generated a fear of loss of job and hence led to the unethical compromise with the management. All these reasons led to the decline of the trade union movement and its bargaining capacity.

The author also suggests for the enactment of an act and strict rules so that capitalists' exploitative ways could be kept in check. The unity among trade unions and their social concern should be made stronger and they should have a substantial bargaining capacity.

Rakhi Singh in 'Waiting for a Movement: The Plight of Banarasi Saree Weavers' focuses on the working conditions and difficulties of the workers engaged in Banarasi Saree production activities with highlights on the conditions of child labour, including the exploitation and oppression that the workers face.

The saree production was dominated by the upper caste Hindus earlier but replaced by Muslims in contemporary times. However, the major composition of the production process consists of non-upper caste social groups. Muslims, Harijans and Yadavs are the major participants either as employers or employees. The Harjans, in particular, prefer to join weaving industries not only for the economic reasons such as lack of opportunities in agricultural field and wages in cash, but also to escape from the trauma of caste discrimination.

The author discusses the strengthening of multiculturalism through mixing and mingling of Hindus and Muslims on different occasions while emphasizing on the poor and pitiable condition of workers—poor education and health, social stigma, denial to their political rights, including their condition like bonded labourers. Their poor conditions lead to their self-alienation and create a feeling of sub-ordination and inability in them. They lead a life of confinement, separation, isolation, non-participation in public life and no enthusiasm in political activities.

Fourth part of the book is entitled 'Emergence and Struggle of Rural Working Class'. It begins with the paper presented by Kumar Shiralkar and Uday Narkar. In their paper titled 'Sugar Industry and Working Masses: Prospects and Challenges' the authors discuss the struggle in sugar industry of Maharashtra between monopolist-capitalist forces and working masses—the actual producers, especially during the period of imperialist globalization in the post-1990 period. They also make comparative references to the movements in other states, including global aspects of production, export and import factors, etc. During the period of neoliberal economic policies and globalization, the significant increase in the number of privately-owned sugar factories focusing on profit-making by ruling elites and corrupt politicians at the expense of the interests of workers and producer-peasants constituted a new feature of the sugar sector, particularly, in Maharashtra.

As a consequence of a major change in policy and growth of sugar industry which is dominated by big business class and politicians, a position of dominance has been provided to private sector. The changed situation which was created under the impact of neoliberal economic policies at global level provided propitious ground for the emergence and growth of the struggle between monopolist-capitalist forces and toiling working class. The struggle between the capitalist elements and working class intensified in the post-globalized phase because of the corrupt practices, such as political opportunism, mismanagement, including fraud and profiteering to amass huge wealth by a handful of powerful persons.

In 1945, a conference of farmers adopted a resolution to establish a sugar factory in a cooperative sector and the Pravara Cooperative Sugar Factory was set-up at Loni in Ahmednagar district. The sugar industry in cooperative sector continued developing until the advent of the era of LPG in 1990s after which privately-owned industry began developing and growing in number and capacity. Sugar factories in cooperative sector contributed to the integrated development of rural Maharashtra, especially under the leadership of visionary personalities, like Vikhe Patil, Vasantdada Patil, Yashwantrao Chavan and Nagnathanna Naikwadi. Later, the industry came under control of some powerful politicians and exploitative business barons who aimed at profit-making at the expense of workers-peasants' interests, thus, necessitating the protest movements in which producer-farmers and toiling working masses actively participated.

The major issues of the workers' struggle have been the wage rates, use of machines as it replaces the need of human labour causing employment and sufferings to the workers, especially those who are skilled in sugar cane cutting occupation, control over market as open market benefits capitalist-business class and harms the interests of working class by affecting pricing.

Ramakumar in 'A Brief History of Dalit Agricultural Labourers' Resistance in Kerala' focuses on the processes that have led to the changes in socio-economic conditions of the most oppressed section within Dalits—the Dalit agricultural labourers—in the history of Kerala. He argues that the decisive advancement in socio-economic freedoms of people belonging, especially to lower strata of society has been one of the significant features of the development experience in Kerala during the twentieth century. The standard of living, education, health, wage rate and conditions of employments of Dalit agricultural labourers in Kerala are better than their counterparts in other states of the country.

Besides these, they have the privilege of agricultural labour pensions (after the age of 60 years) from the state governments and also the medical allowances from the labour welfare funds. The expansion of freedom of Dalits was made possible by weakening the material basis of caste discrimination through change in land relations in which the struggles of Dalits in Kerala. The author contends that the improvement in the condition of Dalits in Kerala is a result of the labour and peasant movement in Malabar and Travancore regions, mainly under the leadership of communist parties.

The enactment and effective implementation of the land reforms measures in the state despite a number of attempts to manipulate and circumvent land reforms laws by the landed gentry interests groups during and after mid-1960s brought about a positive change in the socio-economic conditions of people belonging to lower rungs of society, thus enabling them to lead a dignified life. However, in today's period, Dalits need a special attention and protective measures such as employment, health improvement, skill upgradation, land distribution, etc., to enhance their capacity—including capacity-building programmes keeping in view of the larger interests of society for an equitable and sustainable development.

Manoj Kumar in 'The Radicalism in Agrarian Structure for Social Transformation: The Case of Bihar' discusses the struggle waged by the rural landless labourers and poor peasantry mostly belonging to lower castes, especially Dalits, for social transformation. The paper makes an attempt to understand the causes, nature, scope and aims of this agrarian radicalism. Besides, it also examines the causes of the underdevelopment of the state that have generated caste-class contradictions in the society of Bihar, creating a suitable ground for emergence of armed anti-feudal struggle with an aim to achieve the goal of social transformation and ensure peace and harmony in society on the basis of distributive justice.

In 1967, the Naxalbari region of West Bengal turned into a hotbed of agrarian radicalism under the guidance of Maoist philosophy. Despite the glorious history of Bihar, it has been suffering from a number of socio-economic evils and it is one of the most backward states of India. These socio-economic conditions made a propitious ground for causing widespread violence in the rural agrarian structure along the caste and class lines, especially since the late 1960s under the leadership of Naxalite organizations.

This movement of poor peasantry, belonging mostly to lower caste-classes, spread to the central regions of Bihar and grew intense in 1980s, turning rural Bihar into 'flaming fields' which aimed at liberation of masses through anti-feudal struggle based on the issues of land, wage and social dignity.

Part five of the book is entitled 'Working Class in the Era of Liberalization, Globalization and Privatization'. It analyses the trade union movements and the rights of unions against the backdrop of

LPG. Abdulrahim P. Vijapur in his 'Laying the Foundations of Rights: The Role of ILO in Evolving Rights of Working Class' discusses the role of the International Labour Organization (ILO) established in 1919 in laying and consolidating the foundation of the rights of working class by framing and enacting various laws and rules through the methods of organizing conventions in the interest of the labour class. The ILO emerged as an effective organization on the issue of social and economical rights of workers, besides promoting human rights in general.

It is a permanent intergovernmental organization with global objectives for amelioration of the condition of workers such as (1) employment and the raising of standards of living;(2) the employment of workers in occupations in which they can have the satisfaction of giving the fullest measure of their skill and attainments and can make their contribution to the common well-being; (3) facilities for training and the transfer of labour, including migration for employment and settlement; policies in regard to wages and earnings, hours and other conditions of work, calculated to insure a just share of the fruits of progress to all, and a minimum living wage to all employed; (4) the effective recognition of the right of collective bargaining, the co-operation of management and labour in the continuous improvement of productive efficiency, and the collaboration of workers in the preparation and application of social and economic measures; (5) the extension of social security measures to provide a basic income to all in need of such protection and comprehensive medical care; (6) adequate protection for the life and health of workers in all occupations; (7) provision of child welfare and maternity protection; (8) the provision of adequate nutrition, housing, and facilities for recreation and culture; and (9) the assurance of equality of educational and vocational opportunity.

The ILO adopted the mechanism of tripartism in securing fine balance between the interests of workers and employer, of course, under the mediating and monitoring control of the governing structures. The constitution along with a number of conventions of the ILO provides provisions and mechanisms for the protection of the rights of workers, children, women, disabled and migrant labourers. All the ratifying member countries of the ILO are obliged to submit report on the status of the implementations of the provisions of the ILO Conventions within one to five years and the government representatives are made accountable in case of violation or non-compliance of the provisions of the conventions. The ILO with its conventions and recommendations along with its supervisory mechanism has made remarkable achievements by influencing the labour legislation in all the member countries and promoting human rights while improving the lives and working conditions of people all over the world.

B.N. Mehrish in 'Impact of Globalization on Trade Union Movements' examines the impact of globalization process on trade union movements in India and analyses how this process affects the rights of workers in both public and private sectors. It also highlights the role of the working class in the freedom struggle of India.

Initially, the main objective of trade unionism was to achieve some welfare measures related to wage, hours of work, conditions of employment and other related economic issues. In many cases, such needs of toiling workers were subordinated to political objectives as a result of which workers sought the help of unofficial leaders to champion their most urgent needs.

The process of globalization made a clear division between those who are in favour of globalization policies and those who oppose and this is a consequence of interaction between trade unions and political parties. The aims of the trade union movements have not been confined only to the achievement of immediate economic goals. The trade union policies have been largely conditioned by the association of unions with political parties committed to diverse ideologies. The Congress party and Indian National Trade Union Congress (INTUC) had progressively focused on the socialist pattern of society as the national goal before globalization. In the post-1990s, the Congress government has given more emphasis on economic growth and considered that the actual role of trade unions in India includes persuading workers to forgo immediate economic demands while urging to maintain restraint and discipline so as to achieve the goal of increasing the rate of economic growth and check inflationary pressures. Hence, their trade union party, the INTUC, remained aloof from some national level political agitations. Now the situation is such that the union leaders in India in the globalized phase, can even face imprisonment for an allegedly 'political offence' for going on an illegal strike.

Sangeeta N. Pawar in 'Working Class Movement: Modern Economic System, Social Structure and Power Conflict' discusses the emergence of a new economic system integrating domestic market with global economy. The agriculture-based economy had become industry-based economy with a rise in the gross domestic product and per capita income. The power struggle among various interest groups has intensified as a consequence of the process of globalization and policy of liberalization and privatization for the protection and promotion of their respective interests.

The process of the liberalization has adversely affected the prospects of employment opportunities in public sector and the population, belonging to scheduled castes, scheduled tribes and backward classes. The lack of provision of reservation in private sector has also a negative impact. The flexible labour practices such as, casualization, feminization, use of contract labour, job contracting, relocation of production, deskilling of labour, etc., have become the main characteristics of today's socio-economic reality. The unemployment has been increased due to the adoption of flexible practices of employers, which bypass the labour laws. Besides these, absence of provision of insurance, social security and lack of job security, including weakening and declining bargaining power of trade unions are among the negative effects of the liberalization policies.

Therefore, the author recommends awareness campaign in collaboration with voluntary organizations and trade unions. The existing institutional laws and programmes should be restructured, and social measures should be adopted. And she also highlights the importance of vocational training system for the betterment of working class.

'Trade Unionism at Cross Roads: Impact of Liberalization Reforms in Kerala' by B. Venugopal discusses the impact of neoliberal reform policies and measures on the functioning and efficacy of trade unionism in Kerala. He contends that India adopted a strategy of mixed economy and provided a dominant role in the public sector enterprises in pursuant to the principles of socialism which remained effectively in existence until the 1990s. The trade unionism in India, particularly in Kerala did not remain confined to achieving some benefits and rights for itself but participated actively in almost every movement that concerned with the weaker and marginalized sections of society and was regarded as an agent for social change and transformation.

After the process of globalization, the agenda of liberalization and privatization took the centrestage. The period of post-1990 began witnessing its decline and weakening under the impact of neoliberal policies adopted at national and international level and also due to its own internal weaknesses. In the liberalized phase, the emphasis shifted from the state to the market and non-state actors began emerging as dominant actors and sharing the social responsibilities which, previously, used to constitute a part of principal functions of the state. The attitude of the state underwent a remarkable change with regard to its relation with the labour. In the changed situation, the role and significance of the public and services sectors was reduced while the private sector was encouraged to grow and flourish. Retrenchment of workers and increase in the number of the unemployed became a common feature that led to other social problems. The workers' unions were compelled to accept the retrenchments and the reduction in wages. The idea of collective bargaining was transformed into bargaining for concession, such as, wages, dearness allowances, incentives, etc. The attitude of the management became more authoritative and aggressive. The labour laws were amended to suit the interests of the owners and managers of the industries at the expense of the welfare of the workers.

Trade unions are facing difficulties in sustaining their organizational base now. They seem to have lost their vision and historic responsibilities as they focus merely on protecting the rights of their member workers and improving their wages and living conditions. From 1980 onwards, the trade union movement in Kerala has undergone remarkable changes as a result of the process of liberalization that has created an anti-union atmosphere in the state. Policies like import liberalization, tariff reduction and removal of subsidies affected even the traditional and small-scale industries in the state leading to de-industrialization with almost all the public sector units on the verge of disinvestment and closure. A large number of industrial units grew sick and unable to pay the minimum wages to the workers. The liberalization policies of the government and their impact have immensely affected the industrial organization and management, with severe consequences for the working class. The employer-employee relations have undergone drastic changes, widening the way for the master-slave system instead of the old practices of cooperation and negotiations. The workers and their unions became ineffective to counter the anti-labour policies while the consequences of the impact of the liberalization led to the fragmentation of working class and emergence of social tensions in the name of caste, region, religion, etc., and revival of sectarian identity politics.

NOTES

1. At the end of the Second World War, the big victorious imperialistic powers, especially United Kingdom and the United States took initiatives to establish global-based financial (World Bank), monetary (International Monetary Fund) and trade related institutions (General Agreement on Tariff and Trade which, later was reconstituted as World Trade Organization in 1995) to facilitate free trading and serving the interest of powerful countries with imperialistic ambitions in the name of global economic cooperation and integration. These organizations have always been dominated by the Western, industrially and economically developed countries serving the economic and expansionist ambitions of the US, UK and other powerful European countries, while creating an illusion of economic development among less developed countries of global South. It is a widely known fact that the president of the World Bank has been always from among the American citizens nominated by the President of the US while the IMF has been headed by citizens of European countries. WTO is under the influence of economically developed countries constantly striving to facilitate free trading at international level in the name of global economic and trade efficiency by putting pressures on the national governments of the countries across the world to relax their rules and policies pertaining to the trade and tariff, exchange values of their currencies and other associated regulations which pave the way for the multinational companies to expand and monopolize the world economy at the expense of the interests of the host countries, rights of the workers and environmental protection. Many times, these multinational companies take the help of their home countries' governments and intelligence agencies to deal with the unfavourable or unfriendly host governments. The US has always, particularly after 1920s, framed its foreign policy to pursue its national economic policies and protect the interests of the US multinationals. Thus, the international organizations, particularly, economic and financial institutions and MNCs are neo-imperialistic tools in the hands of economically powerful countries that continue to have the ambitions to establish and maintain hegemony in the world by adopting sophisticated and indirect methods of imperialism and colonialism which essentially constitute a part of strategy of neo-imperialism. One of the elements of the imperialistic strategy seems to be the efforts of the imperialistic forces to destroy the working class movements across the globe.
2. When industrial workers were agitating for their rights and against the exploitative capitalist elements in urban areas, small, marginal and landless peasants (a major portion of them belonged to lower caste and classes) were struggling in rural regions of the country against the exploitative and oppressive feudal elements on the issue of land, wage and social dignity. Besides struggling on economic issues, the rural poor fought against social

discrimination and oppression by upper caste feudal landlords. The struggle of peasantry for social honour in rural Bihar has been described as being *izzat ki ladai* (struggle for dignity).

3. The first industrial unit in the country was a textile mill, Bombay Spinning and Weaving Mills, which was started by Kowasji Nanabhai Dawar in 1854 at Tardeo in Mumbai. The number of establishment of the factories kept on increasing with passage of time, and therefore, the need of the better life and working condition (the feeling of protest against the exploitative working conditions, including lack of safeguards for the workers was expressed at various occasions before the formation of the formal trade union). The workers used to stop working and sit in open space of the compound of the factory to express their protest until they were assured by the manager or supervisor of the satisfactory redressal of their grievances. Narayan Meghaji Lokhande, who was working as a storekeeper in Madavi Mills formed the Bombay Mill Hands Association in 1884. In mid-1850s, jute mill was started in Calcutta. The railways service was also started in Bombay and the workers in this sector formed their own association, the Amalgamated Society of Railway Servants of India and Burma in 1897. The emergence of the workers' union was concomitant with the development of industrial firms. Usually, the workers used to express their protest by going on strikes and their demands, many times, were conceded by the employers, especially demands for weekly holidays, working hours and health-related safety measures. The Madras Labour Union of the workers of Buckingham and Carnatic Mills emerged in the then Madras Presidency. In Ahmedabad also textile mills were started and workers' organization, the Textile Labour Association was formed. In July 1920, the AITUC was formed at Parel (in Bombay) under the leadership of N.M. Joshi. Lala Lajpat Rai who was a prominent leader of the Indian national movement became its first president. In 1926, the Trade Union Act was passed by the Central Legislative Assembly providing workers' right to form their trade unions and raise their demands. Their major demands were on the issues of hours of work, wage, bonus, compensation on accidents, fair price shops for workers, provident fund, dearness allowances, leave, etc. The non-communist, national leaders too provided support and leadership to the workers' associations. Workers too played important roles in advancing the cause of India's struggle for freedom. The railway men went on strike under the leadership of All India Railway Men's Federation, defence employees under the banner of All India Defence Employees Federation, central government employees, including an agitation of Godrej and Boyce Company workers signalled the assertion of workers' rights. Besides these major strikes, there were large numbers of minor agitations, *morchas*, processions, conferences, *dharnas*, etc.
4. The war between India and China in 1962, Indo-Pak war in 1965, food crisis, increase in the cost of essential commodities, including poor

implementation of the land reform measures provided propitious ground for people's movement against the prevailing political system at that time. The radical communist elements broke away from the CPI and formed the CPI(M). Again, CPI(M) got split and a new party, the Communist Party of India (Marxist Leninist) was emerged. The CPI(ML) relied on armed peasant struggle and rejected trade unionism as mere economics.

5. The major portion of proletariat belongs to the non-industrial sectors. Therefore, there is a great responsibility on the workers of the more organized sectors to organize themselves and provide leadership to the large majority of unorganized workers while taking up the causes of the large numbers of poor and landless peasantry and tribal people and winning them over to the cause of socialist transformation.
6. See C.N. Subramanian, 'Labour Movement in India as Reflected in the Indian Labour Year Book 1997', http://www.revolutionarydemocracy.org/rdv6n2/labour.htm, accessed on 28 May 2011, A. Roy, 'The Working Class Movement in the Dhanbad-Durgapur Area', http://www.revolutionarydemocracy.org/rdv6n1/workclass.htm, accessed on 28 May 2011 for more information on problems of labour and challenges of the working class movement in India.

PART I

EMERGENCE AND GROWTH OF WORKING CLASS MOVEMENT IN INDIA

CHAPTER 2

Trade Union Movement in India at a Glance

M.K. PANDHE

The trade union movement in India is at crossroads today. Though working class constitutes the most organized detachment of our society, the serious division in the trade union movement has reduced its bargaining power. It is facing several challenges today in a period of globalization and its future depends on how it is poised to meet these challenges.

ORIGIN AND RISE OF MODERN WORKING CLASS

The modern industrial working class in India is a creation of industrial capitalism. The industrial revolution of England which commenced in the second half of the eighteenth century required a big market for its large-scale production. The East India Company developed in India as their market by destroying the age-old base of India's traditional handicraft industry and village economy.

L.C.A. Knowles (1924) in his book *Economic Development of the British Overseas Empire* has noted, that the importance of India to England in the first half of the [nineteenth] century lay in the fact that India supplied some of the essential raw materials—hides, oil, dyes, jute and cotton—required for the industrial revolution in England, and at the same time, afforded a growing market for English manufacturers of iron and cotton (p. 305).

While the exports of food grains from India were high, severe famines occurred in several parts of India. According to official estimates during the first half of nineteenth century, there were seven famines resulting in deaths of 15 lakh persons, while during the second half there were 24 famines resulting in deaths of over two crore people. *Indian Famine Commission Report*, Part 1 (Calcutta) in 1880 stated,

> . . . no remedy for present evils can be complete which does not include the introduction of a diversity of occupations, through which the surplus population may be drawn from agricultural pursuits and led to find the means of sustenance from manufactures or some such employers.

The East India Company felt that the developments of some modern industries in India would augment their profits. Some of the officials of the company had garnered huge financial resources through the loot of the Indian people, who preferred to have investments in India to add to their earnings.

The first coal mine was developed in Raniganj in 1832. The tea plantation started developing in Assam at the same period. The famines provided them availability of labour at cheap rates. The first cotton textile mill started in Bombay in 1854, while the first jute mill commenced production in the same year. In 1853, the first railway line was developed between Calcutta and Raniganj as well as from Bombay to Thane.

Thus, the modern working class was born in India. The working conditions were indeed shocking. There was no limit to hours of work, no holidays for workers, no compensation for injuries and maternity benefit, etc. The workers and their families were living in shanties constructed by them without any hygienic conditions, while no educational facilities were available for their children. The question of retirement benefit was not known to them. The tea plantation workers were whipped by the officers and beating of workers by jobbers and *mukadams* was common in factories.

The workers were working for extremely low wages and in bad working conditions. A British delegation visited Indian coal mines in the second half of nineteenth century reported that the workers were naked while working underground since they could not afford to spoil their clothes in mines. They reported that the workers were paid 5 annas per week as wages. The delegation expressed surprise how they could survive with such ridiculously low wages.

When conditions became unbearable, preliminary resistance of the workers were reported in the historic records. The workers thought that the machines were responsible for their bad working conditions and they resorted to destroy machines, unmindful of the consequences. There were also instances of workers beating their supervisors when they found working conditions intolerable. An attempt to leave the job by running away was difficult because the workers were punished for violating the contract of employment. A law relating to breach of contract was passed by the British government to prevent the workers from leaving the job.

Several lakhs of workers were recruited as indentured labour from famine-stricken areas on false promises and taken by force to Mauritius, British Guyana, West Indies, Fiji, Malaysia and South Africa. Several died while travelling and those who reached the destination had to adjust in a totally different environment, losing total contact with their motherland. Modern capitalism grew in India under such harrowing conditions for the working class.

ORIGIN AND GROWTH OF TRADE UNION MOVEMENT

The historical outline of the trade union movement can be understood properly by dividing it into three phases.

1. First phase till the formation of national trade union centre till 1920.
2. The second phase since 1920 till India attains Independence in 1947.
3. The third post-Independence phase till the period of commencement of globalization.

The period of globalization can be considered in the topic of present situation of the trade union movement. In this paper it is possible to cover only the general aspects of the movement without going into details of events in the trade union movement.

The early strike actions of the workers were spontaneous outbursts against the extremely bad working conditions. The work stoppages were of smaller duration and were either suppressed by brute police force or were settled by accepting some improvement in the working conditions by the representative of the management.

Reports indicate that in Bombay, in the early stage of the movement, if the conditions became intolerable, workers used to stop work and sit in an open space in the compound of the factory. This action was popularly known as *adda* (centre of activity) of workers. There were no speeches or slogans, while workers would silently sit in *adda*. The representative of the management would then come and enquire about the matter, then the workers would speak. He would then assure them something. If the workers got satisfied, then they would go back to work or sit till the management revised the offer. There are reports that some of the *addas* resulted in clashes inside the factory between the management, security personnel and the workers when police would intervene most of the time in favour of the management. Some of the *addas* belonged to the workers of only one department of the factory.

The first recorded industrial strike was reported in 1862 when 1,200 railwaymen at Howrah station struck work demanding eight hours a day workday. The strike lasted for some days but did not achieve the demand of the workers.

Another major strike reported was in Tata's Empress Mill at Nagpur in 1877 demanding a rise in wages which lasted for four days. However, formation of unions was not recorded till that time.

The conditions in Indian factories were so bad and the wages were so poor that in British parliament, the representatives of Lancashire mill owners, who were finding it difficult to compete with newly emerging textile industries in India, spoke at length about the shocking working conditions in the Indian industries and criticized the British government for not enacting labour laws to regulate the working conditions. As a result, in 1884, a Factory Commission was sent by the British government to study the conditions in Indian factories and suggest measures to improve them.

When the Factory Commission visited Bombay a demonstration was organized by Bombay Mill-hands Associations led by N.M. Lokhande, a philanthropist who submitted a memorandum as president of the association, demanding reduction in hours of work, weekly off, wage increase and compensation for injuries during accidents. Though this was considered as the first union in India, it was having no regular membership but was working to take up the grievances of the workers. Lokhande edited a newspaper in Marathi entitled *Dinbandhu* (friend of the poor) during that period.

Between 1882 and 1890, 25 major strikes had been reported in Bombay and Madras presidencies. As reported by the chief inspector of factories, Bombay,

> strikes have been many. Two should be put down every year for each factory, but all of them have been short lived and in the end it is always the operatives who have given in, in many cases with fines and in some cases loss of arrear wages. The reasons for strike are mostly temporary reduction of wages

without any notice whatsoever. (Annual Report of the Chief Inspector of Factories and Workshops for the Year 1918)

Strikes had been reported in several jute mills in Bengal during this period. As a result of the growing labour discontent reflected in a series of strike actions, the British government enacted the Factories Act in 1891, which fixed daily nine hours work for children and 11 hours for women with half an hour for lunch break. The Act did not provide any working hours for male workers, but allowed one day weekly rest compulsorily. This was the first labour law passed by the colonial power to regulate working conditions in the factories.

In 1897, due to an outbreak of bubonic plague in Bombay, Kanpur and other industrial centres, large number of workers lost their lives and many had fled to rural areas. To motivate workers to remain at work, the mill owners announced a bonus to workers known as 'plague bonus'.

At the turn of the century, leaders like Bal Gangadhar Tilak and Lala Lajpat Rai gave a call for Swadeshi movement which influenced the working classes. It spread widely in Bombay, Madras and Calcutta, and gradually the trade unions began to be formed in these areas.

The six-day strike in 1908 of more than 1 lakh workers of Bombay, in a protest against the six years imprisonment of Bal Gangadhar Tilak for stating 'swaraj is my birth right and I shall have it', was the first political action of the Indian working class. The workers braved police repression and resisted heroically all repressive action of the policemen. The strike received popular support among the citizens of Bombay which became a popular upsurge against imperialist domination.

The Russian Revolution in 1917 which established the rule of the working class and by abolishing the capitalist system, ushered in a new era of socialism that inspired the working class all over the world to fight against capitalist exploitation. Trade union movement got impetus everywhere including India. To stem the tide of revolutionary movement after the First World War, the League of Nations decided to form the International Labour Organization (ILO) in 1918 to propose labour legislation to improve the working and living conditions of the workers.

When the British government nominated workers representatives for the ILO meet, it was objected in India. Since there was no central trade union, it was decided to hold all-India trade union congress in October 1920 at Bombay. Lala Lajpat Rai presided over it, while several national leaders participated in it. Thus, the All-India Trade Union Congress (AITUC) was formed in India. There were 125 unions affiliated to AITUC which showed the growth of the trade union movement during this period.

TRADE UNION MOVEMENT PRIOR TO INDEPENDENCE

In 1918, B.P. Wadia, a philanthropist belonging to the Theosophical Society of Madras founded Madras Labour Union with regular membership. It is considered to be the first systematic formation of a trade union. In the year 1921, he led a two-day strike of Buckingham Mill and Carnatic Mill which led to his prosecution by the mill owners. The court imposed a heavy fine for causing loss to the company. Wadia was forced to sever his connection with the trade union movement. This episode, however, evoked strong reactions all over India and N.M. Joshi moved a resolution in the central legislative assembly to register a trade union and grant protection to trade union activities. The British government in 1926 passed the Indian Trade Union Act providing for registration of a trade union.

The British imperialism viewed the rising Indian trade union movement as a conspiracy to overthrow their colonial rule. Hence in 1924, four prominent trade union leaders were arrested and involved in Kanpur conspiracy case and sentenced to longer prison terms. Again in 1928, 31 trade unionists from all over the country were involved in Meerut conspiracy case and the trial went on for a longer period. The accused were sentenced to longer prison terms. This, however, created an outcry all over the world as an attack on trade union rights of the working class. In India, the national movement condemned this attack, and ultimately, the prisoners had to be released earlier. Hundreds of trade union leaders were involved in several criminal cases and were imprisoned for merely participating in trade union activities.

The support given by the national movement was an important aspect in survival and growth of the trade union movement. Prominent national leaders like Lala Lajpat Rai, Chittaranjan Das, Jawaharlal Nehru, Subhas Chandra Bose and others were presidents of the AITUC and supported the struggles of the working class.

Several strikes conducted by the working class during 1920s and 1930s compelled the British rule to provide some relief steps for the working class. The passing of the Workmen's Compensation Act

(1923) and Bombay Maternity Benefit Act (1930) were some of the examples. In 1920, the government had to grant food allowance to workers in view of the rise in prices of essential commodities which later became dearness allowance. The government had to prepare cost of living index to assess the rise in prices of essential commodities. The government had to appoint several enquiry committees to investigate into living standards of the working class with a view to provide some relief to them.

The political situation in the country had some impact on the trade union movement. At the end of 1927, the British government nominated Simon Commission to suggest political reforms, while the Indian National Congress decided to boycott it. The country was advancing towards demanding full independence. The British government also appointed another commission under the presidentship of Whitley to investigate into conditions of workers and suggest remedial measure. The majority in the AITUC in 1929 Conference under the presidentship of Jawaharlal Nehru wanted to boycott it, meanwhile, N.M. Joshi, V.V. Giri and others advocated joining it. There was a split in AITUC when the minority group walked out and formed the Indian Trade Union Federation. In 1930, another split also took place when S.C. Bose was the president and the communists walked out of it and formed the Red Trade Union Congress.

The division in the trade union movement immensely harmed the movement when the working class faced a severe wage cut offensive and massive unemployment due to severe global recession. Red Trade Union Congress decided to merge in the AITUC in 1934, while in 1938, the Indian Trade Union Federation merged with the AITUC and again the unity of the trade union movement was restored.

However, due to the outbreak of the Second World War in 1939, the situation again changed and the British government resorted to suppressive measures. In 1941, Germany attacked Soviet Union and Japan attacked Pearl Harbour and declared war against the United States (US) and its allies. Due to war, prices of essential commodities increased and the resistance of the working class was witnessed everywhere. In this situation, the British government convened in 1942 the Tripartite Labour Conference which later on came to be known as the Indian Labour Conference. The Tripartite Conferences were generally called every year though there were several gaps in between.

Conditions of the working class deteriorated during the Second World War. In 1943, due to severe famine in West Bengal, lakhs of people died. The call given by the Indian National Congress for Quit India movement resulted in thousands of national leaders being imprisoned.

In 1945, the Second World War came to an end. In the post-war situation, a new strike wave engulfed the entire country. A big popular upsurge against British imperialism swept through entire India. A demand was raised all over India for the release of the prisoners of the Indian National Army. In February 1946, there was a revolt of the Royal Indian Navy and the Bombay workers supported the navy rebels. British imperialism realized that they could not rule India any more. Negotiations started which led to granting of freedom to India but the country was divided into India and Pakistan.

Trade union movement in India played a notable role in the post-world war upsurge and contributed in achieving national Independence for the country.

POST-INDEPENDENCE PERIOD

Expectation of the workers had risen to a higher level after India attained Independence which was reflected by the activities of the trade unions immediately after Independence, demanding higher wages, better services and social security measures. Though the government passed the Minimum Wages Act, Payment of Wages Act, Employees Provident Fund Act, Employees State Insurance Act, etc., the wage level of Indian workers was extremely low. The government appointed a Fair Wage Committee which recommended fair wages to be fixed higher than the minimum wages, but they were lower than the living wages and decided by the capacity of industry to pay. However, the wage level was still in the lower order and several strikes took place in the country in the early 1950s demanding higher wages. The Fair Wage Committee report was not acceptable to the trade union movement which was pressing the government to fix the minimum wage on the basis of minimum requirements of human existence. Therefore, the government appointed a committee to study these aspects and a formula was worked out to fix the need-based minimum wage. So, in the 15th Indian Labour Conference in 1957, the need-based minimum wage formula was approved according to which the family should be of three consumption units and daily intake of food per person should be 2,700 calories. Cloth requirement to be 72 yards per family with a minimum standard housing to be provided and other expenses should be 20 per cent of the total wage. The conference also decided to fix the need-based minimum wage in 15 industries, and accordingly, wage boards were constituted for the purpose. However, the wage board's decision to work out wages on the basis of 15th Indian Labour Conference was not accepted by any wage board which created a strong resentment among the working class. The Indian Labour Conference also adopted a model agreement for rationalization and a code of discipline in the industry laying down the norms of behaviour by management and trade unions. It also worked out a grievance procedure and finalized inter-union code of conduct which stipulated the relations between different trade union organizations. However, despite these tripartite agreements, conditions could not be improved in the industrial relations. The government felt that this was due to the absence of a statutory backing and it thought of making a legal provision to implement these aspects of the tripartite agreements. The tripartite machinery also worked out a verification procedure for determining the membership of trade unions which would determine the representative character of the unions. Meanwhile, the political differentiation started emerging in the trade unions.

After Independence, the ruling party felt that it should have its own trade union organization. So, in the year 1947, the Indian National Trade Union Congress (INTUC) was founded. In 1948, Hind Maha Sabha (HMS) was constituted by a section coming out from AITUC and another section from INTUC. Later, there was a split in HMS also and the United Trade Union Congress (UTUC) was formed. Thus, multiplicity of trade unions came into existence. Later, UTUC also split up and a section of the organization worked out and formed UTUC (LS). In the year 1957, Bharatiya Mazdoor Sangh (BMS) came into existence. Thus, we find a large number of trade unions started operating in the country instead of a single organization as in the pre-Independence period. In the year 1970, the AITUC was also split and the Centre of Indian Trade Unions (CITU) was formed. Thus, today, there are 12 central trade unions recognized by the Government of India after verification of membership for tripartite consultation.

Seeing the failure of the wage board machinery, public sector undertakings decided to prefer to have a bipartite mechanism to settle the wages and other terms of service conditions. The National Joint Committee of Steel Industry (NJCS) was formed in 1969 which signed an agreement without any third party intervention. This system spread soon to other industries also in the public sector which became a norm for all wage negotiations in public sector undertakings. In the year 1966, the Payment of Bonus Act was passed which provided 4 per cent minimum bonus for workers, irrespective of profit or loss. In the early 1970s, the government appointed a Bonus Review Committee which recommended the minimum bonus to be paid at 8.33 per cent. However, during the emergency, the Act was changed and bonus was restored to 4 per cent. Due to sustained struggle by the trade unions all over the country in the year 1977, the government again had to change the Act and restored 8.33 per cent minimum bonus to workers.

At the instance of the Union Labour Ministry, a national council for trade unions was formed with INTUC, AITUC and HMS. To oppose this combination, other trade unions constituted United Council of Trade Unions (UCTU) in 1973 and started struggles against the government's policies. It opposed compulsory deposit scheme of the government and demanded its withdrawal, and ultimately in the year 1977, the government had to withdraw this scheme. In the year 1971, the government formulated a family pension scheme which was contributory by the workers and the management, but was not giving sufficient family pension to meet the requirement of the workers' families after the death of the earning member. So, a campaign all over the country was launched to change the scheme and the government had to ultimately adopt the employees' pension scheme by merging the family pension scheme into that scheme. At that time, the family pension scheme had Rs 14,000 crore of surplus funds.

When the government prepared the Industrial Relations Bill in 1979, a national convention was held by all the trade unions to oppose the bill and a massive demonstration was held before parliament, and ultimately the government was compelled to withdraw the bill. In the year 1981, in a Bombay convention, the national campaign committee of trade unions was formed which gave call for a nationwide strike in 1982, which was the first nationwide strike of the working class on common issues. Since then, during 1980s the national campaign committee conducted several struggles of the workers of common issues. In the year 1986, the committee of public sector undertakings was formed by several public sector unions and the first strike of public sector workers was organized at the national level in 1987. In this period, except INTUC, all unions could come on a common platform and the national unity could be achieved though partially in the trade union movement.

GLOBALIZATION AND TRADE UNIONS

After the dismantling of socialism in erstwhile Soviet Union and East European countries, the world situation changed radically and the system of capitalism received a big boost. A massive propaganda was launched that socialism had failed and capitalism had reached at the final stage of human civilization.

International finance capital with the help of World Bank and the International Monetary Fund (IMF) developed a structural adjustment programme which came to be popularly known as globalization.

Due to severe foreign exchange crisis during the 1990-1 periods, the Government of India accepted conditionality of the World Bank and the IMF for a loan to meet the foreign exchange crisis. Indian economy faced several changes due to acceptance of those conditionalities. The working class and the trade union movement in India had to meet multifarious challenges due to the structural adjustment programme. The following have been the major aspects:

1. Due to deregulation of economy, the previous licensing policy was reversed and the investors were free to decide the location of industry. It resulted in uneven development of regions and migration of labour in search of job avenues acquired prominence.
2. Downsizing of manpower as a cost cutting measure became universal. It imposed an increase in the workload on the workers. The army of unemployed had swelled in most of the countries including in India. Even in public sector in India due to globalization, the employment declined from 23 to 18 lakh. This caused a decline in trade union membership in the organized sector.
3. The drastic increase in the casual, contractual, outsourced, temporary, short-term jobs resulted in reduction in job security and quality of job. The then ILO director general, Joan Somavia's call for decent work remained only on paper.
4. The World Bank's concept that labour laws should not be punitive, while there should be an emphasis on self-compliance by the

employer, resulted in large-scale violation of labour laws. The inadequate government machinery to ensure implementation had only facilitated this process. The promise of abolition of inspector raj had further aggravated the phenomenon.

5. The drive towards privatization and disinvestment had weakened the public sector. The concept to economic growth with social justice was given a go-bye. Closure of non-profitable units became the order of the day.
6. Social security benefits of workers came under heavy attacks in the name of cutting costs.
7. The liberalization of foreign investment resulted in foreign capital displacing traditional and small-scale units which faced closure and consequent unemployment. The government steps to stop multinational corporations (MNCs) from violating labour laws, etc., became inoperative on the plea that it might result in less foreign direct investment (FDI) in India.
8. The trade union rights of the working class came under ferocious attacks. Right to strike became meaningless. Pressure to grant right to the employers of hire and fire became more prominent and official attempts to marginalize the trade union movement got strengthened.

As a result of global meltdown of economy, the attacks on working and living conditions of the workers became more prominent. While the industrial undertakings got bonanza amounting to crores of rupees, over 30 lakh workers who lost jobs in India due to economic meltdown during 2008-9 did not get any relief whatsoever, though they were in no way responsible for the crisis and downturn.

During the last two decades of globalization, the trade unions had organized 12 nationwide strikes in India against the policies of globalization and attack on trade union rights.

The trade union movement has to come together irrespective of ideological differences today to protect the vital interests of the working class on the following major issues:

1. Rising prices of essential commodities.
2. Growing unemployment and need for unemployment insurance.
3. Ensuring full the implementation of labour laws.Need to create a special fund to ensure social security benefits for the unorganized labour. To amend the law relating to unorganized labour.
4. No to disinvestment in profit-making public sector undertakings.

The policies of globalization have underlined the need for international cooperation by the trade union movement. The coming together by several trade unions under the banner of Southern Initiative on Globalization and Trade Union Rights (SIGTUR) has created a favourable atmosphere for such a cooperation. The congress held in Kochi in April 2008 brought together trade unions from nineteen countries, who expressed their firm determination to resist the policies of globalization and protect the interests of the working class at a global level. Trade unions belong to different international affiliations can come together to oppose the policies of globalization. This positive development should be strengthened so that an international movement can be evolved to stop the intensification of exploitation of the working class all over the world.

MULTIPLICITY OF TRADE UNIONS

One of the specific features of the contemporary trade union movement is its multiplicity. Due to historic reasons trade union movement got divided in India on political lines. Prior to Independence, AITUC was the only one national trade union centre and all political forces were working within it. However, after Independence the ruling party in 1947 thought of having a trade union of its own and decided to form a separate organization Indian National Trade Union Congress (INTUC). This started a process of division of trade unions on political lines and today we have 12 central trade unions recognized by the Government of India for tripartite consultation.

Proliferation of trade unions even on caste lines or craft basis had taken place over a period of time. In Bokaro Steel Plant, there are over 40 registered trade unions. There are several industrial units where 5 to 10 trade unions are operating. This wide division in the trade union movement has considerably reduced bargaining power of the working class.

Formation of company unions by the managements and recognizing them has become a phenomenon in several undertakings in India. All concessions are given only through such a union to prevail upon the workers to accept it as fait accompli. When verification of membership is conducted by the government, management ensures that its union gets the highest membership.

An argument is being advanced that the workers should not involve themselves in political activity with a view to avoid political controversies in the trade union movement. This is practically not possible. As an advanced section of the society, the workers will have their political views. They have the right to vote and several workers contest elections in various forums. Under these circumstances asking workers to keep away from politics is not possible. As a matter of fact, they should play a crucial role in deciding political destiny of the country. The voice of the working class is raised less in parliament and legislative assemblies because the trade union representatives are less in numbers in these forums. Therefore, the workers should take more interest in political developments in the country so that they can play more effective roles to ensuring social justice in the country. However, political differences should not come in the way of trade union unity and struggles of the working class.

Multiplicity of trade unions is an internal problem of the trade union movement and it should be resolved through common dialogue within the trade union movement. It is only through struggles and united actions that mutual faith in the trade union movement will be restored and unification in the trade union movement can be achieved.

No outside efforts and legal measures can effectively check multiplicity of trade union movement. The phenomenon of undemocratic functioning of trade unions has been responsible for some of the splits in the trade union movement. It is also necessary to work out democratic norms for trade union recognition if multiplicity has to be reduced. The recognition of such union by the management has to be stopped if the process of unification has to be strengthened. Individual style of functioning of some of the leaders who want to establish personal control over the union has also added to the phenomenon of multiplicity of trade unions. However, it is only through mutual dialogue that the reduction in multiplicity of trade union is possible.

FUNCTIONING WITHIN LEGAL MACHINERY

In India there are about 50 laws at the central level and 200 laws applicable at the state level. The plethora of labour legislation has not materially helped in improving industrial relations in the country.

The definitions of 'worker' and 'industry' are different in different laws. Despite repeated demand by the employer's organizations and trade unions, the Government of India has not brought uniformity on these definitions so far.

The labour legislation is covering only 7 to 8 per cent of our working class. The limits imposed on employment or salary limit is excluding large section of the workforce from the purview of the labour laws. The payment of Bonus Act and Wages Act has become meaningless due to imposition of ceiling for coverage.

Enforcement machinery of the labour laws is so weak that the labour departments have no adequate staff to ensure their implementation. These laws have several loopholes which enable the employers to avoid their implementation. The power of exemption given to the administration is often misused to avoid implementation by certain sections of employers.

Several labour laws provide imprisonment for their violation but cases of such imprisonment are rarely found in most of the cases. Over Rs 1,500 crore of dues are pending with the employers on provident fund (PF) account, while the Employee's State Insurance (ESI) implementation is suffering from several defects.

The administrative expenditure in some of the welfare laws is so high that not much money is available for welfare. The benefits are received by a small section of workers keeping vast section of workers without any meaningful benefit.

Regarding corruption in the labour administration the less said the better. Employers skilfully use this situation to violate provisions of the labour laws. Only in areas where trade union movement is strong, the benefits of labour legislation reach the workers.

It would not be correct to say that all labour department officers are corrupt. There are many officers who are honest and sincere but the corrupt officers have given a bad name to the entire labour machinery. A strong action by the government against such officers may help in improving the situation.

The industrial relations law is dilatory and delayed justice is denying justice. The conciliation machinery is not time bound and employers can remain absent to delay the settlement of issues. The tribunals take years to settle and employers go to Supreme Court on almost every issue to tire our workers from fighting court case. Several labour courts have no presiding officers for years or so with the result that pending cases are increasing year by year!

On the whole, the law is heavily loaded against the workers who are losing faith in labour judiciary. I had to take up one representation of about 130 lawyers of Chennai with the Union Labour Ministry who complained that one particular presiding officer did not give single judgement in favour of the workers for the whole year!

There is no law at the national level providing for recognition of trade union, though in some states that provision is made to decide after conducting secret ballot of workers in the unit. In the absence of national laws, employers are in a position to recognize a union of their choice ignoring the claim of a real representative union.

The present procedure of verification of membership agreed in the 15th Indian Labour Conference in 1957 is unscientific since it only estimates the membership. It gives wide powers to the verifying officer who is likely to misuse it to advantage of some union. It does not verify the membership of agricultural workers since they change employers as well as place of work periodically. The verification of membership of central trade unions also is suffering from the same defect.

The experience of several countries shows that with less number of labour laws the labour administration has been functioning more effectively.

There is an urgent need to review the working of the labour laws and making them more effective to serve the interests of the working class.

DEMOCRATIC FUNCTIONING OF TRADE UNIONS

Trade union democracy is a crucial prerequisite of a genuine trade union movement. Unless a member of a union feels that she/he has a personal involvement in deciding the policy of the union, we cannot say that real democracy is established in the trade union. Unless the average member of a union is conscious of his right as a member of a union, she/he would not be able to contribute in deciding the policy of the union. For this purpose, a proper education of rank and file workers in the union assumes importance.

In the absence of this, the member of the union does not actively participate in the activity of the union. Her/his participation remains passive. One can witness this phenomenon when one observers the small participation of the workers in the general body meetings of the union.

Even participation of workers in the working committee/executive committee of the unions is below mark and an active participation in union discussion is much inadequate. A handful of leading workers only participate in the discussion, while majority of the workers are silent spectators during the course of discussion. The need to hold the meetings regularly is also an important aspect of trade union democracy.

In my study of trade union functioning in the city of Sholapur for my doctoral thesis, I found this weakness of trade union movement in general.

The union activity is thus carried by handful of individuals, while the majority of the executive committee members as well as rank and file workers remain uninvolved. This results in stagnation of membership in the union.

It has been observed that some unions do not get approval of a well-attended general body of the union before signing an agreement with the management. Commitment of the rank and file workers to the bipartite or tripartite agreement is an important aspect of trade union democracy. I have seen some cases when the productivity agreement could not be implemented since the workers did not agree with the commitment given by the union leadership. Hence, it is important to ensure that agreed norms of production by the members of the union are implemented properly. The practice of signing agreement behind the back of workers is hitting at the very concept of trade union democracy.

Intolerance to any criticism by ordinary workers about the union functioning by a section of leadership is not conducive to healthy growth of trade union movement. Accountability of the leadership to ordinary members of the union is of vital importance to democratic functioning of trade unions. I am informed that when one union in France conducted a study on the reactions of union members towards its functioning, it was found out that the workers were highly critical about the undemocratic methods of trade union functioning.

There are several unions who function democratically but erroneous trends are visible in some trade unions. There is an urgent need to overcome this weakness of the trade union movement so that the qualitative growth of trade union movement in India is ensured to serve the interests of the working class more effectively.

WHITHER TRIPARTISM IN INDIA?

The Union Labour Ministry has about 35 tripartite committees but most of them do not function effectively. Some of the committees have not even met for couple of years! Whenever the meetings are called they are normally half day affair and discuss issues perfunctorily which do not help in solving the problem. Some of the committees function as rituals and defeat the purpose of tripartite consultation. Some trade union leaders have gone to the extent of calling such meetings as 'tea and biscuit committees'. Postponement of already convened meeting is a frequent phenomenon.

It is also seen that the decisions taken in these meeting do not get implemented. Frequent changes in the labour ministry officials as well as ministers are also one of the factors that are making tripartite machinery ineffective.

The Governmet of India has devalued the status of the labour ministry as an institution. This portfolio which was once held by stalwarts like Gulzarilal Nanda, Jagajivan Ram, V.V. Giri and others is now given to a minister of state only. He does not have any authority over the employing ministries whose ministers are holding cabinet status! I have seen in many tripartite committees senior representatives of employing ministries are refusing to attend the meeting.

The Indian Labour Conference and the Standing Labour Committee have been converted into debating societies without arriving at decisions of long-standing importance. During the last 10 years I cannot see a single decision of the Indian Labour Conference which has long-term implications. The Standing Labour Committee which was a committee to review the labour relations scene in the country is being converted into a committee to decide the agenda of the Indian Labour Conference. The devaluation of the tripartite machinery in India is indicative of the thinking of the government to reduce tripartite consultation.

The Government of India is having regular dialogues with the employers' organizations through senior ministers attending meetings convened by employers' organizations but there is no regular dialogue with the central trade unions. The decline of tripartism is in a way adversely affecting the right of trade unions to have a say in industrial relations machinery.

TRADE UNIONS AND WORKING WOMEN

Job opportunity for working women in India is still a distant dream. In the organized sector the employment of women is only 10-11 per cent, while in the unorganized sector it is about 30 per cent. Women are denied job opportunities in several sectors of employment. They are not allowed to work on heavy machines in several industries, while the Planning Commission itself is coming out with the idea of women-oriented jobs like *papad* making, candle manufacturing, etc. In the coal mines, there is a voluntary retirement scheme by which a woman can retire and a male family member can seek her job. Even now in several industries, including some MNCs, pregnant women are denied jobs. The practice of women losing job after marriage continues in some of our industries. The laws concerning the rights of women at work such as Maternity Benefit Act, provision of creche, ban on night shift work, etc., are considered by some to be responsible for less jobs for women in our industrial undertakings.

Some trade unions do not take up working women's problems in their charter of demands. There is a tendency to consider the problems of women workers as their own problem and not the problems of the union. This has resulted in less women membership of trade unions. The issue is more severe in the case of Dalit and minority women. Though formation of coordination committee of working women has created more awareness among the unions to take up the issues of women workers, the task on the whole is sadly neglected.

Trade unions have to strive more to nurture women activists in the unions. Today we find that even industries where women are in a majority in the workforce, the union executive committees are dominated by male workers. In the industry level, state level or the national level the presence of women activists is still insignificant in India. In tripartite committees of the Government of India, the number of women is extremely negligible.

Trade unions have to give a special emphasis to educate women on principles of trade unionism, etc., so that they can discharge union responsibilities more effectively. Many times the union meetings are held at a time not convenient for women due to their domestic responsibilities. Most of the women are at the lower levels of the ladder at the workplace. Their number is reducing at the level of skilled and highly skilled levels as well as executive level.

Sexual harassment of working women at the workplace is widespread in India, but the steps to check the menace are insufficient. Women are reluctant to complain about sexual harassment due to lack of stringent action against the culprits and quite often the complainant's moral character is questioned by the perpetrators of crime. Molestation and rape of working women at the workplace or while travelling to the workplace are quite frequent, yet not much action has been taken by the authorities. Demanding sexual favours to facilitate promotion of a women employee is also common in workplaces.

Despite directive from the Supreme Court, the Government of India has not prepared a law to impose heavy punishment to the criminals. It has only defined what amounts to sexual harassment, but no punishment is prescribed for the criminal acts. The unit level grievance committees are also not functioning properly. Since at times perpetrators of crime are union members, the unions do not take keen interest or try to pressurize the woman employee for mutual settlements in order to avoid punishment against the culprit.

Hence, the trade union movement has to take up the question of ensuring equality for women at the workplace. Increasing participation of women in the trade union movement will further strengthen the movement itself. Trade union movement has to play a crucial role in the general women's movement for liberation and equality with men in all aspects of social life.

CURSE OF CHILD LABOUR

India has the dubious distinction of employing the largest number of child labourers in the world. Though it is difficult to assess the extent of child labour, it is observed that nearly 5 crore children in India are working for a pittance of a wage instead of studying in the school. ILO has funded several projects to create awareness among the workers about the need to abolish the system of child labour. However, there has not been a significant decline in the number of child workers in our industrial undertakings.

Two decades ago the Government of India passed a law prohibiting child labour in jobs of a hazardous nature. However, the law has by and large remained unimplemented and the number of children working in hazardous nature of jobs has increased during the last two decades. The millennium goals specifically stipulate that child labour in hazardous industries should be abolished by 2012. However, the indications point out that the goals are not likely to be achieved in India.

Child labour is a product of poverty prevailing in the social system. As long as poverty remains in the society, child labour cannot be abolished. It is observed that in the US, UK and other advanced countries, the phenomenon of child labour still prevails. Minimum wages in the country are so low that parents find it difficult to maintain their children and educate them. Unless need-based wages are paid to the workers, child labour can never be abolished by legal provisions.

Studies conducted on the working conditions of child labour clearly show that they work in extremely vulnerable conditions and are deprived of an adequate nutritional standard. Child labour prevents the proper development of physique of a child whose health gets impaired for life. The condition of girl child labour is indeed pitiable. They are sexually exploited by employers. Their destiny is doomed at a tender age.

Midday meal schemes have no doubt improved the number of children studying in schools. However, privatization of the preparation of meal has been converted into a source of profit by unscrupulous contractors, who have reduced the nutritional quality and quantity of midday meals. The government should provide proper clothing and educational material to poor children which may help in increasing the students in primary schools.

Trade union movement has to take more interest in the problems of child labour. The parents of child labour are at times members of trade unions, and hence, the question should acquire special significance for trade unions. The struggle to abolish the system of child labour should be closely linked with enhancing the wage level of the working class and abolition of poverty in the society as a whole. Giving sermons to hungry parents about the inhuman nature of the system of child labour will not carry any meaning. No poor father would like his son or daughter remain in poverty conditions.

The conspicuous consumption by the super rich in the Indian society should be treated as an anti-social act as long as the scourge of child labour prevails in Indian society. But today they are the most glorified people in the society!

SHOCKING CONDITIONS IN THE IT SECTOR

The IT sector which has developed faster in India than any other sector employs nearly 15 lakh workers. It is estimated that in the next 3-4 years the number is likely to increase to 20-5 lakh.

A study conducted by V.V. Giri National Labour Institute has highlighted the shocking conditions in the IT sector at NOIDA, near New Delhi. The study compared the conditions with a nineteenth-century prison. In another place the study points out that the IT sector employees are living a life which was last witnessed in the Roman slave ships.

The employees are working in two shifts which compel them to work for 12 hours or more a day. The bigger companies are paying better pay scales, but in call centres the earnings of employees are very poor. Due to constant staring at the computer screen, the cathode rays emitted by the monitor affect the eyes of the employees, while the cases of colour blindness are frequently reported by the employees. Some Australian trade unions have demanded that pregnant women should not be asked to work on the computer since it would affect the health of the baby. Due to excessive stress to the brain, the employees become irritated and many employees have a shattered family life due to continuous working in the night shift.

The IT sector workers do not have job security. At times employees are terminated without even giving notice. There is no uniformity in pay scales and working conditions. The attrition rate is perhaps the highest in the IT sector. Managements do not allow formation of trade unions. Several employees had to face termination notices for forming unions or taking up the grievances of the employees with the management. There are instances of penal actions when employees made collective representation to the management demanding improvement in working conditions. Many jobs from advanced countries are coming to the Indian IT sector since wages in India are one-tenth of the wages available to the workers in advanced countries like the US.

Some organizations have referred this problem in the IT industry to the Government of India, demanding a legislation to govern the working and living conditions for the employees in the sector. The government is refusing to do so, on the plea that any legal mechanism will prevent IT jobs coming to India.

Some state governments offer undue concession to IT sector managements to give encouragement to start IT centres in their states. As a matter of fact, there is a competition going on among different state governments to offer concession to the IT sector. This naturally results in ignoring the conditions of the workers. The trade union movement has to take up the problem in right earnest to ensure proper working conditions to these employees.

In a similar manner the workers working in export processing zones or special economic zones (SEZs) are deprived of benefits of all the labour laws. Some state governments have openly announced the exemption of SEZ from the purview of the labour laws. In a complaint to ILO, CITU criticized the powers given to development commissioners to decide the matters relating to labour. The ILO recommended that there should be an independent mechanism to deal with problems of industrial relations, but the Government of India has not implemented the observations of the ILO.

The workers in SEZs are not allowed to form a union and any worker opposing the exploitation is summarily dismissed from service and the labour department does not consider such cases as industrial dispute. As a result, the working conditions are extremely bad and inhuman.

The united demand made by the trade unions to cover the SEZs by labour laws and that trade unions should be allowed to function in them is not accepted by the government. Only the company unions are allowed to function which make a mockery of trade union movement.

FORMATION OF CONFEDERATION OF TRADE UNIONS

We have already noted that the present disunity in the trade union movement is immensely damaging the collective bargaining strength of the trade union movement. Therefore, there is an urgent need to evolve a common policy framework for the advancement of the working class and the trade union movement. Attempts to merge some trade unions have been made in the past which has not proved to be successful. The talks between AITUC and HMS and talks between HMS and INTUC about merger have not been successful which clearly indicate that an immediate merger of trade unions is not possible in the present Indian context. Therefore, it is necessary to make some interim arrangement for bringing together all trade unions on a common platform, irrespective of ideological affiliations. Workers having ideological moorings should be welcome, but it should not be allowed to come in the way of common struggle of the working class against the attacks on their living standard.

The formation of a confederation of trade unions can be a way to find out an interim arrangement of trade unions to come together on a united platform on common issues facing the working class. The decision of a confederation should be unanimously or by consensus and not by a majority opinion. A confederation can adopt a policy on agreed decision through a process of dialogue among the central unions, while continuing debate on issues on which there are differences within the trade unions. In this way, measures can be taken to evolve a common understanding among the trade unions to strive for a movement on common issues acceptable to all. A recent experience of all central trade unions coming together on a common platform on burning issues of the working class, namely, rise in prices of essential commodities, growing unemployment and the need to extend relief to unemployed persons, non-implementation of labour laws and steps to ensure their full implementation, provision of proper funding for ensuring effective social security schemes for the unorganized workers and opposing the policy of disinvestment of profit-making public sector undertakings. The convention held in Delhi on 14 September 2009 evolved a complete united understanding among all the trade unions, the decision to organize a national protest day on 28 October 2009 and for holding a massive demonstration before parliament during the winter session. As noted earlier, this unity developed from above is to be converted into unity from below, which alone will create a confidence in the minds of the workers that through unity and determination the working class can achieve their demands. Therefore, I consider that formation of a confederation of Indian trade unions can give a concrete organizational shape to the trade unions in India which can strive for better bargaining power for the working class.

Workers can have their political affiliations, they can join political parties, but the confederation will be an agency only to organize struggles on some common issues. There may be occasions when confederation may have to take a stand on political issues but such decisions can be by evolving common understanding within the trade unions. The confederation can take steps for further unification of trade union movement by bringing together all industrywise federations into a common organization and also take positive measures to strengthen trade unionism in the unorganized and rural sector. Already a welcome trend is emerging in the country when all industrywise federations are coming together on common issues and achieving their demands through joint movements and struggles.

If confidence is restored among the trade unions, then it is possible to take measures to unify the local unions in a phased manner by adopting a principle of merging of small unions into a large one by deciding its strength through secret ballot.

There is an urgent need to strengthen the democratic functioning of the trade unions, if a confederation is to succeed. There may be difficulties in the formation of a confederation, but trade union organizations will have to be convinced through proper debate and confidence-building measures. The confederation can be formed only after a united understanding is developed among all the trade unions. It is hoped that the trade union movement in India will rise to the occasion and give a positive response to the proposal as a step towards its unification.

Already a campaign is being made by the champions of globalization that the trade union movement has become irrelevant in today's context. Organizational unity of the trade union movement in India will certainly prove that the relevance of the trade union movement is much more today than at any other time in its history.

FORMATION OF ONE UNION IN ONE INDUSTRY

The trade union movement has to properly develop its own perspective in the present challenging situation, while an objective of formation of one union in one industry should be accepted by all. Steps should be taken in the direction of bringing together trade unions with a view to ultimately achieving complete unification of the trade union movement. The formation of a single trade union can be achieved only if democracy is properly introduced within the trade union movement. Many trade unions have split due to undemocratic functioning and individual aggrandisement. Unfortunately, a trend is emerging in India where some persons tried to make trade union functioning a source of personal income. Such trade union leaders will always object to formation of a single trade union within the industry. Therefore, there is a need for development of the consciousness in the working class against such individualistic tendencies. In some sectors, there are only single unions which are in a position to serve the working class better. The present disunity can be reduced by creating awareness among the mass of the workers in favour of building a united trade union movement. If the objective of formation of a single trade union in an industry is accepted, then it is possible to work out the modalities of merger of trade unions on democratic lines. In order to ensure that all groups are given a fair treatment, it would be useful to implement the concept of proportionate representation so that a particular group cannot be kept away from the leadership by a dominant group.

There is a tremendous sentiment of unity within the lower cadres in trade union movement and among the rank and file workers. Every person who has interest in the working class movement at his heart would wholeheartedly welcome the move for unity of trade unions. This sentiment can be utilized for development of common organization of working class by bringing together all the trade unions working in a particular factory or establishment. This would further help in ultimate formation of a single national central trade union in India.

CULTURAL AND SOCIAL ACTIVITIES OF TRADE UNIONS

To improve the quality of life of the working class, mere increase in wages is not enough. Hence, trade union movement will have to pay more attention to improve the cultural and social aspects of workers' livelihood. Very few trade unions in our country keep in touch with the family members of the workers. However, some of the unions which arranged periodic get-together of family members, have received tremendous response from the workers and it helped to improve the social life of the workers. Several workers have got artistic and literary talents, some have composed poems, scripted dramas, wrote articles in magazines, acted in dramas and performed exceedingly well in sports and games. The trade unions, therefore, have to pay special attention to these aspects also to develop their cultural and artistic talents so that the cultural life of the workers and their families are improved radically, otherwise, the relations with workers become impersonal and sometimes even contradictory policies are taken by different sections of the workers. It is our experience that some of our unions have started libraries for the members to improve their reading habits. But such trends to organize workers on the basis of caste and language, which adversely affect the unity and understanding of the workers should be avoided.

Due to poverty conditions, several workers do not get opportunities for their cultural development. Trade unions should help such workers and give them an opportunity to develop cultural values in them.

Trade unions which have taken steps to organize literacy campaigns among the workers with a view to make all workers literate had helped the unions in improving the quality of their membership. The trade unions have to play a role in removing false notions and illusions prevailing in their minds due to their social backwardness. Development of social and scientific outlook among the members of the union enhances the quality of the union activities.

TRADE UNIONS AND COOPERATIVE MOVEMENT

Many trade unions have started cooperatives to help the workers in improving their living conditions. Cooperative credit societies are being run by several unions to meet the credit needs of members of the unions. There are multi-purpose cooperative societies run by the unions such as supply of provision and other essential commodities, arranging transport facilities, running canteen for the workers in establishments, provision of holiday homes for workers at concessional rates for the members of the union. Some of the unions have also started developing cooperative banks and doing good work to help the members of the union. However, there are several complaints of corruption also in some of the societies and legal actions have to be taken against some of them. There should be a better social control over the functioning of the societies and there is an urgent need to make the workers vigilant about the working of the societies. Unless and until the societies are run democratically, they cannot be successful.

In some undertakings, the managements have taken initiatives in forming workers cooperatives which are, in fact, not strictly cooperative societies of the workers, but are management-run organizations which have been formed to avoid the implementation of the provisions of the Contract Labour (Regulation and Abolition) Act. The trade unions should object to formation of such fictitious cooperative societies, which are in practice, agencies built to exploit them. There are examples of leaders keeping their control over the unions through their control over the societies having turnover of crores of rupees in some of the major public- and private-sector undertakings. Leaving aside these aberrations, the cooperative movement can play an important role in helping the working class in improving their standard of living if properly organized.

SOCIAL RESPONSIBILITY OF TRADE UNIONS

The trade unions being the most advanced section of the society, should also have an attitude of doing positive work to help the needy people in the society. Some of the unions are doing good social activities like helping the poor people around the industrial areas by providing them medical facilities and trying to help them in organizing their struggles for better living conditions. Some of the unions have even participated in gram panchayat activities and trying to help the rural poor in giving them better quality of life. Such activities will popularize the union among the poorer section of the society. During national calamities or certain mishaps, trade unions have contributed good amount of money collected from the workers which reflects the social consciousness in the minds of the workers and their responsibility towards deprived sections of the society. The trade union cadres should be encouraged to help the poorer sections of the society whose standard of living is extremely low and who find it exceedingly difficult to make both the ends meet. Some of the trade unions do not educate workers to create awareness about their social responsibility. Trade union movement should not make the working class a selfish class which looks after their personal interests alone and not fully concerned about the pitiable conditions of their brothers and sisters who live around them. It is necessary to create awareness among the trade union movement in our country so that it can play a much more important role in improving the working and living conditions of the people at large.

RATIFICATION OF CORE CONVENTION OF ILO

The Government of India has been extremely slow in ratifying the ILO conventions. The number of conventions ratified by the British government during twenty-eight years of their colonial rule was about the same ratified by the Government of India during the last sixty-two years of Independence. It had not ratified the conventions relating to freedom of association and right to collective bargaining. The thirty-seven conventions of the ILO ratified by India have also not been implemented in their true spirit.

The ILO has eight conventions as the Core Conventions and it is expected that the Government of India should take steps to ratify them at an early date. In the year of the 90th Anniversary of the ILO, the Government of India is expected to ratify some of the Core

Conventions. But no such steps are forthcoming from the government. The Director General of the ILO, Somavia Juan has visualized that ratification of the Core Conventions is an important prerequisite to ensure work. But the Government of India's positive approach is not forthcoming so far. The Core Conventions of the ILO are as follows:

Nomenclature	Convention No.	Year of Adoption
Freedom of association and protection of the right to organize	87	1948
Right to organize and collective bargaining	98	1949
Forced labour	29	1930
Abolition of forced labour	105	1957
Minimum age	138	1973
Worst form of child labour	182	1999
Equal remuneration	100	1951
Discrimination (employment and occupation)	111	1958

Out of these Core Conventions, the Government of India has so far ratified only four conventions relating to forced labour, equal remuneration, abolition of forced labour and discrimination in employment and occupations. The other four are not being considered for adoption by the government though India is one of the founder members of the ILO.

The trade union movement in the country should unanimously take steps through nationwide campaign and movements to ensure that the government ratifies all the Core Conventions of the ILO. If it takes steps for ratification of the Core Conventions, it would give a positive message to the developing countries all over the world to follow suit and take steps to ratify these conventions.

The advanced countries are advocating a linkage of ratification of the Core Conventions with trade relations. The trade union movement of India while opposing the very concept of linking the trade relations with such ratification, should continue to press the government for an early ratification of the Core Conventions, which will ensure better working and service conditions of the working population of India.

THE ROLE OF MAFIAS

As in several countries in the world, mafias are playing an unsavoury role in trade union movements. In coal mines, for example, mafias are controlling the social life while playing a negative role in the development of the industry. In a study conducted by the Union Labour Ministry during 1970s, several mafias who were parading as trade union leaders were acting as moneylenders and recovering monthly interest amounts from the workers. Some of the trade union leaders are indulging in taking benami contracts and amassing ill-gotten wealth at the cost of development of industry and living conditions of the workers. The existence of mafia is perpetuating in coal mines and other industrial undertakings due to political patronage they receive from several leaders. These mafias have private armies to terrorize workers and the people. Such existence of mafias is depriving the genuine trade unions from carrying out legitimate activities. Several trade union leaders had been brutally murdered by mafias who did not respect any law of the land. Such a detrimental system is allowed to continue in our country because of the secret donations they give to various political parties to enable them to carry forward their depredations. A strong action against such activities in our industrial undertakings is required to stop such gangsterism within the trade union movement.

PROBLEMS OF OCCUPATIONAL HEALTH AND SAFETY

With the advent of modern technology in our industry, several new health hazards have also developed in our industrial undertakings. Thousands of chemicals are being used in our industries which adversely affect the health of our workers. Despite worldwide campaign to ban the use of asbestos, it is still being produced in India and its consumption is increasing year by year. The ship-breaking industry is exposing the workers to several dangerous chemicals adversely affecting their health. In coal industry also, the dreaded disease pneumoconiosis is causing health hazard to thousands of workers every year. Workers are exposed to several carcinogenic substances adversely affecting their health. The Government of India has amended the Factory's Act to provide some measures against occupational hazards, but its implementation is tardy and workers continue to suffer. In road accidents, more than 40,000 workers are dying every year. In the absence of any statutory mechanism to ensure full protection to workers, victims of occupational diseases are suffering.

The multinational companies who observe strict rules regarding occupational safety in their country are not doing so in India. The example of Union Carbide in Bhopal which violated all safety norms which they were implementing in US was sadly neglected in India which must be appropriately stressed in the forthcoming period so that workers are properly informed about the safety norms. India should identify occupational diseases for every industry and adopt suitable measures to protect the workers from these hazards. If any worker becomes a victim of the occupational disease, she/he should be fully rehabilitated by the employers. In the absence of identification of industrywise occupational diseases, the workers are suffering in an acute manner without any rehabilitation attempt. The imposition by some managements to impose voluntary retirement for such workers should be put an end to. It is necessary to ensure full statutory inspections which should not be given up in the name of abolition of inspector raj. Strong measures are necessary if the inspectors misuse their powers and resort to corrupt practices to avoid action against the employer.

In the forthcoming period, steps must be taken to develop an internal safety organization by involving trade unions at all levels. Workers' inspectors should be developed to inspect the working conditions and should point out the neglect of safety at the shop level. Stringent punishment should be provided for violators of all safety norms. Workmen's compensation should be enhanced substantially to fully rehabilitate the workers. International experience in ensuring safe working conditions and knowledge available in different countries should be properly studied and steps should be taken to improve the safe conditions in our industrial undertakings. Cost considerations should not come in the way of taking measures to provide safe working conditions for our working class.

SIMPLIFICATION OF LABOUR LAWS

The plethora of labour legislation in India is causing several problems for the trade union movement in dealing with labour relations machinery in tackling the problems of the workers. Even employers are sometimes saying that it is difficult for them to deal with all the labour laws. There is an urgent need to plug the loopholes of the labour legislations which enable the employers to find ways and means to avoid their implementation, e.g. there is a ceiling of wages for coverage of workmen in several legislations which prevents large sections of the workmen from coming within the purview of the law. Then several laws provide arbitrary powers to the administration to exempt certain units from the purview of the labour law. This power is misused rampantly and corruption is also involved in granting exemption to certain units from the purview of the law. Moreover, certain clauses in the law remain so vague that they are liable to be interpreted in different ways which only encourage litigation. The First National Labour Commission tried to prepare a labour code by bringing several laws under common umbrella legislation. However, it was actually an amalgamation of various labour laws and no attempt was made to improve their content. As a result, it was not acceptable to the trade union movement. In many countries, there are only limited numbers of labour laws, but they are implemented strictly by the governments while in India, there are plenty of labour laws, but most of them have remained unimplemented. It is necessary to have a detailed discussion to improve the present labour legislation and consolidated them on five major topics, viz.

1. Wages and other terms of service conditions
2. Social security
3. Industrial relations
4. Welfare measure
5. Vocational training and employment guarantee

If comprehensive labour laws are prepared and they are properly administered, it will certainly help make the labour laws beneficial to the working class. It is, therefore, necessary to increase the coverage of the labour legislation in a phased manner so as to ultimately cover all workers to ensure that nobody is excluded from the purview of the Act.

The trade union movement should initiate detailed discussions on the issues and prepare concrete proposals to see that the laws become more effective and beneficial to the interests of the workers. Then, attempts can be made collectively to pressurize the Government of India to introduce such beneficial labour legislation. At a certain stage, there may be a resistance from the side of employers to implement some of the progressive provisions, but united assertion by the trade union movement will ultimately result in taking effective measures to reform the present labour legislation.

TRADE UNIONS ARE INSTRUMENTAL IN SOCIAL CHANGES

The present society is based on the economic inequality and political discrimination. The prevailing corruption in the bureaucracy and political leadership is coming in the way of accelerating social progress and the bottlenecks in eliminating poverty in the society. In the Indian context, when the profits of big business houses are increasing sky-high and the poor people are committing suicides and killing their kith and kin just because they are unable to provide them with the elementary needs of human existence. The present capitalist society is based on exploitation of the working class and the toiling people of our country and the trade union movement is resisting the very basis of the exploitation. In such a situation, the trade unions have an important role to play in changing the present society into a more progressive and toiling people-oriented society. Today, the profits and share markets are given more priority than the needs of the common people. The conspicuous consumption of the upper strata of the society is increasing at a faster rate while the poverty and destitution is growing day by day. Under these circumstances, the trade unions and the working class have a social responsibility to champion the cause of the toiling masses and leading them for a social change in favour of the poor people and take the stringent measures against exploitation. Here, the trade unions can play their role effectively. They would be able to perform their historic responsibility in deciding the destiny of the common people of India. The World Social Forum has given a slogan 'Another World is Possible'. The working class has to play a leading role in bringing about such a new world order. India has accepted a socialist pattern of society, but it is essentially building a capitalist society. The trade unions have to struggle to bring a genuine socialist system in India which will ensure happiness for all. As the Indian philosophy has advocated:

> *sarve bhavantu sukhinah, sarve santu niramaya,*
> *sarve bhadrani pashyantu, maa kashchid-dukhabhavbhaveta!*
>
> May all beings be happy, may all be healthy, may people have the well-being of all in mind, may nobody suffer in any way.

This concept can be implemented in its true spirit only under a socialist system which abolishes exploitation of man by man. It is hoped that the trade union movement of tomorrow should reorient to approach and strive for such a social transformation. History has given this responsibility to the working class. Let us prepare the working class to discharge its historic mission.

CHAPTER 3

Working Class Movement in Kerala

M.M. LAWRENCE

In simple terms, a person who directs the organization of an industry is a capitalist. A person who is hired to perform work in the industry is a worker. A formation of industrial workers, having the objective to promote welfare of workers in broad terms, can be called working class. The object of this essay is to briefly trace the working class movement in Kerala from around a century ago to the present times.

Conceptually, as viewed from the points of view of the Western thinkers, a capitalist normally inherits or has an access to wealth. He does not need to work to meet the bare necessities of life. On the contrary, a worker has neither any inherited wealth nor has any access to wealth. A worker works for his livelihood. Capitalist class and working class are not based on rigidities. At times, though rarely, cross migration occur between these classes. Such rare happening occurs, for example, when a capitalist loses his capital, he would be forced to seek any work for his living. Conversely, a worker may become successful in selling a profitable idea and thus may assume the role of a capitalist through partnership or by borrowing capital.

Prior to the end of British rule in India, in 1947, Kerala was divided into three princely states: Travancore, Cochin and parts of Malabar of Madras presidency. Traditionally, the social order in Kerala closely resembled the feudal order of the West. However, unlike in the West, slavery was not imposed on anybody. The society was organized in such a way that one could assume his role in the society by birth itself. Caste system was prevalent all over India and each caste was assigned to do a particular work traditionally. Caste rigidities were firmly entrenched so that cross migration, as in the West, was impossible. The caste was built into economic and social system in such a way that the landholdings were not allowed to fritter away. The Namboodiris of Kerala, unlike the Brahmins in the rest of India, were predominantly landholders. Nairs, who were considered as forward caste, people to a lesser extent, were also landholders. A system of matrimonial and semi-matrimonial alliances was intricately built into social mores of these two communities in such a way that both Namboodiris and Nairs held on to their respective inherited land without being fractured thorough inheritance. All other backward castes and Dalits were firmly entrenched with stiff rigidities, such as for example, certain barber castes rendered services solely to Brahmins and Nairs; while certain other barber castes rendered services only to backward castes. Other religious communities such as Muslims and Christians moderately influenced social mores. At the same time, converts to these religious groups carried with them some of the vestiges of caste traditions to which they belonged prior to their religious conversion.

Against this backdrop, naturally reforms took place, especially, in the caste system during the initial stages. Many of the reformers were belonged to elite classes. V.T. Bhattathiripad was a Namboodiri; Sree Narayana Guru Swami was from the Eezhava caste; Mannathu Padmanabhan was a Nair, meanwhile, Ayyanjkali was a Dalit. They strived to put an end to the oppressiveness of the caste system. Certain reformers, especially, Sree Narayana Guru Swami, sought to uplift Eezhavas to the status of Brahmins by imbibing in the Eezhava community some of the desirable traits of good living of Brahmin caste.

INDUSTRIAL ERA

Kerala's industrial era had begun in the coir and tile factories and also in the tea plantations. According to a study conducted by T.V. Ushadevi and V.N. Jayachandran,[1] tea industry was introduced in Travancore in Calvyooni coffee estate in Kollam. The first tea estate in Travancore at Penchurst estate was started by F.M. Parker in 1875. During the initial periods, the total area of tea cultivation was on 200-500 acres. When labourers from Ceylon were brought for work, the area of cultivation increased tremendously.

In 1894, John Muir of the House of Finlays of Glasgow bought a large tract of high altitude virgin jungle in the state of Travancore.

Between 1896 and 1898, a reorganization of the estates owned by Muir, or managed by the Finlay Muir & Co. resulted in the formation of the tea estates like the Consolidated Tea and Lands Co. Limited, the Amalgamated Tea Estates Co. Limited, the Kanan Devan Hills Produce Co. Limited and the Anglo-American Direct Tea Trading Co. Limited, all of which were floated on the stock market. In 1900, Kanan Devan Tea Company alone had 19 estates. The area of cultivation jumped from 3,352 acres (during 1885-90) and 34,555 acres in 1914. Finlays finally divested itself of its Indian tea estates, when its shareholdings were sold to the Tatas, with whom the company had been in partnership for some years.

Though industrial employment in large scale in Kerala began with plantations, the coir factory workers of Alleppey took the initiative to form trade unions in Kerala. The 'Travancore Labour Association', the first labour organization in Kerala was formed in Alleppey in April 1922. In the plantation sector, trade unions emerged much later in 1930 with the formation of an organization for plantation labourers at Mundakayam.

Convinced by the business prospects of coir fibre and yarn, James Darragh, an American of Irish origin came to Alleppey, which was the main port in Travancore at that time and started a manufacturing unit there with the establishment of the first coir factory in 1859. He enlisted the help of the foreign trader called Henry Smail and the factory became known as 'Darragh, Smail & Company'. Later, other industrial heavyweights of the time, followed in establishing coir factories in Alleppey, Kollam, Kozhikode, Kochi and other parts of Kerala. The first labour strike took place in Kerala in the year 1907, in protest against the 12-hour work norm prevalent in the Derragh, Smail & Company. Consequently, the working hours got reduced by one and a half hours.

Tracing the early history of trade unions, it can be said that Vadapuram B.K. Bava, who belonged to the Eezhava caste, used his position as *Muppan*, the designation for yard superintendent in the Empire Coir Works, to form a union of workers in Alleppey as he was inspired by the teachings of Sree Narayana Guru Swami. This organization was called 'Labour Union'. Initially, the workers looked upon his organization with suspicion and only a few workers joined just to please the *Muppan*. A more serious attempt to form the union was undertaken, in April 1922, when the general body of workers adopted the name 'Travancore Labour Association' (TLA). The TLA was later registered under the Travancore Trade Union Act of 1937. At the time of registration, TLA was renamed as the Travancore Coir Factory Workers' Union (TCFWU).

The demands of the TCFWU were increase in wages, improvement in the working conditions, guaranteed minimum earnings, abolition of contract labour and prohibition of unauthorized deduction from the wages of *Muppans* and labourers by the contractors and recognition of the union. The Dewan of Travancore took keen interest in the settlement of strike and the government appointed the Board of Conciliation. Later, industrial relations worsened more in 1938. The police unleashed terror. Bava was killed in this lathi-charge and he became the first martyr of the labour movement in Travancore.

The death of Bava made the situation explosive. Later on, the All Travancore Trade Union Congress (ATTUC) was formed in Kerala. By this time, the communists were guiding the trade union movement. The ATTUC emerged as a platform for all shades of the Left wing unions in the state. The communists' approach to Quit India movement led to split into radical Left and Left socialists. The communists got well entrenched in the working class and the student community. Class struggle, violent agitations, and even mass armed revolts were considered appropriate to achieve social change. Alleppey became the centre of the communist movement.

The Punnappra-Vayalar revolt of 1946 was an important historical event in the history of trade union movement in Kerala. The workers in Alleppey declared a general strike in September 1946. The police and the workers clashed against each other. On 24 October 1946 armed conflict took place between the organized group of workers and police. Though started as a trade union agitation, the Punnappra-Vayalar revolt formed part of the political struggle for achieving freedom and responsible government.

The Dewan's attitude to trade unionism and industrial relations was probably ambivalent. Personally, he seemed to have had a soft corner for the working class. He used to encourage the growth of unionism, by influencing employers to give recognition to major unions. He strongly held the view that industrial disputes should be settled through joint consultations. He took an initiative in setting up a tripartite system and formed a labour department as well as the Industrial Relation Committees (IRCs). But the Dewan was strongly opposed to the mixing up of unionism with politics. Therefore, he held that Punnappra-Vayalar revolt as a political struggle against the established government. Considering the many aspects of trade union involvement in politics, the Dewan banned the Communist Party and pro-communist trade unions in the state.

During the period 1930-1 a labour strike took place in the Kozhikode Commonwealth Cotton Mill. Tile factories and power loom textile sector also witnessed labour strikes. These strikes were not held under the banner of any trade union.

Another major industry that dawned in Kerala during that era was the tile industry. In 1928 the workers in the tile industry in Quilon came together to form the Quilon Labour Union.

The cashew sector in Kerala was another important sector where trade union had large number of members. Female cashew workers, whose number range between 2,00,000 and 4,00,000, depending on the availability of work, form the majority of the factory workers in the state. Most of them had been organized into trade unions since the 1940s or 1950s. They were very militant, if militancy could be measured in terms of man-days lost due to strikes.

According to a study by Anna Lindberg (2005),[2] by the 1960s, the prominence of trade unions in cashew industry became too strong that a few factory owners began to shift their plants to neighbouring states, mainly in Tamil Nadu. At the same time, the owners began using whatever means they could to side-step the labour laws. One stratagem was to close down a factory every few months and reopen it under a new name.

Another was to open *kudivarappus*, non-registered, illegal factories in which no labour laws were followed and wages stood at about half the legal minimum wage for women. Illegal *kudivarappus* are said to have become rampant. Several cashew factories in Tamil Nadu are said to be owned by the same people who closed their factory in Kerala.

The Left parties and the unions were ultimately successful in nationalizing some of the cashew factories. At the end of the 1970s, Kerala became the largest employer in the cashew sector. However, although the state-owned factories were successful in the beginning, the success could not be sustained. Eventually, the factories were only opened for short periods each year. Moreover, the gender discrimination with regard to wages and unemployment benefits was almost as conspicuous even in the nationalized factories as in the private factories. The trade unions had limited success to eradicate this discrimination or for action against the illegal *kudivarappus.*

P. Krishna Pillai (1906-48) was one of the pioneers in organizing the coir workers in Alappuzha, cotton mill workers in Kozhikkode, beedi and weaving workers in Kannur and the peasants in Malabar.

TRADE UNION MOVEMENT AFTER INDEPENDENCE

Just as in rest of India, All India Trade Union Congress (AITUC), a Leftist central trade union organization, was prominent for several decades until the ideological split of the Communist Party. It forced grassroot level workers to form the Centre of Indian Trade Unions (CITU) in 1970 with B.T. Ranadive as president and P. Rama Murthy as general secretary. Since Independence, trade unions began to be organized into political groupings, which were either Leftists or Rightists. In Kerala for the last over three decades the state is ruled alternately by Leftist coalition (Left Democratic Front) and Rightist coalition (United Democratic Front) by turn. In all sectors there exists multiplicity of trade unions organized with an affiliation to all shades of Right or Left trade union movement.

Prominent central trade union organizations include CITU, AITUC and Hind Mazdoor Sabha (HMS)—all of them are ideologically Leftist organizations. No workers' organization claim to be rightist. However, the Indian National Trade Union Congress (INTUC) and Bharatiya Mazdoor Sangh (BMS) are alternatives to Leftist trade unions.

POLITICS, CASTE MINORITY AND IDEOLOGY

As mentioned in the beginning, reforms took place to eradicate caste-based oppressions. The reforms, however, failed to bring about a casteless society. The numerical balance in terms of votes in general election between the ideological Left and the ideological Right in Kerala is almost even. Therefore, the caste groupings try to tilt the balance either way. Similarly, Christians and Muslims though minorities in India, have almost equal numerical strength in Kerala. These religious groups together with Eezhavas have the numerical strength to sway political power to swing between ideological Left and Right.

Unlike the happenings in trade union movement in Tamil Nadu, trade unions in Kerala, however, relatively distanced themselves from caste strings. This probably is the silver lining in trade union movement.

CURRENT STATE OF TRADE UNIONS

All prominent trade unions in Kerala are normally led by the leaders from political parties that the trade unions may choose to elect. Organized labour are powerful in almost all sectors of industry, trade and services sectors. They include traditional industries like coir, cashew, plantations, and services like ports, road transport and shipping. Other industries like brick and mortar too have a strong trade union presence. However, in the Information and Communication Technology, a sun-rise industry, trade unions have no significant presence.

At the same time, the self-employed and artisans have trade unions. Landless agricultural workers and farmers have also formed their own organizations. Yet, there exists several workers who are not organized. They include migrant workers, whose number is steadily growing in Kerala. CITU has initiated mass contact programme with migrant workers to help them organized. New entrants to labour market are not concerned about regular jobs or trade unions. Even young workers who join the trade unions prefer to stay away from being active. Ideological leanings are steadily wakening amongst new generation of workers.

NOTES

1. http://www.scribd.com/doc/35221503/TEAWORKER-2.
2. Anna Lindberg (2005): *Modernisation and Effeminisation in India: Kerala Cashew Workers since 1930* (Copenhagen, Denmark: Nordic Institute of Asian Studies).

CHAPTER 4

Workers' Struggles and Challenges Ahead

V.B. ATHREYA

One of the key impacts of colonial rule in India was the process of decimation, through most of the nineteenth century, and especially, in its first half, of artisanal industries which led to the large-scale shift of population from urban areas to rural India. This had immense political and economic significance.

COLONIAL RULE

The emergence of the modern working class was an enormously complex and protracted process, especially under unfavourable circumstances characterized by the threefold exploitation of labour: pre-capitalist, colonial and capitalist. Following the development of the railways and associated engineering industries in the 1850s, first, the cotton textile industry, and later, jute, sugar and cement industries had rapidly increased constituting tremendous growth in the number of the industrial workforce.

This workforce was drawn from the distressed rural population, decimated by the colonial land and agricultural policies. This working class people were having extremely low wages, miserable living standards and highly exploitative working conditions. They also had steeped in pre-capitalist relations, both in terms of economic ties, linked with land and agriculture, and in terms of caste and other obscurantist structures. Even the recruitment process of workers to any factories for jobs through labour contractors was compartmentalization in terms of religion, caste and location of origin. This situation, of course, had posed huge challenges to the working class movement in its efforts to organize workers into unions and to develop their political and class consciousness.

Under these circumstances, it was no surprise that, while the political organization of the Indian bourgeoisie had already taken a concrete shape in the formation of the Indian National Congress by the mid-1880s, the first modern trade union emerged only in the second decade of the twentieth century in the shape of the Madras Labour Union of the workers of Buckingham Mill and Carnatic Mill in the Madras Presidency.

The first national conference of the All India Trade Union Congress took place only in 1920s, inspired both by the Russian Revolution of October 1917 and the mass national movement against colonial rule. Plagued by internal divisions and the systematic repression of trade unions by the colonial rulers, who foisted conspiracy cases against prominent trade union leaders and working class militants, the movement of the working class suffered several setbacks in the 1930s, but managed to survive and then gradually strengthen itself under the leadership of the political Left, with intermittent and inconsistent support from a section of the leaders of the Indian National Congress. The working class played an important role in the transition to freedom from colonial rule, a wave of industrial actions being the prominent feature of the two years on the eve of independence, 1945 and 1946.

WORKING CLASS MOVEMENT (1950 TO 1990)

The national and international context at the time of India's Independence was conductive to the relatively autonomous development of capitalism in India. For over three decades, the Indian ruling class attempted several development processes, although they were based on the stimulus to growth from public investment, import substitution and limited land reforms and produced an impressive rate of economic growth and diversification of industrial activities in comparison with the stagnation of the colonial period. However, the country ran into crisis by the mid-1960s, and the economy was characterized by relative stagnation from the mid-1960s to the end of the 1970s. The root of the crisis lies in the fact that the Indian bourgeoisie compromised with landlordism and imperialism, with the result that neither the agrarian revolution could be completed nor the fight against imperialism carried forward consistently.

However, during this phase of economic development from the early 1950s to the end of the 1970s, the working class expanded significantly and the working class movement made rapid strides as well. The impressive achievements of the working class and the trade union movement in this phase became evident when one recalls that, during the colonial rule, well into the twentieth century, 15-hour working days were common in factories and the daily real wage was often poorer than the daily prison rations. Despite the systematic attempt by the Congress after Independence to split each mass organization that had been under one banner during the freedom movement, and despite serious ideological differences within the Left movement itself, militant and united trade union struggles took place through the turbulent 1970s, thanks to the maturity of the leadership of the most militant segment of the trade union movement in that period, the high points of the decade being the formation of the Union Front of Trade Unions (UFTU) and the historic strike of railway workers.

By the end of the 1970s, major changes occurred in the international economy. Massive building up of financial surpluses in the hands of the global transnational corporations following 30 years of uninterrupted growth at about 5 per cent per annum compound of the world from the end of the Second World War, the petro-dollar accumulation in the metropolitan banking system following the massive increase in the price of crude oil in 1973 and 1978, and the vast expansion in the various funds emerging from the savings of workers and employees for the post-retirement phase of their lives, all led to the rise of finance capital on an unprecedented scale. The breakdown of the international monetary system evolved at the Bretton Woods conference of 1944, where the World Bank and the International Monetary Fund (IMF) were created, and the simultaneous revolution in information and communications technology led to the emergence of a world economy in which highly centralized, large finance capital acquired enormous power.

The 1980s witnessed both the rise of finance capital and the massive attack on trade unions and working class rights on both sides of the Atlantic—the United States (US) and the United Kingdom (UK). The new international conjuncture provided the Indian bourgeoisie an opportunity to borrow from international financial institutions (World Bank, IMF, etc.), both official and private (such as commercial banks), and embark upon a loan-financed expansion of government expenditure to stimulate the economic growth. Acceptance of large-scale international loans, beginning with the 5 billion SDR loan from the IMF in 1981, brought with them a strong conditionality requiring reining in of wages and rising administered prices.

The early 1980s saw a major attack on trade union rights in India, with the passing of the National Security Act and the Essential Services Maintenance Act. Sustained and militant struggles of the working class sought to stem the rising tide of repression.

NEOLIBERAL REFORMS (1991-2009)

By the end of the 1980s, the global tide of reaction had been greatly strengthened by the smashing of militant trade unions in the US and the UK and the weakening and ultimate collapse of the socialist economics of Eastern Europe, with imperialism playing a key role in these events. The restoration of capitalism in Russia and the break-up of the Union of Soviet Socialist Republics by 1991 made the international situation dramatically different from what it had been between 1950 and 1980. Meanwhile, the policies of loan-financed government expenditure and import liberalization of the 1980s led India into twin crisis—a fiscal crunch and collapse of the balance of payments—by 1991, brought forward by massive capital flight in early 1991. This provided the minority Congress government of Narasimha Rao, the excuse to make a major shift in economic policies in favour of foreign finance capital.

The economic reforms with liberalization, privatization and globalization (LPG) policies, had entailed the removal of most norms of accountability of private capital in the name of deregulation, opening up of vast new spaces for profit-centred operations in such fields as diverse as education, health and infrastructure in the name of privatization, and the relatively unrestricted movement of goods, services and finance into and out of India.

The period of neoliberal reforms has been by far the most challenging period for the Indian working class movement. With the state lining up strongly behind both large international and domestic capital and ignoring the interests of working people, both rural and urban, altogether, the working class has had to fight a defensive battle, especially with the collapse of socialism in many countries and a strong ideological offensive mounted by a triumphant capitalist order. In retrospect, and contrary to claims made sometimes that the neoliberal order has more or less eliminated resistance, with even such a resistance as has been mounted by the political Left being largely 'tokenist'. It is remarkable that the working class movement in India under Left leadership has managed to sustain its struggles and retain its base amount working people, having successfully carried out major partial and general industrial strikes over the last decade and a half. The electoral verdict of 2004 and the impact of the Left on government policies in the period 2004-9 stand testimony to the resilience of the Indian working class movement under trying conditions. While the neoliberal policy framework remains in place, the ruling classes have also had to concede ground in a number of instances.

Thus, the United Progressive Alliance (UPA) regime, which began by notifying the Fiscal Responsibility and Budget Management Act, three days before presenting its first budget in July 2004, ended its first term by passing two important Acts—the National Rural Employment Guarantee Act (NREGA) and the Tribal Forests Rights Act (TFRA)—in versions that had been improved substantially by the intervention of progressive forces both inside and outside the parliament. The UPA began its second term in office by admitting the role of such measures as the NREGS and the farm loan waiver in its electoral victory, thus, attributing the victory not to neoliberal policies, but to potentially pro-people interventions.

It would, of course, be completely wrong to consider that the government has moved away from neoliberal policies. On the contrary, its panic-stricken measures to further liberalize the financial sector and open it up to speculative forces of global finance indicate that even while advanced capitalist economies are seeking greater regulation of private players in the wake of the global economic crisis, our rulers remain firmly committed to disastrous neoliberal policies. But it is important to understand that the slowing down of the reform juggernaut preceded the global economic crisis and is in substantial measure due to the active resistance put up against these policies by the working class movement led by the political Left in our country.

CHALLENGES AHEAD

The point of the foregoing narrative is not to encourage any sense of complacency about the progress of the working class movement, but merely to recall its resilience during a phase when objective conditions, both national and international, have forced it to be on the defensive.

In fact, as should be obvious, the working class movement in India faces immense challenges. First of all, the very structure of India's workforce highlights the complexity that the movement has to confront. As of 2004-5, India's workforce was estimated at nearly 460 million. Of these, only 70 million were in any kind of regular employment. Another 130 million were casual or contract wage workers. But the majority of India's working people, the remaining 260 million, were in fact 'self-employed', mostly tiny producers or persons, forced to be engaged in some income-earning activity on their own for a pittance, given the absence of any kind of social security for the poor in our country.

A significant part of this workforce—including the wage employed—is having very low level education. A substantial part of the working population is linked to land and to pre-capitalist relations. Ideologically, the forces of obscurantism and of identity politics continue to exercise a strong influence even in the segments of the working population, including industrial workers that are part of the technologically advanced sectors of the economy. Divisions of caste, religion, language and ethnicity have not disappeared, and continue to influence the consciousness of workers, thus, making the task of developing the class and political consciousness of the working class a major challenge. Where the democratic movement has advanced through decades of struggle, an all-in unity of the most reactionary forces against it is emerging.

Neoliberal policies, while deepening the crisis of working people's lives, also provide a fertile soil for growth of divisive forces that make it even more difficult to build the unity of the working class and of the broader sections of working people. It is only through a relentless struggle against both neoliberal policies and obscurantist forces of all hues that the working class movement will be able to go forward. The current global economic crisis and the neoliberal bankruptcy that it has exposed can be considered as an opportunity for the working class people to go ahead with their movements. However, the working class movement must carry with it the overwhelming mass of petty producers including the peasantry, but without succumbing to the political illusions of petty commodity production or romantic conceptions concerning the dynamics of social change that tends to underplay the role of science and productive forces.

CHAPTER 5

Movement of Left Trade Unions in French India

B. KRISHNAMURTHY

The French in India had five settlements and eleven *loges* comprising an area of about 500 sq km. They were under the control of the French government for more than two centuries. The natives had lost their political and socio-cultural rights under the colonial yoke, and especially, the working class felt the heat of the colonial exploitation more. A strong labour movement was started in Pondicherry and which fought for the rights and privileges of the working class. After many efforts and sacrifices on the part of the working class, the French imperialists relented at the end and extended progressive labour rights to their colonies in India, which was considered as something superior to the then prevailing Asian standards. Soon, the working class clamoured for political independence from the French colonial masters, who resorted to suppress the movement and to weaken it through division among the nationalist elements. In the end, the French Indians succeeded in getting their territories transferred to the Indian Union. As such, the working class had played a significant role in the freedom movement in French India.

INDUSTRIAL ECONOMY OF FRENCH INDIA

Industrialization of France in the mid-nineteenth century influenced French India as well. Usine Gaebelé, a textile mill, was established in 1892 at Mudaliyarpettai in Pondicherry and Rodier Mill was founded in 1898. Savana Mill owned by a company in Bordeaux in France followed suit. The Gaebelé Mill was later acquired by Ehny and came to be known as Ehny Mill. All these mills belonged to the French and British capitalists. Gondalpara Jute Mill in Chandernagore too came into existence in due course of time. Big export enterprises like Ralley Brothers, Volkar and East Asiatic Company too were present at Pondicherry. However, in the other French Indian settlements like Karaikal, Yanam and Mahe, there was no significant industrialization. These developments brought into existence an industrial working class in Pondicherry, who were treated by their employers as bonded labourers (Subbaiah 1985: 10-11).[1] The workers were given a paltry sum by way of wages. They had neither job security, nor compensation in case of accident and were forced to work daily for about 12 to 14 hours without even weekly holidays, under poor working conditions. Child and female labour was also widely prevalent in the French Indian colonies benefiting the colonial masters. In brief, the labour laws, which protected the interests of the working community in France, were deliberately not extended to their colonies in India (Subbaiah 1990: 57-8).[2]

YOUTH AND WORKING CLASS MOVEMENT

In any society, the youth and the working class always spearhead any political and socio-economic movement and the labour population of French India was no exception to this general rule. In 1908, the workers of the Rodier Mill organized a strike in support of their demand for a slight increase in their wages and against the retrenchment of some of their colleagues. In spite of some initial success, they could not achieve much due to the adamant attitude of the mill owners, who had succeeded in breaking the unity among the workers by planting and patronizing a few black legs among them. In May 1920, when the workers of Savana Mill resorted to strike, by way of retaliation, the owners settled all their accounts and threw them all out of the mill. Then they started fresh recruitment and imposed several stringent conditions on the new workers. Since the former workers of the mill had no other alternative, they joined the mill as fresh hands, accepting all the conditions imposed by the owners. The same tactics was followed by other mills also in suppressing the workers' movement in their organizations and the working class itself was divided by the creation of workers who were more loyal to the owners than to the interest and welfare of co-workers. The Civil Disobedience movement launched in the 1930s opened the eyes of the French Indian youth. This helped in awakening the political and social consciousness among the people, who demanded social reforms and the end of alien rule in India. Harijana Seva Sangam was established by the French Indian youth in Pondicherry in December 1933. Branches of the Sangam were also established in other French Indian establishments like Karaikal. In February 1935, 3,000 workers of the Savana Mill started an agitation demanding an increase in wages and decrease in the working hours. They had succeeded in wresting an increase in daily wages from 3 to 6 annas and a reduction in the working hours from 12-14 hours to 10 hours. They also demanded that women should not be asked to work during night times and they should be given one month paid leave with half pay during confinement. There was also a demand to ban child labour, especially for children below 14 years old (Subbaiah 1990: 49). With the active backing of the French Indian authorities, the mill owners resorted to dismiss the leaders and active participants of the movement. However, in the end, they had to revoke their earlier orders to appease the working classes.

In June 1936, the mill workers resumed their movement clamouring for the right to form labour unions, 8-hours work, the right to collective bargaining, increase in wages and weekly holidays. The governor initially accepted to promulgate all progressive labour legislations after due consultation with the French government and requested the labour leaders to stop their agitations. But he failed to fulfil his promise by the end of the stipulated period and the labour leaders had to resort to their agitations. On 30 July 1936, the French military was deployed to suppress the labour movement and in a firing, 12 workers lost their life.

The labour leaders like Subbaiah maintained contacts with Jawaharlal Nehru. Nehru was a trade union leader in his own right, who assisted labourers to gain contacts with their comrades in France. This enabled the workers in securing their helping hand in their ongoing struggles for protecting labour rights and those, liberal and progressive labour laws of France were introduced and implemented in the French Indian settlements (Vijayalakshmi 2008: 41-58).

Meanwhile, in June 1936, the Popular Front, a joint forum of the French Communist Party and the Socialist Party came to power in France. The French Communist Party members and labour leaders demanded for the extension of progressive labour laws of the French Republic to the Indian colonies as well. Justin Gaudart, a former minister in the French government, came to Pondicherry as a special envoy to the President of the French Republic to study the problems of workers in the French Indian colonies.[3] On his recommendation the decree of 5 April 1937, hailed as Workers' Charter was passed in France and was promulgated in French India in May 1937.[4] Taking benefit of this Act, numerous trade unions came into existence in all the settlements of French India, and they were brought together under one central federation called the French India Labour Federation. Most of them were affiliated to the French Federation of Labour in Paris individually or collectively, thus, cementing the fraternal unity of working class of French India with those of France.

The success of the labour movement and the rights secured by the industrial workers encouraged the public and they came to realize the strength of united action. The struggle for economic rights transformed and developed into clamouring for political privileges and right for self-determination, in due course.

MOVEMENT FOR POLITICAL RIGHTS

This was followed by the establishment of Mahajana Party in 1937, by Subbaiah and other politically volatile elements like Marie Savary, Dorairaj and Purushotama Reddiar and they wanted to take away the inordinate power enjoyed by the governor of French India on the strength of the *Ordonnance organique*. They also demanded the removal of the existing anomaly of two-list voter system and ensure the conduct of free and fair elections (Subbaiah 1990: 145).[5] Subsequently, the branches of Mahajana Party were established in the other French Indian settlements as well.In the municipal elections of 2 May 1937, the Franco-Hindu Party, which was supported by the French Indian authorities, with their police and administrative machinery and the Mahajana Party contested. Although, the latter could gain popular support, through sheer muscle power and governmental support, the Franco-Hindu Party was declared elected and Mahajana Party disputed the veracity of the results. The ruling party used police and its goonda elements to terrorize all remnants of opposition and the labour leaders. The mill workers had to fight pitched battles with them, and in the end, the government had to come to terms with the working class leaders. However, even in the elections for the *Conseil General*, which was held on 10 October 1937, Mahajana Party lost due to the political manoeuvring of Crocicchia, the then governor of French India.

Mahajana Party and other democratic elements retaliated by

launching a non-cooperation movement. They established gram panchayats, sealed the civil registries and government offices, disregarded the authority and orders of the police and judiciary and started running a parallel government (GoI 1982: 245). As part of the no-tax campaign, the people refused to pay taxes to the government. The French Indian administration came to a standstill. Moreover, the people demonstrated in front of the houses of the municipal councillors, who were declared elected by the government and demanded their immediate resignation. As a result, few councillors resigned their office. The government had to come into terms with the popular leaders and agreed to conduct free and fair elections within six months. About this time, the popular front government in France was dissolved and the reactionary Radical Socialist Party came to power on 16 April 1938. As a fall out, the French Indian authorities threw their assurances to the wind. They resorted to the policy of repression against the workers. A French army battalion was brought from Indo-China to Pondicherry to suppress any political agitation. Several mass leaders were imprisoned. Gram panchayats and village libraries were destroyed. Thousands of people had to leave Pondicherry and took asylum in the surrounding Indian territories.

The use of force proved to be counter-productive and resulted in the eruption of political violence. There was an unsuccessful attempt on Joseph David, one of the leaders of the ruling Franco-Hindu Party. Selvaradjulu Chettiar, another pro-French leader, who led the suppression of the working class elements, was assassinated by Ramaiah, a worker of Savana Mill on 16 December 1938 (Subbaiah n.d.: 16-17). Later, he shot himself to death and joined the band of martyrs of the ilk of Bhagat Singh of Punjab and Vanchinatha Iyer of the Thirunelveli district of Tamil Nadu. Ramaiah's action aimed at warning the natives, who turned out to be more pro-French than the French themselves and traitors to the native cause, by and joining hands with the colonial oppressors in suppressing the working class movement.

FRENCH INDIA COMMUNIST PARTY

The French India Communist Party came into existence in early 1940s and along with other progressive democratic forces it formed the National Democratic Front (NDF), which demanded the right to have self-rule, adult suffrage to both men and women and the introduction of fundamental and democratic rights to the colonies. When the Nazi army entered into war with Russia in June 1941, the French India Communist Party launched its campaign against Nazi Germany and joined hands with other democratic forces[6] at Pondicherry in April 1944 and Subbaiah was elected as its chairman. However, Louis Bonvin, the then governor of Pondicherry, charged him as an undesirable element and expelled him from the French Indian settlements.

In 1944, Zivarattinam, the representative of the French India in the Consultative Assembly in Paris, demanded a single list of voters and called for the abolition of the reserved seats or separate electorates for the Europeans and their descendants. On 3 August 1945, separate electorates were abolished and a single list of voters came into force in the French colonies in India. The Fourth French Republic under General de Gaulle revoked the expulsion order against Subbaiah on 11 September 1945 and allowed him to continue to work at Pondicherry. This political change in France and in the French Indian settlements augured well for the freedom movement in the following years. In the municipal elections held on 23 June 1946, in the five French Indian territories, on the basis of universal adult franchise and a single electoral list, the NDF triumphed. It captured power in all the 22 municipal councils of French India, winning 101 out of 122 municipal seats and its candidates were elected as mayors (More 2001: 93). Its election manifesto proclaimed in favour of French India remaining fully a self-governing national unit within the French republic (*Communaute Française Republicaine*) and demanded adequate representation for French India in the representative institutions to be newly formed in France. Even in the elections held to elect a member to the national assembly in Paris on 10 November 1946, the candidate of NDF, Lambert Saravane, a professor of French at the Colonial College, had won. In the elections for the new *Assemblée Representative* (representative assembly) held on 15 December 1946 also, the NDF won 34 seats out of 44. On 26 January 1947, for the first time, two Indian candidates of the NDF were elected to the senate in Paris by the representative assembly of Pondicherry (ibid.: 96-7). However, by the end of 1946, there was a split among the constituents of the front and some moderates, who were estranged by the radical policies of the French India Communist Party, formed the French India National Congress and All French India Congress.[7] On 1 January 1947, another moderate leader,

S.R. Subramanyam organized the Congress Socialist Party to continue the struggle for the freedom of French Indian settlements. In January 1947, there was a change in the stand of the NDF. It stood for the status of a self-governing national unit within the French republic in 1946, started clamouring for *purna swaraj* (complete independence) and for an immediate merger with the Indian Union. The leaders of the front presented similar demand for independence to Maurice Moutet, the then French overseas minister, when he visited Pondicherry on his way back from Indo-China. Moutet seemed to be evasive on the question of independence. The nationalist elements of Pondicherry observed 17 February 1947 as the first anniversary of the rebellion of the naval cadets at Bombay. More than 10,000 workers, peasants, students and others took out a procession in Pondicherry. A peaceful bandh was also organized and mills, shops and educational institutions remained closed. The police and the pro-French goonda elements obstructed the procession by pelting stones and by spraying boiled oil. Police resorted to firing on the mob and one man was killed. Popular support to the freedom movement and the electoral success of the NDF was resented by the French Indian authorities and Governor Baron tried to weaken the movement by creating divisions among the rank and file of the front. He lured a few of its leaders like Lambert Saravane, Counouma, André, Edouard Goubert and Mouthu Poulle out of it and encouraged them to form a new political outfit and to please Baron, who was a socialist, these leaders formed the French India Socialist Party in July 1947.[8] Lambert Saravane, who got elected as the candidate of the NDF, was declared as the representative of the Socialist Party. Baron supported and backed the new party with all the strength of the government machinery—administrative, police and judicial. Goubert considered the communists as his first and foremost enemies and started oppressing the working class with brute force and muscle power. The French India Socialist Party took a more liberal and pro-French stand of favouring the French Indian settlements to continue under the French union, while other nationalist elements clamoured for the immediate withdrawal of the French from India. However, the announcement of the Mountbatten Plan of 3 June 1947, which envisaged withdrawal of the British from India before August 1947, electrified the whole Indian environment. The news that the British had decided to leave the shores of India for good, came as a bolt from the blue for the nationalist movement in the French Indian colonies. The locals expected that the French would follow suit and allow them to join the free united India. On 3 August 1947, people of Pondicherry gheraoed the government offices and demanded freedom from the French rule. The workers, students and the general public organized strikes and called for bandhs. Kamal Prasad Ghosh, the mayor of Chandernagore, declared on 4 August 1947: 'Chandernagore forms an integral part of Bengal and has every right to break its links with imperialist France'. On 9 August the French Indians took a direct action to achieve their goal. The public agitation brought the French India administration to a standstill at Chandernagore, where the people sealed the government offices, forced the police to lay down their arms and drove away the French administrator. The French India Communist Party and the French India Farmer's Federation requested its members to haul down the French flag on 15 August and to hoist the Indian national flag. At Pondicherry, those who attempted to do so were brutally attacked by the police and goonda elements. Rangasamy Naicker, the president of the Thirunallar Commune, was sacked from his post for hoisting the Indian national flag over the municipal office building (Ramasamy 1987: 159). However, soon there was a change in the stand of French India Communist Party, as a result of the anti-communist activities of the Indian Union government. It started criticizing both the governments of France and India and their willing instruments in the French Indian scene, French India Socialist Party and French India National Congress, respectively, for not arriving at an early solution to the French Indian issue.[9] It gave a call to the French India National Congress to join the popular movement and promised that it would not do anything to spoil the Indo-French dialogue to find a peaceful solution for the French Indian problem. But, when it found that the Indian government would not say or do anything that would create problem for its French counterpart and would not hesitate to sacrifice the interests of the French Indian colonies for the benefit of the Indian capitalists, the French India Communist Party openly declared that it had lost its faith in the Government of India.[10] The communists condemned the latter as the government of neo-fascist exploiters and stooges of Anglo-American imperialists who were bent upon suppressing the human rights of their people and announced that they would try to avoid the merger of the French Indian settlements with the Indian Union, as they doubted the very genuineness of the Indian Independence.[11] By taking such a pro-French stand, the communists believed that they could persuade the French government to extend the human rights laws of the Constitution of the Fourth Republic to French India.[12] The leaders of the French India Socialist Party started camouflaging the situation at Pondicherry and tried to gamble with both the French and Indian governments, to achieve their personal ends (Raj Kumar 1951: 73). In July 1949, delegations were sent to Paris as well as to Delhi to find out the stand of the respective governments. While the French government assured an autonomous status for the establishments within the framework of the French union after the referendum,[13] the Government of India promised that after the merger any changes in the administrative set-up of the settlements would be carried out only in consultation with the public. On its return to Pondicherry, the Goubert group, which dominated the municipal councils, resolved to indefinitely postpone the referendum and to accept autonomy offer of the French government and urged the people to approve it. This was due to behind-the-curtain manoeuvres of the French Indian authorities, who tried to keep the socialists under their tutelage and the latter's ability to change colour, as and when required. Moreover, the fear that following the Chandernagore example, the people of the other settlements too would vote them out of the Indian soil would have prompted the French Indian authorities and their local supporters to postpone the conduct of referendum in other settlements.

The French and pro-French elements on the one hand tried to hoodwink the Indian government by dishonourable and deceptive political gimmicks and to suppress the nationalist elements at Pondicherry with an iron hand on the other. Political violence was patronized and so flourished as a profession in the French Indian settlements. The police and army, at the disposal of the French Indian authorities and the anti-social goonda elements, at the employ of the ruling party indulged in subversive and coercive measures. On 13 January 1950, the headquarters of the French India Communist Party at Pondicherry was burnt down, which resulted in considerable damage to *Sudandiram*, the party organ, which voiced for the economic liberation of the working classes and the political liberation of the French Indian settlements since 1934 (Subbaiah 1885: 21). More than hundred shops and houses of the nationalist leaders and those of the merchants' association were set on fire (Raj Kumar 1951: 79-80). To counter the influence of the French India Communist Party on the working classes, the socialists organized rival labour unions, thereby tried to disunite and weaken the labour movement. Thousands of employees were thrown out of jobs. This resulted in the mass exodus in thousands from Pondicherry and the French Indians and took asylum in the neighbouring Indian territories. The estrangement of the French India Communist Party and the Dravidian leaders from the Indian cause had already weakened the struggle for merger with India. All this resulted in a lull in the mass movement. Working class leaders of India like V.V. Giri intervened and brought a compromise between the Government of India and the labour leaders of French India. As a result, by the end of 1953, the French India Communist Party called for united action among all the nationalist elements and to accelerate the phase of the movement. An all-party conference was held at Cuddalore to coordinate the freedom struggle. The French India Communist Party launched its direct action on 6 April 1954 and in the following days its volunteers stormed in the Thirubhuvani police station and municipal office. Administration of the municipality was taken over by the representatives of the people (Subbaiah 1985: 62). A couple of communist cadres lost their life when they tried to free Kallaye village in the Mahe region from the French rule. The nationalist leaders organized demonstrations and processions demanding the merger of the settlements with the Indian Union. While the Indian government hesitated to take action in this regard, the French Indian government deployed the army brought from Saigon to assist the police and tried to crush the popular upsurge.

Meanwhile, the French India Socialist Party leaders switched over their loyalty to the Indian Union and Nehru had not hesitated to embrace them into the Congress fold.[14] His government started negotiating with its French counterpart, which was forced to accept the writing on the wall in the end. The agreement for the *de facto* transfer of the French Indian colonies to the Indian Union was signed in New Delhi on 21 October and came into force on 1 November 1954.

CONCLUSION

It may be concluded that the working class played a notable and meritorious role in the popular movement for the restoration of political and socio-economic rights of the people of French India. The stand that they had taken differed at different times as its leaders were acting or reacting to various international, national and domestic developments and compulsions.

The governments of French India tried to weaken the labour movement by creating and patronizing divisions among the Leftist camps and Goubert and his French India Socialist Party was the outcome of such a political manoeuvring. The French wanted to delay the inevitable transfer of their colonial possessions to the Indian Union. Nehru too patronized Goubert at the cost of the real freedom fighters who toiled and toiled for liberating French India from the hands of the French colonial masters. In this regard, it may be concluded that Nehru turned out to be a prisoner of circumstances that prevailed in Pondicherry at that juncture. With all his weakness and wickedness, no one can deny; that Goubert was very clear about his political career in the post-1954 period than anybody else in French India. He was a shrewd politician, who was clear about the game from 1947 onwards. In the pamphlet published by the French India Socialist Party in 1947, Goubert made it clear that French India should become part of the Indian Union some time in the future. However, he believed that the time had not ripened yet, since he feared that in case French India joined the Indian Union at that juncture, it would have to lose its separate identity. So, his idea was to wait for as long as it was needed so that the Indian government would offer a political status, which would ensure the separate identity of French India. He was pro-French till it was profitable and switched side at the right moment and was rewarded by Nehru, as he expected. This was, no doubt, political opportunism, practised and patronized. As far as the choice of Goubert at the cost of other freedom fighters, Nehru was forced to accept him since the pro-Indian elements were weak and divided. The Congress party in French India was weak and was not ready to join hands with the communists and Dravidian parties, which were ready to play a role of their choice and intent. Nehru was not happy or prepared to allow the communists to lead the movement and to take credit for securing Independence. In the end, he had to accept and recognize Goubert, who could face the communists squarely as the leader of Congress party in Pondicherry. It appears that Goubert's virtue was his anti-communism and his ability to face and to pay the communists back in their own coin. To be precise, Goubert was successful in his political game and it was the French on the one hand, and Nehru on the other, who made him possible for their own vested interests.

NOTES

1. Subbaiah was a well-known leader of the Communist Party of India and considered as the Father of the Freedom Movement in French India. The term 'French India' is used in this paper just to denote those territories which remained under the colonial administration of France on Indian soil and not at all as the 'France in India'.
2. Subbaiah brought out the French duplicity very clearly and maintained: By Article 421 of the Treaty of Versailles of 28 June 1919, the French government had agreed to apply ratified conventions of the International Labour Organizations to its colonies, protectorates and possessions, which were self-governing, except where owing to the local conditions, the provisions were inapplicable or local conditions required any modifications. The French government took recourse to this exceptional clause and justified the non-enforcement of the conventions in French India on the ground that the provisions of the conventions were inapplicable owing to local conditions. Since the French Indian workers were denied of right to association, they were not in a position to take benefit of the provisions contained in Article 409 of part XIII (Labour) of the Treaty of Versailles of June 1919 to make necessary representation to the International Labour Office directly. The nationalist and pro-labour newspapers like *Sudandiram* highly criticized the anti-labour policies of the French Indian government and accused it for deliberately withholding the promulgation of progressive labour laws of the French Republic in its Indian colonies.
3. Documents preserved in the collection of National Archives of India (NAI) 463-X/Secret/1936 and NAI.313-X/Secret/36, Government of India —Foreign and Political Department — External Branch, throw interesting light on the labour movement in French India and the response of the Government of France in this regard.
4. This French India Labour Code provided rights to industrial and agricultural labourers to organize themselves into trade unions. Even the government employees including the policemen secured the right to collective bargaining under this code. The first Article provided for the right to collective contract of labour. This was a unique feature which provided for a mutual discussion between the representatives of the trade union and employers and reached a settlement across the table. There were also provisions for conciliation and arbitration. The right to strike work was the most significant provision of the code.

   Another important provision was the restriction of working hours to nine hours till December 1937 and to eight hours from 1 January 1938. For overtime work, an employee was entitled to one and a half times of his wages and for work during night times between 9 p.m. to 6 a.m. twice the wages. Industries were prohibited from employing women during night times. Moreover, maternity leave with half wages for eight weeks was provided under this code. Again, 30 minutes per day was granted to mothers to feed their babies during the course of work. Compulsory weekly holidays on Sundays and a fair compensation against accidents too were provided. The most important provision of the Act was that the employers were subjected to severe punishment if they were found to have failed to enforce any of its provisions.

5. Subbaiah (1990: 145) maintained that the nationalist leaders of Pondicherry were actually interested in establishing the Pondicherry branch of the Indian National Congress, but in deference to the advice of Nehru they started the Mahajana Party.
6. 'Combat' (to fight) was organized in Algeria to free France from the control of Germany during the course of Second World War. A branch of it was organized in Pondicherry by Julien Adocéam, who came from Algeria. It was in support of 'Free France' movement of Charles de Gaulle and recruited volunteers in French India with a slogan *partent pour de Gaulle* (to join de Gaulle) to free France from Nazi control.
7. Subbaiah, however, accuses Baron, the then Governor of Pondicherry as the initiator of this political development with the hope of shattering the strength of the freedom movement. He visualized the conspiracy of the Indian capitalists in the move of the intellectuals and capitalist elements of French India in opening the branch of Indian National Congress in Pondicherry, at this juncture. Nehru's refusal to such a move of Subbaiah in late 1930s, of which reference had been made earlier (n. 5), need to be juxtaposed against this new development (Subbaiah 1985: 20).
8. It is an irony that the French India Socialist Party was neither ideologically oriented towards socialism nor affiliated to either French or Indian socialist parties. It turned out to be a group of political opportunists and self-seekers and promoters.
9. *Sudandiram* (Pondicherry), 23 January 1948.
10. *Sudandriam*, 9, 15 and 30 March 1948; *Sudesamitran* (Madras), 26 March 1948; *Dinamani* (Madras), 25 March 1948.
11. *Sudandiram* 7 and 26 April 1948; 15 May 1948.
12. *Sudandiram*, 10 August 1948.
13. By the terms of the Indo-French Agreement of 8 June 1948, which aimed to settle the future status of the French Indian settlements to the satisfaction of all concerned, the Indian government agreed to the French government's contention that the future status of the French Indian territories should be left to the decision of the people concerned and that their wishes would be ascertained by means of a referendum, the modalities of which were left to be finalized by the municipal councils of all the settlements.
14. *Bombay Chronicle* (Bombay), 18 October 1954. Muthukumarappa Reddiar, one of the leaders of the French India Socialist Party had the audacity to claim that the recent political history of the French Indian

settlements had largely been the history of the French India Socialist Party and the purpose of his party's historic meeting at Madukkarai on 17 October was 'no less than to cease as a party and to re-awaken as the Congress of the new State'. He also claimed: 'This party took great initiative in the final and only practical phase of the liberation movement'.

REFERENCES

GoI (1982): *Gazetteer of India : Union Territory of Pondicherry*, ed. Francis Cyril Antony, vol. 1, Pondicherry.

More, J.B.P. (2001): *Freedom Movement in French India: The Mahe Revolt of 1948* (Tellicherry: IRISH).

Raj Kumar, N.V. (1951): *The Problem of French India* (New Delhi: Novin Press).

Ramasamy, A. (1987): *History of Pondicherry* (NewDelhi: Stosius Inc/Advent Books Division).

Subbaiah, V. (1985): *Puthuvai Manila Desiya Iyakkam, Iymbathandu Sudandira Varalaru 1935-1985* (Tamil), Pondicherry.

——— (1990): *Saga of Freedom of French India (Testament of My Life)* (Madras: New Century Book House).

Vijayalakshmi, S. (2006): 'Jawaharlal Nehru's Visit to Pondicherry in 1936 and the Labour Movement in French India', in B. Krishnamurthy (ed.), *India and France: Past, Present and Future* (Pondicherry: Centre for Nehru Studies, Pondicherry University).

CHAPTER 6

Peasants' Struggle and Freedom Movement

ASHOK KUMAR SINGH

Capitalism, with high production, technology and speedy development, replaced feudalism in modern world history. In a short time, it covered long distance, but could not change the piteous conditions of the working class. Exploitation continued in a full swing. People's revolt against capitalism was based on the socialist theories. Socialism supported national freedom movements and all other people's revolutions against imperialism to end exploitation of labours, barbarous attitude of zamindars in villages, poverty of peasants, base-less working class and exploitation of minority classes. The political leadership of different countries understood the historical possibilities of struggle for their own common people through Marxism and Leninism. Jawaharlal Nehru, who was highly influenced by Karl Marx, wrote that 'Marxism helped us understand social circumstances of our time and it showed the way for the freedom and progress in the direction of work' (Nehru 1953: 592). Earlier, even before Nehru, Har Dayal Lal had written an essay in March 1912 issue of *Modern Review* (Calcutta) titled 'Karl-Marx: Modern Rishi' (cited in Adhikari 1971: 5).

INSTANT PEASANT MOVEMENTS

India had a self-sufficient village community system before the British disintegrated it. A new form of landlordship was introduced changing the whole concept of ownership of land (Nehru 1985: 303). The land became a private property of newly-created landowners. Charles Metcalfe, who was appointed as the Governor-General of India in 1935, had also described the self-dependant village community system (cited in Desai 1976: 6). As the object of the British was to collect money in the shape of revenue, enhancement in revenue took place from time to time. If the farmers failed to pay revenue, their land was taken away from them. The British rulers also banned all other foreign traders and vigorous measures were taken to prevent the flow of industrial goods within the country itself, making craftsmen and artisans jobless. India became an agricultural colony of industrial England, supplying raw materials and providing market for England's industrial goods. More than half of the entire population, which was subjected to exploitation, in one form or another, ultimately, participated in agrarian revolution against imperialism.

Before the First World War, Indian peasant's revolutionary responses to British authorities and Indian landlords as well as moneylenders came in the form of indigo planters revolt in Bengal (1859-60), Kuki revolt (1860-90) in Assam, indigo peasant's revolt in Darabhanga and Champaran (1866-8) and again in East Bengal (1870) (Pawana peasant revolt of 1872-3 now in Bangladesh), Kuka revolt of Punjab (1869-72), peasant revolt in Ahmednagar, Maharashtra (1875), Poona revolt of 1879 and Rampa revolt (1879-80) of Madras Presidency (Desai 1976). Mahatma Gandhi led some revolts of communities of poor Indian farmers against the tyranny of British government and allied landlords in Champaran (Bihar) and Kheda (Gujarat) successfully.

Although, these early movements and riots of peasants did not create any threat to the British rule, they proved that the Indian peasant's reactions were instant and spontaneous to every situation. Every time they were tortured adversely that they had to rebel. This showed that, in practical, the illiterate and ignorant people performed acts of appreciation against the menace of the increasing British colonialism that even while the upper class and educated could not perform (Singh 1987: 69). The Indian National Congress could not attach itself with all these peasant's movements because of their violent and revolutionary nature, but passed some resolutions regarding a just and legal *lagaan*. Bal Gangadhar Tilak tried to unite the exploited and oppressed peasants and labours first time in the history of Indian National Congress and requested the peasants of Maharashtra not to pay *lagaan* at the time of drought or loss of crop.[1]

SPREAD OF CLASS CONSCIOUSNESS

After the First World War, the Bolshevik revolution of Russia under the leadership of Lenin and the worldwide economic depression of

1929-32 organized peasants to form different peasant fronts. The Bolshevik revolution spread a class consciousness among peasants and they felt that only just rights and the end of exploitation were not enough, the end of imperialism was also essential. As the Congress was coming close to the common people, it also showed affinity with peasants, who were more than half of the total population. However, it was very conscious towards the class nature and revolutionary ideas of peasants and did not support the end of imperialism at this juncture. Peasants' movement was guided and supported mostly by the communist ideology. Although, in the Gaya Session of the Indian National Congress, in 1922, its president Chitranjan Das felt the need for a separate association for peasants and labourers under the garb of Congress. In 1927, the Congress committee directed the working committee to appoint some party activists to work among the industrial and farm labourers and to prepare a proposal for their associations.

Due to the great economic depression, peasants were bound to sell their lands or take loans, as the price of agriculture products came down sharply. In June 1922, the price of the agriculture commodities was 50 per cent more than that of the price in September 1929 (Mahendra 1988: 23). Zamindars and moneylenders exploited the situation in their own interest and compelled the peasants for a sharp revolt to end exploitation. During 1920-1, centres of these peasant revolutions were Punjab, Malabar, Eastern United Province and Bengal (Singh 1987: 416). In the peasant movement of Punjab, the Congress party and the communists participated all together. The police suppressed the movement. In September 1922, the Congress Working Committee in its meeting at Amritsar condemned the exploitation and the Akalis supported the peasants. However, the movement was a failure under the leadership of the Congress party.

Moplah rebellion (1921) (Namboodiripad 1968: 141) broke out at the time when the non-cooperation and Khilafat movements were gaining ground in Malabar (Madras Presidency). The rebellion was initially directed against the landlords and their British patterns, but later took on a communal character. Unlike the other earlier rebellions of the nineteenth century, which were localized in extent and unlimited in scope, the Moplah rebellion was far more intense and widespread. It embraced in it entirely the Moplah peasant population of Eranadu and Valluvanadu talukas.

Another major centre of peasant movement was Awadh region of United Province (Kapoor and Gupta 2004: 306). Although peasants of all districts of the United Province were disappointed by British rule, the peasants of Awadh region were more suppressed, so they reacted sharply. Faizabad, Sultanpur, Rae Bareli and Pratapgarh were the centres of the movement. Baba Ramchandra led this movement comparatively more in a mature and an organized manner in which Jawaharlal Nehru also participated (Chandra 2002: 145). Later this movement spread in Bareilly and Gorakhpur too. But during this revolt, the Congress Working Committee in Bardoli, after the Chauri-Chaura incident, passed a resolution saying that the non-payment of *lagaan* was against the national interest. Congress told the zamindars that their conflicts with peasants would be solved by mutual discussions. Agitating peasants were upset and lost faith in the leadership of Gandhi. Awadh peasants' movement became more strong and the British government took military action against the unarmed rebels.

Bardoli satyagrah of 1925 (Mahendra 1988: 56), in the state of Gujarat, was a major episode of civil disobedience during the independence movement. In 1925, the taluka of Bardoli was affected by severe flood and famine, which damaged the crop production, leaving the farmers facing great financial troubles. However, the government of Bombay presidency had raised the tax rate by 30 per cent that year and despite the petitions from civic groups, it refused to cancel the rise even in calamities. The situation for farmers was grave, that they barely had enough property and crops to pay off the tax, let alone for feeding themselves. The Government of Bombay ignored the request of Vallabhbhai Patel to reduce taxes but reciprocated by announcing the date of collection. Patel instructed all the farmers of Bardoli to refuse the payment of their taxes and remain completely non-violent. He reassured that the struggle would not end until the cancellation of all taxes for the year and all seized properties as well as land were returned to the owners. The government declared that it would suppress the revolt. But under the pressure of the Members of Legislative Council of Bombay, the government had to return the confiscated lands and properties as well as cancel the revenue payment not only for that year, but also the 30 per cent rise of tax in the succeeding year. In the support of Bardoli farmers, demonstrations were organized in different parts of the country. In the meetings conducted in Bombay and United Province, peasants declared that they would fight against the increase of *lagaan* following

Bardoli. On the appeal of Gandhi, Bardoli Day was organized on 12 June 1928. On this occasion, while addressing a meeting, the then Congress president Ansari told that Bardoli people had showed us the way against the long slavery of our people.[2]

THE CONGRESS ATTITUDE

With the active cooperation of the communist groups in India, the peasant movement became more organized and aggressive. They demanded the end of imperialism for total freedom. In India, it was not possible for the communist groups to participate actively due to the pressure of British government, so with the advice of M.N. Roy, worker-peasant associations were formed during 1925-7(Singh 1987: 526). The first worker-peasant party was formed in Bengal in November 1925.[3] Meanwhile in Bombay the worker-peasant party started working in March 1927. In Punjab it was formed in December 1927 and in the United Province on 14 October 1928. By uniting all these regional parties, All India Workers and Peasants Party was formed in Calcutta in December 1928. Peasants' party supported the Congress resolution of Madras session of December 1927 to boycott the Simon Commission in Calcutta. The peasants-workers party opposed the commission with slogans—'Establish People's Socialist Republic' and 'Long Live the Revolution'. Peasants-workers party tried to convert this agitation into a countywide national liberation movement. In December 1928, during the session of the Indian National Congress at the Park Circus ground of Calcutta, a huge number of Peasants and Workers Party members marched in a procession and captured the stage of the Congress and shouted slogans for India's freedom and an independent socialist republic. But Congress was not ready to pass the resolution in favour of India's Independence. Under the leadership of the communists, Peasants and Workers Party mobilized people's opinion regarding the demand of complete freedom. The Lahore Session (December 1929) of Indian National Congress adopted a resolution for 'Purna Swaraj' (Sarkar 1985). Nehru attacked Gandhi's 'trusteeship' solution for zamindar and peasant conflict. Subhas Chandra Bose proposed for an immediate 'non-payment of taxes'.

Till the Non-Cooperation movement of 1930, peasants were more organized and aggressive against their exploitation. The centre of peasants' movement during this period was the Awadh region of United Province. Peasants were struggling against the removal of them from their land as they were not able to pay *lagaan* due to low prices of crops. During 1930-1, only in Allahabad, 12,000 farmers were removed from the land. Till early 1931, 16,000 cases of removal were registered in the Awadh region.[4]

Peasants' movement also spread in different parts of the country to stop *lagaan*. Kishoreganj and Buldana regions, north region of Kanara district (Karnataka), Bihar, Madhya Pradesh, Kashmir and Gujarat were the main centres of this movement. Rulers of Kashmir and Dogra zamindars tried to give this revolution a communal colour. Communal differences of Hindu and Muslim gave British a new weapon to break the national movement in India.[5] Peasants' movement was also spread in the princely states of Alwar, Pulsar and *tehri riyasats* (princely states) of the western frontier province during 1932-3.

Although, the peasants of the entire country fought for India's absolute freedom during 1929-33 against the imperialist rulers, they failed due to revisionist and compromizing attitude of the leadership. Afraid of revolt, this leadership broke the revolution and limited the national movement.

RISE OF KISAN SABHA

After the success of Congress in 1937 election, peasants were highly hopeful regarding their demands. In June 1937, All India Kisan Sabha demanded the Congress government of all states to save farmers from the exploitation of zamindars and moneylenders and implement the Rent Act. As the Congress could not support these demands, peasant movement started again in different parts of the country. In Bihar more than 60,000 farmers agitated under the banner of the Kisan Sabha. The peasants of United Province, Madras, Bombay, Orissa, Madhya Pradesh, Bengal and Punjab also agitated. Peasant movements compelled the revisionist Congress to split the Kisan Sabha. Parallel to Kisan Sabha, the farm workers' associations were also formed. The Bihar Regional Congress Committee issued an order that no Congressman will participate in the agitations of the Kisan Sabha. The National Congress Working Committee, in January 1938, supported this restriction. Although Congress was more close with people's revolution and more powerful than before, they could not change their revisionist attitude towards zamindars. But a good number of Congressmen were with the peasants and in February 1938, at the Haripur session of the Congress, the revisionists accepted that the Congress had the right to participate in the working of the

Kisan Sabha. Due to the peasant movements, the Congress chief minister's conference of May 1938 decided to form some laws for peasants. With these laws *lagaan* was reduced and payment of loan was stopped for some time. But this could not end the sufferings of peasants.

Under the communist framework, Swami Sahajanand Saraswati and Rahul Sankrityayan organized the peasant movement in Bihar. Swami Sahajanand was highly influenced with Gandhian philosophy from 1920 to 1934 and was an active member of the Indian National Congress. But after 1928, he felt that most of the Congress leaders were anti-peasants. A high intensity earthquake occurred in 1934 in Bihar and during the relief works Sahajanand met Gandhi at the Patna relief camp and requested for a peasant movement against the exploitation of landlords in Bihar (Sharma 2001: 20). But Gandhi was against such a movement. This hurt Swamiji to such an extent that he decided to oppose Gandhian attitude of conciliation. He was clear that only Marxist ideology of class struggle was the ultimate solution of peasant's problems. In the meeting of Bihar provincial Kisan Sabha, November 1935, he shouted for socialism. Bihar provincial Kisan Sabha was formed by Swami in 1929. He was nominated as the first president of All India Kisan Sabha in 1936 at Lucknow.[6] Again, in the third session of All India Kisan Sabha, held in Komilla (Bengal) from 13 to 15 May 1938, he was nominated as the president. In March 1944 Swami presided the All India Kisan Sabha held in Madras Presidency (Mahendra 1988: 131).

As a great intellectual and as a rigid Marxist, Rahul Sankrityayan also fought for the peasants in Bihar. He was one of the founder members of the Bihar Communist Party established on 20 October 1939 against the backdrop of intense peasant movements, student's agitations and trade union activities (Bhushan 1988: 130). Sankrityayan was the frontline leader who made the Bihar peasant movement an issue-based movement and organized it. He led the Amabari Kisan struggle (Prasad 1994: 148) and agitations in Saran, Bihar in February 1939 in which he was beaten brutally and thrown into jail. Earlier, he participated in zamindar-kisan struggle after the formation of the Congress ministry in Bihar. Sankrityayan was nominated as the president of Fifth All India Kisan Sabha Session organized in Visakhapatnam on 26-7 March 1940. But he could not participate as he was arrested by the Bihar government. He presided over Bihar provincial Kisan Sabha in 1940 and also supported the peasants' movement in Gaya and Munger (Bihar). Sankrityayan was clear in view that without throwing out feudalism and capitalism, freedom in real sense is not possible and as Congress cannot do this, only Marxist approach can solve people's suffering.

Between the two world wars, although the Congress supported the peasants' movement, it could not lead them. Gandhi wrote in the *Harijan* on 5 December 1936 that 'I do not think to abolish zamindari system, but at the same time, I feel that its survival is not necessary. Farmer is the real owner of crop and property. If he is united, exploitation will finish itself.' Other than Gandhi, a large section of the Congress leadership was of the opinion that the real cause of suffering of India was imperialism and zamindars, and they supported the peasant movement. It the 49th session of the Indian National Congress in Lucknow (March 1936), as president, Nehru talked about the middle class and workers and peasants. Nehru's proposal to affiliate worker-peasant organizations with Congress was not supported by the majority (Singh 1987: 611). This session got importance as the Congress started discussions on the economic demands of the working people. It was felt that only with the upper classes, Congress could not gain momentum. In the Ambari Kisan struggle in December 1936, the Congress, under the leadership of Nehru, adopted a 13-point programme which included the maximum number of demands from peasants (Singh 1987: 612). This new direction of the Congress increased the popularity and strength of the party. Before the Faizpur session, its membership was merely 6,36,000 which increased in 1937 up to 30,00,000 and in 1938 it was about 40,000,00 in which 12.5 lakh were from the united province (Singh 1987: 612).

THE SECOND WORLD WAR

The Second World War further increased the sufferings of peasants as within three months the prices of essential commodities increased by 37 per cent. Peasants of the United Province agitated in October 1939. As Hitler attacked the communist Russia on 22 June 1941 and the British Prime Minister Winston Churchill declared British-Russia friendship, the whole nature of the war changed with his declaration. The imperial war changed into a people's war against fascism.

At the end of 1945, crisis of food grains emerged due to poor production in Madhya Pradesh, Bombay Province, Hyderabad, middle

India and the Rajputana region. On the other hand, exploitation of zamindars and his allies was on peak. Peasants fought against them mainly in Telangana, Tebhaga (Bengal) region and Punnappra-Vayalar, Kerala (Singh 1987: 763). Peasants' agitation spread in Punjab, United Province, Bihar and Maharashtra also. In the United Province, farmers struggled in an organized way against the anti-auction of land in Ballia, Basti, Azamgarh, Aligarh and Unnao. In Maharashtra, an intense peasant movement was started in 1947 by the Warli farmers. Farmers of Satara and Karwar division also agitated.

The historical analysis of peasants' movement in India, after the First World War, shows that it started against the politics of British imperialism. In India it created a huge number of workless, jobless citizens and left them on the mercy of a new class of zamindars and moneylenders. The British policy was to extract as much as tax they could, under the protection of the government, zamindars started endless exploitation of peasants in different parts of the country. Early peasant revolts against exploitation were unorganized, self-stimulated and local in nature. At this stage, although Congress passed some resolutions in favour of peasants, it could not do much for them. Congress was afraid of the aggressive nature of peasants and was not ready to go against zamindars.

After the First World War, especially after the Bolshevik revolution of Russia, Indian Leftists supported peasants and peasants' organizations in different forms. All India Kisan Sabha, came into existence which worked specially for peasants. Many Congress people also supported peasants' movements. Gandhi on 7 August 1942, in Bombay, asked farmers not to pay taxes. He said that the land belonged to those who were directly attached to land and doing farming. During the Quit India movement of 1942, peasants from all over India actively participated in the freedom movement. Small zamindars of United Province and Bihar were also with the national stream. The specialty of the revolution was that peasants did not use their energy against zamindars but wholeheartedly supported Congress against British imperialism.

NOTES

1. Indianetzone/History of India/Peasant movement and Uprising in India: www.concern:net, p. 2.
2. Wikipedia: *Farmers Movements in India*, p. 2.

3. *Peasants and Workers Party of Bengal Report, 1927 and 1928.*
4. Provincial Congress Committee, Agrarian Distress in United Province, Allahabad, 1931, p. 26.
5. *Civil and Military Gazette*, 8 November 1931.
6. Wikipedia: The Free Encyclopedia: *Farmers Movements in India*, p. 1.

REFERENCES

Adhikari, Gangadhar (1971): *Documents of the History of the Communist Party of India*, pt. I (New Delhi: People's Publishing House).

Bhushan, Chandra (1988): 'Rahul Tere Roop', *Sancha*, Bimonthly, Delhi, June-July.

Chandra, Bipin (2002): *Bharat Ka Swatantrata Sangrash* (Delhi: University of Delhi).

Desai, A.R. (1976): *Social Background of Indian Nationalism* (New Delhi: Macmillan).

Kapoor, A.N. and V.P. Gupta (2004): *An Encyclopedic Dictionary of Freedom Movement, 1757-1947* (New Delhi: Radha Publications).

Kulkarni, K.R. (1951): *Agricultural Marketing in India* (Bombay: The Cooperative Book Depot).

Namboodiripad, E.M.S. (1968): *Kerala: Yesterday, Today and Tomorrow* (Calcutta: National Book Agency).

Nehru, Jawaharlal (1953): *An Autobiography* (London: The Bodley Head Publishers).

——— (1985): *The Discovery of India* (New Delhi: Oxford University).

Prasad, Kamala (1994) (ed.): *Maha Pandit Rahul* (Allahabad: Parimal Prakash).

Pratap, Mahendra (1988): *Uttar Pradesh Mein Kisan Andolan* (New Delhi: Vani Press).

Ranga, N.G. (n.d.): *Kisan Hand Book* (Madras: Kisan Publications).

Sarkar, Sumit (1885): *Modern India, 1885-1947* (New Delhi: Macmillan).

Sharma, D.P. (2001): 'Swami Sahajanand, Gandhi and Subhas', *Collected Lectures of Swami Sahajanand Saraswati* (Ghazipur: Swami Sahajanand Saraswati Smriti Kendra).

Singh, Ayodhya (1987): *Bharat Ka Mukti Sangram* (New Delhi: Macmillan).

PART II

ASPECTS OF IDEOLOGY, PROGRAMME AND STRATEGY OF WORKING CLASS MOVEMENT

CHAPTER 7

Working Class and the Insecurity Hypothesis

ANURADHA KALHAN

The central claim of the Insecurity Hypothesis (IH) is that insecurity is deepening and widening even across sectors traditionally considered secure in terms of employment, e.g. the public sector, unionized sectors and white-collared service sector and it is empirically measurable.

STATEMENT OF THE HYPOTHESIS

Between the end of the 1980s and early 1990s, intensification of global competition and recurrent recessions led broadly to three types of organizational transitions in the Organization for Economic Cooperation and Development (OECD) countries—restructuring and downsizing, mergers and acquisitions and privatization (Burke and Cooper 2000; Cooper Burke 2002). These changes were an attempt to increase sagging comparative productivity. This direction of change too has been globally and variedly examined and it is commonplace for the workforce of even the developed world to be described as increasingly insecure (Heery and Salmon 2000). This view is global in scope and embraces international commentators in a range of countries and over a wide range of interests (Baker and Christensen 1998; OECD 1997; Standing 1997; Deshpande et al. 1998; Blanchard and Islam 2001). For some, we live in the 'age of insecurity' and risk and instability have become the defining features of contemporary social life (Elliot and Atkinson 1998; Beck 1992)—a coherent set of statements about the nature, causes and impacts of recent changes in employment relations, which is referred to as the 'Insecurity Hypothesis'.

Reports of this are available from a number of empirical studies conducted in OECD countries like the United Kingdom (UK), the United States (US) and a few in developing countries like India. Some of these studies are summarized here.

From these, it is possible to extract the concepts and the measures of insecurity experienced by the workers. Concepts like increasing spells of unemployment, number of job changes, contingent employment, institutional and legal changes that reduce the job protection, working hours, shorter job tenures, declining real wage rates experienced after spells of unemployment.

There is an association between wages and various kinds of flexibilities—organizational, technological and functional, numerical—and there is also a correspondence between flexibility and insecurity. Detrimental, psychological, social, political and economic consequences are associated with increasing job insecurity. The empirical work was done on similar lines as the later part of this study shows.

The central proposition of the IH is that the economic risk of increased global competition is being progressively passed on from the employer to the employee, variously using above features and reduced the protection and bargaining power of employee in the workplace.

The corollary is that widespread insecurity is damaging. In the short run, it promotes an employment relationship based on opportunism, distrust and low commitment. The medium to long-term consequence is underinvestment by employers in skill formation and training because of uncertain tenures; even when this is obviously critical to competitive advantage. Additionally, the widespread insecurity weakens institutions of collective action bargaining that act as networks of trust and cooperation. The feeble trade unions become both a cause and a consequence of mounting insecurity.

In the long term, it undermines productivity and economic performance because in times of rapid economic and technological change, insufficient management of social and human capital can become the limiting factor to growth. The danger of disregarding to the medium and long-term consequences is greater in countries like India.

All its expressions taken together provide the breadth of coverage and connect developments in the world of work with changes beyond, and embody concerns of labour economics, development economics, social psychology, sociology and political science.

PROMINENT PROPOSITIONS OF THE HYPOTHESIS

Employment and job security can be defined and measured. Some of its indicators are lower median job tenures, increase in involuntary job separations, growth in the use of contingent workers such as fixed-term contract, freelance, agency; temporary workers; use of variable performance linked pays (neither consolidated nor pensionable), and the rising work flexibility in affected countries (Nickell et al. 2002). Equally measurable are: spells of unemployment, number of jobs changed due to organizational decisions, time for searching another job, time period of unemployment, decreasing or stagnant real wages, hours of work, contingent employment, etc. All or many of these symptoms may occur together to make the worker insecure.

Employment in the developed countries has become insecure both in continuity and level of remuneration and for factors outside the control of the employee. A clear shift has taken place from the earlier dominant pattern in which internal labour markets shielded workers from market forces (Cappelli et al. 1997). The OECD report, an analysis of nine European Union (EU) countries, reveals that the difficulty of finding replacement work has risen since the early 1980s, even when the impacts of economic cycles are taken into account (OECD 1997). Also when new job is found, earnings may be substantially lower than in the previous job. The difference is substantial and enduring even in the UK and the US (Faber 1993: 73-132).

The insecurity trend has been compounded by changes in factors external to the labour market and national systems of employment regulation. The external factors at work here are the heightened global competition and structural and technological changes in the economy. The national systems of regulation have moved towards creating flexible labour markets. In Britain, for example, this included adverse changes in benefit systems and pressure to accept flexible terms of employment, attenuation of individual employment rights, increase in the qualifying period for the right, not to be unfairly dismissed (from six months to two years), severe and continuous decline in trade union density and coverage by bargaining power (Heery and Abbott 2000).

Previously secure groups are now finding themselves in a precarious position. The current list includes middle managers, public service professionals and older workers. Each of these categories may continue to enjoy higher security than non-management employees, private sector, younger workers and women, but their relative position is becoming less favourable. The trend is secular and not temporary or sector-specific (Cappelli 1995: 563-602). These trends are in the direction of what has been termed the contingent workforce—an army of blue collar, white-collar and managerial temps (Rousseau 1996: 50-61). This trend is likely to replicate itself in the organized manufacturing and services sectors in the developing countries as well.

EXPLANATORY FACTORS

Increasing insecurity has been traced to two causal factors:

(1) *Globalization of the economy*: In an era of 'market deregulation', the capitalist economies have entered a new stage at the heart of which is increasing competition and a new management-model characterized by the identification of 'core-competencies' and restructuring for flexibility (Standing 1997: 7-37). All operations and services outside this core competency can be performed by non-core contingent workforce (Guest 2000).

(2) *National systems of capitalism*: It promotes the dominance by a system of financial interest and the short-term management of company assets in the interest of shareholder values. This argument touches upon corporate governance and financing and emphasizes the different experiences of labour across national economies. It also highlights the significance of national systems of labour market regulation in increasing or moderating the pressure of insecurity (Wickham 1997: 133-51).

THE CONSEQUENCES

The consequences of increasing insecurity in the workforce are wide ranging and they have economic, psychological, social and political facets.

Psychological contract at workplace begins to resemble a spot market where workers are encouraged to focus on their immediate self-interest and employers undertake to do the same (Cappelli et al. 1997; Beynon 1997; Brown 1997). Disadvantages of this breakdown include low levels of employee commitment, unwillingness to work beyond contract, and high transaction cost associated with the monitoring and enforcement of contracts.

Right sizing, restructuring and downsizing were corporate slogans in the 1980s and 1990s in the US, especially in the manufacturing sector. It was supposed to be the fastest and the easiest way to cut business costs, be more competitive and raise profits.

Evidence is that such labour policy mostly backfired and firms failed to record sustained increase in earnings and their ability to compete eroded even further. One of the unintended effects of downsizing was that employees who survived were insecure, had to work longer and felt less loyal towards the firm. They also reported a loss of creativity under the high levels of stress.

The American Management Association, in 1992, surveyed more than 500 firms which had downsized since 1987 (Baumohal 1993). More than 75 per cent reported that employee morale had collapsed. Two-thirds showed no increase in efficiency and less than half showed any increase in profits.

This also works as a disincentive for employers to invest in training and employee involvement (Broadbent et al. 1998; Cappelli et al. 1997; Kelly 1997: 393-8; Legge 1998). Cappelli et al. (1997) argue that new forms of high performance work organization, for global competition, require committed, flexible and highly trained employees, the very factors whose growth is hampered by worker insecurity. Paradoxically, an essential precondition for business strategy, which emphasizes quality enhancement, productivity growth and flexibility is a stable, secure and trained workforce (Brown et al. 1993: 247-75; Edwards et al. 1998: 449-75).

The skill premium had increased at the end of the last century, unlike the earlier part of the century when it fell as a result of Fordist organization of production (Bound and Johnson 1992: 371-2). When production had become organized in large mass-producing plants, jobs became routinized, favouring less-skilled workers. Manufacturing could absorb a large number of workers from the rural sector. The nature of technological change was different in the second half of the twentieth century.

The recent experience of manufacturing is that flexible, numerically-controlled machines have allowed plants to operate at a smaller scale. Batch production has replaced mass production. Each batch may be highly customized and require workers who can manipulate the machines to perform the wide variety of tasks that it can perform. In data samples from 1977 to 1994 downsizing is related to decrease in plant size, increase in the average industry wage, productivity and employment of more skilled rather than unskilled labour (Mitchell 2005: 935-55).

Skill formation has been identified as the main collective goal of economic policy and an effective system of vocational educational training is viewed as a necessary condition for maintenance of a high wage economy (Crouch 1997: 367-84; Lane 1990: 247-59; Streeck 1989: 89-104; Brown et al. 2001). The more flexible systems of production actually require increased involvement of enterprises in the design and development of programmes of training and development. But a more contingent employment relationship and collapse of internal labour market inhibit this. The risks are passed on via outsourcing, subcontracting, just-in-time (JIT) inventory systems, network of subsidiary firms and contingent labour strategies.

Just as all production inputs are being purchased on the market and only in sufficient quantities, so too the labour market is being shaped along similar lines where labour is purchased on the market on an as-needed basis via labour contractors.

In addition, employers now require labour to enter the labour market with a higher level of generalized skills, which labour is increasingly acquiring via temporary agency training programmes or vocational schools. This reduces employer's investment in labour skills, and therefore, reduces the employer's interest in holding on to employees (Christopherson 1997). Therefore, a smaller work-force is being compelled to work more intensively by means of both speed-up and stretch-out, while millions of unemployed accept worse jobs or no jobs. So the profits increase as employment and wages decline.

The threat of being fired instils fear which inhibits learning and systemic improvements; furthermore, incentive, quota and piecework system of pays all foster competition rather than team work among workers and undermine morale because of their inherent arbitrary nature (Best 1990: 160).

Education and training, in other words, learning, are the basis of individual, organizational, and national growth. Since the skill, knowledge and experience of each individual contributes to economic growth of the organization and cumulatively the national economy, economists talk in terms of human capital as the primary requirement for national economic development. The main effect of accumulative knowledge and capital has been to accelerate change, over time this has reduced the number of low skill jobs. So that, the acquisition of knowledge is today the key to value addition and wealth creation globally just as control over raw materials was in the age of industrial capitalism.

Social scientists see society deeply divided into three knowledge-based classes—the symbolic analyst who creates and manipulates knowledge, a service class to support them and a large number of people who have no economic role at all. There is a tendency like never before to polarize the working class. The technological and organizational changes in the post-industrial economy are occurring so rapidly that there is an urgent and growing need to constantly train and retrain workers to prevent any long-term exclusion/marginalization of workers from the market.

As it stands, in 1993, the OECD job study survey had estimated that the average individual leaving school in the developed world would have five separate jobs in a working life; for each job major retraining would be required.

The critical question, therefore, is who will bear the cost of this learning and relearning over a lifetime? Whether an increasingly insecure workforce can remain employable? Since education is a very long-term investment, the typical market-driven firm will train its employees only if urgently required for the briefest period and this is most likely in the case of absence of long-term retention and employment.

It is even more likely in the case of low skilled peripheral/non-permanent workers. Hence, the possibility of cumulative causations that keeps the low skilled in a trap, unemployable and poor. There is a further likelihood of the developing countries getting trapped in a vicious cycle of cheap labour advantage in global trade, low skill, low productivity, low wage circuit, unless state policy induces/compels firms to train and upgrade workforce (Kalhan 2004).

Life-long learning and empowerment needs a dynamic process of devolving power and responsibility downward in organizations to harness creative energies of workforce. The essence of empowerment, lies in the growth of knowledge, training, analytical skills, experience and motivation of workers (Blanchard et al. 1999). Organizations grow and technology and processes become more complex. A class of workers called professionals comes into existence, and, they exercise power within organizations. Empowerment occurs simultaneously in the social and business processes with the spread of education. Nowadays, human resource policy makers talk of the Dawn of the Age of Learning and the necessity of life-long learning in a knowledge-driven society. At a micro level, this translates into the character of human resource management (HRM) policies of the firm and its culture that may or may not induce life-long learning. It implies that workers will have to learn throughout their working life and should view every new task as an opportunity to learn afresh (Jarvis 2000).

Firms in England and the US, for example, were spending 1 to 2 per cent of their salary bills on formal training in 1994-5. In addition, informal training would amount to six times the amount spent on formal training. Training or staff development itself is a growing industry. It caters to a growing number of firms and other organizations that may need outside help/decentralized training to prevent staff obsolescence in a competitive market (Hargreaves and Jarvis 1998). Employment stability, measured as the average employment tenure, is now considered important for achieving high levels of productivity. While a degree of job mobility is necessary for increasing productivity, this has to be distinguished from employment instability and insecurity.

The prime source of productivity growth is a technological innovation, which itself is influenced by an array of institutions, the quality and quantity of human capital, spending on research and development (R&D), competitive pressures in the market and the levels of investment in general.

That changes in the organization of work and production have a profound effect on productivity has been long acknowledged, from Adam Smith 250 years ago in his study of the growth of division of labour, specialization and rising productivity in the factory system down to present discussions on generating high performance work systems. The Human Capital Theory also tells us that much of how workers learn to do their job better comes from formal training plus the training they receive on the job from more experienced workers, simply called learning by doing. Employer has no incentive to invest in workers training if the contract between employer and worker is an uncertain and short one. Workers on the other hand, have no reason to develop and acquire more productive ways of doing things as either teams or individuals if they fear that they will work themselves out of a job. Employment stability promotes productivity growth and the reverse is also true that productivity growth can improve employment stability with the help of appropriate institutional arrangements like in-place employment protection legislation (ILO 2005).

Increasingly insecure workforce is also associated with polarization of labour market. At one end, are the high-skill, high-wage workers, and at the other, low-skill, low-wage insecure workforce, the latter numerically larger than the former. This increasing inequality in income and wealth reduces social cohesion and has been linked to criminality, family breakdown and political alienation (Beynon 1997; Gray 1995; Luttwak 1994: 3, 6; Hutton 1995).

The increasingly insecure workforce is making a demand for protective regulation, because, the job and everything organized around the job—the friends at work, the after work meeting places, even group transport—are losing their social function. These are becoming as permanently temporary as the work itself. The new workplace is destabilizing the family, degrading the very institution critical for social reproduction (Carnoy 1995: 411-29).

It is being argued that while there is a new and increasing opportunities for trade unionism, trade unions must affect a realignment of their policies and structures. For example, pursuit of collective bargain in which job security is exchanged for union cooperation for raising productivity and company performance has to be circumvented. Also, union must pay an increasing attention to organizing contingent workforce in old and new sectors of economy. Since the demographic characteristics of the current workforce include larger number of women, migrants and the youth, this segment must be adequately represented within union policy making (Heery and Abbott 2000; Leisink 1997: 534-50; Wever 1998: 388-407).

Social scientists, sociologists and political scientists have also suggested that this central problem of our day, 'personal economic insecurity of working people', might be distancing a growing percentage of population from conventional politics and fostering support for extremist politics of all types (Gray 1995). This is a view that is supported by a growing number of social commentators.

In India, for example, the growth of identity politics and vandalism in Maharashtra in the shape of the politics of a political party called the Shiv Sena over a period 1966-84 is studied by Shaikh (2005) and linked to the slowdown in the growth of jobs in Mumbai textile mills, immigration into Mumbai, growth of the partially, temporary and self-employed in a growing informal economy and the increasing economic insecurity of workers (Shaikh 2005: 1893-1999; Breman 1996). According to the author: this transformation of the workers' psyche away from class-based formations to right wing identity based regional chauvinism occurs in central Mumbai, the heartland of left unions, speaks a lot for the possible consequences of insecurity.

The French riots of November 2005 and the Los Angeles riots earlier had also been attributed to the same process of alienation, polarization and insecurity (Srinivas 1992: 2388). Silver (2003) also makes a similar observation when she says that, insecure labour may have a good reason to seek identity in non-class boundaries and borders, e.g. race, citizenship and gender as a way of making claims for privileged protection from the maelstrom created by the de-socialization of the state. Just because capital finds it in its interest to treat labour as interchangeable commodities, the workers may not find it in their interest to accept this paradigm (Silver 2003). The initial impact of globalization could well mean an intensification of identity-based rather than class-based politics.

One of the effects of the spread of insecure employment is work intensification, i.e. reduction in access to holiday, sick pay and increase in hours of work and abuse of managerial authority (Dex and McCulloch 1997; Engberg 1993). This intensification is directly associated with the loss of democratic space.

Social scientists have also attributed the loss of social capital, i.e. public indifference to socio-political causes and declining public participation in collective action to the new work conditions like work intensification and insecurity. The middle class is caught between the pressures to maintain their standard of living and an increasingly insecure labour market (Frank 2004).

Costs for employees of job insecurity extend beyond the work-place and include physical and psychological stress and ill-health, which are as great as that associated with unemployment (Nolan et al. 1997; Dex and McCulloch 1997; Gallie et al. 1998). All industrial countries have experienced sizeable changes in their labour markets over the past two decades and one of the most significant recurrent themes in this upheaval has been the reduction of employee security. Many social psychologists have also examined the phenomenon and from their perspective job insecurity is very stressful, it affects the motivation and attitudes of employees, and it spills over into family, the basic unit of social reproduction (Nolan et al. 2000). The psychological effects of stress are often visible in the decreased quality of life and decreased levels of psychological well-being like increased anxiety level and depression, a sense of uselessness, lack of self-confidence and dissatisfaction with one's environment. Studies have shown that anticipation or concern about job loss may be as damaging as job loss itself (Latack and Dozier 1986: 375-92). Job insecurity has been found to be associated with increasing medical consultation for psychological distress. In studies on job insecurity, psychological well-being has been measured on a number of scales and indicators and found to be negatively related to insecurity (Vuuren et al. 1991). Macho cultures in lean and mean workplaces requiring long hours of work in an insecure job environment are especially hard on women with young children (Collinson and Collinson 1995).

Insecurity ultimately has consequences for the social reproduction of labour. Social reproduction refers to all those activities and processes, by which, human beings are sustained materially and psychologically, directly and indirectly. In simple terms, it means how labour power is reproduced over every generation to sustain economic activity, which in turn, sustains it. These activities and processes of social reproduction have been historically embedded in social and cultural structures like the tribe, the family, community, market and state. Economists focus on production and not on social reproduction, which is assumed to be autonomous. In fact, the process by which labour is produced and maintained as a commodity has not been considered important enough even in Marxist literature. This tends to assign the social organization of childbirth, infant care and domestic socialization to the realm of nature or some intermediate location and sees the real dynamic of society as stemming from production. The concept, therefore, figures mainly in feminist discourses and sociology. But if one takes labour power seriously as a productive force in all modes of production, the question of the specific relations within which it is produced and reproduced must be centrally addressed (Secombe 1986: 56-84).

In the period before the industrial revolution and the reorientation of values that held the individuals responsible for sustaining themselves, the individual was not threatened by starvation unless the community as a whole was in a likewise predicament (Polanyi 1957). The unpaid domestic labour of women also serves to lower the cost of all wage labour (Castells and Alejandro 1989). Historically, the ties of reciprocity took care of social reproduction. In the period after that, instability of market conditions brought about the dilution of community ties and increasing insecurity. And it became apparent that the capitalist system was unable to provide for the reproduction of its own labour force. Because workers have only one way to live under capitalism—by selling their own labour power—a reserve army necessitates some mechanism for maintaining the unemployed and those earning poverty wages in a condition in which they are ready to work when capital calls. It must be pointed out that social reproduction requires not just physical reproduction of labour in required quantities for work, but, with higher/diverse levels of knowledge and skills commensurate with technology. Hence, social reproduction presupposes training and upskilling as well. As long as the cost of maintaining these reserve armies of workers could be diffused through religious charity and the community reciprocity the market system could survive.

Under capitalism, social reproduction refers to the reproduction of the capital-wage labour relationship, and thereby, the construction of labour power as commodity. However, there are three peculiarities of labour, first, the commodity labour power is inseparable from the human being, as Marx said that labour power is the capacity of a living person to labour, which in turn, depends on labour's productive consumption. Second, there is a historical, social and cultural basis of determining the value of labour power. It would differ in time and place. Third, of all the commodities produced in a capitalistic society, labour is the only one that cannot be produced capitalistically based on wage labour and the extraction of surplus value. It is produced outside the ambit of the market in the household and family, which may be penetrated, by the market and state but lies outside it (Dickinson 1986).

The state interfaces social reproduction through industrial policies, labour market regulations and social and redistribution policies. The welfare state can be understood in that context—it sought to stabilize and reproduce the workforce to meet the needs of an increasingly well-organized and highly productive factory organization, which had evolved over 150 years since Adam Smith first wrote about it. The welfare system was to provide the reserve army and the non-wage earning dependents of wage earners—family unit within which labour is reproduced—some form of security (Harris 1995: 157-85). The welfare state was a struggle within capitalism for a transfer of value led by the workers themselves for whom the insufficiency and insecurity of wage is a threat to survival and reproduction (Wayne 1986: 56-84).

Globalization and the restructuring of production have changed the premise of the state. The state is now a partner with the capital to weaken the welfare structures that made social reproduction possible in capitalism. That has set into process cumulative causative forces that bring down the price of labour even below its real cost for super profits. A process of recasualization/normalization has set in across the globe and workers from developed/developing countries, both skilled and unskilled are experiencing the pressures. Non-standard employment, with uncertain or limited duration, i.e. work assignment other than full-time-wage job, is a commonly used source of flexibility by firms now. The casual, informal worker works at low wages outside the parameters of state mandated labour regulations regarding wages, lay off wages, retrenchment compensation, work hours, work environment, health insurance and any other forms of security. The only recourse now for social reproduction for these contingent workers is the family, since the community solidarity, NGOs; self-help groups are proving to be inadequate (Tabak and Crichlow 2000: 133-265).

Globalization of economy and the accompanying deregulation of financial, product markets has thus significantly altered the employment patterns and aggravated insecurity. This has wide-ranging, multidimensional consequences affecting working people everywhere. The resistance to globalization may be understood in the context of these changes.

POLITICAL IMPLICATIONS OF INSECURITY HYPOTHESIS

Pervasive insecurity underscores the need for innovative policies to intervene in the labour market and reform the system of employment. Policies, which include legal regulations of the terms and conditions of employment, reform of corporate governance and human resource policies of employers so as to build skills, employability and income security (Wright 2000). Evidence suggests that there is a strong and positive correlation between country's openness to trade and how much a country spends on active labour market policies as a percentage of gross domestic product (GDP). Countries have to find a workable balance between the micro level stability and macro level employment security that a system affords. Workers' perception of their employment security provides a basis for strong aggregate demand in the economy to sustain equitable economic growth (ILO 2005).

Both welfare state capitalism and state socialism of the twentieth century aimed at de-commodification of labour. Both offered full employment, individual and collective security to a lesser or greater extent. Macroeconomic policies were employed to maintain security. This era saw the introduction of all those above-mentioned multiple-dimensions of security mentioned earlier, namely (1) labour market security—state guaranteed employment or income, (2) employment security—protection from arbitrary dismissal, retrenchment and layoff or in cases of accident or sickness, (3) job security—protection of an occupation or skill, (4) skill reproduction security—improved access to training and apprenticeship, and (5) representational security—protection of collective voice of labour.

There is a need to revisit these policies in new ways. Some of the best practices to deal with insecurity across the globe are discussed later in the study under the heading of 'Active Labour Market Policies'.

A CRITIQUE OF INSECURITY HYPOTHESIS

A critique of IH has also emerged and has the following core arguments:

The first argument attacks the root proposition that the labour market is changing in a fundamental way and that employment is becoming more insecure in an objective sense (Heery and Salmon 2000: 11). According to this, there is limited empirical support for growing job instability. Some modest changes may have occurred, but there is a moral panic over insecurity, which will turn out to be temporary. Insecurity sceptics include Burgess and Rees (1996), Goddard Spencer (1996 and 1998), and Guest (1997) (Burgess and Rees 1996: 334-44; Goddard 1998: 501-3; Guest 1997: 344-52).

The second line of criticism is in defence of the government policies of deregulation and flexibilization of labour markets (Smith 1997). Essentially, it accepts that job insecurity is rising and imposes a cost on a portion of the workforce, but there are compensatory benefits to society that outweigh these costs.

Alan Greenspan, ex-chairman of the US Federal Reserve Board is on record as attributing America's prolonged non-inflationary upward swing during the 1990s to a growing sense of insecurity in the US workforce. Similar claims have been made in the UK, where the death of inflation is judged to be a result of market reforms of the 1980s, which removed the protective shield of trade unionism from a large percentage of the labour force (Bootle 1996). Consequently, the macroeconomic policy can be set within a looser framework with low interest rates and lower level Non-Accelerating Inflation Rate of Unemployment (NAIRU). The insecurity serves to improve the rest of the economy. The rest of the economy here could well refer to the corporate interests as against that of the working class.

A third line of criticism emphasizes the structural nature of changes induced by globalization in the economies of the developed countries as they shift away from labour-intensive manufacturing towards knowledge-based manufacturing and services sector growth. Calculations by *The Economist* indicate that manufacturing now accounts for less than 10 per cent of the jobs in America (*The Economist* 2005). In 1820, agriculture accounted for 80 per cent of the jobs and today it accounts for less than 2 per cent. If all those workers had remained tilling the land, America would have been poorer. On the other hand, labour-intensive manufacturing continues to grow in all developing countries. In America, as well, manufacturing sector grew at 4 per cent per year since 1991, although the growth there is oriented away from labour-intensive low value added industries like textiles or computer assembly, towards high value added products like pharmaceuticals, aviation or computer design. America is the world's biggest manufacturer in value terms producing about twice as much as China, even if American markets are flooded with cheaper Chinese consumer products. Services sector employment continues to grow in DCs.

Even in the case of the latter, the shift is towards knowledge-based high value added services, which are not outsourced and have stayed at home, e.g. services like research and development (R&D), patenting of new designs, product marketing and financial services. Low rates of unemployment in America and the UK today suggest that those who lost their jobs in manufacturing have got new ones over time. Developed countries will be forced to move towards higher skilled jobs and countries that prevent this shift will be left behind. The low value added manufacturing will shift to lower cost countries like China. The current rate of growth of the Chinese economy suggests that it will outsize the American by 2050. Even as changes cause pain for some and are resisted, the government can facilitate change by providing assistance in the form of temporary unemployment benefits and retraining for those who lose their jobs. In the long run, economists like Bootle (2001) are optimistic about the prospects of the truly global economy, as the division of labour is made possible on a grand international scale (Bootle 2001). Europe should not mourn the hollowing out of manufacturing jobs, but specialize in knowledge-based high-technology industry.

In the developing countries, the same prescription of flexibility for economic health (albeit in very different circumstances) is being recommended. It is claimed that free trade will generate jobs in the medium to long-term in labour-intensive sectors. The IH may be irrelevant in developing countries like India because 90 per cent of the workforce is in the informal sector, where even today, there is labour flexibility and there has never been any security. Poor implementation of labour laws has in any case made security in the organized sector a paper tiger. Regulatory attempts to protect employment security have so far restricted the overall growth of organized sector employment and succeeded only in creating islands of security. Flexibility will support growth, international trade and investment. It will stimulate employment growth, which has been lagging, and benefit workers and the firms in the long run. Examples of newly industrialized economies of East Asia are given to endorse flexibility as a means of promoting employment, increasing productivity and real wages.

Critics either allege lack of convincing data to support a conclusion of increasing insecurity or else treat it as a transient but essential and inevitable phenomenon.

INSECURITY HYPOTHESIS AND LABOUR MARKET FLEXIBILITY

The inference that jobs for life are a thing of the past, and insecure workforce is on the rise has coincided with rapid growth in 'flexible' forms of work in the developed countries. While insecurity can be measured in terms of unemployment, redundancy, falling real income, etc., the term flexibility is used in the context of growth in forms of non-standard employment, wage flexibility and functional flexibility (Robinson 2000). The non-standard forms of employment like part-time and temporary employees are perceived to be inherently inferior and less secure than full-time permanent jobs for employees (Felstead et al. 1998: 180-4). Technically, it is important to note that growth in part-time work in the OECD countries was first linked to the feminization of the workforce and the growth of the services sector that took place after the Second World War. New ways of working or new labour styles are not absolutely new. Home working, temporary work and shift working supported the early phases of the Industrial Revolution, while job sharing and flexi time arrived as early as the 1950s. Team working and multi-skilling, teleworking, annual time, V-time, zero-hours, gain sharing, flexible benefits, virtual office, call centres have made their appearance in a formal way in the last twenty years in the OECD countries and now in the developing countries as well (Stredwick and Ellis 1998).

Countries like the US and the UK with less regulated labour markets than France and Germany also have a higher category of flexible workers. The flexible American style labour markets are promoted in the name of increasing employment, it is based on a fragile theory that interventions to enhance job security or pay roll taxes to improve pension benefits would lead to inefficiency and increase in unemployment. The highly deregulated US economy is characterized by stagnant or falling real wages for a significant percentage of the low-skilled workers. The high-skilled workers have super-charged work schedules, for outcompeting others and meeting deadlines at all costs. They earn more but at the cost of more intensified work schedules, job security, individual stress and social isolation. The flexible model of labour market is making sustained inroads into social Europe and secure Japan under the guise of competitiveness, efficiency and increased investments (Stiglitz 2002: 9-29).

The origins of flexible production and organization precede the current wave of globalization and also precede the rapid growth in flexible employment. Not all OECD based firms, seeking to overcome the rigidities of Taylorism, turned to low wage production sites off-shore. Some of the firms succeeded in developing more flexible forms of production organizations at home. Toyota started in the late 1950s, and the clusters of small- and medium-size firms in Italy, which developed during 1960-70, are probably the best-known early examples (Piore and Sable 1984). As the late 1970s and early 1980s marked the watershed, the formidable dynamism and competitive strength of flexible producers led many Taylorist firms to start talking about the new rules of global competition. Above all, they were reacting to the much greater capacity of flexible producers to profitably exploit the flexible automation technologies that began emerging in the late 1970s (Womack et al. 1990). The first sign of crisis of Taylorism, therefore, predate the current wave of globalization and are more closely linked to events like slowing down of the US productivity growth in the late 1960s, the spectacular growth of Japanese flexible automaker's share of the US auto market following the second oil-shock and the deregulation of global competition. Even though this may not be well-appreciated by economists, the crisis of Taylorism is an important cause of the structural labour market problems in OECD countries (Best 1990).

There are broadly two types of flexible organizations. One is the large firm variety in terms of financial or marketing strength or what is called 'intra-group approach to flexibility', i.e. like Japan's automobile and electronics producers, large firms in Germany and American firms like HP and Motorola. The second type is the district of industrial clusters, where a number of relatively small, independently owned firms compete and cooperate with each other in close physical proximity.

Their principal differences from Taylorist firms are (a) they claim to integrate thinking and do so at all levels of operations, (b) harness human capability of their workers, especially for anticipating and diagnosing problems, finding solutions and adapting to changing circumstances, (c) they organize work in teams that avoid excessive specialization and compartmentalization, (d) continuously innovate, which contrasts with Taylor's 'one best way', (e) higher degree of customization as against mass production, (f) higher productivity by exploiting economies of scope and quicker response to changes in market demands, (g) only a core group of relatively higher skilled workers, who are treated as long-term assets, and are trained continuously, and compensated as per the performance of their teams/groups, (h) lean middle level management, and (i) high dependence on infrastructure support.

In the automobile industry, which has been most extensively studied, the leading flexible producers in the mid-1980s (for example, Toyota) were found to have productivity levels twice those of leading European and US manufacturers. Equally, impressive differences in productivity and competitiveness have been reported by studies in other flexibly organized industries (Cooper 1995).

Flexible production is no longer limited to assembly type manufacturing, but also exists in processing industries like chemical, steel, ceramics, textile, high-fashion, modern services like insurance, banking, telecommunications and even in traditional public monopolies like power distribution and postal services. Implications of flexibility for developed countries are more serious for the workers used to the Taylorist organization, most significantly, for unskilled workers because flexible organizations have little use for workers who lack strong basic literacy, numeric, social and interpersonal social skills and general trainability. Other category of workers affected are (a) highly skilled and too narrowly specialized, (b) middle management and (c) low-skilled. Their jobs are likely to disappear.

Developing countries like India already have a large number of small or tiny firms/unorganized sector and these tend to fall into the second type of flexibility offered in clusters albeit rudimentary type and here flexible organization offers considerably greater possibilities to adapt output levels and product features for relatively small markets with lower quality requirements. They also have a minimum efficient level (break-even level) of production, which is significantly lower than that of Taylorist type. This is suited to a smaller market, where number of medium size producers can compete (Caplinsky 1993). They also have greater employment potential.

It is not as if Taylorist firms are entirely redundant or irrelevant, and in fact, they account for one-third to half of all manufacturing in OECD countries. They also have considerable potential in developing countries because of their robustness in terms of economies of scale and scope, financial strength and their capacity to create transportation, communications and power infrastructure, etc., to meet their own requirements. They can also absorb a fairly large number of unskilled, low-skilled workers. The successful use of this model over the past twenty years in China is a testimony to its advantage.

It needs to be understood that increasing flexibility from the point of view of the organization of production of goods and services implies insecurity of employment from the point of view of the workforce.

TYPES OF LABOUR FLEXIBILITIES

The World Bank has also broadened the concept of flexibility. Many kinds of labour flexibility now find mention in the literature and are identified by Standing as below (Standing 1999; Deshpande et al. 1998).

ORGANIZATIONAL FLEXIBILITY

Large firms have extended their division of labour by linking activities between firms and by outsourcing. By adopting flexible organizational structures that are decentralized (small firms are also building flexible specialization in turn), they are engaged in downloading risk and uncertainty to smaller firms. With the death of 'Fordism', as far as labour is concerned, the decentralization, i.e. organizational flexibility has increased (Holmstorm and Tirole 1989). The defining characteristics of labour markets in the global era are smaller workplaces, fewer rules in the workplace, weaker unions and wages tied to business cycles (Munck 2002: 72-3). The US has used spatial dispersion and geographical isolation of employees as one of its prime but subtle mechanisms of labour control. But the recent transformation of the industrial organization, flexible location choices and deregulation have been turned into a totally obvious form of coercive exploitation and capitalistic control, which is pre-rather than post-Fordist in the organizational form (Harvey 1993).

WORK PROCESS OR FUNCTIONAL FLEXIBILITY

Changes in the market or technology occur rapidly. The speeds with which the firm can bring about internal changes in the organization of work are called functional flexibilities. This is also referred to as vertical and horizontal flexibility so that workers carry out jobs above their level or below their level and accept lateral shifts. Here again, flexibility implies multi-skilling of workers, teamwork, work intensification, variable working hours, overtime, teamwork and shift work.

NUMERICAL FLEXIBILITY

This refers to the ability of the firm to reduce or increase the workforce with minimum cost. They rely on flexible or contingent workers. In case of statutory regulations that make such flexibility difficult and costly, the firm has two set of responses (a) look for loopholes in regulations and creates new labour categories, which are flexible, or (b) shift to capital-intensive technologies. Growing tribe of flexible categories include the casual, temporary and permanently temporary workers. Casual workers are hired for fixed hours and paid on a piece rates. Temporary workers have a fixed term contract, and the permanently temporary workers are long-term workers but lack the benefits-entitlements of the permanent workers. Then there are subcontractors, agency workers, home workers, teleworkers, part-time workers, consultants, associates and concealed workers. The new systems that emphasize the working flexibility have been introduced in an incremental way in three stages, first, they have been introduced to save money for the firms, second, they are associated with downsizing to deal with crisis, third, they have been expanded and retained as a business advantage for the firm leading to improvements in the bottom line.

WAGE FLEXIBILITY

Wage flexibility is critical to a flexible labour market. This wage flexibility is ensured by a decline of the fixed wage component in the total income of an employee. Wide wage differentials separate the core from the peripheral, permanent from temporary, formal sector workers in the core activities of the firm from informal set of workers in the non-core outsourced work sites. So that workers fall into categories of increasing insecurity. The core being the most secure consisting of full-time, high wage-cum-benefit, permanent workers who are trained, multi-skilled and functionally flexible, followed by the first periphery, second periphery and external groups providing the numerical flexibility. This also results in total wage bill flexibility, wide wage differentials and low labour cost as a proportion of the total cost. In the neo-classical economics, mass unemployment is considered as a positive proof of the absence of downwards wage flexibility. Absence of wage flexibility consequently causes unemployment, inflation, stagnation in growth and lack of structural adjustment.

While the trend for greater flexibility continues and wage differentials widen, underpinned by performance related pay. The low wages and insecurity at the periphery are such that the Confederation of British Industry-commissioned a report into flexible labour markets (CBI 1996) pointing out the vital question of 'who pays for the training of atypical workers' (CBI 1996).

FLEXIBLE TECHNOLOGIES

As a popular concept, flexible specialization implies that the Fordist mass production is being replaced, in successful industrial economies, by decentralized production and less hierarchical management. Firms in the new industrial clusters innovate constantly—using multi-purpose machinery like CNC, CAD, CAM and workers who are always learning new skills—to supply fragmented and rapidly changing markets. Large firms are broken down into smaller decision-making units, while networks of small firms, often but not always, concentrated in industrial districts, achieve collective efficiency by working together using complementary technologies, products and skills (Cadene and Holmstrom 1998).

There is another way in which flexibility can be understood—as the converse of inflexibility. A labour market is inflexible for re-structuring to bring about organizational flexibility of business firms if the level of unemployment insurance benefits is too high or their duration is too long, or if there are many restrictions on the freedom of employers to fire and hire or if the permissible hours of work are too tightly regulated, or if excessive generous compensation for over-time work is mandated or if trade unions have too much power to protect incumbent workers against competition and to control the flow of work at the site of production, or perhaps, if the statutory health and safety regulations are too stringent (Solow 2005). Hence, job security legislation refers to all the legal provisions that raise the cost of dismissing a worker and those that regulate the hiring of particular types of labour.

Flexibility is now so varied and widespread that the ILO has framed International Conventions to deal with it (Shyam Sundar 2005: 4-10). Concept of flexibility has been widely applied to organizational-structure, workplace-functionality, size of the workforce, wage-benefit differentials, and flexible production or service technologies. It is a fundamental link between the pressures of global competition on firms on the one hand, and insecurity of workers on the other.

CRITIQUE OF FLEXIBILITY

There has been a strong defence of flexibility on the grounds that it is an imperative for survival in competitive conditions, where demand is volatile and technologies change rapidly (Forrester 1994: 221-42). Management has usually tried to adopt Japanese style at work and manufacturing in which Japan held a salient position in the 1980s. Others have looked at flexibilities from labour's point of view, on effort-rate, skills, employee autonomy, shop floor empowerment, and social relations between the workforce, unions and management. These studies understand flexibility as a continuum of capitalistic exploitation and subordination of labour accompanied by an inherent process of class struggle and resistance.

Japanization has been described as the application of full repertoire of production practices like total quality management, continuous improvement, statistical quality control, just in time production, labour flexibility, multi-skill, job rotation, organization of labour into teams/groups, progressive substitution of labour union's influence by direct management control. In the first category, i.e. the management view, Womack et al. (1990) present lean production as a pre-eminent high productivity manufacturing system dominant in Japan, which the West and the rest must emulate, because it removes all slack, human and material waste (Womack et al. 1990). The dynamic work-team at the heart of the lean factory enriches the work environment, which compels workers to think and address challenges that arise at work.

Kenny and Florida (1993) make similar arguments and they argue that Japanization is an inevitable outcome of the capitalistic dynamics of technological and organizational progress (Kenny and Florida 1993). They conceptualize the practices within a framework of innovation-mediated production, characterized by integration and harnessing of the intelligence and knowledge of the R&D staff, design engineers and the shop floor workers. Through the mechanism of mutli-functional team, the shop floor is transformed into a continuously innovative production laboratory. On the basis of some case studies, Oliver and Wilkinson (1992), assert that the Japanization of the British industry is still in progress (Oliver and Wilkinson 1992). This system completely synchronizes production with the demands of the market, by using human resource management practices such as long-term job security for a lean core of skilled workers, careful employee recruitment and selection techniques, performance related pay, direct communication and enterprise unionism. The implications of worker resistance to these far-reaching changes are, however, noted by the authors.

In the second category of studies (worker's point of view), Ackroyd et al. (1998) argue that fundamental differences between an integrated Japanese economy characterized by high level of coordination between banking, manufacturing and traditional capital and a high fragmented British economy imply a limit to Japanization of British industry and economy (Ackroyd et al. 1998: 23). In their study of the Nissan car assembly transplant in Sunderland, Garrhan and Stewart (1992) provide an influential analysis of managerial endeavours to control and subordinate the workforce by mobilizing an ideology built on the appealing principle of consensus and participation (Garrhan and Stewart 1992). According to the authors, despite the highly exploitative nature of the production system—labour intensification, low skill job enlargement—the workers display a corporate consciousness and identify with the objectives of their employers in the absence of independent trade union. An ideology of consent works at two levels, first, through social form such as teamwork and Kaizen, and second, through a wider organizational vision of a classless factory. But the authors convey a mixed picture of complete worker subordination and total management control instead of participation and consensus.

Similar conclusions emerge from the study of Danford (1999). Operating within an economic environment of intensive global competitive pressure, managers of these firms were not interested in enriching the lives of their employees (Danford 1999). They regarded the notion that the assembly line workers could enjoy meaningful empowerment and self-management as nonsensical. Their labour control priority reflected the timeless capitalistic exigencies of efficient surplus extraction and capital accumulation. Globalization of economy and its resulting intense competition are central to compulsions behind flexibility of labour and political consent for these changes.

From the point of view of the developing countries, evidence seems to be different. It indicates that the characteristics of the flexible specialization model, like multipurpose machines, broad skills, varied products, innovations and local policy forces, which channel the competitive pressure towards permanent innovation, are based on the experiences of some developed countries like Italy and Japan. But due to labour surplus, lax labour regulations, and inadequate growth of trade unions, the competitive advantage frequently results from the sweating of labour rather than innovation. Schmitz (1989) gives examples from the hammock making industry in Brazil, knitting and clothing industry in Sao Paulo and garment industry in India to show the dynamics towards low wage, low technology and low quality. He raises doubts about the replicability of the model of advanced countries to the cluster of small firms in labour surplus third world countries (Schmitz 1989: 27-33).

Flexibility within the Japanese model works well in a cultural context that has strong elements of feudalism and patriarchy, it may not be possible to replicate Japanese type of flexibility in another cultural context, e.g. Germany without resistance from the workers. While in 'labour surplus' India, it may impose a distinct penalty upon the workers.

INSECURITY HYPOTHESIS: SOME EMPIRICAL STUDIES AND SUBSTANTIATION

The US, along with the UK is recognized as the leading deregulator of the labour markets. Flexible work practices (FWP) are common and some studies have evaluated the resulting insecurity. In India too there have been studies to examine flexibility of employment in the organized sector.

THE UNITED STATES OF AMERICA

The US leads the world in making labour markets flexible. The Bureau of Labour Statistics (BLS) has noted a sectoral shift in employment in the US from manufacturing to services sector since the beginning of the 1970s. Initially, this shift was linked to expansion of the public sectors like health services, education. However, in 1985, it was estimated that the most rapidly growing sector in the American economy till 1995 would be janitor, fast food workers, nurses, aides and clerical workers. They expected a demand for only 120,000 computer programmers. In the category of business services, work increasingly consisted of feeding data into computers on a piece rate basis (Kolko 2000).

Besides this, part-time, homework and temporary had replaced traditional employment in both services and manufacturing. In America, a worker is statistically employed if he or she works for three hours a day and for at least three days a week, or if the work is categorized as temporary. From 1980 to 1995, the number of part-time workers has grown 58 per cent, and they account for one-fourth of the total employed. Part-time work is especially prevalent in the new high-tech sunrise industries. In California's Silicon Valley, part-timers are 30 per cent of the total workers. The workers in this flexible work forms make up the bulk of what is called the working poor. The advantages of flexibility to the employers are obvious; there are no costs such as sickness pay, insurance, health cover, training or vacation. Wages are nearly one-half of full-time workers. This transient labour force is usually unorganized and exists because there is a large pool of the unemployed. The above-cited norms account for the faster expansion of employment in the US compared to other industrial countries because of the absence of so-called rigidity in the labour market.

FLEXIBILITY AND IH IN INDIA

Although the entire IH has been stated and tested in the developed countries where labour market conditions are vastly different, IH has relevance and applications in the context of developing countries—perhaps more so (Das and Panayiotopoulos 1996: 56-71; Ramaswamy 1999: 363-8).

The first and the most obvious difference in the labour market of developed and the developing countries, is in the percentage of labour employed in the formal, and organized sectors of economy. Ninety per cent of employment in the developed countries is in this sector. Organized sector here implies formally registered firms, obliged to keep accounts and pay taxes. The opposite is true in India where the organized sector employment accounts for less than 10 per cent of the total employment.

The second important difference is the quality, extent and efficiency of regulation of the labour market, which is far greater in the developed countries, for example, in the most basic aspect of implementation of the minimum wages, regulation against unfair dismissal, against discrimination at workplace and severance or redundancy payments.

The third difference, which is the cause and consequence of the first two, is in the trade union density in the labour markets of the developed countries where typical coverage is over 33 per cent as against less than 10 per cent for India. These differences notwithstanding, the flexibility and IH are becoming the debated terms in labour economics in India (Deshpande et al. 1998). This is happening in the context of globalization and liberalization.

EVIDENCE OF FLEXIBILITY FROM INDIA

The published studies indicate the true extent of flexibility and insecurity in the workforce. The case for deregulation of the labour market was orchestrated on the basis of the evidence, that organized sector was growing slower than the GDP, population, workforce and the labour force. The lag between the rate of employment and output was analysed from 1977-8 to 1999-2000, and it has been widening as evident from the following table.

RATE OF GROWTH IN OUTPUT, ORGANIZED SECTOR EMPLOYMENT, LABOUR FORCE, WORKFORCE AND UNEMPLOYMENT FROM 1977-8 TO 1999-2000 (PER CENT)

Variable	1977-8 to 1983	1983 to 1987-8	–	1993-4 to 1999-2000
GDP at 1993-4 prices	3.8	4.1	5.6	6.5
Organized sector employment total	2.0	1.1	1.0	0.7
Public sector	2.6	1.5	1.0	0.1
Private sector	0.6	0.1	1.2	2.2
Population	2.0	2.4	2.1	1.8
Workforce (P+S)	2.1	1.8	2.1	0.8
Labour force (T+S)	2.0	2.0	2.2	0.9
Workforce (P)	2.6	2.0	2.3	1.3
Labour force (P)	1.8	2.2	2.2	1.3
Unemployment (live register)	10.3	6.1	3.3	1.9
Unemployment (estimated from NSSO data)	–11.8	9.1	–2.7	1.2

Source: NSSO, data from 32nd, 38th, 43rd, and 50th, 55th rounds.

The elasticity of employment with respect to output in manufacturing steadily declined from 1.14 per cent (1973-8) to 0.33 per cent (1988-94). Although, the elasticity of employment in manufacturing was declining, the manufacturing employment grew faster at 3.3 per cent per annum compounded for the period 1991-2 to 1997-8 compared to 1.5 per cent per annum during 1985-6 to 1991-2.

Fallon and Lucas estimate that an amendment in 1976 of the exit clause of the Industrial Dispute Act 1947 prohibited the employers of 300 or more workers to retrench or close down without permission. Actually the demand for labour fell by 17.5 per cent. In 1984, another amendment lowered the employment limit to 100 workers. This reduced the potential employment more drastically (Fallon and Lucas 1991: 121-34).

Based on the Annual Survey of Industries (ASI) data, T.S. Papola

(1994) reports a decline in unit labour cost from 1971 to 1987-8. The labour productivity in manufacturing sector increased ahead of real wages with a high correlation between productivity and wages. In the same period, the capital intensity with respect to labour did increase, probably in anticipation of increasing real cost of labour and to support the demand for deregulation of the labour market.

Roy analysing the ASI data for the period 1960-1 to 1993-4, finds that job security regulations were not responsible for slowdown in employment growth (Roy 1998; Nagraj 1994: 177-86). Nagraj finds that higher wages were a result of increases in productivity or increase in working hours. Goldar (2000) shows that, despite the presence of unaltered job security regulations, employment in organized manufacturing sector grew at 4.03 per cent per annum during the first half of 1990s. Micro level study supports the macro level finding that employment growth had taken place during early 1990s and as per Nagraj 1.3 million employees (13 per cent of the workforce) lost job in the organized sector during the later period 1995-6 to 2001 (Nagraj 2004: 3387-90). So, either way through the 1990s, firms could increase or decrease their workforce despite the job security provisions.

A large scale study, funded by the ILO, of flexible labour practices conducted by Deshpande et al., is also relevant to the IH and flexibility in India (Deshpande et al. 1998). The study concludes that Mumbai, the industrial and financial capital of the country, experienced a decline of employment in the whole modern sector during the 1980s and not just in the factories. Registered unemployment, informal employment and *badli*, contract labour and women employment increased. The study also concluded that although regulations are often blamed for unemployment, the employers in Mumbai enjoyed much greater flexibility as far as use of non-permanent labour is concerned than those in Malaysia (ibid.: 83). Larger employers who are allegedly more regulated by law from retrenching their workers are in fact able to do so as freely as small employers. The growth in flexible labour category will represent much of the growth in employment in future and this portends ill for the maintenance of minimum labour standards in private factory employment as also for the union movement in the future (ibid.: 46-9). The government policies and overall macro conditions created by increasing liberalization and deregulation of the industrial sector were found to be closely related to the factors responsible for this state of affairs.

A pertinent study based on 1,300 firms belonging to nine industries in 10 states and eight different size groups of employment was undertaken to find out the determinant of levels and change in employment between 1991 and 1998 (Deshpande and Deshpande 2002). The determinants were identified as (a) employment flexibility, (b) wage flexibility, (c) labour process flexibility, (d) impact of union collective bargaining, (e) impact of state regulation, impact of ideology and administrative action. Some findings of this study are: total employment in the sampled firms belonging to the factory sector increased at 2.84 per cent per annum compounded during 1991-8; non-manual employment increased at 5 per cent per annum—manual at 2.20 per cent per annum, majority of the employers (60 per cent) increased total employment, only 27 per cent decreased; employers increased total employment by increasing the share of non-permanent employees and women workers and .in the nine manufacturing industries investigated, employment increased by 3 per cent per annum.

In the wage analysis confined to unskilled male manual workers, the study showed that four out of five firms paid a consolidated wage. Typically, wage has three components. The basic wage is a fixed component, whereas dearness allowance (DA) and bonus are variable. The higher the component of the fixed wage, the more secure is the worker. Basic wages are determined largely by the minimum wage law, and to a smaller extent, by collective bargaining. In the textile firms of the sample, other factors determined the basic wage in a majority of cases. These included experience, qualification, job evaluation and adjudication. The textile industry was the most unionized. Proportionately more of the larger firms reported that the basic wages were determined by collective bargaining. Payment of separate DA was reported by only 12 per cent of the firms and that the larger firms were more likely to pay the DA. One-third of the employees were paid bonus at the minimum rate and the union presence was associated with higher bonus rates. In all 80 per cent of the firms paid consolidated wages and collective bargaining was associated with other allowances. By and large, for manual labour, the compensation tends to be close to the minimum wage and not flexible.

The study found that over the seven-year liberalization period, the share of permanent manual workers declined from close to 68 per cent in 1991 to 64 per cent in 1998. It increased only in two categories, non-metallic minerals, beverages and tobacco. In the category of non-permanent employment, casual workers increased the fastest making them the most insecure category. The big firms resorted to greater use of non-permanent workers—33 per cent non-permanent and 8 per cent contract. Relationship between location and share of non-permanent workers was not significant in the case of manual workers.

Another aspect, which could be used to indicate the increasing flexibilization and insecurity in employment, in the Indian context, is the quantitative growth of the informal/unorganized (IFS) sector. In manufacturing, it may be defined as not registered under the Factories Act, and in the service defined as employing less than seven persons. In this context, the studies of Kundu, Nagamine and Mukherjee are important (Kundu 1993a; 1993b: 1785-93; Nagamine 1993, 2004; Mukherjee 2004: 293-310). All these studies indicate the significance of the informal sector. The size and growth of the small-scale and the informal sector share a relationship to the increasing organizational, numerical, wage and work flexibility sought by the organized manufacturing and services sectors in India. As per the National Sample Survey Organization (NSSO) and the Central Statistical Organization (CSO) surveys, the size of the informal sector (IFS) has not changed appreciably since 1984. Examining four successive NSSO surveys, Mukherjee observes that in terms of enterprise numbers and employment, the sector has experienced a marginal decline in 1984-9, but recovered after that, and by 2000, there were 17 million enterprises and 37 million employees. The sector's heterogeneous growth pattern and recent revival and growth cannot be simply imputed to the distress factor of the unemployed, but there is a dynamic factor, especially in the sub-segments of urban non-directory manufacturing enterprises (NDMEs) and directory manufacturing enterprises (DMEs), employing less than six workers including household workers and DME units employing six or more workers with at least one hired worker, which are linked to the growth of outsourcing and other linkages with the organized factory sector. Rural NDME and DME are linked to the growth of agricultural productivity and per capita income. In the post-reform period, there was a strong revival of the IFS, and the number of enterprises and employment (grew at the rate of 2.85 per cent per annum over 1994-2000) increased in all segments except rural NDMEs and DMEs. In fact, the share of own account manufacturing enterprises (OAMEs) units operating with no hired labour have increased during this period indicating that the distress factor of unemployment may also be working along with the retrenchment from and restructuring of large and small manufacturing enterprises.

Add to the above situation, the fact that the small scale, as distinct from the IFS, has always been a large employer of insecure labour, the overall picture of insecurity is complete. The small- scale accounts for an astounding 95 per cent of all industrial units in the economy and for 40 per cent of the value added, 34 per cent of the total exports and 7 per cent of the gross domestic product. A study of small-scale industry (SSI) units based in Mumbai Metropolitan Region (MMR) highlights the state of employees in the sector. Although the number of closures have increased after the reforms, mainly due to lockouts, the SSIs are able to survive more easily when they are captive to the medium and large units through the system of putting out and sub-contracting (Diwan 2004: 1039-52). The study provides a graphic picture of the quality of employment, as; according to the Bombay Small Scale Industries Association (BSSIA) data only 5.6 per cent workers were registered, while the rest 94.5 per cent were daily voucher workers. In her sample of 446 workers, working in 109 SSIs, located in the 33 industrial estates surveyed, three-fifths of the workers had not found secure employment in the SSIs, in that they had been employed for less than five years. Only seven workers in the sample had a provident fund and the rest had regular weekly lay offs. All of them were multi-tasking in the units. Forty-five per cent of the workers had shifted job at least once in the last decade. Of this half used to be employed in the informal sector before they came into the SSIs, while 37 per cent were (mainly temporary employees in the formal sector) from organized sector mills and factories and had come into the SSI due to closures, voluntary retirement schemes (VRS) and retrenchments. This signifies that, perhaps as literature also suggests, restructuring in the formal manufacturing sector in Mumbai had begun more than a decade ago.

Three important studies therefore provide conclusive evidence on the high degree of flexibility of all types in India namely: (1) Sharma and Sasikumar surveyed firms in Ghaziabad 1991-5 (Sharma and Sasikumar 1996); (2) Sudha Deshpande et al. studied labour flexibility 1997-8 (Deshpande et al. 1998); Lalit Deshpande et al. studied labour flexibility practices in 10 states and nine industries in India during 1991-8 (Deshpande et al. 2004). The main findings are as follows (Shyam Sundar 2005: 4-10).

Firms increased their total employment during the period (1987-

2004) of all three studies. Lalit Deshpande found that total employment grew by 3 per cent, manual employment by 2.29 per cent and non-manual by over 5 per cent. Only 13 per cent firms surveyed did not change employment, 60 per cent increased employment and 27 per cent decreased the jobs.

All firms—small, medium and large—that increased employment did so by hiring primarily non-permanent workers. Firms employing 200-499 workers registered the largest employment increase. These are the firms supposedly constrained by restrictive laws and trade unions. The percentage share of permanent manual employment decreased during 1991-8, while the percentage of non-casual belonging to the non-permanent category increased to more than one-third of manual employment. If contract labour is added then the share of non-regular, i.e. non-permanent plus contract was as high as 42 per cent. Large firms (100 plus workers) used more non-permanent labour.

Basic wages of unskilled male workers were based on the minimum wage law and not on the basis of collective bargaining. The law has many loopholes and is revised very infrequently with the result that the new minimum wage rates are lower in real terms than the pre-revision rates. In most cases, these minimum wages are below the poverty line as reported by the ILO (ILO-FATT 1996). Three-fourths of the firms in Lalit's survey paid a consolidated wage only and only 12 per cent, mostly large firms, paid a separate dearness allowance. Sudha notes that the Indian employers enjoy tremendous wage flexibility, and the labour institutions do not in practice enforce any rigidity.

Deshpande's study found that the unions were present in only a little over one-fourth of the surveyed firms, and this presence was not a deterrent to changing employment in either direction. She found that the unionized firms were more likely to introduce technological changes, alter the product range, and improve the quality of the product. Venkatratnam, by studying 204 collective agreements in 1990, finds that unions were not a hindrance to introducing labour flexibility measures in the firm (Venkataratnam 2004). He cites several clauses of understanding reached between the unions and management, where flexibility, quality and productivity yardsticks were spelled out. This is in tune with the international trend cited by researchers like Ozaki, who has noted that in recent years trade unions have toned down their resistance to flexibility in this age of intense competition (Ozaki 1999). The changing balance of power is evident in the fact that in the post-Mumbai textile strike (early 1980s), there had been more lockouts than strikes. The former is an important managerial strategy to weaken the union power and introduce flexibility (Shyam Sundar 2003: 679-88).

The studies underscore the fact that labour market flexibility in India is extensive and perhaps more than all the countries cited above.

CONCLUSION

We have stated the Insecurity Hypothesis, its corollaries, its relationship with flexibility and summary evidence of increasing flexibly in some OECD countries and India. The OECD studies use a wider variety of concepts and data, like number of job losses, impact of job losses on future income, occupational downgrading and elements of job protection, loss of real wages and average tenure of employees in the organized sector. Flexibility is also viewed from the worker's perspective and related to the concept of insecurity. The Indian studies are at a more basic stage, they estimate the reduction in organized sector employment, numbers of non-permanent and the casual workers. In the vast informal sector on the other hand, non-permanent and atypical workers are the norm.

Despite the need to extend the empirical evidence and to generate more comprehensive data to support the hypothesis and its outcome over time, there seems to be adequate evidence to indicate a pervasive phenomenon of widening flexibility in even the erstwhile 'secure' sectors, and a further deepening as the informal sector grows in India.

REFERENCES

Ackroyd, S., G. Burrell, M. Hugh and A. Whitaker (1998): 'The Japanisation of the British Industry', *Industrial Relations Journal*, 19, 1.

Baker, K. and K. Christensen (1998): *Contingent Work: American Employment Relations in Transition* (New York: Cornell University Press).

Baumohl, Bernard (1993): 'When Downsizing Becomes Dumb Sizing', *Time Magazine*, 15 March.

Beck, U. (1992): *Risk Society: Towards a New Modernity* (London: Sage).

Best, M. (1990): *The New Competition: Institutions of Industrial Restructuring* (Cambridge: Polity Press and Harvard University Press).

Beynon, H. (1997): 'The Changing Practices of Work', in R.K. Brown (ed.), *The Changing Shape of Work* (Basingstoke: Macmillan).

Blanchard, Gordon and Rizwanul Islam (2001): *East Asia Labour Markets* (Geneva: ILO).

Blanchard, K., J.P. Carlos and A. Randolph (1999): *The Three Keys to Empowerment* (San Francisco: Berret-Koehler).

Bootle, R. (1996): *The Death of Inflation: The Surviving and Thriving in the Zero Era* (London: Nicholas Brealey).

Bootle, Roger (2001): *Money for Nothing: Real Wealth, Financial Fantasies and The Economy of the Future* (London: Nicholas Brealey).

Bound, J. and G. Johnson (1992): 'Changes in the Structure of Wages in the 1980s: An Evaluation of Alternative Explanation', *American Economic Review*, 82.

Breman, Jan (1996): *Footloose Labour: Working in India's Informal Economy* (Cambridge: Cambridge University Press).

Broadbent, J., M. Dietrich and J. Robert (1998): 'The End of Profession?', in J. Broadbent, M. Dietrich and J. Robert (eds.), *The End of Profession?: The Restructuring of Professional Work* (London: Routledge).

Brown, C., M. Reich and D. Stern (1993): 'Becoming a High Performance Work Organisation: The Role of Security, Employee Involvement and Training', *International Journal of Human Resource Management*, 4, 2.

Brown, Philip, Andy Green and Hugh Lauder (2001): *High Skills: Globalisation, Competitiveness and Skill Formation* (Oxford: Oxford University Press).

Brown, R.K. (1997): 'Flexibility and Security: Contradictions in the Contemporary Labour Market', in Brown (ed.), *The Changing Shape of Work*.

Burgess, S. and H. Rees (1996): 'Job Tenure in Britain 1975-92', *The Economic Journal*, 106.

Burke, R.J. and C.L. Cooper (2000): *The Organisation in Crisis: Downsizing, Restructuring and Privatisation* (Oxford: Blackwell Publishers).

Cadene, Philippe and Mark Holmstrom (1998): *Decentralised Production in India* (New Delhi: Sage).

Caplinsky, R. (1993): 'Is Flexible Production Relevant to Less Developed Countries', *OECD Development Centre Working Paper* (Paris: OECD).

Cappelli, P. (1995): 'Rethinking Employment', *British Journal of Industrial Relations*, 33, 34.

Cappelli, P., L. Bassi, H. Katz, D. Knoke and M. Useem (1997): *Change at Work* (New York: Oxford University Press).

Castells, Manuel and Alejandro Portes (1989): 'World Underneath: The Origins, Dynamics and Effects of the Informal Economy', in Alejandro Portes, Manuel Castells and Lauren A. Benton (eds.), *Informal Economy: Studies in Advanced and Less Developed Countries* (Baltimore: John Hopkins University Press).

CBI (1996): *Flexible Labour Markets* (London: Confederation of British Industry).

Christopherson, Susan (1987): 'Workforce Flexibility: Implications for Women Workers', *ISSR Working Paper* 3 (2).

Collinson, D. and M. Collinson (1995): 'Corporate Liposuction and the Re-Masculinisation of Management', Keynote address at Gender and Life in Organisations Conference, University of Portsmouth, The UK.

Cooper, C.L. and R.J. Burke (2002): 'Introduction: The New World of Work', in Cooper and Burke (ed.), *The New World of Work* (Oxford: Blackwell).

Cooper, R. (1995): *When Lean Enterprises Collide* (Boston: Harvard Business School Press).

Crouch, C. (1997): 'Skill-based Full Employment: The Latest Philosopher's Stone', *The British Journal of Industrial Relations*, 35, 3.

Danford, Andy (1999): *Management Techniques and British Workers* (London/New York: Mansell).

Das, K. and Panayiotopoulos (1996): 'Flexible Specialisation: New Paradigm for Industrialisation for Developing Countries', *Economic and Political Weekly*, vol. 31, no. 52, 28 December.

Deshpande, Lalit, Alakh N. Sharma, A. Karan and S. Sarkar (2004): *Liberalisation and Labour: Labour Flexibility in Manufacturing* (New Delhi: Institute for Human Development).

Deshpande, Sudha, Guy Standing and Lalit Deshpande (1998): *Labour Flexibility in Third World: A Case Study of Bombay* (New Delhi: Commonwealth Publications).

Deshpande, Sudha and L.K. Deshpande (2002): 'Reform and Labour Market in India', *Reform and Employment: Institute of Applied Manpower Research* (New Delhi: Concept).

Dex, S. and McCulloch (1997): *Flexible Employment: The Future of Britain's Jobs* (London: Macmillan Press).

Dickinson, James (1986): *From Poor Law to Social Insurance: The Periodisation of State Intervention in the Reproduction Process* (London: Routledge).

Diwan, Ritu (2004): 'Captive Workers in Captive Small Scale Factories', *Indian Journal of Labour Economics*, vol. 47, no. 4.

Edwards, P., M. Collinson and C. Reese (1998): 'The Determinants of Employee Responses to Total Quality Management: Six Case Studies', *Organisation Studies*.

Elliot, L. and D. Atkinson (1998): *The Age of Insecurity* (London: Verso).

Engberg, E. (1993): 'Union Responses to the Contingent Work Force', in D.S. Cobble (ed.), *Women in Union: Forging a Partnership* (Ithaca, New York: ILR Press).

Faber, H. (1993): 'The Incidence and the Cost of Job Loss 1982-91', Bookings Papers on Economic Activity, Microeconomics.

Fallon, P. and R. Lucas (1991): 'Impact of Changes in Job Security Regulation in India and Zimbabwe', *World Bank Economic Review*, vol. 5, no. 3.

Felstead, A., B. Burchell and F. Green (1998): 'Insecurity at Work: Is Job Insecurity Really Much Worse than Before', *New Economy 5.*

Forrester, P. (1994): 'Flexibility, Politics and Strategy: In Defence of the Model of the Flexible Firm', *Work Employment and Society*, vol. 8, no. 2.

Frank, Thomas (2004): *What's the Matter with Kansas? Metropolitan* (New York: Owl).

Gallie, Duncan, Michael White, Yuan Cheng and Mark Tomlinson (1998): *Restructuring the Employment Relationship* (New York: Oxford University Press).

Garrhan, P. and T. Stewart (1992): *The Nissan Enigma-Flexibility at Work in Local Economy* (London: Mansell).

Goddard, J. (1998): 'Review of Change at Work', *British Journal of Industrial Relations*, 36.

Gray, J. (1995): 'The Undoing of Conservatism', in J. Gray (ed.), *Enlightenment Wake: Politics and Culture at the End of the Modern Age* (London: Routledge).

Guest, D. (1997): 'Towards Jobs and Justice in Europe: A Research Agenda', *Industrial Relations Journal*, 28, 4.

Guest, David (2000): 'Management and the Insecure Workforce', in Edmund Heery and John Salmon (eds.), *The Insecure Workforce* (London: Routledge).

Hargreaves, P. and Peter Jarvis (1998): *The Human Resource Development Handbook* (London: Kogan Page).

Harris, N. (1995): 'The Reproduction of Labour Force', in N. Harris (ed.), *The New Untouchables: Immigration and the New World Worker* (London: I.B. Tauris Publishers).

Harvey, David (1993): 'Class Relations, Social Justice and Politics of Difference', in Michael and Pile (eds.), *Place and Politics of Identity* (London: Routledge).

Heery, Edmond and John Salmon (2000): 'Introduction', *The Insecure Workforce* (London: Routledge Press).

Heery, Edmund and Brian Abbott (2000): 'Trade Unions and the Insecure Workforce', in *The Insecure Workforce* (London: Routledge).

Heery, Edmund and John Salmon (2000): 'The Insecurity Thesis', in *The Insecurity Thesis* (London: Routledge).

Holmstrom, B.R. and J. Tirole (1989): 'The Theory of the Firm', in R. Schmalensee and R.D. Willing (eds.), *Handbook of Industrial Organisation* (Amsterdam: North Holland).

Hutton, W. (1995): *The State We're In* (London: Johnathan Cape).

ILO-FAAT (1996): *Indian Economic Reforms and Labour Policy* (New Delhi: ILO-FAAT).

ILO (2005): *World Employment Report 2004-05* (Geneva: ILO).

Jarvis, Peter (2000): 'The Age of Learning', in Peter Jarvis (ed.), *Continuing Education at the University of Surrey* (London: Oxford University Press).

Kalhan, A. (2004): 'Life Long Learning for What?', in *Teachers of the World*, July-September, vol. 5, no. 7.

Kelly, J. (1997): 'Industrial Relation: Looking to the Future', *British Journal of Industrial Relations*, 33, 3.

Kenny, M. and T. Florida (1993): *Beyond Mass Production the Japanese System and its Transfer to the USA* (New York: Oxford University Press).

Kolko, Joyce (2000): 'Restructuring the Working Classes', in Harry Dahms (ed.), *Transformations of Capitalism* (London: Macmillan Press).

Kundu, A. (1993): 'Trends and Patterns of Female Employment in India: A Case of Organised Informalisation', *Indian Journal of Labour Economics*, vol. 40, no. 3, July-September.

——— (1993): 'Urban Informal Sector: An Overview of Macro Dimensions, Socio-economic Correlates and Policy Perspectives in India', in H. Nagamine (ed.), *Urban Informal Sector Employment: A Cross-national Comparison Study* (Nagoya, Japan: Institute for Regional Planning and Development).

Lane, C. (1990): 'Vocational Training, Employment Training and New Production Concepts: Some Lessons for Britain', *International Review Journal*, 21, 4.

Latack, J.C. and R.B. Dozier (1986): 'After the Axe Falls: Job Loss as a Career Transition', *Academy of Management Review*, 11, pp. 375-92.

Legge, K. (1998): 'Flexibility: The Gift-wrapping of Employment, Degradation', in P. Sparrow and M. Marchington (eds.), *Human Resource Management: The New Agenda* (London: Pitman Publishing).

Leisink, P. (1997): 'New Union Constituency Call for Differentiated Agenda and Democratic Participation', *Transfer*, 3.

Luttwak, E. (1994): 'Why Fascism is the Wave of the Future', *London Review of Book*, 7 April.

Martin, Carnoy (1999): 'The Family, Flexible Work and Social Cohesion at Risk', *International Labour Review*, vol. 138, no. 4.

Mitchell, M.F. (2005): 'Specialisation and the Skill Premium in the 20th Century', *International Economic Review*, vol. 46, August.

Mukherjee (2004): 'Informal Manufacturing Sector in India: Pre- and Post-Reform Growth Dynamics', *Indian Journal of Labour Economics*, vol. 47, no. 2.

Munck, Ronald (2002): *Globalisation and Labour* (Delhi: Madhyam Books).

Nagamine, H. (1993): *Urban Informal Sector Employment: A Cross-national Comparative Study* (Nagoya, Japan: Research Institute for Planning and Development).

Nagraj, R. (1994): 'Employment and Wages in Manufacturing Industry: Trends

Hypothesis and Evidence', *Economic and Political Weekly*, vol. 29, no. 4, 22 January.

——— (2004): 'Fall in the Organised Employment a Brief Note', *Economic and Political Weekly*, 24 July.

Nickell, Stephen, Patricia Jones and Leanda Quintini (2002): 'Picture of Job Insecurity Facing British Men', *The Economic Journal of Royal Economic Society*, vol. 112, no. 476.

Nolan, Jane , I. Wichert and B. Burchell (2000): 'Job Insecurity, Psychological Well-Being and Family Life', in Edmund Heery and Salmon Jon (eds.), *The Insecure Workforce.*

OECD (1997): *Employment Outlook: Organisation for Economic Co-operation and Development* (Paris: OECD).

Oliver, N. and B. Wilkinson (1992): *The Japanisation of British Industry* (Oxford: Blackwell).

Ozaki, Muneto (1999): *Negotiating Flexibility the Role of the Social Partner and the State* (Geneva: ILO).

Piore, N. and C. Sable (1984): *The Second Industrial Divide* (New York: Basic Books).

Polanyi, Karl (1957): *The Great Transformation* (Boston: Beacon Press).

Ramaswamy, K.V. (1999): 'The Search for Flexibility in Indian Manufacturing', *Economic and Political Weekly*, vol. 34, no. 30, 6 February.

Robinson, Peter (2000): 'Insecurity and the Flexible Workforce, Measuring the Ill-defined', in Heery and Solomon (eds.), *The Insecure Workforce.*

Rousseau, D.M. (1996): 'Changing the Deal while Keeping the People', *Academy of Management Executive*, vol. 10.

Roy, Sudita (1998): 'Lags in Employment Adjustment and Inter-industry Differential: An Analysis Using Dynamic Inter-related Factor Demand Function', Discussion Paper No. 199, IGIDR, Bombay.

Schmitz, H. (1989): 'Flexible Specialisation: A New Paradigm of Small Scale Industrialisation', *Institute of Development Studies*, Paper No. 324.

Secombe, W. (1986): 'Marxism and Demography, Family, Economy and State: The Social Reproduction Process under Capitalism', in J. Dickinson and Bob Russell (eds.), *Social Welfare* (London: Routledge).

Shaikh, Juned (2005): 'Worker Politics, Trade Unions and the Shiv Sena's Rise in Central Bombay', *Economic and Political Weekly*, 30 April-6 May, 2005, vol. 40, no. 18.

Sharma, Alakh and S.K. Sasikumar (1996): *Structural Adjustments and Labour* (NOIDA: V.V. Giri National Labour Institute (mimeo).

Shyam Sundar, K.R. (2003): 'Flexibility and Rigidity in Labour Market: Towards Balanced Prospective', *Journal of Indian School of Political Economy*, vol. 15.3.

——— (2005): 'Labour Flexibility Debate in India', *Economic and Political Weekly*, vol. XL, no. 22, 23 May, no. 23, 28 June.

Silver, B.J. (2003): *Forces of Labour: Cambridge Studies in Comparative Politics* (Cambridge, The UK: Cambridge University Press).

Smith, D. (1997): *Job Insecurity versus Labour Market Flexibility* (London: Social Market Foundation).

Solow, Robert M. (2005): *What is Labour Market Flexibility?: What is it Good for?* Internet site www:// Britac.uk/pubs/src/keynes97/text. html.

Srinivas, Ravi K. (1992): 'Underclass, Hi-Technology and Los Angeles Uprising', *Economic and Political Weekly*, 24-31 October.

Standing, Guy (1997): 'Globalisation, Labour Flexibility and Insecurity: The Era of Market Regulation', *European Journal of Industrial Relations*, 3, 1.

——— (1999): *Global Labour Flexibility: Thinking Distributive Justice* (London: Macmillan Press).

Stiglitz, J.E. (2002): 'Employment, Social Justice and Societal Well-being', *International Labour Review*, vol. 141, nos. 1-2.

Stredwick, J. and Steve Ellis (1998): *Flexible Working Practices: Techniques and Innovations* (London: Institute of Personnel and Development).

Streeck, W. (1989): 'Skills and the Limits of Neo Liberalism: Enterprise of the Future as a Place of Learning', *Work Employment and Society*, 3, 1, pp. 89-104.

Tabak, F. and M.A. Crichlow (2000): *Normalistion: Process and Structure* (Baltimore and London: John Hopkins University Press).

The Economist (2005): 'The Great Job Switch', 1-7 October.

Venkatranam, C.S. (2004): *Negotiated Change, Collective Bargaining, Liberalisation and Restructuring in India* (New Delhi/London: Response Books and Sage).

Vuuren, T. (1991): 'Employee Reactions to Job Insecurity', in J. Hartley, D. Jacobson, B. Klandermans and T. Van Vuuren (eds.), *Job Insecurity: Coping With Jobs At Risk 9* (London: Sage).

Wayne, J. (1986): 'Function of Social Welfare in a Capitalist Economy', in Dickinson and Russell (eds.), *Social Welfare.*

Wever, K. (1998): 'International Labour Revitalisation: Enlarging the Playing Field', *Industrial Relations*, 37, 3.

Wickham, J. (1997): 'Part-time Work in Ireland and Europe: Who Wants What Where?', *Work: Employment and Society*, 11. 1.

Womack, James P., Daniel T. Jones and Daniel Roos (1990): *The Machine that Changed the World: The Story of Lean Production* (New York: Rawson/Macmillan).

Wright, Martin (2000): *Managing Competitive Prices* (New York: Cambridge University Press.

CHAPTER 8

The Working Class in Mumbai: A Perspective

D.K. OJHA

The historic image of Bombay's (now it is Mumbai) working class people is in disarray due to the onslaught of financial capital policies. This vibrant metropolis has now become a city of decadent cultural and social life. The reasons are many and this paper delineates some of the key factors which led to such a situation.

The life and activities of working class people in Bombay can be divided into three phases: (1) till 1947, (2) from 1947 to 1990 and (3) after 1990.

EMERGENCE OF THE MODERN WORKING CLASS

When the seven different islands of Bombay were handed over to British by the Portuguese rulers as a dowry for the marriage of English King Charles II to Catherine of Braganza of Portugal in 1661, they were merely scattered colonies of local fishermen. The credit for making Bombay as an industrial city goes to erstwhile British rulers who had seen the big potential of developing this coastal zone of India. Strategically, this was located at a very favourable point, a centre to all maritime activities to Africa, Gulf and other places.

There was no confusion for the East India Company that only through industrialization, it could generate maximum profit out of this country. In 1853, the first railway line was constructed between Bombay and Thane, and also between Calcutta and Raniganj. Both eastern and western centres were in the throes of rapid development. In 1854, the first cotton textile mill was opened in Bombay and thus emerged a new class of modern industrial workers in India.

Soon the British rulers had introduced a new tax system for rural India, which paved the way for the systemic ruin of peasantry and thus created wage earners in the industry.

The famine occurred in the major parts of India during that time forced the rulers to think about some welfare measures for working class people. Efforts were made to improve public health, sanitary conditions and living conditions in the workers' colonies. The company's basic concern was that working class people should at least be in a position to work so as surplus generation machinery would continue. The working conditions were shockingly bad, with unlimited hours of work, no holidays and nothing as compensation in case of injury. These conditions were imposed on the working class people who were entirely new and workers did not know what to do. So, sometimes they damaged machinery, sometimes they were beaten up by supervisors.

HISTORICAL PERSPECTIVE

Against the backdrop of this historical perspective, it is necessary to see the present-day condition of working class people in Mumbai, so that the evolution and growth can be comprehended in the interplay of national and international political situation. The British rule in India had already broken the peace and self-sufficiency of Indian villages. The new tax system imposed on the Indian peasantry, made the mass proletarians jobless and they were forced to migrate to cities to sell their labour power so as to survive. There were two distinct phases for their movement before 1947: (1) initial phase of unorganized and spontaneous protest till 1920; more organized and effective movement till 1947.

During the early years of industrialization, especially in the textile sector, newly-employed labourers had to face many challenges both mentally and physically as they were transformed from poor peasantry to industrial workers. The work in mills and factories was more tiring. Thus, bagan their simple forms of associations like *adda* where they could share their miseries and anger. They protested against the existing conditions in their *addas*. The British rulers were aware of these *addas* and gatherings. So when the rulers indirectly helped the formation of the Indian National Congress in 1885, they might have considered that, an organization like the Indian National Congress could calm the sparks of the agitated labourers. But the workers were becoming more and more conscious about their pathetic conditions. The Swadeshi movement led by Bal Gangadhar Tilak had a profound influence on the working class people during that time. In 1908, more than 1 lakh workers of Bombay stopped working as a protest against the six years imprisonment of Tilak for stating 'Swaraj is my birth right and I shall have it'. This was the first political action of the Indian working class.

The year 1917 had witnessed the beginning of a new era in the world political system when the working class people in Russia under the leadership of the Bolshevik Party established a communist rule, after defeating and overthrowing the tsar and the provisional government. British imperialism was aware of the dangers of widespread communist ideology in India. After the First World War, the League of Nations decided to form the International Labour Organization (ILO) in 1918. The ILO proposed new labour legislations for the member states to improve the working and living conditions of the workers, so that under the guise of welfare schemes, the political forms of protest could be curtailed. In October 1920, a meeting of all scattered working class unions of India was arranged in Bombay. Lala Lajpat Rai presided over that meeting in which All India Trade Union Congress (AITUC) was formed. Thus Bombay had become the historical place in shaping and guiding the working class movement of India.

During the period from 1920 to 1947, the working class people of Bombay played a significant role in the struggle against British imperialism. Despite the unwillingness of Congress party, a large section of working class population followed the communist leadership.

ECONOMIC CONDITIONS IN MUMBAI

The class composition of present Mumbai population clearly demonstrates that it is the only city in India where society is so clearly divided and visible in terms of economic classes. The top 5-7 per cent of the population belongs to the ruling bourgeoisie who have their secured area for living and activities. This class consists of industrialists, members of corporate houses, multinational corporation heads, big trading houses, production houses, etc. The basic distinguishing criterion is that they do not work and they own all means of production. They are distinguished mostly by their residential locations which are spread from Malabar Hill to Worli. Around 18-20 per cent of the population belongs to the middle class. This class has further sub-categories, like upper, middle and lower middle class.

The government ministers, politicians, high-ranking executives, government and private company upper rank officers, small businessmen, traders, brokers, film personnel, etc., constitute the upper middle class. The distinguishing feature is that they are working for their livelihood and in most cases and are not the owners of any means of production themselves. The middle class is consisting of government/private officers, middle level traders, businessmen, artists, etc. This class is mostly mobile, fluid and under pressure. They need to work overtime, simply to maintain their status in society. This class is fragmented on regional, linguistic, religious and on caste basis and it is the feeder of all reactions in society. Their intra-competition to increase respective share of social wealth by any means is one of the reasons for existence and growth of parochial movements in contemporary Mumbai society. They also have marked areas of presence, in the areas from Dadar to Borivali on western side, and Dadar to Vashi on the central side. The lower middle class is almost half the middle class and is the most stressed and cynical class of Mumbai. It consists of low level executives and government officers, small business people, agents, small traders, etc. Their life is a constant struggle to fight with the economic pressure in order to stop sliding down to working class position.

Next on the social ladder, at bottom is the working class population which constitutes around 75 per cent of the society. Out of them, almost 80 per cent people are working in the unorganized sectors and lead a miserable life. This working class consists of a broad category of workers, skilled and unskilled, employees of government and private companies, drivers, office assistants, construction workers, etc. This class is rather carrying the whole burden of Mumbai on their shoulders and daily sinking further downwards! They either live in slums near their working places or cover the satellite or the suburbs in New Bombay, Thane or Raigada districts. This population can be seen struggling to cope up with local train travel, daily making 4-5 hours of to and fro journey for jobs and then facing the tough life at home. Sizeable portions of the working population even commute from such far off places like Surat and Manmad, which takes 4-5 hours for one way travelling. With non-existent public distribution system (PDS), this section of the working class population is worst affected by inflationary pressures on food prices. They get good and nutritional food only at the time of their festivals. The irregular nature of salary makes their life tougher. There is no social security for health services and even young people are subjected to real hard taste of inhuman system, once they fall sick. For older and poor people, life is simply a hell in Mumbai. The reports from tribal areas embedded in Mumbai city say shocking stories of poverty, ill-health and destitution. The moment one passes through Palghar and Dahanu districts of Maharashtra, one gets a true picture of the working class hutments. They are excluded from many of the welfare programmes of the government. Earlier, till 1990, the state governments as well as the union government were keen in the implementation of at least some welfare programmes, although they had not reached the people beyond a limit. The governments were bound to take some successful measures like PDS and ration cards in order to gain poor people's faith in its trickling down welfare schemes. The government had given subsidies in the economic sectors where poor labourers were having a direct link with their livelihood. Everything in the economic sector seemed to be working, and welfare model of the state was active to ideologically counter the constant communist criticisms. But after the 1990s, especially the collapse of Union of Soviet Socialist Republics (USSR), a tectonic shift happened worldwide. Since then capitalism has no fear to hide its inhuman face. Everything has been left for the markets and accordingly two major capitalist institutions, the International Monetary Fund (IMF) and the World Bank impose pressure on all countries to get rid of welfare schemes and subsidies in the name of Structural Adjustment Programme (SAP) and liberalization. India too was subjected to such harsh economic prescriptions of finance capital and results are too clear to see. All ruling political parties in India, Congress, Bharatiya Janata Party and the regional parties had to welcome SAP and open the gates for the free flow of capital. Parliamentarians of Left parties had protested many times but after the collapse of USSR, they have become ideologically weak.

The point is that the whole economic life of Mumbai took a shift after the 1990s. The mill workers' history also has been changed, the capitalist rulers could suppress their demands more easily and their strikes were unsuccessful. Due to advancement of technology and worldwide overproduction in the textile sectors, Bombay mills also needed immediate upgradation or closures. Owners opted for closures as it was more profitable for them to close. The mills had received the status of sick industrial units and received relief from the banks and the owners got rid of payment burdens of workers.

This single event killed the very essence of Bombay and had far-reaching effects on all aspects of social life. Industries slowly started moving to the areas where labour power was cheap and Bombay was slowly becoming a services centre for international finance capital. Outsourcing, ancillarization and fragmentation of production process started as they gave better option to create more surplus value from the working people, with no accountability from the employers. Slowly most industrially active centres were deserted. Now mills are changing into malls, offices, hotels, business process outsourcing firms and IT parks. In the old Bombay a major metamorphosis took place in its economic life and it became Mumbai and the city looks more alien to its own people.

POLITICAL CONDITION

Politically, working class people of Mumbai do not have their own representation as a class and so are an appendage to various ruling class parties. The historic presence of leaders like Tilak, B.T. Randive, S.A. Dange, who were representing the working class interests had faded and now there is no single party or a leader in Mumbai who can claim to represent their interests. During the freedom movement and after Independence too, the Communist Party of India (CPI) had a massive base and support among the working class population. Trade union activities reached on peak in the textile industries at that time. But ruling class was shrewder than trade unions. Politically, it suits best to the existing system of rule of capitalists, that working class never gets even closer to its class consciousness. It is aware of the dangers inherent in this consciousness which creates the will and action for changing the system based on wage slavery. To keep this current tendency, ruling class continuously impresses on its ideologues, mentors, writers, media, etc., to create issues which are non-economic in nature and which can convert superficial issues into core issues. Earlier, the British imperialism had done a favour to the ruling class here by creating division among working people on religious lines. Pakistan was created and so the whole of India's population was under the influence of this false consciousness. Not content with this, it was required to further break the unity of working class people on regional or chauvinist lines. Keeping this in mind, a whole series of movements started in India to reorganize states on a linguistic basis. Gujarat, Maharashtra, Andhra Pradesh, Tamil Nadu, Karnataka got entangled with each other. On the behalf of language and culture, regional disparities and interstate disputes had begun, which were led by the local bourgeois and petty-bourgeoisie sections of particular regions for their own interests. Naturally, these interests were in conflict with each other all the time. As such movements grew stronger, the political initiative had been taken away from the working class and they became just fence sitters. In Mumbai too, this happened.

There are many working class people in Mumbai belonging to different regions of India. They have genuine common grievances. But due to the aspect of regionalism, they have lost the unity among them and this regionalism splits the people. Capitalist rulers could flare up this regionalism in Mumbai too.

The real political question is to fight against the rule of capitalism and not to go for fratricidal wars! Recent events in Iraq, Afghanistan are examples for how imperialism as a system works. How it breaks nationalities and creates sub-nationalities, tribes, etc. To put it simply, it is against the civil society and against anything which unites people on class considerations. It never calls the people on what their economic category of existence is; rather it differentiates on region, religion, tribe, caste, etc. This is the genesis and reason why there is no political space left among the working class people to act for their own class interests under the existing system. Without any exception, all divisive and retrograde movements in society have support, both financially and politically, by the ruling class. Same social prescription is being applied in African, Gulf, Latin American and East European countries.

Against this backdrop, it is not difficult to understand why working class politics had failed in Mumbai. The role of individuals and the parties are not so important in this grand scheme of the rule of finance capital. Everyone has been assigned to a historical role to play and masters write script and play! In India, the ruling Congress party, the best representative of finance capital has been involved in creating and developing such regional or chauvinistic groups right from the beginning, like in Maharashtra, Punjab, Assam and Kerala and other places. This serves two purposes, first it keeps them in control of social movements to see that they never question the basic economic issues or question the property relations prevalent in society, and second, it helps them to manipulate the opposition space too in parliamentary form of rule.

Against this backdrop, Shiv Sena was formed in 1966 in Bombay. It got the direct patronage of the then Congress leadership and was well suited to grand design of future political life of Bombay. Its first target was to get hold of Bombay working class support base and Lalbagh was the first casuality.

Lalbagh name itself symbolized the domination of communists in that area. It had seen several communist leaders speaking there in all movements, symbolizing the hopes and aspirations of working class people; it grew an inspiration directly from Russia and China and was aspiring to be red. It was unacceptable for the ruling class to have such presence of communists at the centre of the city and at right time. First the headquarters of the CPI at Dalwi building was attacked and ransacked in December 1967 to give a signal of things to come. Baharatiya Kamgar Sena (BKS) was formed in 1968. Later on 6 June 1970, Krishna Desai, the militant and most popular leader of CPI was murdered in broad day light. He had been very active in textile industries and was regarded as one of the most popular and militant trade union leaders. He had a large support base and four times he was chosen as corporator, before elected to Maharashtra assembly in 1967. This was the first political murder and was a turning point in Bombay working class politics. Once defeated in its fort and not in a position to defend itself on the streets, the communist leadership's influence on the working class started diminishing. There were ideological issues too involved in such state of affairs in the communist leadership. With the guidance and reference from Moscow, they followed the revisionist line of Khrushchev era and believed that under socialism, there is no requirement of class struggle and that there is scope for peaceful transition to socialism, etc.

Adherence to this revisionist ideology made the communist leadership toothless and once the state realized this, it remained just a spectator to such attacks (similar incidents happened in Delhi when Safdar Hashmi was killed and thereafter the communist leadership lost its moral authority to lead masses in Delhi). There were demonstrations against the murder but working people base got fractured and it was a shock that in the next assembly election, the Shiv Sena candidate defeated the CPI candidate, who was the wife of Krishna Desai. Today it is no surprise that Left parties do not represent a single corporation constituency in Brihan Mumbai Municipal Corporation, forget about representation in assembly and parliament.

Interestingly, Shiv Sena came to the position of the communist organizations and inserted their own content. Soon after its formation, it knew that the surest way to survive politically in Mumbai was to get hold of working class leadership, and thus, it destroyed the Left working class base and created its own organizations. It also took welfare measures like providing ambulances, health support and instilled a sense of confidence among working people who were so much alienated in this big city. For the working class also, the change was not too negative; they could get more benefits from employers, under the leadership of the BKS sponsored by Shiv Sena. It was more militant and suited to the then requirements of the working class. Another issue which had affected the growth of political consciousness as a class was the rule of capitalists. The existing Left leadership was best involved in raising trade union consciousness which later slipped into struggle for economic issues only and not for any larger political issues for social or system change. Though they were carrying red flags, but in content there was always scope of changing into a saffron flag. They never told of the bigger political mission they were capable of achieving as a political class. This is not the case of Mumbai alone, but the same story is repeated all over India. The leadership section of the working class had never told to have a class identity and consciousness, and in lieu of this all prevalent social consciousness of religion, region, caste, tribe, were forced to carry forward. Exactly at this point, the communist leadership failed to act and the results were alarming. Working class in Mumbai has been divided on the lines of religion, region, caste and tribes. This makes them weaker and in the political sense, they are appendages for different ruling class parties. They are influenced by all political parties but are particularly indifferent to Left parties when it comes to voting. About the unorganized sections of the working class, they are non-existent politically in the absence of any political party serving the interests of the working class. Mumbai, New Mumbai, Thane district—everywhere it is the rule of either Shiv Sena-BJP combine or Cong-Nationalist Congress Party (NCP), nowhere does the working class have any say politically as a distinct political category.

SOCIAL AND CULTURAL CONDITIONS

The social life of Mumbai's working class represents the scene of a mini India and its poorest strata of society. People from every part of country are coming to Mumbai in search of a livelihood and better life. They make this city vibrant. But this is the most troublesome place as far as the life conditions are concerned. More than half of the population is living in slums and basties. The tough economic conditions and day-to-day dependence on the market for survival puts majority of Mumbai working class families in a continuous stress. The wounds of communal riots are still in their mind, so they prefer to live safely in their own groups.

Their life was more safe earlier in the days when textile mills were functioning. The city was more safe for women to live and work. After the disappearance of textile workers from the social scene, Mumbai slowly turned into a centre of services industry which brought along its own anarchy and chaos. The 1992 Hindu-Muslim riots and the riots against the Hindi-speaking Indians occurred after the collapse of mills. Even then the city celebrates the festivals like Dahi Handi, Ganesh Puja, Chhat Puja, Diwali, Navratri on a grand scale without any bias of caste and region. Similarly, the festivities of other religions too are celebrated in a good way and the city shows a great degree of tolerance and acceptance. Be in slums or poorer residential areas, under normal circumstances, there is a sense of cooperation. Only by provocation or outside interference, they lose their existing calm and transform into hostility. It is a class in flux, under the pressure of living conditions and daily struggle. Added to it, the ruling parties' apathy makes their life more vulnerable to any disorder.

Meanwhile, the lumpen sections of the working class provides fodder for all petty or big crimes in the city on cheaper terms. This section is not involved in any productive economic activity, and in general, is used against its own people by the organizers of crime syndicates.

Generally, the working class people of Mumbai are in perpetual conflict with their past and present. They are not satisfied with the present life in which they are forced to live, but when they see their native villages or their roots, they cannot go back to the deserted villages as there is no life. This conflict is seen in the cultural life of the working class. They posit and carry all the trends with which they were attached earlier.

All print and electronic media is silent on the news or stories about working people. Working people and their life are seldom the issue of any cultural production. The government does not want to face the reality that 80 per cent of their own people are forced to lead a wretched life. This simple fact is unexplainable by any existing theories of ruling class and so there is always a hidden guideline which does not portray anything real about the common people. They put a distorted mirror towards the society so that one cannot see one's real face in it.

To summarize, the working class in Mumbai presents a picture of chaos in contemporary society. They find no hope of life anywhere and are immersed in dejection and despair. They see their life daily sinking from them under the burden of wage slavery, but they do not know the way out of their struggle. Life is a big cruel joke to them.

CHAPTER 9

Capitalist Labour Processes and its Consequences

ASHOK BANERJI

Labour processes are dealt within sociological studies as well as in political economy. It is an integral part of the mode of production. This topic is specific to the changes effected in the labour process in keeping with development of capitalist mode of production of commodities and its consequences on the forces of labour.

In order to live people should have food, clothes, shelter and other material values. The production of material values constitutes the basis of the society's life and development.

Production of material values always includes three components: human labour, objects of labour and means of labour. Objects and means of labour are used to make products. Together they constitute the means of production, and the people who have production experience and set the production in motion constitute society's productive forces. Taken all together, the components of labour process form in general preconditions of all production.

Social relations among people in the process of the production, distribution, exchange and consumption of material values are called relations of production. The type of production relations primarily depends on who is the proprietor of the means of production, whose interest does the production process serve and on who owns the results. Relations among the people concerning the means of production, i.e. relations of property in the means of production are the basis of whole system of production relations in the society.

The productive forces and the relations of production constitute the mode of production of material values. There are four consecutive modes of production historically: primitive-communal, slaveholding, feudal and capitalist. In modern times, the new entrant in the field is the socialist mode of production. This article concerns the capitalist mode of production.

The specific features of the capitalism are derived from the capitalist purchasing of the various components of labour process—the means of production and labour power—setting one to work on the other. The capitalist mode of production is based on further development of private property in the means of production and exploitation of wage labour. The growing economic requirements for material production lead to the emergence and use of new means of labour, i.e. the machines.

The transition from manual means of labour to machines radically altered the working person's labour functions in the production process. When the capitalists began to bring independent craftsmen in a workshop under their control, the nature of production changed, even when the same commodity which the independent craftsmen produce, was being produced in the workshop. The forms of co-operation and division of labour inevitably bore the imprint of capital in its search for greater productivity and in turn profit. This affected the nature and use of tools, machinery and the means of production in general.

The form of work unionism in the early or even pre-capitalist periods survived sometimes in later circumstances. There were artisans and other skilled workers. Workers used informal job practices and craft unionism to maintain their degree of work control, consequently limiting changes in technology and labour process restructuring.

The production of commodities with the use values is not the sole goal of the capitalist. He needs to exchange those commodities for a price greater in value than the cost incurred in production. The process of production is, therefore, to combine the labour process with the creation of greater value. Hence the labour process becomes inextricably linked to the struggle for profitable production. To ensure profitability, it is vital that in the work of transforming the product into commodity for the market, no more time is consumed than is necessary under the given social conditions. It is not enough to create value that is equivalent to the payment for labour power. Production must be extended into surplus value, which although created by labour power, becomes distinctively capitalist; therefore, when it is combined with what Karl Marx called valorization—the process of creating surplus value.

In the early period of industrial revolution, employers relied heavily on handicraft and domestic production. Therefore, machinery and division of tasks were insignificant, and in spite of despotic authority, the real power of capital over labour tended to be limited. Large-scale workshops gradually replaced domestic work. At this stage, there was more emphasis on reorganizing work than on mechanizing it. Mechanized factories and the beginning of the assembly-line production needed further technological and economic change and this was not to reach its peak until the heyday of the factory system in the mid-nineteenth century. Such changes were described by Marx as a particular stage in the development of the labour process, from cooperation to manufacture and then to large-scale industry.

In the first stage of capitalism, the traditional works of the craftsman were subdivided into its constituent tasks and were performed in a series by a chain of detail workers, so that the process was little changed; what had changed is the organization of labour.

Writing on the division of labour, Harry Braverman (1998) states that the earliest innovative principle of the capitalist mode of production was the manufacturing division of labour, and in one form or another, the division of labour has remained the fundamental principle of an industrial organization. The division of labour in capitalist industry is not at all identical with the phenomenon of the distribution of tasks, crafts or specialities of production in the earlier societies. Because, while all known societies have divided their work into production specialities. No society before capitalism systematically subdivided the work of each productive specialty into limited operations. This form of division of labour is generalized only with capitalism.

Advantages of this form of organization of labour, i.e. the division of labour, according to Adam Smith (*The Wealth of Nation*, 1776), are savings in labour obtained through maximization of learning acquired by doing. Each individual worker theoretically becomes more adept at a given task, when the work is sub-divided, with each worker responsible for a single operation. In Smith's famous example of 'pin manufacture', one man draws out the wire, another straightens it, a third cuts it, a fourth points it . . . and the important business of making pins in this manner, divided into about 18 distinct operations are all performed by distinct hands. Smith considered the process embodied an increased dexterity on the part of the individual worker and the saving in labour time through the elimination of time previously spent going from task to task and the ease with which the division of labour facilitated the introduction of machinery. For Smith, this kind of detailed division of labour was a mere matter of technical efficiency, promotion of job-specific work skill led in each and every case to 'a proportionate increase of the productive process of labour'. Advantages arising from the division of labour have traditionally been extolled in these terms introduced by Adam Smith.

The division of labour as practised within the factory meant for the vast majority of workers was not so much the creation of job-specific work skills, but the breaking down of previous skills—a process that could only be justified by the greater profits it brought to employers. Classical liberal theorists of management Charles Babbage and Andrew Ure, writing half a century after Smith, contradicted Smith's assumption of skill enhancement through job specialization. Deliberately choosing the very same example of pin-making as Smith, Babbage argued in *On the Economy of Machinery and Manufacture* (1832) that, the most important and influential cause of the division of labour under capitalism was to be found in the minimization of job-specific knowledge on the part of the worker. 'By dividing the work to be performed into different processes each requiring different degrees of skill or of force.' Babbage wrote, the owner, 'can purchase exactly that precise quantity of both which is necessary for each process: whereas if the whole work were executed by one workman, that person must possess sufficient skill to perform the most difficult and sufficient strength to execute the most laborious of the operations into which the art is divided'. Babbage further argued that higher the worker's skill level, the higher the wages that had to be paid, this process of systematic deskilling by breaking down work tasks into simpler components had the effect of cheapening labour.

Andrew Ure identified the same overall tendency towards diminishing skill requirements for the great bulk of workers in his *Philosophy of Manufactures* (1835).

These criticisms of Smithian theory of division of labour by the early proponents of capitalist management were subsequently incorporated by Marx in his critique of capitalist political economy. He argues that the key to understanding the detailed division of labour under capitalism was not found in Smith's 'learning by doing' which demanded an ever greater specialization as a means of enhancing the skill levels of workmen. But in the opposite principle enunciated by Babbage and Ure in the early nineteenth century there was division of labour by reducing labour cost through systematic degradation of human labour.

The development of division of labour as Adam Smith observed was dependent on the extent of the market and the scale of production. Its full development was, therefore, impracticable for the small family firms that still dominated in the nineteenth century.

Between what Charles Babbage and Andrew Ure wrote and the next step in the development of labour process, a period of more than half a century elapsed. In this period of half a century, there was enormous growth in the size of enterprises. There was also a beginning of the monopolistic organization of industry and also a systematic application of science to production. Against this background, a comprehensive theory of management developed. These forces brought into being the 'scientific management' started by Frederick Winslow Taylor (1911). F.W. Taylor dealt with the fundamentals of the organization of the labour process and control over it.

Taylorism was summarized by Braverman in the form of three distinct principles: dissociation of the labour process from the skills of the workers, separation of conception from execution and use of this monopoly over knowledge to control each step of the labour process and its mode of execution. Taylor himself in his book *Shop Management* admitted that the full possibilities of his system would not have been realized until machines in the shop were run by men who were of smaller calibre and attainments and who were therefore cheaper than those required under the old system. What Taylor articulated was a full-scale job control by managers, primarily through deskilling. Hence, Braverman maintains that within Taylorism lies a theory which is nothing less than the explicit verbalization of the capitalist mode of production. Thus, it was found that 43 per cent of the workers in the Ford Works in the United States of America require but one day's tuition, 36 per cent from one to eight days, 6 per cent from one to two weeks, 14 per cent from one month to a year; and only 1 per cent from one to six years (cited from Wolfram 1976).

An orthodox view of work relations was continued to be propounded and propagated in academia as well as by sociologists. In the early post-Second World War years, a pre-eminent interpretation of work in modern society was presented by John Kerr et al. in their article published in the *International Labour Review* (1960: 238). These authors have described industrial society, asserting amongst others, that: (1) industrialization has displaced capitalism, (2) new technology requires rising levels of skill and responsibility, (3) new wealth and leisure mean increased well-being rather than increased misery, (4) there is decline of overt protest, (5) the state is omnipresent and modern industry demands bureaucratization, (6) classes are eternal, (7) industrialization is pluralistic, and power is diffused.

The sociologist Robert Blauner argued in his study, *Alienation and Freedom: The Factory Worker and His Industry* (1964) that the technological change is shaped by three factors: the state of scientific and mechanical processes, the nature of product and the engineering and economic resources specific to particular firms. Blauner wrote, 'Alienation has travelled a course that could be charted on a graph by means of an inverted U-curve. It reached its height,' he suggested, 'with the assembly-line industries of the early twentieth century. But as more and more industries have become automated, alienation has diminished—thus the inverted U.'

This orthodox view of 'Industrialism and Industrial Man' was difficult to maintain in view of mounting dissatisfaction among a significant number of workers by the quality of their working lives. A special task force selected by the then US Secretary of Health, Education and Welfare, declared in its 1973 report on Work in America that the 'significant numbers of American workers are dissatisfied by the quality of their working lives. As a result, the productivity of the worker is low—as measured by absenteeism, turnover rate, wildcat strikes, sabotage, poor-quality products, and reluctance by workers to commit themselves to their work tasks.'

In this context, Braverman has written in his *Labour and Monopoly Capital* (1974) that 'more I read in the formal literature of occupations, more I become aware of a contradiction that marks much of the current writing in this area'. On the one hand, it is emphasized that modern work, as a result of scientific-technical revolution and 'automation', requires ever higher levels of education, training, the greater exercise of intelligence and mental effort in general. At the same time, a mounting dissatisfaction with the conditions of industrial and office labour appears to contradict this view. For it is also said—sometimes by the same people who at other times support the first view—the work has become increasingly sub-divided into petty operations that fail to sustain the interest or engage the capacities of human being with the current levels of education; that these petty operations demand less skill and training; and that the modern trend of work by its 'mindlessness' and 'bureaucratization' is alienating larger sections of the working population.

The division of labour simplified each operation in the labour process which made it possible to substitute machine for human skill. The broad range of earlier machinery had been general purpose equipment, adapted not to a particular product or to a specialized operation, but to a range of operations. Lathes existed for metal turning not for manufacture of a particular size or class of screw or shaft; presses were adapted to a variety of forming operations, not to a particular part. As the machinery underwent its first phase of progress towards an increase in control, this took the form of fixed arrangements adapting the machine to a particular product or for an operation. In an advanced stage, such as the machining of an automobile engine block, a single machine drills scores of holes from various angles, mills surfaces to final finish, counter-bores, taps, threads, etc., performing these operations simultaneously or in a rapid sequence.

Pins are no longer produced by workers divided into discrete tasks. Rather the entire process is re-unified in a single machine which transforms great coils of wire into millions of pins each day already papered and ready for sale. The re-unified process in which the execution of all the 18 and odd steps is built into the working mechanism of a single machine. In modern machine shop, which remains the fundamental branch of all industry, not only because of the great role which machine tools play in great many areas of production, but also because it is in the machine shop that the machinery of the industry itself is fabricated. It is also particularly important because of the great innovation in machine control is undertaken here. It is interesting to note here what the American writer Arthur Pound described in his book *The Iron Man in Industry* (1922): '. . . the most valuable man in the automatic machine workshop is the man without imagination and in general a man below average intelligence.'

Insofar as the management has found an answer to the problem of cheapening labour and controlling production, it has taken the form, on the one hand, of breaking down the machinists' craft among operators specializing in the lathe, milling machine and other individual machines, and making machine set-up itself a speciality; and on the other hand, of predetermining operations according to the management standard in the Taylor tradition.

The mechanical solution to the problem of controlling labour has taken the form of 'numerical control', which has been called 'probably the most significant new development in manufacturing technology since Henry Ford introduced the concept of the moving assemble line'.

With a numerical control, the machine process is subjected to the control of a separate unit, which receives instructions from two sources: in numerical form from an external source and in the form of signals from monitoring devices which check the ongoing process at the point of contract between tool and work. Using this information, the control unit originates signals which activate power drives controlling the work tool, coolant, etc.

The numerical control is used to divide the process among separate operations, each representing far less in terms of training, abilities and hourly labour costs than does the competent machinist. The process has become more complex, but this is lost to the workers, who do not rise with the process but sink beneath it. Each of these workers is required to know and understand not more than the single worker before, but much less. The skilled machinist is, by this innovation, deliberately rendered as obsolete as was the glass-blower or Morse code telegrapher (Braverman). In a survey of companies by the University of Michigan it has revealed that the cost of developing and training an operator to produce identical parts by conventional methods and machines compared with numerical controlled machining system is approximately 12 to 1.

Control in this form and other forms that are developing out of it, is by no means, limited to metal-cutting machinery. The principle has general applicability in many crafts. The philosophy of this control system is separation of 'intellectual work from the work of execution'. There is no spread of knowledge or skill; there is polarization of knowledge and skill. A few have it and the vast numbers are deprived of it.

Braverman points out that the way in which functions are distributed and the effect of them upon the world of work is the important aspect which must not be lost. Such a separation of intellectual work from the work of execution is indeed a technical condition best adapted to a hierarchical organization, best adapted to the control of both the hand and the brain worker, best adapted to profitability, best adapted to everything but the needs of the people. These needs, however, are in the words of economists 'externalities', a notion that is absolutely incomprehensible from the human point of view, but from the capitalist point of view, is perfectly clear and precise since it simply means external to the balance sheet.

Another important feature of the capitalist labour process is rationalization. Rationalization primarily entails intensification of labour. Intensity of labour is its concentration or compression in definite working time. The quantity of energy spent by the worker in an hour for more intensive labour is equal to so many hours of less-intensive labour. Intensity of labour denotes the condition of work when the 'speeding up' system is used which compels the worker to render (say) double the quantity of products even while the technical working conditions remain otherwise the same. When the intensity of labour is raised, the worker has to spend more energy; and this is equivalent to the lengthening of the working day with the maintenance of the previous intensity. The capitalists use two methods of augmenting the intensity of labour: first is the method of wage-payment and second is the machinery.

At this stage it will be proper to have an overview of what the labour process has come to with regards to white-collar labour in office work. Suffice would be to quote from Joan Greenbaum's study *Windows on the Workplace: Technology, Jobs and the Organisation of Office Work*. The study, she writes, developed and illustrated through examples, the following four themes:

1. The management reorganizes work before new technology is introduced. This is accomplished, in part, by analysing work and cutting it up into specific tasks. These small units of work then can be more clearly specified and coded into software and database (rationalization of work).
2. People applying for jobs are expected to have more skills and more experience; however, these skills (including programming and job design) are often devalued in order to rein in salaries (lowering wages).
3. Organizations and consultants reorganize work, through both specialization and integration of the work tasks that they divided up in the first place, so that fewer please can do more work (increasing productivity).
4. Companies and government agencies are increasingly carving up services into smaller units (as they do with work tasks) so that these services (such as insurance policies) can be sold as products

on the web, on the phone, and anywhere in the world (commoditization of services).

This thumb-nail sketch of the themes gives us an idea that the capitalist labour process has not remained confined to manufacturing of commodities through blue-collar labour in the factories, but has now engulfed the white-collar labour in the offices. Greenbaum's research study looks into the changes in labour process and labour markets and concludes that these changes wrought three major global economic changes, viz.,

(1) *Global economy*, which she explains: this part of which economists call flexible accumulation, because it means that both capital and labour can be flexibly divided up and parcelled out among different workforces. The current form of flexible accumulation is based on something mainstream economists call market liberalization.
(2) *Commodification of services*, which she explains: for much of the twentieth century, economists and business managers argued that services were not open to the same division of labour as tangible products, such as automobiles, because services involved non-quantifiable professional and administrative labour. But by the 1970s and 1980s major employment sectors like finance (banking) insurance, real estate and law were turning services into products that could then be sold as commodities. These commodities—everything from computer programme or designing kitchens to bank transactions—could then be made and sold in many countries. They also could be produced more quickly and cheaply as the labour process of creating them were being made more productive.
(3) *Digital exchange*—The 20-20 hindsight lets us see how the changes in labour process, coupled with computer technology in the second half of the twentieth century, were slowly but surely making a paper-based economy into a digital one. The digital infrastructure of the global economy is not, however, the so-called new economy promised in the 1990s. Digital exchange is built on labour processes that have been divided into pieces and these pieces carved out into products. Now 50 years after the birth of computer age, the exchange of products and labour is increasingly supported by an electronic infrastructure rather than paper documents or paper money.

Greenbaum further points out that in some ways this combination of changing production and changing technology is not very different from the processes that Karl Marx described in the early industrial period in his *The Communist Manifesto*:

> Constant revolutionising of production, uninterrupted disturbance of all social conditions, everlasting uncertainty and agitation distinguished the bourgeois epoch from all earlier ones. All fixed, fast frozen relations, with their train of ancient and venerable prejudices and opinions, are swept away, all new-formed ones become antiquated before they can ossify. All that is solid melts into air, all that is holy is profaned, and man is at last compelled to face with sober senses his real condition of life and his relations with his kind.

REFERENCES

Babbage, Charles (1832): *On the Economy of Machinery and Manufacture* (London: R. Clay, Bread Street Hill).

Blauner, Robert (1964): *Alienation and Freedom: The Factory Worker and His Industry* (Chicago: University of Chicago Press).

Braverman, Harry (1998): *Labour and Monopoly Capital: The Degradation of Work in the Twentieth Century*, 1998 [1974] (New York: Monthly Review Press).

Department of Health, Education and Welfare (1973): *Work in America: Report on a Special Task to the Department of Health, Education and Welfare* (Cambridge, MA: MIT Press).

Greenbaum, Joan (1979, 2004): *Windows on the Workplace: Technology, Jobs and the Organisation of Office Work* (New York: Monthly Review Press).

Kerr, John, Clark Dunlop, Frederick T. Harbison, and Charles A. Myers, (1960): 'Industrialism and Industrial Man', *International Labour Review*, vol. LXXXII, no. 13.

Marx, Karl and Friedrich Engels (1969): 'The Communist Manifesto' *Marx/ Engels Selected Works*, vol. 1 (Moscow: Progress Publishers).

Pound, Arthur (1922): *The Iron Man in Industry* (Boston: Atlantic Monthly Press).

Smith, Adam (1776): *The Wealth of Nations* (London: W. Strahan and T. Cadell).

Taylor, Frederick Winslow (1911): *Shop Management* (London: Harper and Brothers).

Ure, Andrew (1967) (1st edn. 1835): *Philosophy of Manufactures* (London: Routledge).

Wolfram, Michael (1976): *Political Economy: A Marxist Study Courses* (New York: Banner Press).

CHAPTER 10

Teachers' Movement as a Potential Ally of the Working Class Movement

K.K. THECKEDATH

Teachers are not workers, and the teaching community cannot be considered as a part of the working class. The working class, in the words of Marx and Engels, is the special and essential product of capitalism, its own creation. The teachers belong to the strata of middle classes having their origin in the petty bourgeoisie and the pre-capitalist formations. However, there is a great similarity between the working class movement and the movement of the teachers worldwide. The teachers' movement can be considered as an ally of the workers' movement for better working conditions and in the achievement of the historic task of the revolutionary overthrow of the capitalist system and the building up of a socialist society.

First, although they are not a part of the working class, the capitalist system is rapidly converting teachers into wage labour. In the Communist Manifesto, Marx and Engels state:

> The lower strata of the middle class—the small trades people, shopkeepers, and retired tradesmen, generally the handicraftsmen and peasants, all these sink gradually into the proletariat, partly because their diminutive capital does not suffice for the scale on which modern industry is carried on, and is swamped in the competition with the large capitalists, partly because their specialised skill is rendered worthless by new methods of production. . . .

Further they add: 'The bourgeoisie has stripped of its halo every occupation hitherto honoured and looked up to with reverent awe. It has converted the physician, the lawyer, the priest, the poet, the man of science, into its paid wage-labourers.'

Second, in the creation of surplus value, which is the essence of human labour power for capital, teaching plays a role unlike such sectors as trade, banking, advertising, where other sections of the middle classes are employed. In advertising, for example, value is transferred from the production sphere where it has already been created, and in banking and credit, value is transferred from the future that is yet to create the value (Mohun 2003). Regarding teaching and education Marx says in *Capital*, vol. I:

> In order to modify the human organism, so that it may acquire skill and handiness in a given branch of industry, and become labour-power of a special kind, a special education or training is requisite, and this on its part, costs an equivalent in commodities of a greater or less amount. This amount varies according to the more or less complicated character of the labour-power. The expenses of this education (excessively small in the case of ordinary labour-power), enter *pro tanto* (for so much) into the total value spent in its production. (Marx and Engels 1971: 168-9)

Many so-called Marxists are taken in by the phrase 'education as human capital', but they are unable to understand that this input of education goes into forming variable capital and not constant capital, and it is therefore, part of the value increasing (valorizing) input. It should never be treated as another input like investing in machines for a factory or 'lavatories for schools'. Hence, unlike other sections of the middle classes engaged in trade, banking and credit, advertising, and other such professions, teachers create surplus value, in the sphere of production, and do not just take part in the transfer of value in the sphere of distribution. This makes the teacher a special stake holder and an ally of the workers in the process of creating surplus value.

A third point is that, historically, in the development of the teachers' movement also, we see a similarity. In India, the first teachers' organizations, like the West Bengal College and University Teachers Association or the Greater Bombay Secondary Teachers' Association, were formed in the early years of the decade 1920-30. This is contemporaneous with the formation of the all-India trade union federation under the inspiration of Lokmanya Bal Gangadhar Tilak in the first year of the same decade.

Fourth, in the capacity to fight prolonged struggles also the teachers' movement is a good example. While the all-India railway strike of 1975 went on for 26 days, the all-India college and university teachers' strike of 1987 went on for 34 days, and in Mumbai, the strike was extended by another 20 to 54 days. In Andhra Pradesh, the college teachers' strike went on 45 days in 1986. In Maharashtra, recently the college and university teachers went on a 44-day long strike. The school teachers of Maharashtra went on a 54-day strike along with the state government employees in the year 1977. The junior college teachers in the state went on a 42-day strike in the year 1991. In 1992, the college teachers of Bihar went on a 90-day strike. Although this is an incomplete list, it shows the power and resilience of the teaching community to fight doggedly for their trade union demands.

The potential of the teaching community to be an ally of the working class politically in the first phase of the Indian revolution, namely, the stage of people's democratic revolution, has been recognized by certain political parties in India. For example, the Communist Party of India (Marxist) [CPI (M)] states in its programme that both the urban and rural middle class suffer heavily under the capitalist landlord rule. The large number of white-collar employees, teachers, professionals, engineers, doctors and new strata of intelligentsia constitute a significant and influential section, the bulk of this section is plagued by ever rising prices. These sections can and will be an ally in the people's democratic front and every attempt should be made to win them for the revolution. The role of the progressive intelligentsia in mobilizing this strata for democratic causes is an important one.

This classification refers mainly to sections of the urban and rural middle class, and only parenthetically, to the teaching fraternity. Before we come to the potential of the general class of intellectuals, it is necessary to point out recent history, and specifically, the close connection that the teachers' movement has had with the working class movement.

In April 2001, a total bandh was organized in the state of Maharashtra to protest against the proposal of the government to introduce new labour laws in the state. Under the impact of the neo-liberal policy changes, it was felt necessary for the rulers to make labour laws flexible, with easy hire and fire clauses. This was why the bill was brought in. This protest strike and bandh programme was organized by different trade unions' joint action committees. An important and leading role in this strike was played by the teachers' organizations. In Mumbai, all the constituents of the teachers' coordination committee from the primary teachers to the college and university teachers participated in this strike.

Coming to the all-India movement of trade unions against the Government of India's neoliberal policies, it may be noted that during the past one decade there have been nearly a dozen trade union actions in the form of one-day strike, processions, squatting, and so on. In everyone of these actions the teachers' organizations have been in the forefront. There were all-India strikes on 14 December 2006 and 20 August 2008. In spite of difficulties of a logistic nature, the teachers had participated in both strikes. Thus, whether it is an action of the working class, or a wider action of the democratic sections like the state and central government employees, we see the active role played by the teachers' organizations.

Before moving on to the potential role of the intelligentsia, let us note that the active role of teachers' organizations has been worldwide. In the United Kingdom, the coordinated and united movement of teachers is so well-established that the name of their united forum, the National Union of Teachers (NUT), has entered the *Concise Oxford Dictionary* as an English word NUT.

POSSIBLE ROLE OF THE INTELLIGENTSIA

A large proportion of the intelligentsia belongs to the class of teachers, especially at the level of higher education. The trade union movement has in recent times expanded to include large sections of the intelligentsia. One such strong current is the all-India movement of teachers, and especially, of the college and university teachers. The members of the intelligentsia are often passive members of the teachers' unions and hardly take a leading role in the organizations. However, they are sympathetic when there is a movement and tend to move into action if properly approached.

The intelligentsia has an important role to play in the revolutionary struggles of the working class and the working class leadership cannot afford to ignore this section, especially as the battle reaches its critical stage. The intellectuals are generally neutral as far as class struggle goes. However, it is necessary to note that the stratum of the intellectuals is important for the working class-led revolution, for its potential, as a reserve force and an ally in the class war. It is a reserve force which should be retained with us, rather than be allowed to be used by the bourgeois class on their side and against the working class.

In the present ideological struggle which is being waged by the bourgeoisie against socialism, the largest sections of the intellectuals are being utilized by the bourgeoisie to strengthen their ideological positions.

THE QUESTION OF IDEOLOGY

Let us begin with the ideological struggle. In his work *What is to be Done?*, Lenin has pointed out that 'Without revolutionary theory no revolutionary movement is possible'. Giving a long quotation from Engels, he writes: 'Engels recognises, *not two* forms of the great struggle of social democracy, political and economic, as is the fashion among us, but three, placing the theoretical struggle on par with the first two'.

Lenin continues:

> Writing to the German workers, Engels says that the important role of the German workers, who had the heritage of the great philosophy of Hegel and others, demands study. This demands redoubled efforts in every field of struggle and agitation. In particular, it will be the duty of the leaders to gain an ever clearer insight into all theoretical questions, to free themselves more and more from the old world outlook, and constantly to keep in mind that socialism, since it has become a science, demands that it is pursued as a science, ie., that *it be studied*.

On the importance of this book of Lenin, which was written in 1903, Stalin says (1945): the historic significance of Lenin's celebrated book *What is to be Done?* lies in the fact that:

(1) It laid bare the ideological roots of opportunism which stressed only spontaneous movement and belittled the role of *socialist consciousness* in the working class movement;
(2) It brought out the great importance of *theory* as a guiding force of the working class movement;
(3) It substantiated the fundamental Marxist thesis that the Marxist Party is a union of the working class movement with socialism;
(4) It gave a brilliant exposition of the ideological foundation of working class movement and the Marxist Party.

It must also be noted that Lenin showed that socialist ideology does not arise spontaneously from the working class movement, but it arises from outside the working class movement, namely, in science.

Going back to understand the roots of this science of socialism, which lie outside the working class movement, we may refer to the precise formulation by Marx and Engels in the *Communist Manifesto* of 1848:

> Altogether collisions between the classes of the old society further, in many ways, the course of development of the proletariat. The bourgeoisie finds

itself in a constant battle. At first with the Aristocracy: later on, with those portions of the bourgeoisie itself, whose interests have become antagonistic to the progress of industries: at all times, with the bourgeoisie of foreign countries. In all these battles it sees itself compelled to appeal to the proletariat, to ask for its help, and thus to drag it into the political arena. The bourgeoisie itself, therefore, supplies the proletariat with its own elements of political and general education, in other words, it furnishes the proletariat with weapon for fighting the bourgeoisie.

. . . Further, as we have already seen, entire sections of the ruling classes are, by the advance of industry, precipitated into the proletariat, or are at least threatened in their conditions of existence. These also supply the proletariat with fresh elements of enlightenment and progress.

. . . Finally, in times when the class struggle nears the decisive hour, the process of dissolution going on within the ruling class, in fact, within the whole range of old society, assumes such a violent, glaring character, that a small section of the ruling class, cuts itself adrift, and joins the revolutionary class, the class that holds the future in its hands. Just as, therefore, at an earlier period, a section of the nobility went over to the bourgeoisie, a portion of the bourgeoisie ideologists goes over the proletariat, who have raised themselves to the *level of comprehending theoretically the historical movement as a whole.* (emphasis added)

According to Marx and Engels, it is this portion of the bourgeois ideologists, who had raised themselves to the level of comprehending theoretically the movement as a whole, who gave the science of socialism to the working class movement. It may be said that, in fact, Marx and Engels themselves were representatives of this process. Historically, they became the first and the greatest teachers of the working class.

A RESERVE FORCE

Apart from the role that intellectuals have played in the historical task of giving to the working class movement, the science of socialism, this stratum of society has a role to play in the ideological struggles against the bourgeoisie which tries to demolish the theory of the working class. They represent a reserve force and can be of help for the working class movement in countering the ideological attacks on socialism. After the revolution, the leadership of the working class can be sustained only on the basis of the assimilation of the intellectuals into the socialist system.

In the middle ages, the church was able to hold its sway, and feudal relations could dominate social life, because they were able to absorb the most intelligent people into the system. Marx says:

> . . . the circumstance that the Catholic Church in the Middle Ages formed its hierarchy out of the best brains in the land, regardless of their estate, birth or fortune, was one of the principal means of consolidating ecclesiastical rule and suppressing the laity. The more a ruling class is able to assimilate the foremost minds of a ruled class, the more stable and dangerous becomes its rule. (Marx and Engels 1971: 601)

A similar situation is to be found in the history of the growth of capitalism with the extension of the institution of credit. Marx says:

> What distinguishes interest-bearing capital, insofar as it is an element of the capitalist mode of production, . . . is the altered condition in which it operates, and consequently, also the totally transformed character of the borrower who confronts the moneylender. Even when a man without fortune receives credit in his capacity of industrialist or merchant, it occurs with the expectation that he will function as a capitalist. . . . The circumstance that a man without fortune but possessing energy, solidity, ability and business acumen may become a capitalist in this manner . . . is greatly admired by apologists of the capitalist system. . . . It also reinforces the supremacy of capital itself, expands its base and enables it to recruit ever new forces for itself out of this substratum of society. (ibid.: 600)

Thus, both feudalism and capitalism are seen to have recruited and relied on this substratum, or the foremost minds in the land, to consolidate their rule, and to work as supporters, apologists and ideologues of the respective systems. The foremost minds, although belonging to no class in particular, yet form a substratum which is a reserve force in the ideological struggle. The working class and its party should learn from this historical experience and ensure that this reserve force comes as an ally of the working class rather than remains an ally of the bourgeoisie in the coming revolution.

TODAY'S REALITY

The reality today, however, is that the intellectuals have been captured by the bourgeois class and they represent the ideological force in the bourgeoisie's struggle against socialism. It is this stratum which is used for running down socialism by means of lies and slander. More and more sophisticated means are invented by this stratum in the vicious ideological warfare. A list of such issues in the ideological field has been given in the book *Leninism: An Effective Ideological Weapon* (Novosti 1969). Especially important in this book is the chapter entitled 'The Contemporary Struggle of Ideas and the Concept of Ideological Disarmament'.

One such ideological attack consists in the attempt today to show that, with the new changes in technology, there is an emerging unity between the two systems of capitalism and socialism. This is the so-called convergence theory. According to this theory the contemporary world is pictured as a sum total of states differing in economic, military and scientific-technological potential. No account is taken of the opposition between socialism and capitalism. According to this theory, there will take place a rapprochement between capitalism and socialism, and their transformation into a de-ideologized society.

The argument is that the countries with capitalist and socialist systems are both industrialized countries. Their systems work to increase productivity, and in the process they open up, so that the world becomes an integrated system. The problems of one country affect all other countries. Such is the picture presented by this convergence theory.

In the current financial crisis, which has been triggered by the speculative lending by the banks of the United States of America, the attempt by the ideologues of the capitalist system is to cover up the innate tendency of capitalism to break out into crises again and again. The concentration is on the immediate cause of the crisis in the financial sector. It is then pointed out that this crisis affects all the countries in the world. The financial crisis is admitted to be mainly a crisis in the Western advanced economies, but it is pointed out in the same breath that the crisis will affect the developing countries like India and China.

By combining India and China as two powerful developing countries, the attempt is to play up the convergence arguments of an integrated world. The special feature of the socialist country China, where the main sectors of the economy are state-owned, and only a small part of the gross domestic product is produced in the private sector and the fact that it differs from India, are both deliberately suppressed. It must be noted that in a socialist country, it is very easy to deal with problems arising out of external causes such as the inability to export in the same old way. State intervention by a socialist country is done in a scientific way, because the disturbance from the fluctuating market is minimal.

Here we find an example of the subtle, but a pernicious attempt to stress on globalized economics and to suppress the redeeming features of socialist planning and development. Such propaganda is the handiwork of the intellectuals who are working overtime for the capitalist class. This is precisely where the need is felt for having intellectuals working for the socialist cause and on the side of the working class.

CONCLUSION

In India, the freedom struggle and the struggle of the downtrodden under the leadership of Babasaheb Ambedkar, have led to a considerable expansion of education in general, and higher education in particular, because of the provision of reservations for the common people. Large numbers of young people from the working class and those belonging to the reserved categories have been able to raise themselves to the level of intellectuals. However, these people coming out of our educational institutions are imbued with a consciousness which is alien. As products of the present bourgeois educational system, these intellectuals tend to identify themselves with the present bourgeois system.

But as we have seen, these people coming out of our educational system are also being drawn in their hundreds into the democratic movement in general and the teachers' movement in particular. This is the great treasure house from which the working class leadership has to recruit the ideological defenders of socialism. The working class movement and its politically mature leadership should also recognize the reality that without philosophy the movement is blind and cannot move towards the historic role of the working class. It should thus recognize that in this march the teachers' movement is a potential ally.

REFERENCES

Lenin, V.I. (1975): 'What is to be Done?', in *Lenin Selected Works*, vol. 1, pp. 110-12 (Moscow: Progress Publishers).

Marx, Karl and Friedrich Engels (1965): *The Communist Manifesto* (Moscow: Progress Publishers), pp. 45, 57.

Marx, Karl (1971): *Capital* (Moscow: Progress Publishers), vol. I, pp. 168-9 and vol. III, pp. 600-1.

Mohun, Simon (2003): 'Does Labour Create Value?', in A. Saad-Filho (ed.), *Anti-capitalism: A Marxist Introduction* (London: Pluto Press).

Novosti (1969): *Leninism: An Effective Ideological Weapon* (Moscow: Novosti Press Agency).

Stalin (1945): *History of the CPSU (Bolshevik)* (Moscow: Foreign Languages Publishing House), p. 38.

CHAPTER 11

Need for Social Scientific Studies for Organizing the Unorganized Sector in India

VIVEK MONTEIRO

Neoliberal policies of liberalization, privatization and globalization (LPG) are visibly failing in various parts of the globe including India. The failure of market fundamentalism in the financial sector is now followed by failures in other key sectors such as energy and power and in the aviation sector.

ANTI-LABOUR POLICIES

The Indian trade union movement's persistent resistance together with the opposition of the Left parties to the LPG policies had succeeded in partially checking their advance in India and averting collapse of the nation's financial, energy and infrastructural sectors. India remained relatively insulated from the ravages of the global capitalist crisis because of the defence of the public sector by the trade unions and the Left.

It must be realized that the LPG policies are hostile to the interests of workers belonging to both organized and unorganized sectors. In the name of deregulation of the labour markets and making labour markets more flexible, during the tenure of the Bharatiya Janata Party (BJP)-led National Democratic Alliance (NDA) government, the 2nd National Labour Commission (NLC), sought to play the unorganized sector against the organized sector to undermine labour rights of both sectors. The NDA government paid the price of its anti-labour policies and was voted out of power in 2004.

The 2nd NLC study was a classic example of an unscientific study. It was wrong in its both factual matrix and conclusions, such as:

(1) That labour laws are not working, therefore, labour laws are irrelevant.
(2) Non-governmental organizations (NGOs) are doing more important work as compared to trade unions in organizing the unorganized sector workers.
(3) The Contract Labour Act needed to be further diluted.

It is worthwhile to examine the methodology of the 2nd NLC study. It was predisposed to arrive at certain conclusions. Facts were chosen to suit these conclusions. In science, it must be the other way around, facts have to be noted comprehensively and accurately. Conclusions must emerge from the facts.

A second point which needs to be made here is the deliberate attempt made by the 2nd NLC to bypass the Directive Principles of the Indian Constitution. This is clear when we compare the report of the 1st NLC with the 2nd NLC report. The questionnaire circulated by the 2nd NLC was virtually a copy of the questionnaire of the 1st NLC, with one conspicuous difference: all the questions referring to the Directive Principles were carefully excluded.

NCEUS REPORTS

Under the pressure of the Left parties, when the United Progressive Alliance (UPA) government came into power in 2004, the Common Minimum Programme was introduced for the first time in India. The agenda of this programme contained certain matters of the Directive Principles of the Indian Constitution such as the right to employment and the right to social security in old age. These along with other issues like the public distribution system (PDS), universal access to education are other crucial issues in the unorganized sector.

For the first time, the unorganized sector began to receive some more serious study such as in the various reports of the National Council for Enterprises in Unorganized Sector (NCEUS). The reports of the NCEUS are qualitatively different and far superior to the studies performed by the 2nd NLC.

The workers of organized and unorganized sectors have a common interest in defending the public sector, strengthening labour market regulation and in preventing the dilution of labour laws. These interests along with the demands of the unorganized sector like strengthening and extending the National Rural Employment

Guarantee Act (NREGA), and strengthening the PDS run counter to the current of the LPG programme. Thus, a vigorous struggle is on the national agenda. This is a struggle for ensuring the basic needs for all Indian citizens—for ensuring the mandate of the Directive Principles of the Indian Constitution.

The problem of providing basic needs for all Indian citizens is the most important problem facing our nation. It is the most important scientific problem, having both technical and social science dimensions. It will require alternative policies—a Left and democratic restructuring.

Organizing the unorganized sector is a necessary condition for bringing out the political change which is the precondition for alternative policies to provide basic needs for all.

The formulation of and promotion of feasible alternative policies is an important input. This struggle is also an ideological struggle. There are several issues which require serious social scientific studies in this context. These include the problem of accounting by occupational category, more rigorous studies on living and working conditions in various sectors, issues of productivity and viability, scientific study of failures of LPG policies in various public services and the working out of specific practical alternatives in each area.

This struggle will require the intellectual support of social scientific community through their in-depth analyses of the struggles of working class people of both the organized and unorganized sectors against LPG and in favour of pro-people democratic alternatives for fulfilling the constitutional mandate. In the following part we identify 10 important problems which need scientific studies by the social scientific academic community. These studies will be very useful to those who are working to organize the unorganized sector, and working for alternative pro-people policies.

TEN PROBLEMS FOR SOCIAL SCIENTIFIC STUDY

(1) *The Human Accounting Problem*: What is the anatomy of the unorganized sector in India today? How many domestic workers, street vendors, small retailers, waste reprocessing workers, safai workers, agricultural workers, the number of workers in mixed employments (agricultural plus construction) are in the country? What is a scientific occupational classification of the unorganized sector? How does the average Indian citizen survive and make his/

her living? This question is important because of the extremely unsatisfactory state of primary data collection as regards to occupational status in the country.

(2) *The Problem of Universalization of Basic Needs*: The Directive Principles of the Constitution contain right to employment, right to a living wage, right to social security in the old age. What is the *status quo* in respect of these basic needs for different sections of the Indian citizenry?

(3) *Productivity Problem*: Productivity is intimately related to energy consumption. What is the relation between development and energy consumption? Can we tackle the problem of development separately with relatively low commercial fossil fuel energy consumption? If development has to be taken place with average per capita energy consumption managed within certain limits, then how can productivity be enhanced sufficiently to deliver universalization of the basic needs? Is it human energy *vs* fossil-fuel energy? We need in-depth studies on the role of organization and education in enhancing productivity and development based on renewable energy.

(4) *Resource Problem*: How can we use nation's resources for fulfilling the constitutional mandate? As in the case of a beedi industry or a construction industry, how can we raise the cess for providing universal social security? For example, how can the wealth contained in our fossil fuel resources be used for social sector expenditure including building universal social security and employment guarantee?

(5) *Labour Market Regulation*: What is the role of labour market condition in improving the living conditions and services in the different sections of the unorganized sector? Social security legislation is implemented in different parts of the country. Further studies have to be conducted to analyse the relation between enabling legislation and the organization of the unorganized sector.

(6) *Food Security*: The problem of food security and the strengthening process of PDS also have to be analysed. The Food Corporation of India has been weakened by both the NDA and the UPA governments. Therefore, we need alternative policies for food security.

(7) *Legislations in Energy Sector*: An examination of the working of legislations like the post-liberalization electricity sector legislation

and the amendments and restructuring is needed to ensure social objectives like affordability and universal access.

(8) *Social Justice Problem*: The interplay between issues of social justice and the problems of the unorganized sector is to be analysed. It is urgent to study the relations between economic inequality and social discrimination based on caste, religion and gender.

(9) *Problem of Restructuring*: Left and democratic restructuring is needed for providing basic needs to all citizens and fulfilling the mandates of the Indian Constitution.

(10) *Study of Workers*: A study of the commonality of the interests of workers belonging to both organized sector and unorganized sectors in the present context, particularly in the context of defending the public sector and in alternative Left and democratic restructuring to be conducted.

In conclusion, an excerpt from the inaugural address by Jyoti Basu at the 47th Annual Conference of the Indian Society of Labour Economics in December 2005 is highly relevant:

> As a trade unionist myself I can vouch for the fact that the working class needs the academic support of bodies such as this. They do not have to be overtly partisan in any sense. All they have to do is honest academic work, and objective scientific research free of prejudices. Scientific honesty is an ally of the working class, while false theories, advanced either owing to erroneous conceptions, or owing to ignorance or prejudice or with the deliberate intent of promoting the interests of the employers, have been great practical hindrances to the amelioration of the suffering of the workers. History is replete with examples of such theories.

CHAPTER 12

Broken Pledges of the Constitutional Mandates and Anti-People Role of the Judiciary

P.R. KRISHNAN

India, after Independence, has so far tried to copy down and build-up a three-wing system of governance based mostly on the Western parliamentary model. In framing the Constitution for the country, importance was given to a system and practice of governance in Britain.

The three-wing system of governance which our country adopted after Independence is categorized as legislative, executive and judiciary. The functioning of these arms of administration is founded in the Constitution which the historic constituent assembly passed on 6 November 1949. The people of India have solemnly accepted the same since then. After Independence in 1947 and since adoption of the Constitution by the constituent assembly of India in November 1949, we became a sovereign, democratic republic on 26 January 1950. However, the words 'socialist' and 'secular' came to be incorporated in the Constitution by the 42nd Amendment Act passed by the Parliament in March 1977, and India became a sovereign socialist secular democratic republic.

CONSTITUTIONAL PLEDGES

It is widely acknowledged that this Constitution is based on the declaration of a resolution passed in the 1930 at the historic Karachi session of the Indian National Congress. This well-acclaimed resolution was a declaration of pledges and promises that were to be kept up and implemented after Independence. To be brief, what this meant was to secure basic and essential conditions for the people to live a dignified life. Accordingly, the preamble to the Constitution summarizes the aims and proclaims:

We, THE PEOPLE OF INDIA, having solemnly resolved to constitute India into a (SOVEREIGN SOCIALIST SECULAR DEMOCRATIC REPUBLIC) and to secure to all its citizens:

JUSTICE, social, economic and political;

LIBERTY of thought, expression, belief, faith and worship;

EQUALITY of status and of opportunity; and to promote among them all;

FRATERNITY assuring and of the dignity of the individual and the (unity and integrity of the Nation);

IN OUR CONSTITUENT ASSEMBLY this twenty-sixth day of November, 1949, do HEREBY ADOPT, ENACT AND GIVE TO OURSELVES THIS CONSTITUTION.

It is in consonance with the above preamble that a separate chapter Part IV, is included in the Constitution. This chapter is for solving grievances of the people and for fulfilling the constitutional pledges. Some of these articles which deal with problems of the people require a special mention here. Foremost amongst them is Article 14. This Article under the title 'Equality before the Law', unequivocally declares and lays down that the state shall not deny to any person equality before the law or the equal protection of the laws within the territory of India. The next, Article 15, 'Prohibition of Discrimination on Grounds of Religion, Race, Caste, Sex or Place of Birth' is very important. It declares that the state shall not discriminate against any citizen on grounds only of religion, race, caste, sex, place of birth or any of them. Article 16, 'Equality of Opportunity in Matters of Public Employment' states that, there shall be quality of opportunity for all citizens in matters relating to employment or appointment to any office under the state. Article 17 is under the caption 'Abolition of Untouchability'. It directs that untouchability is abolished and its practice in any form is forbidden. It further says that, untouchability if practised in any form shall be an offence and be punishable in accordance with law. Article 19, 'Protection of Certain Rights Regarding Freedom of Speech, etc.', deals with protection of certain rights and says that all citizens shall have the right to (a) freedom of speech and expression, (b) freedom to assemble peacefully and without arms, (c) freedom to form associations or unions, (d) freedom to move freely throughout the territory of India, and (e) freedom to reside and settle in any part of the territory of India. Most important is that Article 21, 'Protection of Life and Personal Liberty' mandates that no person shall be deprived of his life and personal liberty, except according to procedure established by law. Article 23,'Prohibition of Traffic in Human Beings and Forced Labour' is meant to prohibit traffic in human beings and beggars and other similar forms of forced labour in the country. Article 24 is under the caption 'Prohibition of Employment of Children in Factories', etc. This article makes it clear that no child below the age of 14 years shall be employed to work in any factory or mine or engaged in any other hazardous employment.

Article 25 is 'Freedom of Conscience and Free Profession, Practice and Propagation of Religion'. There are two parts, two sub-parts and two explanations under this Article. The main part lays down that subject to public order, morality and health and to the other provisions of this part, all persons are equally entitled to freedom of conscience and the right to profess freely, practise and propagate religion. Together with this, when we go to Article 29, 'Protection of Interests of Minorities', it says that any section of the citizens residing in the territory of India or any part thereof having a distinct language, script or culture of its own, shall have the right to conserve the same. This Article further says that, no citizen shall be denied admission into any educational institution maintained by the state or receiving aid out of state funds on grounds only of religion, race, caste, language or any of them. Article 30 provides 'the Right of Minorities to Establish and Administer Educational Institutions'. It says that all minorities, based on religion or language, shall have the right to establish and administer educational institutions of their choice.

Article 38, mandates the 'State to Secure a Social Order for the Promotion of Welfare of the People'. It says that the state shall strive to promote the welfare of the people by securing and protecting as effectively as it may a social order in which justice, social, economic and political, shall inform all the institutions of the national life. When we then go to Article 41, under the headline, 'Right to Work, to Education and to Public Assistance in Certain Cases' directs that the state shall, within the limits of its economic capacity and development, make effective provisions for securing the right to work, to education and to public assistance in cases of unemployment, old age, sickness and disablement. Article 42 deals with the 'Provision for Just and Humane Conditions of Work and Maternity Relief'. Article 43 is

'Living Wage, etc., for Workers'. It says that the state shall endeavour to secure by suitable legislation or economic organization or in an other way, to all workers, agricultural, industrial or otherwise work, a living wage, conditions of work ensuring a decent standard of life and full enjoyment of leisure and social and cultural opportunities, and in particular, the state shall endeavour to promote cottage industries on an individual or cooperative basis in rural areas. Article 43(A) is 'Participation of Workers in Management of Industries'. This Article directs that the state shall take steps, by suitable legislation or in any other way, to secure the participation of workers in the management of undertakings, establishments or other organizations engaged in any industry.

I have quoted a few of the Articles from the Constitution as above with the original headlines and captions. All these articles, though are separate, they are complimentary to and supportive of each other.

A PERUSAL OF ARTICLES

A perusal of these Articles will reveal that while some are on political rights of the citizens, some are for protection of minorities and their interests. Some are meant for promotion of the interests of scheduled castes. But all other Articles are for making provisions for social and economic justice to the people. It is highly regrettable that despite the fact that we are, in the 64th year of freedom hardly any of these Articles have been implemented in its true spirit.

In the scheme of things that our Constitution has accepted and the three-wing system of governance that we are following through the parliamentary democratic process, the judicial system of the country occupies a place of pride. It is, therefore, of crucial importance. Any citizen, group of people, body, party, company organization or institution can move the high court of any state or the Supreme Court and seek remedy if any injustice and injury has been caused to them by the executive, i.e. the state government, union territory government or the central government or by state legislatures or Parliament.

There are many examples when people have, in the midst of utter injustice and the wrongs perpetrated on them by the executive, got them undone and got protected by the judiciary. Also there were occasions when some of the provisions of laws proposed by the governments and passed by the legislative assemblies and parliament were declared as *ultra-vires* of the Constitution by the high courts and Supreme Court. It was in several such legal battles that some of the high bureaucrats, state and central ministers and chief ministers had to quit. This also holds good so far as arrests and detentions of political functionaries and trade union leaders are concerned. So also is the case with regard to corrupt practices in the electoral system. There were several instances when the Supreme Court and high courts found that the arrests and detentions of political leaders, civil liberty functionaries and trade union activists were illegal and *malafide* and they were ordered to be freed.

Similarly, if any of the elected members, right from gram panchayats to state assemblies or even the parliament was found to have committed corrupt practices in the election campaign, her/his election has been held to be null and void. In some cases even the dissolved assemblies came to be restored. A famous example in this glorious heritage is the Allahabad High Court's judgement in 1975, disqualifying the former Prime Minister Indira Gandhi for corrupt electoral practices. However, on appeal, the Supreme Court stayed the operation of this judgement and allowed Indira Gandhi to continue as prime minister. What thereafter followed was declaration of national emergency and mass arrests and detentions of thousands of political opponents, abrogation of legal rights and civil liberties. A very glaring example in the history of our elected legislatures is the judgement of a five-member constitution bench of the Supreme Court which struck down the action of the Bihar governor Buta Singh recommending dissolvement of the state assembly as unconstitutional. There are also examples when the Supreme Court had declared some of the provisions contained in the legislative enactments in regard to industry and labour as unconstitutional. There were also occasions when the high court and Supreme Court have delivered landmark judgements granting relief to the working class and upholding their contentions for economic and social justice.

NON-ADHERENCE TO ARTICLES

Sad, however, is the fact that the executive, i.e. the state and central governments have not taken sufficient steps to implement those Articles which aim at and deals with social and economic progress of the people. Had these provisions been implemented, India could have achieved far greater progress in all fronts than what we see today. Non-adherence to these Articles has made our country lag far behind. In addition, the advent of globalization has further worsened the situation. However, glamorously presented, the hidden features of globalization have now started surfacing and hitting the common man below his belt. The new policy has also started creating havoc in the economic, industrial, agricultural, employment, health, education and environment fields. In a situation like this, instead of the judiciary coming to the rescue of the common people, it has started to show a new twist to the past judicial precedents. This makes the people feel that the glory of our judicial system is getting tainted.

This is undoubtedly because the World Bank, International Monetary Fund, the World Trade Organization and multinational corporations have started penetrating into and influencing the judiciary's mind in India. One is forced to say this, because, some of the judgements which the high courts and Supreme Court have delivered in recent period negate the protective legislations and the precedents laid down through judicial pronouncements in the past.

The most glaring and astonishing example in the series is the judgement of the Supreme Court regarding contract workers in the Steel Authority of India [*SAIL* vs *National Union of Water Front Workers* (2001-II L.L.J.1087)]. By this single judgement the Supreme Court has made millions of contract workers defenceless. It is clear that this judgement contradicts all the previous judgements of the federal court and Supreme Court. By this very judgement, the highest forum of judiciary has helped the capitalist class to perpetuate its exploitation. Other instances are the judgements of Kerala High Court, Bombay High Court and Calcutta High Court regarding the rights of the toiling people to take our processions, staging of protest demonstrations, organizing strikes and bandhs. Still shocking is the Supreme Court judgement of August 2003, regarding the 12 lakh Tamil Nadu State Government employees' strike. It is a different matter that the government terminated the services of these employees who voted out the government in the state assembly election which took place a year after its draconian action.

But a precedent having, thus, laid down by the Apex Court, had its repercussion inasmuch as the Bombay High Court by its judgement on 17 July 2004 ordered the Shiv Sena and Bharatiya Janata Party (BJP) to deposit Rs 40 lakh as damage for the *bandh* called following the Ghatkopar blast in 2002. On appeal, the Supreme Court by its interim order in September 2005 asked these parties to first comply with the high court directive before the appeal being heard. This speaks volumes about the direction to which the judiciary has moved. By these judgements, the Supreme Court and high courts are taking away the rights of the toiling masses to demonstrate their protest which they have achieved through decades of struggles and sacrifices.

As stated hereinbefore, this is because a new thinking is being sought to be imposed by the World Bank, International Monetary Fund and World Trade Organization as a part of its globalization, liberalization and privatization policies. This has its origin in the 1991 Congress government led by Narasimha Rao. The BJP, then in opposition, had objected for this policy. But when it came to power, the Vajpayee-led government started vigorously implementing it. The present United Progressive Alliance (UPA) government led by Manmohan Singh has not made any difference.

The numerous other measures being implemented by the UPA government at the centre will go to reveal that the rulers have scant respect for the people's aspirations and the words 'secularism' and 'democracy' inscribed in the Constitution. All these principles highlighted in the Constitution are being breached by the same people, who at the time of assuming ministerial positions and prime ministership have taken an oath to strive to achieve its goal. Examples are, the large-scale privatization of public sector industries and nationalized banking and insurance sectors. The central government previously led by A.B. Vajpayee and presently led by Manmohan Singh also allowed large-scale contract system in all government services and public sector industries including defence departments. It is in our record that the central government on 2 September 2005 had decided to privatize the security presses and mints which print currency notes, coins and stamps papers. The departments within these mints and presses which produce weights and measures will also be privatized as per this decision.

DISCRETIONARY POWERS OF LABOUR COURTS

Now I come to the discretionary powers of labour courts and industrial courts in giving a reinstatement of employees wrongly dismissed or terminated from services. The law laid down by the Supreme Court and high courts till the advent of globalization was that if the trial courts find that the dismissal, discharge, termination, suspension or retrenchment as the case may be, is arbitrary, capricious or in violation of the provisions of the Industrial Employment Standing Orders or against the provisions of the Industrial Disputes Act or any other relevant law in force, the relief of reinstatement and full back wages can be granted. But the Supreme Court has now started to give a new twist to these previous judgements and has in a number of cases set aside such awards during the period after the onset of globalization. The message is clear that the judiciary has to change and fall in line with the demands of big capital gradually to do away with the protective labour legislations of post-Independent India.

Coming to the wage fixation cases of workers before industrial tribunals, the picture is quite alarming. The practice till recently followed by the adjudicating authorities was to grant at least some monetary relief to the workers in wage demand matters. The factors such as (a) change in circumstances from the time of last revision, (b) the rise in cost of living indices, (c) erosion in the money value, (d) fall in purchasing capacity, (e) rise in price of essential commodities, (f) the improvement in the financial conditions of the employers, (g) the price rise effected in the products of the employer companies, (h) the increase given in the remunerations of the executives, etc., were considered by industrial courts and tribunals in wage demand matters. The recommendations of the 15th Indian Labour Conference of the year 1960 were also considered as relevant factors for the purpose of revision of wages. These principles were laid down by the Supreme Court in a number of cases and were followed by the high courts and adjudicating authorities. The Articles quoted from the Constitution as above were the guiding directions for the courts to lay down such principles. For example, this is what in that context the Supreme Court in *Hindustan Times* case as far back as in 1963 observed (*The Hindustan Times Ltd, New Delhi* vs *Their Workmen* on 14/12/1962):

> The tribunal has not accepted the company's contention that the existing wage-structure is fair, though at the same time, it has held that the wage-system needs no such radical change as alleged by the union. Mr Pathak, who appeared before us for the company, did not seriously suggest that the present wage-structure gives the employees 'a fair wage'. He argued generally that no case was made out for any revision of the wage-structure. Such an extreme proposition has only to be mentioned to deserve rejection. At the

time the tribunal was dealing with this question the wage scale of the workmen in this concern had remained practically unaltered for almost twelve years—twelve years of momentous change through which social ideas have moved forward in favour of workmen getting a better share of the national income; twelve years during which the new India was born and a Constitution was framed for this new democracy 'to secure to all its citizens, justice, social and economic and political' and enshrining in its Article 43, the principle that the State shall endeavour to secure by suitable legislation or economic organisation or in any other way to all workers agricultural, industrial or otherwise among other things, 'a living wage and conditions of work ensuring a decent standard of life and full enjoyment of labour and social and cultural opportunities . . .'.

But what we see in the adjudication matters since the recent period is a complete negation of these principles to reject the workers' case for wage increase. Added to these onslaughts on the people are the disclosure made at the conference of chief justices, chief ministers and law ministers chaired by the then chief justice K.G. Balakrishnan and inaugurated by the Prime Minister Manmohan Singh in Delhi. The disclosure had sent shock waves. According to the information furnished in this conference, there are more than three and a half crore cases pending in various courts stretching from the lowest courts to the high courts and the apex courts in the country. This is further complicated by the fact that there are large number of vacancies of judges right from the munsif courts to the high courts and Supreme Court. It may here be noted that a substantial number of this backlog cases are of the workers pending since five to 20 years. India is the only country in the world where so much and the highest number of cases are pending in courts. And yet we profess to be a democracy.

These are dangerous signs. This trend needs to be reversed. For that needs greater and wider unity within the working class, apart from widespread struggles and mass actions. Realization of the call given by the Centre of Indian Trade Unions for a National Confederations of Trade Unions is a step forward in this direction.

CHAPTER 13

Work Processes: Insights from Theatre of the Oppressed

SRINATH JAGANNATHAN

This paper, is based on some informal interviews conducted during my fieldwork between June 2009 and September 2010 with 202 workers about their experiential insights pertaining to workers' insecurity. The workers were from four different industrial relations contexts—stateless refugees, unorganized sector workers, contract workers and organized sector workers. It presents how work processes understood in the form of an encompassing labour process which creates insecurities for workers. Workers do not accept these insecurities silently and their resistances are presented here through the frame of the theatre of the oppressed.

The aims of the theatre of the oppressed and its relevance for workers are forcefully articulated by Augusto Boal (1979: 105):

> Brecht was a Marxist; therefore, for him, a theatrical work cannot end in repose, in equilibrium. It must, on the contrary, show the ways in which society loses its equilibrium, which way society is moving, and how to hasten the transition. Brecht contends that the popular artist must abandon the downtown stages and go to the neighbourhoods, because only there will he find people who are truly interested in changing society: in the neighbourhoods he should show his images of social life to the workers who are interested in changing that social life, because they are its victims. A theatre that attempts to change the changers of society cannot lead to repose, cannot re-establish equilibrium. The bourgeois police try to re-establish equilibrium, to enforce repose: a Marxist artist, on the other hand, must promote the movement toward national liberation.

The theatre of the oppressed is thus an attempt to transform society, taking an art to the neighbourhoods and giving courage to workers, the victims of capital, through that art. It is this sense of art and aesthetic articulation of the victim that workers are capable of instilling in work processes.

Conrow and Delp (1999) suggest that when workers are brought together as a collective, and the Freirian process of conscientization is not enacted, then workers are merely mobilized. They are mobilized for the purposes of organizational and trade union elite and their creative energies are subordinated. Meisiek and Barry (2007: 1807-8) suggest that Boalian techniques of theatre make the audience an active participant and encourage her to shape the contours of the contradictions that are being enacted on stage. This has a therapeutic effect for the oppressed as they are able to assert their voice and seek justice for the numerous violence that have been imposed on them. Pratt and Johnston (2007) indicate how elite or governmental co-optation of the theatre of the oppressed can simply reproduce the rational expertise of the elite. For Guardialo-Rivera (2010: 187) the theatre of the oppressed offers the prospects of a view from the below to complete ongoing projects of decolonization. The theatre of the oppressed is an opportunity for the oppressed to understand the tensions that emerge in the project of emancipation and find creative solutions to these problems.

This paper shows how work processes can become a site for aesthetic introspection for workers, as they seek to conscientize themselves, understand the contradictions at play and take creative positions in them, resist elite cooptation of their aesthetic participation in work processes and seek creative solutions for the problems that arise in the processes of emancipation. The immersion of the worker in everyday aesthetics is a programme of theatre of the oppressed at play. In seeking to come to terms with her state as a victim of insecurity, the worker seeks to transform the oppressive work processes in which she participates and transforms them through an everyday aesthetic practice. In essence, work processes are a theatre in which the workers, who are oppressed by insecurity, can creatively discover liberating practices. The lens of the theatre of the oppressed is adopted here to understand the subversive enactments of workers.

NARRATIVE OF A STATELESS WORKER

In the context of stateless workers, their refusal to accept injustice quietly and resist it reinforces the idea of Boalesque protest. The workers are not a passive audience when injustice is inflicted on them, but they enter into the enactment of the theatre and confront with the contradictions that are sought to be closed to establish equilibrium of exploitation. The moment of confronting exploitation is also an aesthetic moment of regenerating the humanity of existence. A Tamil refugee (whom I met during my visit to a refugee camp) narrated his experiences of trying to look for better jobs in another city away from the refugee camp. With better wages, he would be able to send his children to a good school and educate them well. Also, he would be able to take care of his own deteriorating health. He has been regularly coughing blood and sometimes he gets fever and severe headache. The local doctors near his refugee camp are unable to diagnose his condition. He has to skip work on many days due to his ill-health. He came to India when he was only seven years old along with his father. After his father died, he could not continue his studies beyond fourth standard. His elder brother had taken care of him. He now works as a mason. His account is quoted below:

> I have tried to obtain employment outside. But there is no guarantee that contractors in other cities and towns would pay me properly. Going to Chennai is a problem because I would be immediately identified as an outsider. If I go to some other city, then the contractor might cheat me. I have also heard of people dying in accidents at the sites of contractors and receiving nothing in return. Once my elder brother and I had decided to go outside and try to get work. We accompanied a contractor to a place in Kerala. Once we reached there, the contractor told us that he would not be able to make any payments to us. He would only give us food and accommodation. My elder brother and I protested. We told him that we had left our families behind. If wages were not provided to us, then we would not be able to send anything back which would affect our families badly. So after fighting with the contractor, my elder brother, I and seven to eight others left Kerala. We had no money with us. So we travelled outside with great difficulty. We boarded a train. We reached a district in Tamil Nadu by the train. We had nothing to eat or drink for four to five days. After reaching Tirupur, we approached the collector's office. We told him our story. The collector treated us with sympathy. He immediately arranged our food and paid for it himself. He also arranged for our travel back to the refugee camp through train.

The work processes which seek to exploit the worker construct the contractor as a paternal actor, who will take care of the food and housing needs of workers. These processes construct places where the political silence of the refugee is sought to be enforced, in this case, the place of work, where the refugee is a marginal and ethnic subject, for whom dominant political actors have little concern. The idea of such a difficult place where the worker is not an active participant in social politics reinforces the paternal project of the contractor/manager, as the worker has no material alternatives but to submit to such paternal care. The paternal person of the contractor is experienced by the workers in the form of abuse and exploitation. In the phase of these work processes of paternalism and marginalization, workers do not accept their exploitation silently. In this case, the Tamil refugee refuses to accept their position as silent political actors in the theatre of work and society. From the position of the audience, who is acted upon by the theatre, a passive audience who only consumes the theater, the Tamil refugee decides to come on to the stage, and articulate her own arguments of emancipation in the theatre. Creating the theatre of the oppressed means that, the refugee refuses to be an object of paternal care. The refugees indicate to the contractor that they want wages, and it is materially important for them and their families. They decide to leave the place which marginalizes them politically and go to another place where political actors will listen to their voice with sympathy. This flight from the place of oppression indicates the refusal of human beings to accept indignity and the search for places in their life worlds, which will respect their dignities. When they visit the collector, are the refugees reinscribing paternalism and simply substituting the contractor with the state? Rather than reading these testimonials of oppression as the seeking of paternal help, I read them as an appeal to the conscience of another human being, the project of the aesthetics of emancipation. The action of refugees is thus their attempt to ask the state to take the role of human being's conscience, rather than other roles of control, oppression and apathy.

Exploitation of refugees at work has been detailed by many studies. de Vriese (2006: 7) refers to

> . . . absence of civil, social and economic rights including freedom of movement and residence, freedom of speech and assembly, fair trial, property rights, the right to engage in wage labour, self-employment and the conclusion of valid contracts, access to school education, access to credit; protection against physical and sexual abuse, harassment, unlawful detention and deportation.

An approach towards refugee studies has been the articulation of universalist human rights (UNHCR 2002). One of the central features of international human rights is to persuade 'government and other actors to encourage and enable refugees to develop their livelihood security . . .' (Stone and de Vriese 2004: 11). But such an approach is immersed in liberal moorings and its inherent theoretical and empirical character is to exclude the emancipation of refugees, as it individualizes and de-politicizes them. Particular problems arise for refugees when they are denied the permission to work pending the processing of their papers through time-consuming bureaucratic processes (Horst 2001). The failure to give refugees the right to work means that they often have to search for illegal avenues for earning a sustainable livelihood, this only increases their exploitation and sense of insecurity (Macchiavello 2003). Much of the ethnographic data accessed by me reveals that the discursive practice of illegality relies on modernist and liberal principles to affect the marginalization of subaltern workers. The theatre of the oppressed and reading locally situated enactments of resistance by stateless workers, is another approach for political emancipation that transcends liberal and modern approaches. Commitment to the lens of the theatre of the oppressed can create new discursive resources which vulnerable stateless workers can use. Alternatively, there is a lot we can already learn from the refugee practice of the theatre of the oppressed.

NARRATIVE OF AN UNORGANIZED SECTOR WORKER

Reading the resistances of workers in the unorganized sector helps us in understanding the alternative ways of living and organizing that can help in the process of our emancipation. While workers are rendered homeless and even this homelessness is assaulted by municipal agencies and the police which enforce the discourse of illegality with respect to vulnerable workers, workers do not accept these enforcements as silent spectators. For instance, when I was conducting my fieldwork, a community of pavement dwellers had completed 400 continuous days of organizing protests, agitations, relay fasts and submitting memorandums to the government. And the community members told that they had to sustain this agitation till the government gave a principled commitment that they would not demolish the homes that they had built on the pavement. Creative slogans, songs and militant speeches preserved the ethics of resistance of the unorganized sector workers, who earned their livelihoods through tremendous resilience. These resistances identified locally situated oppressions and actors and did not rely on structural instruments of modernity and liberal thought to improve their lives. An account of one such locally situated oppression is given next, that of a woman in Mumbai, whose differences with a local politician who later became the city mayor, have been the basis of exploitation:

> There are people who use the name of the poor to advance in their own lives. When she became the mayor, she immediately cancelled the no objection certificate (NOC) that had been given to me to earn my living as a hawker. For ten years before that my NOC had been renewed. But after she became mayor it was cancelled. I agree that I have not been in the political party. But my mother gave her entire life to the political party. Is this the reward one gets for spending one's entire life for the party? I went to the mayor and told her that please give water connections to the homes in my locality. Now, even the bore wells have been stopped. So if you give water connections, many problems that families face will be solved. The families will be extremely grateful to you. But she refused. I told her that she need not give a water connection to me. She could give water connections to the remaining thirty homes in my locality. But she did not budge. She told the officers that so long as that woman remains in the locality nobody will get water connection. Now, what crime have I committed or what crime have the others committed? Is this the way you treat poor people? Did you become mayor for this reason?

This is the staging of the theatre of the oppressed, where the spectator, who was the victim, is now on the stage in full public glare, and demanding justice for the oppressions that have been perpetrated against her. The moment of being in the public and vigorously asserting the call for justice is the moment of poetry, subversion and transformation. The victim is at the centre of the stage of political theatre and accusing all of us for participating in the infliction of injustice. How could we silently watch when these injustices were being inflicted on her? The hegemonic work processes that are at play here, are the attempts to dislocate poor workers from the city and place them at more distant margins of political society. What is being attempted here by hegemony is the instituting of a colonial labour process. Currently, workers live in interdependent communities in the city, the place of the colonialist and the colonized is not clearly demarcated within the city. For instance, the roads in which the elites ply their cars are the same roads in which the poor live on the street. Colonial imagery does come into play when liberal public anger that is available for middle-class victims such as Jessica Lal, Shanmugam Manjunath and Ruchika Gehrotra is not available for the subaltern poor whose homes are constantly demolished, who are constantly run over by young, rich people driving their cars under the influence of alcohol. To return to the point of the colonial labour process, once the poor are dislocated to the physical margins of the city, the place of the colonialist and the colonized is distinguished more clearly. Now all the practices of the colonialism which seek to exploit the colonized can be inflicted on the worker at the margins of the city. It is this violent reinscribing of the practice of colonial labour processes that are being confronted by workers through alternative processes of the theatre of the oppressed.

The assaults of the state against informal workers such as hawkers have been documented well in literature. Anjaria (2006: 2142) reads the way dominant descriptions seek to marginalize unorganized sector workers,

> Modernist ideals regarding the city and city spaces are dominant . . . these groups rely on orthodox modernist principles regarding the functioning of the city, most notably, the privileging of movement and flow over other concerns. Neighbourhood by neighbourhood, the city's footpaths must be reconfigured, disorderly footpaths must be made mono functional. The crime of the hawker is to contradict this dream. And thus, they have become a 'public nuisance' because, by working on the street, they are engaged in an activity that contradicts the supposed universal ideals of the modern public space.

In the face of urban poverty and the loss of jobs in textile mills, workers were forced to take up work in the unorganized sector for the sake of livelihood and survival (Bhowmik and More 2001). The marginalization of unorganized sector workers is authored in the name of world-class cities ('Vision Mumbai' 2003), with segregated spaces, where the rights of the poor to inhabit the city are sought to be suppressed. Yet workers from the unorganized sector play vital, creative roles in retaining the public spirit of the city (Davis 2000), and preventing the city from becoming habitus of isolated and disconnected individualism. Jacobs (1961) puts forward arguments about how the presence of subaltern communities on the street sustains these streets as safe, creative, human spaces where the solidarity of other human beings is easily available. These articulations demonstrate the creative potential and practice of unorganized sector workers. This section urges the presence of these articulations in the labour process of the city as an enactment of the theatre of the oppressed. Unorganized sector workers through their locally situated resistances are preventing imposed labour processes from coming into play and creatively confronting locally enacted injustices.

NARRATIVE OF A CONTRACT WORKER

Work processes are eventually statements about legitimacies, certain ways for human beings to come together are articulated as legitimate and human beings are expected to work within the algorithms of these legitimacies. In order to sustain these legitimacies in human society, the norms of justice that a human being can expect, are articulated and there is a promise that work processes will not vitiate these norms. That is the structural logic of work processes. In a post-structural sense, processes are being constantly remade and rearticulated by workers in engagement with each other, algorithms are only ideals, they are discursive resources anticipating a plurality of practices and constraining several others. The theatre of the oppressed urges workers to not be passive recipients of dictated processes, but enter the enactments of these processes and voice their concerns, arguments and passions. There are many instances when the injustices are intolerable, and workers resist and protest against the way in which processes become inhuman. Given below is a quote from the protests of contract teachers who used to teach physically handicapped children in different schools. Their salaries were supported by the central government of India to promote the education of physically disabled children. Suddenly, without notice, the central government stopped giving aid in 2009, and the salaries of the teachers stopped. The managements of these schools refused to pay salaries arguing that they had admitted physically handicapped children in their schools, and recruited teachers, only on the premise that the central government would aid their salaries. The state government was also not willing to bear the responsibility of paying salaries. Thus, even the fundamental process of receiving wages for the work done by them was violated. For 16 months, these teachers had been working without wages, in the hope that the state government would take over the administration of their wages. I met them during their protests and agitations. The experiences of one of the teachers (who works in Aurangabad in Maharashtra, I met him in Mumbai) is given here:

> Earlier the central government had started the scheme of teachers for handicapped children. Then it transferred it to the state government. And from 2009, we have not been getting any payments. As a consequence the condition of teachers is extremely bad. We are almost starving. Many issues have arisen because of us not getting payments. We have had to borrow money even to eat. There are many issues pertaining to food. There is nothing in the kitchen. We don't even have the money to buy tea. When we borrowed

money we told them that we will return it in some months. But after a couple of months when we were not able to return the money, they refused to give us any further money. Neither our friends nor the shops from which we buy provisions were willing to give us any further loans. For 16 months we have not been getting any payments. After the central government transferred the scheme to the state government, it is the responsibility of the state government to pay the teachers. This scheme was for all types of disabled children whether they be visually or aurally impaired or any other form of disability. So the teachers are doing an extremely important job of showing the right path to the disabled children. They are showing them the path of national unity. They are enabling them to have a good life. Now for such teachers, if the time of starvation has arrived then the teachers who were teaching the disabled children have themselves been made disabled by the government. When the teachers come to the schools to teach the children they face many difficulties. They are not able to teach them properly as they are under a lot of tensions. They are reminded of the problems in their home, there is no foodgrain, no oil, no vegetables. There are several other tensions at home. They have to worry about their wife. So the teachers are not able to teach the children because they are under tremendous mental distress. This must be kept in mind by the government. The regular teachers who teach the regular kids get their salaries between the 3rd and 5th of every month, but the teachers who teach the disabled children have not got salaries for the past 16 months. This is a matter of great shame for the state government. Whether it be the chief minister or the education minister, they must take note of this and act on it. It is a matter of shame for them. Even for the central government it is a matter of shame as they stopped the scheme without giving any notice. At least the central government should have intimated this earlier that the scheme will be from this period to this period only, after that the funds will cease. We were given no such prior intimation. We had no prior anticipation of the fact that the funds for this scheme are going to be stopped by the central government. . . . The homes of teachers are also crumbling. The wives are leaving their husbands. Suppose if the wife is working as a teacher, then their husbands are leaving them. And there are other teachers who live alone who have not married, their parents are growing older, so they have to take care of them. All these issues are there. When they are not receiving any payments, it becomes difficult for them to take care of their parents. Then there are younger brothers whose education needs to be taken care of. And there is children's education that needs to be taken care of. Because of not receiving payments for 16 months, they are not able to take care of these needs. As a result of all these things their families are crumbling.

The politics of the theatre of the oppressed is the politics of making the perpetrator of oppression feel ashamed. The intense deprivations experienced by these teachers are expressed, as there is not even money to buy food and friends have stopped giving them loans. The crumbling of their families as a result of these intense deprivations is also expressed. Even the basic norms of justice and decency such as a prior notice or an intimation, were also not issued. The central government, state government and ministers are sought to be shamed through the public transcript of resistance. The labour process of accessing justice being sought here is the politics of shame and the shame seeks to destabilize the legitimacy apparatus of the state, for failing to behave responsibly towards its constituents. The theatrical practice of shaming the oppressor is the assertion of the humanity of the oppressed and their refusal to be subordinated by hegemonic practices.

In the vein of the scientific socialism project of the Indian revolutionary Bhagat Singh, the labour process of the theatre of the oppressed is an attempt to make the deaf hear (Habib 2010). The literature on contract work suggests that the temporary nature of work is experienced as alienating by workers and they prefer full-time regular employment (Rogers 1995). Literature on industrial relations has presented this insecurity as the explicit influence of external labour and product markets on the internal labour markets of a firm and the consequent rise of contingent and contract work (Cappelli et al. 1997). Heery and Salmon (2000: 18) call for a shift away from how insecurity may affect company and business performance to a discussion about what are the experiences of workers in the context of insecurity. The central concepts of such industrial relations' investigation into insecurity are the definition and measurement of insecurity, evidence of increases in insecurity, causes and consequences of insecurity (ibid.: 2000). The concern is in understanding how changes in structure of the job such as shifts away from permanent employment to part-time and short-term contract work qualify as objective measures of increase in job insecurity (Robinson 2000). This study agrees with the importance of understanding the material deprivations of workers, and they are accessed through locally situated data. Reading insecurity from macroeconomic data has the possibility of valorizing the job within capitalist processes of subordination, as security is defined as the entitlement of a permanent job. The lens of the theatre of the oppressed meanwhile critiques these processes of subordination and attempts to discern how workers raise their conscientized voices to transform these work processes of subordination. The conscientized pedagogy of the oppressed is the labour process of 'learning to perceive social, political and economic contradictions and to take action against the oppressive elements of reality' (Freire 1970: 35).

CONCLUSION

Ethnographic data accessed from the organized sector workers, indicates that resistance which reflects the concepts of the theatre of the oppressed, is an important avenue for regenerating their humanity. The literatures of liberation theology, theatre of the oppressed, Zapatista militancy, Gandhian satyagraha and poetic dissent are absent in the Foucaldian turn of organization studies. And there is a limitless world of possibility of what they can do to post-structural approaches to worker resistance, and the ways in which militant hope can be introduced into human action. For instance, Thomas and Davies (2005) suggest that worker resistance can re-inscribe the practices that are resisted, even while generative resistance occurs and emerges out of the trap of resistance being a response to oppression, and therefore, the prevalence of a counteracting equilibrium. The politics of shame and the aesthetics of conscience have not yet entered the practices of critical management studies. It is this possibility that is indicated here by drawing upon the imagery of the theatre of the oppressed, while understanding the ways in which dominant work processes are resisted and alternative processes are proposed. An introduction of the themes of the theatre of the oppressed can effectively challenge structural Marxist thought which accuses Foucaldian ideas of resistance to be determinist and nihilist (Thompson and Ackroyd 1995). The theatre of the oppressed can effectively aid the project of problematizing genderless realities of resistances such as factory strikes (Hyman 1972; Beynon 1973) by carefully understanding what the practices of resistance are doing to work processes. It can help us create new concepts about the ways in which colonization of the self of the worker through engineering her attitudes and values, is resisted (du Gay 1996; Clarke and Newman 1997).

The aims of the theatre of the oppressed are a method for reading and enacting worker's actions that seek to humanize the work processes in which they are situated. Thus, stateless workers seek to humanize work processes by protesting against the marginalizations that they are subjected to and refusing to accept these marginalizations.

Unorganized sector workers also refuse to see themselves merely as spectators in the enactment of the city's universalist ideals, which renders them homeless and poor, but see themselves as creative actors who contribute to the city, and therefore, resist domination and injustice. Contract workers also contest the unacceptable deprivations that they are subjected to and refuse to accept the injustices of insecurity as natural. Organized sector workers seek to subvert the processes that subordinate them and undertake fearless projects of resistance to transform the conventional configurations of work processes. These are some of the empirical possibilities that emerge from the lived experiences of workers. From the imagery of the theatre of the oppressed, workers are articulating the wounds that they have suffered, they are asking questions of society by coming onto public stages, they intend to shame the oppressor and appeal to her conscience, even as they themselves discern the contradictions embedded in work processes and seek a humanist transformation of these processes.

REFERENCES

Anjaria, J.S. (2006): 'Street Hawkers and Public Space in Mumbai', *Economic and Political Weekly*, 41(21), 2140-6.

Beynan, H. (1973): *Working for Ford* (Harmondsworth: Penguin).

Bhowmik, S.K. and N. More (2001): 'Coping with Urban Poverty', *Economic and Political Weekly*, 37(35), 4822-7.

Boal, A. (1979): *Theatre of the Oppressed* (London: Pluto).

Cappelli, P., L. Bassi, H. Kats, D. Knoke, P. Osterman and M. Useem (1997): *Change at Work* (New York: Oxford University Press).

Clarke, J. and J. Newman (1997): *The Managerial State* (London: Sage).

Conrow, T. and L. Delp (1999): 'Teaching Organising through Workers' Experiences', *Labor Studies Journal*, 24(1), 42-57.

Davis, M. (2000): *Magical Urbanism: Latinos Reinvent the US Big City* (London: Verso).

de Vriese, M. (2006): *Refugee Livelihoods: A Review of the Evidence* (Geneva: United Nations High Commissioner for Refugees).

du Gay, P. (1996): *Consumption and Identity at Work* (London: Sage).

Freire, P. (1970): *Pedagogy of the Oppressed* (tr. M.B. Ramos) (New York: Continuum).

Guardialo-Rivera, O. (2010): 'What Comes after Sovereignty?', *Law, Culture and the Humanities* 6(2), 185-207.

Habib, S.I. (2010): *To Make the Deaf Hear: Ideology and Programme of Bhagat Singh and his Comrades* (New Delhi: Three Essays Collective).

Heery, E. and J. Salmon (2000): 'The Insecurity Thesis', in E. Heery and J. Salmon (eds.), *The Insecure Workforce* (London: Routledge), pp. 1-24.

Horst, C. (2001): 'Vital Links in Social Security: Somali Refugees in the Dadaab Camps, Kenya', *New Issues in Refugee Research, Working Paper* No. 38 (Geneva: United Nations High Commissioner for Refugees).

Hyman, R. (1972): *Strikes* (Glasgow: Fontana).

Jacobs, J. (1961): *The Death and Life of Great American Cities* (New York: Vintage).

Machiavello, M. (2003): 'Forced Migrants as an Under-utilised Asset: Refugee Skills, Livelihoods and Achievements in Kampala, Uganda', *New Issues in Refugee Research*, Working Paper No. 95 (Geneva: United Nations High Commissioner for Refugees).

Meisiek, S. and D. Barry (2007): 'Through the Looking Glass of Organisational Theatre: Analogically Mediated Inquiry in Organisations', *Organisation Studies*, 28(12), 1805-27.

Pratt, G., and C. Johnston (2007): 'Turning Theatre into Law and Other Spaces of Politics', *Cultural Geographies* 14(1), 92-113.

Robinson, P. (2000): 'Insecurity and the Flexible Workforce: Measuring the Ill Defined', in E. Heery and J. Salmon (eds.), *The Insecure Workforce* (pp. 25-38) (London: Routledge).

Rogers, K.K. (1995): 'Experience and Structure of Alienation in Temporary Clerical Employment', *Work and Occupations* 22(2), 137-66.

Stone, D. and M. de Vriese (2004): *Refugee Livelihoods: Livelihood Strategies and Options for Congolese Refugees in Gabon* (Geneva: United Nations High Commissioner for Refugees).

Thomas, R. and A. Davies (2005): 'Theorising the Micro-politics of Resistance: New Public Management and Managerial Identities in the UK Public Services', *Organisation Studies*, 26(5), 683-706.

Thompson, P. and S. Ackroyd (1995): 'All Quiet on the Workplace Front?: A Critique of Recent Trends in British Industrial Sociology', *Sociology*, 29(4), 615-33.

UNHCR (2002): *A Human Rights Approach to Poverty Reduction Strategies* (Geneva: United Nations High Commissioner of Refugees).

Vision Mumbai (2003): 'Transforming Mumbai into a World-Class City: A Summary of Recommendations' (Mumbai: Bombay First and McKinsey & Company).

PART III

EXPERIENCE OF WORKING CLASS MOVEMENT: URBAN INDUSTRIAL SECTOR

CHAPTER 14

Democratization of Industrial Management: The Kamani Experience from Mumbai

JOSE GEORGE AND MANOJ KUMAR

Karl Marx's analysis of the different phases of the human history emphasizes the scientific process of constant change in social system through class struggle due to class contradictions in the changing context of material conditions. The emerging and fast-growing trends of democratic movements (bourgeois democracy as leaders and beneficiaries of the movements belonged to bourgeois class) in different parts of the world and their interface with the communist movement at global scale initiated a new phase of human civilization marked by the destruction of bourgeois-dominated social system for creation of an egalitarian socio-economic structure. The changed socio-economic order promised people-oriented governance and development. The nature of state and pattern of its administrative functioning underwent a radical change.

The international working class movement evoked an intense curiosity and interest as well as hope and enthusiasm for a system which aimed at building an equitable society. Under the pressure of agitations and demands raised by the toiling masses, most of the countries adopted welfare policies and measures to improve the conditions of underprivileged working class and blunt the movement supported by them as the capitalists-dominated state felt threatened and their hegemonic position came under severe strain at many places. The only way out, in their opinions, was to do something for the poor people's betterment, at least, by adopting policies and programmes to create illusions. One of the strategic options to sail through such situations was to provide space to the workers' participation in the management of industries, particularly, ailing or loss-making industries. In different parts of the world, working class was given an opportunity to participate in the management-tasks of the industry on various terms and conditions in different countries. India could not remain as an exception to it.

The workers' takeover of the Kamani Tubes Limited (KTL), Mumbai, when it was closed down by its owners, for its revival and management, marked a turning point in the history of the trade union movement in India. The Kamani Employees Union (KEU) led by a prominent trade union leader, D. Thankappan, initiated and proposed the takeover of management of the KTL, which was successfully achieved despite a number of hurdles in the process of takeover. However, the initial euphoria, hope and expectation of the workers did not last long and their sky-rocketing dreams shattered within the short span of almost five years owing to the inability of the KTL to withstand the onslaught of globalization, privatization and liberalization, including the uncooperative state administrative apparatus and communal riots in the post-Babri Masjid demolition period. However, the workers continued their struggle to get their due and to save the property of the industry from being usurped by the manipulative and greedy promoters. The case of Kamani raises a number of questions that need to be systematically researched. The viability of such an experiment needs to be examined on the basis of the analysis of various phases and aspects of the management of the KTL by workers' cooperative.

The industrial units incurring continuous losses and sufferings from the financial crunch, mismanagement, non-payment of salaries and wages to employees, non-availability of raw material and the problems of marketing of products for a certain period are generally known as sick industries.[1] To revive such industrial units and make them operational and profitable, a bill was introduced in 1985, which was assented to, by the President of India in 1987, and came to be known as the Sick Industrial Companies (Special Provisions) Act (SICA), 1987. Under the provisions of this Act, the KTL (established in 1959, by Ramjibhai Kamani, and closed down in 1985, because of various reasons) was taken over by the workers' cooperative society of the KEU. It was a unique experiment of management of a sick industry by the workers in the history of the trade union movement in India. The workers had high level of zeal and enthusiasm on attaining the ownership of an industrial unit and pinned high hopes to make a substantial gain. In the beginning, after the takeover of the company, satisfactory progress was made, but soon it began petering out and started facing a number of crises in the early 1990s[2] leading to its virtual closure in 1997. Since then no concrete step was taken to bring it back into operation and the employees' union was mainly fighting for arrears and dues of workers based on their arguments on the plea that the unit was never officially closed down.[3]

There were many sick companies spread all over the country, some of which were taken over by the workers cooperatives, but most of them failed to survive for long time due to a number of reasons.[4] This has necessitated debates on the feasibility of workers' takeover of sick industries. It is in this context that this study is focused upon.

BACKGROUND OF THE KAMANI INDUSTRIES

An industrialist, Ramjibhai H. Kamani, who belonged to the Kamani family (earlier they had established the Kamani Engineering Corporation Limited (KEC, now KEC International Limited) and the Kamani Metals and Alloys Limited (KMA) in 1944 and 1945, respectively), formed an industrial firm, the KTL in 1959 in Kurla, Mumbai to manufacture non-ferrous tubes. It made high profits over a decade which had been increasing since its inception and reached its peak in 1972. The main customers of its copper-based alloy tubes and rods were the sugar industries, thermal power stations and the defence establishments. The demise of Ramjibhai H. Kamani and ensuing feuds among Kamani brothers paved the way for decline of this highly profitable industrial unit. The decline of this company began in 1973, which led to its closure in 1985, after water and power supply to it was disconnected due to non-payment of bills (Srinivas 1993; Palande 1991: 2). In 1984, just before its closure, the company had shown all time low performance with huge loss. The situation of continued losses led finally to the closure occurred as a consequence of feuds in Kamani family, problems in management, prolonged litigation and appropriation of finance resulting in shortage of requisite amount of working capital.

THE RESEARCH PROBLEM

The issue of workers' takeover of the KTL and its management by the workers cooperative society generated curiosity, debates and discussions among various segments of society, especially the activists, intellectuals, academicians and policy makers, regarding the viability of this kind of experiment in which the mass media also played an important role (Palande 1991; Srinivas 1993: Thankappan 1992; Aarti Dua 1993; Dutta 1993; Ramaswamy 1998). The minds of workers and their leaders were filled with zeal and enthusiasm which proved to be short-lived and this historic experiment could not withstand the multifaceted challenges that it encountered. Its decline began since the early phase of 1990s due to a number of reasons mainly unfavourable market conditions, lack of inherent capability (lack of its own financial resources and credit support) of such experiments to withstand the liberal economic policies of the state in post-globalized period. The indifferent attitude of the bureaucratic bourgeois besides the breakdown of the social peace in the aftermath of the Babri Masjid demolition in 1992 were other reasons of the failure of the company's take over by the employees. The confusion among workers and their separation from their parent union created more complications for the workers' cooperative management process. All the efforts to revive and consolidate the workers' control over the management of this industrial unit failed and unofficially it was closed in 1997 because of the absence of crisis management ability and support from the state apparatus. The workers still continue their struggle to get their entitlements.

The whole story of the takeover experiment of the sick industries by the workers, particularly, of the KTL, raises many questions, such as, is the phenomenon of sickness of an industrial unit inevitable in the capitalist mode of production? What were the problems that the workers' cooperative faced in the process of takeover of the management of the KTL? What was the role of state administration in revival of the sick industry? Were the workers sufficiently indoctrinated and trained in handling the management tasks? Were the leaders not responsible for the failure of the experiment? What are the factors that can successfully lead to the effective control of management of such industries by the workers? Is the workers' management of the sick industry feasible in the capitalist mode of production system, wherein the nature of the state predominantly remains oriented towards the patronization of the interests of the capitalist class, while retaining an elusive welfare characteristic for the toiling masses, the workers, especially those at the lower rungs in formal and informal sectors? This study examines the case of the KTL and explores the feasibility of workers' successful participation in the management within the capitalist system with an aim to develop an effective strategy for peaceful transformation of society.

RATIONALE AND SIGNIFICANCE OF THE STUDY

The concept and practice of the workers' participation in management which promised a radical transformation in the socio-economic order in a peaceful means, unfortunately, proved to be short-lived and even illusory. The euphoria of potential-beneficiary working class turned into disappointment and frustration when the historic experiment did not withstand the unfavourable situations and collapsed in the mid-1990s. The equitable change expected through this experiment could not be achieved. This in-depth analysis of the case of Kamani experiment is expected to help in understanding and identifying the factors of the failure of the experiment, and thus, can contribute to the construction of strategic formulations to efficiently protect the interests of working class and improve their socio-economic and political conditions.

The significance of the study lies in the fact that this kind of experiment of control of industrial units by working class promises restructuring of socio-economic order of Indian society along the lines of democratic and socialist principles. Moreover, such experiments can reduce the degree of unjust economic inequalities in the society by ensuring the protection and promotion of the interests of marginalized sections, like industrial workers. It is important to identify the key factors that were responsible for the failure of the management of this sick industry by the workers of the company. This study also suggests the elements of success in reviving and managing sick industries by workers' cooperative societies. The literature on this subject is available, but most of them have focused on the historical perspective of the cases of workers' takeover of the sick industries for their revival and rejuvenation, including the causes of the failure, while putting forward an argument that such experiments collapse under the weight of their own and enter into the phase of natural decline.

RESEARCH OBJECTIVES AND SCOPE

Besides, the descriptive and analytical understanding of the various aspects of the workers' management of KTL, particularly, the sickness of the industry, problems and processes of the takeover of the KTL by the workers' cooperative, this study examines the factors that led to the decline of influence and control of the workers on the management aspect of the industry, while linking the failure of the experiment with the neo-emergent general situation of the decline of the trade union movement at a larger scale.

This paper looks at the whole story of KTL with an emphasis to analyse and locate the unrevealed causes of the decline of the Kamani industry, especially after the industry was taken over by the workers' union of the KTL, the problems faced during the process of takeover of the industry, including its management, and finally, the major causes of the failure of this experiment. The study also examines the role played by various leaders, bureaucrats, bankers and management bosses (including promoters) in the revival and management process of this unique experiment and ascertains the factors for success of such industries.

HYPOTHESIS

The hypothesis, this paper tries to test, is this that the experiments of takeover of a sick industry for revival and management by workers' cooperatives are found to fail in the bourgeois socio-economic system in the absence of favourable government policies as well as the policies (and also attitudes) of other related-institutions and agencies (which is rather often regressive and prejudiced in nature than cooperative and encouraging). The hypotheses that needs to be tested are:

(1) the sickness of the industries is a natural outcome in the capitalist system of production due to inherent contradictions within the monopolistic capitalist culture;
(2) the sick industries, under the managerial control of the workers, can be revived and brought back in the mode of efficient productivity, provided state policy is favourable and administrative agencies are committed to provide much needed support keeping in view the socialist principles of the Directive Principles of the State policies enshrined in Part IV of the Constitution to promote and protect the interest of the working class;
(3) the workers are adequately indoctrinated and trained in the understanding and practice of capitalist culture as well as in successful performance of management task after the takeover process is over.

METHODOLOGY

This study is descriptive, analytical and explorative in nature and the sources of data are official and organizational published/unpublished documents, news articles and reports published in journals, magazines and newspapers, documents of court cases related to this matter, including interviews with the leaders of Kamani Employees' Union (KMU), Kamgar Ekta and creditor bank officials. The reports and documents prepared by the workers' union and other institutions, like the Board of Industrial and Financial Reconstruction (BIFR) and banks concerned, including the petitions filed by the KEU in recent past along with the schemes framed by the financial institutions and other associated agencies have been referred. The secondary source-literature on the subject and related issues, such as theoretical, conceptual and such experiments at other places, within the country and outside of it, has also been referred for analysis for developing sound understanding of the theory and practice of this historic model of workers' participation in management.

THEORETICAL AND CONCEPTUAL ISSUES

The case of workers' management of KTL, a unique and the first experiment of the workers' participation and control on the management and functioning of this sick industry, has been examined in the broad framework of changing industrial relations and workers' participation in the decision-making process of the management of an industry. The experiments of this kind are considered and adopted as an alternative strategy to revive, consolidate and sustain the productive functioning of the industrial unit. The discussions in this study have been made in the framework of industrial socialist democratic operation and management with the help of some important conceptual tools, such as, workers' participation in the industrial management, their control on the industrial management, and the takeover of management by the workers' cooperatives.

These conceptual terms have been used interchangeably implying the same notion in the context of this research project. The 'workers' participation', 'workers control' and 'workers' takeover' here imply an awareness and realization of the workers' rights and the need to participate in decision-making structures of the industrial management which includes the notion of self-management of the industrial unit they work in and contribute in production and gain of the industry.

The increasing level of consciousness and assertiveness of their right in the management of the industrial units are essential elements of the concept of workers' participation in management. This signifies a major shift from workers' bargaining tactics to the strategy of participation in the management itself with a view to protect and promote their interests through the practice of industrial democracy (democratization of industrial relation).

The concept originates from the workers' ardent desire to overcome the stress and suffering which they have been experiencing and their realization of the need of self-management or governance of the industry. The participation in the management yields a sense of ownership in the minds of workers and also the sense of security of job and wage which keeps them in higher level of motivation to work for the higher productivity of the industry. This strategy has a special significance from the point of view of democratization of the place and an atmosphere where the workers invest their labour and spend a bigger part of their life working for production.

This strategy makes the workers not only managers and owners of the industry, but also makes them responsible for operation and production. It signifies bilateral process making industrial firms accountable to their employees, and at the same time, holding workers for their responsibility towards these firms. This concept could be seen in contrast of ownership of means of production by the capitalists. The labouring class which plays an important role in production process is entitled to the natural right of controlling and managing the industrial unit. In such an arrangement, workers take collective decisions that are deeply connected with their destiny. This is an outcome of workers' radical consciousness and the growing realization of humanist priorities, which ultimately, reshapes the personality and contributes towards social transformation.

The concept emerges as the necessity in a changing situation of nature of work, particularly, in the exploitative work environment of the industries wherein a number of conditions are imposed on workers which make them agitate and crave for control of the industrial management. The rationale of the ground on which the strategy of workers' management evolved, is based on the premises of three major factors, insecurity of employment and wage of the workers, alienation of labourers and moral principle that a group of workers who invest their labour in the industrial production and business has every moral right to occupy its due space in decision-making structures and not just those who merely invest their capitals, including a necessity of achieving the target of humanist and equitable justice (Srinivas 1993: 9-16). The necessity of workers' cooperative on industry emerges as a consequence of the sick industrial units under the management of capitalist elements. It was more than a 'pragmatic' response to the emerging phenomenon of the shutting down incidents of industrial units.

WORKERS' PARTICIPATION IN MANAGEMENT: AN OVERVIEW

The root of the growth in assertiveness of working class could be traced in the communist analysis of the social environment and the practice of class struggle of the toiling underprivileged masses. The countries, where industrial growth marked a significant change in the nature of prevalent socio-economic order, witnessed the emergence of the working class movement and trade unionism. The working class movement of European countries, particularly, the movement of workers in England inspired and influenced the trade union movement in other countries, especially India, despite the capitalists' opposition to such workers' movement (which was quite natural for capitalist forces to respond to the growing class consciousness of labour class). England, the birthplace of industrial revolution, became a propitious ground for the emergence of the working class movement which provided an impetus and guidance to the worker's movement in France and Germany (Chetty 2004: 26).

The international working class movement had splits a number of times due to ideological conflicts. However, it provided an inspiration, and to some extent, a guidance to the neo-emergent nation-based working class movement in the third world countries. The workers' movement in India was highly influenced by the working class movement of England. The capitalist-imperialist forces made the life of workers pathetic and profit-making activities were their only concern, not the deteriorating and dehumanizing condition of industrial labouring masses. A concept that the self-interest was the basis of all human relations and that a person alone was responsible for one's own condition became a major contributory factor for deterioration in the condition of working class (Chetty 2004: 31). Industrial capitalists continued exploitation of workers, worsened their conditions; long working hours, poor wages, merciless exploitation of women and children, death, disease and unhygienic conditions which made the life of working class pitiable. Trade union, as a protest organization of industrial workers, grew up in this occasion to protect and promote the interests of workers. The period of the outbreak of the First World War is regarded as the beginning phase of the trade union movement in India when the war situation generated tremendous growth in manufacture of certain products (Chetty 2004: 31-3).

The communist movement and development of democratic process of representative governance awakened workers' consciousness and encouraged them to participate in the political activities as they had come to realize the significance of the political actions. Workers' struggles against the exploitative industrial units began for the protection of their interests and improvement in their conditions in which they were supported by progressive intellectuals and even by some high industrial employers. In the beginning, the trade unions were used to be sporadic, less organized and focused, on no definite ideology, or programme and without any direction and support system. The enactment of labour law by the government, the framing of the Trade Union Act of 1926, the founding of All India Trade Union Congress (AITUC) in 1920, the establishment of the International Labour Organization, including the growing strength of the Indian National Congress provided an inspiration and vigour to the movement of workers (ibid.: 33-4). Ironically, some of the legislations, such as, the Workmen's Breach of Contract Act, the Employers' and Workmen's (Disputes) Act, which were supposed to protect the interests of workers, in true sense, served the interests of employers (ibid.: 36).

The growing incidents of the ailing industrial units created a difficult situation for the working class, threatening even their survival. The increase in the number of ailing industrial firms necessitated a search for an alternative strategic option to revive the industrial firms and secure the job and livelihood of workers. Such conditions prepared a ground for the formation of workers' cooperative and an urge to participate in the managerial work of the industries. The incidents of industrial sickness and the demands by the workers for gaining control of the industrial units led to the enactment of legislation, the Sick Industrial Companies (Special Provisions) Act, 1985, which contained the provision to enable the workers to take control of the management of sick industries to revive and manage. This created euphoria among the workers which, unfortunately, in many cases, proved to be short-lived. The case of Kamani Tubes represents the failure of the experiment, chiefly, due to exploitative and rapacious characteristic of the capitalist system.

The participation of workers' in the management of industry could be realized in different forms: (1) Workers' self-management form which could be seen in Yugoslavia, Peru and Algeria. Producers' cooperatives was an important form of self-management which included workers, owners and managers of the firm managed by a board and management staff either elected or appointed by them (Sahu 1985: 12). (2) The second form was participation of workers' representatives in management organs, implying unity of different class interests and motivating endeavours for cooperation, instances of which could be found in Argentina, Egypt, Italy, Norway and Tanzania. (3) The third form was works councils and similar institutions which emphasized on harmony of interests on important issues. This form of participation of workers in managerial structures was found in Finland, Indonesia, Spain, Sri Lanka, Zambia, Belgium, France, Luxembourg, Netherlands, Britain, Ireland, Denmark and Belgium. (4) The participation through trade union action was the fourth form of workers inclusion in the management of industries which was practised, particularly, in Australia, Canada, United Kingdom, the United States and also in Japan where the tactics of collective bargaining provided an opportunity to workers for participation in management. Meanwhile, in the erstwhile United Soviet Socialist Republic and other Eastern European countries, the objective of enabling workers to participate in management was achieved by increasing the power of trade union committees of the firms. (5) The fifth participatory mechanism was the shop floor level which laid an emphasis on improving the working environment of workplaces as a work humanization programme. This form of workers' participation was adopted in the countries, like United States, Scandinavia, Britain and North America (Sahu 1985: 10-14).

In India, the process of participation could be said to have begun in the early phase of the twentieth century when the informal consultation with the trade union sought in the cotton textile mills in 1910, while in 1919, a works committee was set-up by the Tata Iron and Steel Company Limited which consisted of representatives from the management of the company and trade union. In 1920, the Ahmedabad Textile Industry and Union agreed to form a joint consultation council on the initiation of Mahatma Gandhi to settle industrial disputes, which, could not prove to be effective. The Royal Commission on Labour in 1931 recommended for the formation of works committees. The period of 1932-7 was marked by incidents of wage cuts, retrenchments and agitations of trade unions. The agitations by trade unions were mainly led under the guidance of communist philosophy and organizations. The consultative bodies, Indian National Labour Conference, 1942, Standing Labour Committees, 1942, Industrial Truce Resolution 1947, comprising members belonging to trade unions, industrial owners and government officials, were formed at the national level which aimed at achieving more harmonious industrial relation so as to gain higher productivity. In the late 1940s, some of the companies set-up joint committees for redressal of grievances of workers against the management of companies, while the Government of India enacted an important Act, the Industrial Disputes Act, 1947, which contained the provision for constituting works committees in industrial enterprises that had more than 100 employees. This Act turned out to be a major development in the direction of evolution of the trend of joint consultation. In the forthcoming years, particularly, in the five-year plans, a need of adopting a mechanism resolving the industrial disputes between workers and employers was stressed which paved the way for the emergence of a scope for the workers to participate in management of the industries that affected their life and destiny. In the 1980, the need of making legislative provisions for scheme of workers' participation in industrial management was seriously considered and advocated (Sahu 1985: 19-21).

WORKERS' MANAGEMENT IN KTL

Though KEU had started approaching the Maharashtra government as well as the central government to takeover the management of the company after the mid-1970s, the serious endeavours to takeover the company was made only after the closure of the KTL in 1985. The situation worsened when the company owners expressed their inability to restart it and no one was ready to buy and run it.

The KTL was declared a sick industry under the provisions of the SICA, 1987, and on the basis of the provisions of this Act, the KEU approached Supreme Court in the 1987 with a proposal to takeover, revive and manage the operation of KTL. The Apex Court, after realizing the substance in the proposal, referred this case to the BIFR which was a newly-constituted body to examine the viability of the scheme. As the BIFR did not have many cases pending with it to dispose off, this case was given an early attention and a quick disposal. The Industrial Development Bank of India (IDBI) was appointed as the operating agency (OA) and was directed to submit its report on the viability of the scheme prepared by the KEU.

After submission of report by the IDBI, the BIFR took up this takeover proposal of the KEU with the parties concerned, such as, banks, financial institutions and the state and central governments to confirm and ascertain their commitments for the support in form of concessions and relief to be made available for the smooth operation of the company. The IDBI was asked to revise and make some amendments in its report which was complied by the bank. On the basis of the report prepared by the IDBI and the discussions held with other parties and institutions concerned, the BIFR prepared its own feasibility report and submitted it to the Supreme Court. Originally, the scheme proposed by the KEU for takeover of the sick company was the basis of the report prepared and submitted by the IDBI, and ultimately, sanctioned by the BIFR (Palande 1991: 6).

The main provisions in the scheme sanctioned by them were: (1) the industry would restart in about six months after the completion of required repair works which would incur approximately Rs 60 lakh; (2) the shares of the Kamanis and others of Rs 96 lakh to be transferred to the workers' cooperative at the reduced cost of Re 1 per share against the face value of Rs 10 per share; (3) the KTL to be managed by the board of directors consisting of professionally qualified or experienced persons and two representatives of the workers cooperative; (4) the workers' cooperative to raise an equity capital of Rs 70 lakh. The cooperative, with its membership of nearly 600, was directed to arrange this amount of capital from each of its members who were to contribute Rs 12,000 (each) consisting of Rs 2,000 from their provident fund account and Rs 10,000 by taking loans from urban cooperative banks; (5) the state government to provide an equal amount to augment the share capital after the workers' cooperative collected its share of contribution; (6) the scheme did not make any additional long-term loan from the financial institutions and banks as the requirement of margin money for working capital was to be met from the balance of funds to the extent of Rs 70 lakh (Palande 1991: 6).

The BIFR also assigned certain responsibilities to Bank of India, Canara Bank, Dena Bank, state government, central government, management and shareholders to ensure smooth operation of the industry (Palande 1991: 6). The workers made considerable sacrifices in the process of implementation of the scheme. As the company was officially not closed, the workers were entitled for salary and other wage privileges as per the provisions of the existing legislation related to industrial labour. The arrears that were calculated from December 1984 to August 1988 amounted to Rs 6 crore, exceeding the amount of liabilities of the company which was Rs 5 crore 47 lakh (Srinivas 1993: 90; Palande 1991: 3). Besides this, the scheme settled and approved by the BIFR demanded further sacrifices from the workers such as, the retrenchment of some of the workers, wage freeze for three years, the payment of wages restricted to 75 per cent of the wage amount in the first year of operation and 85 per cent from second year onwards, deferment of the annual increments for a period of two years, postponement of payment of dues of workers during the closure period until all other dues were cleared, linking certain salary/wages with certain production norms, liquidation of loans taken by workers for their contribution through profit-sharing mechanism, stoppage of overtime and ban on strikes, etc. (Palande 1991: 10).

After going through the exhaustive tribulations and the endorsement of the scheme by the Supreme Court on 19 September 1988, the workers' cooperative succeeded in taking over the KTL under the leadership of D. Thankappan in October 1988, under the provisions of the Sick Industry Companies (Special Provision) Act, 1987. After doing required repair works, the company was made operational in April 1989. While making efforts for revival of the KTL, workers had agreed to the provisions of the scheme prepared by the BIFR by which their privileges of arrears and increments in wages were curtailed. Thus, the takeover involved a lot of sacrifices by the workers. In the beginning, the workers and their leaders were overzealous and started the work of production with great enthusiasm and made profits for nearly two and half years. Later, manifold problems started occurring. The main problems were; the shortage of working capital due to dilly-dallying nature of fund provider banks and apathy of the BIFR and the state government. The situation aggravated in the post-1992 period due to the communal riots (as a consequence of Babri Masjid demolition in December 1992), and related problems, besides, the negative impact of the liberal import policy of the government.

In early 1997, the KTL, finally, ceased functioning rendering the workers jobless. Kamgar Ekta, a parallel union has come into existence since 1998. Since then no serious and sincere effort has been made to revive it either by the government institutions or any other agency, like promoters. The promoter, Kalpana Saroj & Associates (KSA), primarily, a developer in construction area, came forward to revive the dying industrial unit but indulged itself in dubious acts of manipulations and manoeuvring to appropriate the assets of the company giving way to dispute litigations involving court cases. The KEU, at present, is making efforts to get the dues and arrears of the workers and rehabilitate them.

EUPHORIA TO DESPAIR

The union of workers and cooperative had to confront a number of problems which was aggravated by the institutional discriminations manifested through inadequate state policies and affirmative endeavours as well as non-cooperative prejudicial attitude of financial institutions like various banks that were supposed to make available the requisite capital support to the KTL for its operation and sustenance under the managerial control of the workers cooperative. The state and its associated institutions showed keenness to help revive the sick industry and assist in its successful operation by making some provisions though enactment of legislations. Their support reflected more on paper than in practice. It would not be an exaggeration to say that this exhibits the classic character of the capitalist system.

Right from the process of takeover of the sick industry by the workers' cooperative to aspects of maintenance, operation and sustenance of the company and finally to secure their equitable arrears after the closure of the industrial unit in 1997, the workers' society had been facing a number of problems which could have been avoided or at least reduced to the comfortable degree by the sincere and favourable policies of state and their proper implementations.

What were the problems that the workers' cooperative faced as a result of which the management of the company by the workers started fizzling out, generating the atmosphere of disappointment, anger and frustration among the workers which resulted in their desertion from their parent union, the KEU, and join a new union, the Kamgar Ekta? Why did the experiment of the management of a sick industry by cooperatives of the working class fail? The answer probably lies in a critical examination of the internal and external factors such as attitude of workers after attaining the ownership of the company, the level of their cooperative culture and consciousness as well as their training and education, and the evaluation of the role of state policies, policies of associated banking institutions and their implementation.

It could be easily realized that the KEU had to face many obstacles before it took over the management of KTL in October 1988 which was due to the exploitative and repressive characteristic of the capitalist socio-political order. It has been observed over the period of centuries that capitalist system tries to create illusion of reforms and welfare of the marginalized sections with sole purpose of containing their outbursts and maintaining its hegemonic position. The story of the experiment of the workers' management of the sick industry, Kamani is no different. The company under the management of workers' society performed well and made profits during 1989-92 period. It was made possible despite the difficulties to successfully re-establish its position in the market after a gap of five years. The company had to face tough competition from the companies operating from Rajasthan. The latter had to pay low sales tax compared to that of KTL and also had an exemption of turnover tax which provided them an edge over the marketing position of the KTL. In the KTL problems started from 1992. The liberal import policies of government and communal riots at large scale crippled the production and market profits of the KTL. The shortage of working capital, lack of efficiency on the part of management and continuous losses faced by the company created a situation leading to its closure in March 1997 when the water and electricity supply to it was disconnected. After the closure of the company in the 1997, dissension came to surface and a separate union of workers, Kamgar Ekta, was formed by the dissident group of the KEU which was joined by many disappointed workers of the KEU. The angry and frustrated workers blamed their earlier leader, D. Thankappan, who had led them in difficult times, for the emergence of new problems in the company. One of the reasons of the formation of the Kamgar Ekta was said to be failure of promises made by the prospective promoter for better arrears and prospect for the workers.

The KTL was in deep trouble from 1995. A management consultant, appointed by the IDBI in August 1996 to assess the viability of the KTL had suggested that the company could be brought back into smooth operational mode by providing an additional amount of Rs 4 crore as working capital and an equal amount of capital investment for modernization of the industry. The consultant valued the surplus assets of KTL at Ballard Estate at a minimum of Rs 26 crore which, after paying tax dues and liabilities of creditor banks that was estimated Rs 10 crore 60 lakh as on 31 December 1996, would leave a comfortable reserve capital for stable operation and investment for modernization (CWM 1999: 13). The plan of selling out the Ballard Estate building could not be implemented because of the difference shown and delaying tactics adopted by the IDBI. However, the IDBI was instructed by the BIFR to honour the report prepared by the consultants.[5] When the plan for the sale of the Ballard Estate was making progress through multilateral discussions, the prices of real estate suddenly crashed as a result of which the party negotiating for the purchase of the building backed out. The attitude of the IDBI was negative in this regard as it did not believe the economic feasibility of the company if investment was made in its revival after the sale of the Ballard Estate building.[6]

Despite the favourable historic judgement of the Supreme Court, support of the financial institutions and the governments in initial phase, supportive mass media coverage, united and committed union membership, good ground in the market even entering the market after the gap of five years, this unique experiment met with an utter failure. The major factors responsible for the failure of this takeover and management experiment included, the attitude of the financial institutional agencies such as, BIFR, Appellate Authority of Industrial and Financial Reconstruction (AAIFR), IDBI,[7] other banking institutions as well as government machinery, the lack of diversification of the products, the lack of an efficient marketing executive, failure of the union to cope up in the changed situation, managerial difficulties, and the lack of development of the cooperative culture and understanding, and some sudden external factors. In the capitalist system of production many of the industrial units cease to operate and sustain due to market competition and only the big monopolist industries survive and maintain their hegemonic position.

In capitalist system of production an impression is created among the workers that the government institutions are meant to look after the interests of the workers and downtrodden. The state uses such tactics to hide its real interests of serving to augment and consolidate the capitalist system. This was evident in the case of KTL even during the phase of process of takeover of management by the workers as the BIFR had sanctioned the scheme after inserting some conditions that loss of wages and arrears of the workers that the latter were entitled to get according to the existing industrial legislation at that time. The fate of such experiments is also determined by the level of class consciousness and the intensity and pattern of mobilization (whether political or economic aspects given priority).[8]

MANIPULATION, LITIGATIONS AND STRUGGLE OF THE KEU

The management of the KTL was run by the workers' cooperative society, the KTL and Kamgar Audyogic Utpadak Sahkari Society Limited. For nearly three years, the company made satisfactory progress and thereafter it started facing crises of various kinds and incurring losses. During the 1994-5, G.D. Apte Consultancy Services Private Limited was appointed to carry out the Techno-Economic Viability (TEVS). On the basis of the report prepared by the consultancy, the BIFR declared that the scheme (of takeover of the KTL by the workers) sanctioned on 6 September 1988 had failed and the board directed the IDBI (OA) to conduct TEVS and submit a long-term revival plan. In May 2000, the BIFR instructed the IDBI to advertise for sale of the company. The IDBI put out advertisements for takeover of the KTL. The Kalpana Saroj & Associate (KSA) group applied but its proposal was not found acceptable, and therefore, this promoter group was asked to resubmit a revised plan. In August 2003, the KEU filed its objections to the proposals submitted by promoters as they were not in favour of workers. In March 2004, the KSA group was given clear control of the management of KTL appointing its chairperson, Kalpana Saroj as the president of the company and employees of KSA as officers of the company. In August 2004, the KSA fraudulently entered into agreements for sale of property belonging to the KTL, though the promoter group was not authorized to do to that. An advance cheque of Rs 50 lakh was issued in the name of M/s Kalpana Saroj and Associates and not in the favour of the KTL. The KEU, after getting this information by end of October 2006, brought it to the notice of the AAIFR. The Kamgar Ekta which was not recognized by the industrial court supported the promoter, KSA.

The KEU had been struggling against the manipulative promoter group and had been raising objections by making several representations in the High Court, Mumbai as well as to various authorities concerned. The KEU lost the case in the court of AAIFR, and thereafter, it has approached the Bombay High Court. The division bench consisting of the chief justice of Bombay High Court, Swatantrakumar and another judge heard the case on 6 February 2008 and stayed the sale of the Bangalore land and Mumbai property of KTL until the disposal of the case/next hearing. Later hearings were held on 15 February 2008 and 18 March 2008. However, the matter remains to be settled finally. The KEU is opposing the unjust method of selling out the real estate assets of KTL which had the value much higher than that what the KSA trying to sell out. And also the union is making its all out efforts to safeguard and secure the interest, wages and arrears of the workers.

CHALLENGES AND WAY-OUT

The takeover of the management of KTL in 1988 was a unique experiment of its kind in annals of the history of the trade union movement in India which, unfortunately, failed due to apathy of the bourgeois democratic social system. The KTL which was established in 1959, grew prosperous and made substantial profits for over a decade. After the death of its founder, Ramajibhai H. Kamani in 1972, the company started petering out as a consequence of, mainly, the family feuds among the Kamani brothers, mismanagement and appropriation of the company's profits by the feuding employers leading, finally, to its complete closure in 1985, however, unofficially, when the supply of water and electricity to it was cut off. The workers union, the KEU, after undergoing the arduous task of the process of takeover of the industry under the provisions of the Sick Industry (Special Provisions) Act, 1987, succeeded in its historic mission of taking over the management of KTL and after a necessary repair works started its operation in April 1989.

The company made satisfactory progress under the management of the workers' society, but after nearly three years, it started confronting a number of internal and external problems. The main causes among them were the lack of sufficient working capital, the institutional discrimination, non-cooperative and prejudicial attitude of the financial institutions like banks that were to support the industry by making required finance available which was aggravated by the sudden outbreak of the communal riots between the Hindu and Muslim communities in December 1992, after the demolition of the Babri Masjid by the Hindu religious fundamentalists, which intermittently continued till March 1993 involving not only in Mumbai, but in many parts of the country, thus, affecting the prospect of trade and commerce very badly. The effort to revive the company and keep it operational began showing signs of its failure in 1995 by making continuous losses resulting, ultimately, in the closure of the company when the water and power supply to it was disconnected in 1997. However, this time too, declaration of closure of the company was officially not made.

No sincere and serious effort was made to bring the company back into life either by any state agency or private promoter. A private promoter, the Kalpana Saroj & Associates, primarily, a developer in the area of construction work, came forward with the declared objective to revive the company, contrary to working towards its official aims, it began indulging in manipulations and manoeuvring activities to appropriate the real assets of KTL even on the expense of the interests of the workers in tacit connivance (it is widely believed by the members of the KEU) with some officials concerned. The KEU has been struggling against such manipulations to secure the arrears of its members and, if possible, help in revival and re-opening of the company (however, the union also does not appear to be too optimistic on this issue). The possibility of revival and re-starting of the company seems to be a distant possibility due to discriminatory and prejudice of the state and its associated financial institutions. The conditions of the institutional constraints, the lack of development of the cooperative culture and class consciousness among the workers, the lack of proper training and education among them, including the lack of modernization and the non-cooperative attitude of the banking institutions and their dilly-dallying behaviour are main causes of the failure of this experiment of the management of a sick industry by the workers' cooperative.

Is the option of the management of a sick industry by the workers cooperative viable in a capitalist system? The analysis of the Kamani experiments suggests that such experiments are bound to fail in bourgeois democratic system unless the state and its related institutions take sincere and active interest in making it a success by ensuring availability of the required infrastructural inputs and also directing its financial institutions to cooperate, or until working class has its own resources, like banking agencies to depend on. The sick industries can be revived and managed successfully only if state is committed to the cause of the worker class along the lines of socialist principles and the workers are adequately indoctrinated and trained in the cooperative culture as well as takeover and management of sick industries.

The excessive emphasis on the economic gains by the trade unions, generally, comprising the industrial workers, ignoring the issues and strategic benefits of the mobilizations of labourers engaged in informal unorganized sector and contradictions of various kinds impeding the prospect of development of class conscious working class, besides the factors of globalization and liberal economic policies which almost destroyed the possibility of the emergence of an effective and capable trade unions that led to weakening of the trade union movement in India. The unions, in general, could have moved to the higher stage of launching a concrete and broad-based people's oriented movement which could not happen due to self-limiting nature of the trade union movement which focused merely on the economic interest of the workers. The absence of radical ideology, the use of union power by the workers for personal gains, frequent call for strikes, association and dependence of unions on political parties, including the manipulative tactical use of workers in the name of participative management rendered the trade union movement weak. Interests of workers, like employment, job security, expansion of the public sector and trade union rights, have suffered. The process of globalization has further weakened it rather rendered it almost irrelevant due to rapid shrinking of the public sector and emergence of the private sector. The strategy of privatization and disinvestments has been adopted on the basis of the argument that the state-controlled industries often make huge losses which consume huge money for its sustenance. The internal differences of working class, formation of caste-based associations, inability to match and cope up with the challenges of modern technologies and change in global economic process aggravate the situation. The changed scenario warrants a suitable and compatible strategic programme, redesigning the scope, structures, method of actions and the process of representation while dealing with the internal (lack of unity, focus on personal interest, affiliation to caste associations) and external factors (capitalist bureaucratic attitude, phase and pattern of globalization, privatization and liberalization, shifting of the industrial units to locations that are comparatively cheaper, expansion and mobility of transnational capital, increasing number of companies whose decision-making centres are out of reach for the trade unions) of the problems of the decline of trade unionism. The change in mode of industrial production and change in labour legislations have been demolishing the very foundation on which trade union had emerged and grown strong (Chetty 2004: 161-9).

The issues of the decreasing number of workers in the public sector due to the process of downsizing and retrenchment, technological changes which are capital-intensive, education, training and health, etc., are some major challenges that the trade union movement has to pay an attention to. The union may benefit by making cooperating arrangements with civil society to get some social supports, like medical aid, insurance, housing, etc., in addition to that, the unions have to extend its areas and reach the unorganized sectors so as to mobilize unorganized labourers by including their issues on agenda of the union which will prove to be beneficial in larger interest of working class in general, and working class in particular. The taking up of the issues concerning various other underprivileged sections, like, women in productive activities, developing managerial capability, instead of merely the leadership support, positive contribution to the development process, strategic alliance with other like-minded national and international organizations, including tie-up with human rights organizations will provide strength and a broader vision to the trade union movement.

NOTES

1. According to the Sick Industrial Companies (Special Provisions) Act, 1987, an industrial unit (registered for not less than five years) which at the end of any financial year has accumulated losses equal to or exceeding its entire net worth and also suffered cash losses in such financial years and the financial year immediately preceding such financial year is defined as a sick industry. Such industries reaches a stage when it is overburdened with debt and do not have sufficient funds to meet its obligations. Symptoms, such as, lower capital turnover, continuing lapse in cash credit, higher returning of bills and cheques deposited by the borrowers, persistent irregularities in accounts, frequent dishonouring of cheques, failure to submit stock and control statement, abnormal inventory, depletion of inventory, low stock turnover, failure to pay dues in time, diversion of funds from productive assets, wide profit fluctuation and too heavy overhead expenses, are some of the major indications for the industries becoming sick. Besides these, low rate of production, sales and profits, high degree of liquidity constraints, labour unrest, high rate of rejection of goods, execution of law suits against the unit, losing grip of the market, too much diversification and expansion within a short span of time, frequent changes in management, etc., are also the signs of sickness of an industry.

The internal causes of industrial sickness are fast changing technology, inadequate technical knowledge, lack of proper management, unplanned extension, diversion of funds for acquiring the luxurious assets, low turnover, faulty purchase and sales policy, lack of harmony with the labour force, uneconomic size of the unit, lack of benefit analysis, lack of innovative approach, lack of overall growing low capacity utilization, lack of control system, low knowledge of market, poor maintenance, unskilled labour, faulty demand forecasting policy, the failure to gain confidence of customer and defective system of internal audit, etc. The external causes comprise detrimental government policies, such as, industry-specific barriers that restrict the choice of capital, technology or labour use, administrative prices of input/output, sudden shift n tariff and indirect tax policies, etc. (Seth 1997: 12-19).

2. The problem was aggravated by the Hindu-Muslim communal riots in aftermath of the Babri Masjid demolition by the Hindu fundamentalists under the leadership of the Bharatiya Janata Party. The supply of raw material needed for the production and also marketing of products were badly affected due to the large scale-disruption of public life and other facilities, like transportation. (Interviews with Comrade Sreedharan, Secretary, KEU, KTL, 20 March 2008, Mumbai and also D. Thankappan, Working President, KEU, on 8 September 2007).
3. Interview with D. Thankappan on 8 September 2007.
4. Ibid.
5. Ibid., 14 February 1999.
6. Interview with K.V. George, general manager, IDBI, on 19 February 1999.
7. Appeal against BIFR's order dated 21 March 2006 in Case No. 218/87, Appeal Nos. 103/06, 125/06, 154/06 & 157/06 addressed to AAIFR (*KEU* vs *BIFR & Ors*); Appellate Authority for Industrial & Financial Reconstruction (AAIFR) (2006): New Delhi, Order No. 18906 dated 18.9.2006 on appeal numbers 103/2006, 154/2006 & 157/2006 (*KEU* vs *BIFR & Ors*); Board for Industrial and Financial Reconstruction (BIFR) (1988) Sanctioned Scheme: Kamani Tubes Limited: No. 218/1987, Kurla, 1988; Board for Industrial and Financial Reconstruction (2006) Case No. 218/87: Kamani Tubes Limited, Bench-1, Summary Records of the Proceedings of the Hearing Held on 21.3.2006 Before S/Shri Ravindra Gupta, Chairman and A.K. Goswami, Member, Reference No. 02/8/87-Bench-II, dated 31 March 2006; BIFR Corrigendum dated 16 October 2007 on Case No. 218/1987.
8. The workers of the KEU comprised various political leanings (leftist and rightist). They could not think beyond the boundary of economic gains, and therefore, could not develop the political consciousness and the consciousness of being 'class for itself'. No effort was made by the leadership to join with other established trade unions having a national

base (and character) and patronized by the party, such as, the CITU or AITUC, as a result of which no concerted endeavour was made to form an alliance with other trade unions and struggle in the interests of working class. The outstanding examples of successful management of industrial and commercial units by the workers in India are the Indian Coffee House Workers' Co-operative functioning in all major cities in India and the Dinesh Beedi Workers' Cooperative functioning in Kerala. These are being successfully managed by the class and politically conscious workers with support from leftist political parties.

REFERENCES

Alexander, K.C. (1972): *Participative Management: The Indian Experience* (New Delhi: Shri Ram Centre for Industrial Relations and Human Resources).

CWM (1999): *Potential for Workers Cooperatives as a Tool for Revival of Sick Industries: An Analytical Study of Kamani Tubes Limited and KMA Limited* (Monograph), New Delhi, Centre for Workers Management.

Chetty, Y. Narayana (2004): *Dynamics of Trade Unionism in India: Sociological Approach* (New Delhi: Anmol Publications).

Derrick, P. and J.F. Phipps (1969): *Co-Ownership, Co-Operation and Control: An Industrial Objective* (London: Longmans).

Dua, Aarti (1993): 'A Management Guru for the Workers', *The Hindu*, 19 October.

Dutta, Kanika (1993): 'A Break with Tradition', *Business Standard*, 6 January.

George, Jose (1984): *Politicisation of Agricultural Workers in Kerala*, (Calcutta: K.P. Bagchi & Company).

Gokak, A.V. (1998): *Industrial Sickness* (Delhi: B.R. Publishing Corporation, Division of BRPC (India) Limited).

Gopal, Vishnu (1984): *Industrial Democracy in India (A Sociological Study of Workers' Participation in Management)* (New Delhi: Chugh Publications).

Hyman, Jeff and Bob Mason (1995): *Managing Employee Involvement and Participation* (London: Sage).

Issac, T.M. Thomas, W. Richard, Franke and Pyaralal Raghavan (1998): *Democracy at Work in an Indian Industrial Cooperative: The Story of Kerala Dinesh Beedi* (Ithaca: ILR Press, An Imprint of Cornell University Press).

Jose, A.V. (2002) (ed.): *Organised Labour in the 21st Century* (Geneva: International Institute of Labour Studies).

Mannan, M.A. (1987): *Workers' Participation in Managerial Decision-Making (A Study in A Developing Country)* (New Delhi: Daya Publishing House).

Masilamani, S. (1993): 'Trade Unions on Defensive', *Sunday Observer*, 21 April.

Mirza, Masood A. (1982): *Workers Participation in Management in India and Abroad* (Aligarh: Printwell Publications).

Nandwani, Deepali and Anamika Rath (1991): 'No Longer a Workforce to Reckon With?', *Sunday Observer*, 16 February.

Narayan, Laxmi (1984): *Worker's Participation in Public Enterprises (A Macro and Micro-Level Survey and Report of a National Seminar)* (Bombay: Himalaya Publishing House).

NTUI (n.d.): *Worker Cooperatives: A Force Resisting Industrial Closure: A Case Study of Kamani Tubes Ltd. and KMA Ltd.* (New Delhi: New Trade Union Initiative).

Palande, P.S. (1991): *Revival of Kamani Tubes Limited (A Report)* (Pune: Indian School of Political Economy).

Panickar, G.K. (1974): *The Story of Kerala Dinesh Beedi: A Thrilling Experience* (Canannore: Kerala Dinesh Beedi).

Prasad, Ch. S. Durga (1995): *Workers' Participation in Management* (New Delhi: Discovery Publishing House).

Ramaswamy, E.A. (1992): 'Can Workers be Owners?', *Business India*, 30 March-12 April.

——— (1993): 'A Glimmer of Hope', *Business India*, 27 September-10 October.

——— (1998): 'Worker Cooperative in India—Lessons from Kamani', paper presented at the workshop held at the ICSSR, Vidyanagari, University of Mumbai, Mumbai, on 28 and 29 December on A Critical Analysis of Kamani Tubes Limited and KMA Limited.

Rao, Purnima and S.T. Sawant (eds.) (1993): *New Economic Policy: Problems and Alternatives* (New Delhi: Friedrich Ebert Stiftung).

Ratnam, C.S. Venkata (2006): *Industrial Relations* (New Delhi: Oxford University Press).

Rehman, M.M. (2007): *Operation of Welfare Fund for Beedi Workers in Madhya Pradesh: Profile, Problems and Prospects* (NODIA: V.V. Giri National Labour).

Seth, P.D. (1997): 'Revival of Sick Public Sector Undertakings and Board for Industrial and Financial Reconstruction: An Empirical Study' (an unpublished M. Phil. dissertation) (New Delhi: Indian Institute of Public Administration).

Singh, Kulbir (1990): 'Workers Participation: Welcome After Gound is Prepared', *The Hindu*, 26 September.

Thankappan, D. (1992): 'Against All Odds', *Business Standard*, 2 September, Calcutta.

Ratnam, Venkata, Gerd Batterwack and Pravin Sinha (eds.) (1994): *Labour and Unions in a Period of Transition* (New Delhi: Friedrich Ebert Stiftung).

Sahu, Bhabatosh (1985): *Dynamics of Participatory Management: Indian Experiences* (Bombay: Himalaya Publishing House).

Seabrook, Jeremy (1992): 'Kamani Tubes: A Hope for Workers', *NFS India*, 1 June.

Srinivas, B. (1993): *Worker Takeover in Industry: The Kamani Tubes Experiment* (New Delhi: Sage).

——— (1987): 'Deccan Textiles: A Case Study in Industrial Sickness' (an unpublished M. Phil. dissertation), Hyderabad, Department of Sociology and Anthropology, School of Social Sciences, University of Hyderabad.

Thomas, C.P. (1995): 'We Need a Uniform Floor Wage', *The Economic Times*, 15 August.

Varandani, Gursharan (n.d.): *Workers' Participation in Management: With Special Reference to India* (New Delhi: Deep and Deep).

Vanek, Jan (1972): *The Economics of Workers Management: A Yugoslav Case Study* (London: George Allen & Unwin Limited).

Virmani, B.R. (ed.) (1972): Workers' *Participation in Management (Proceedings of the Indo-German Seminar)*, Published by Administrative Staff College of India, Hyderabad and Embassy of Federal Republic of Germany, New Delhi.

INTERVIEWS

1. K.L. Bajaj, Secretary, Centre for Indian Trade Union, Maharashtra State Unit, Mumbai, 9 February 1999.
2. Y.V. Chavan, President, Lal Nishan Party, and Sarva Shramik Sangh, Mumbai, 12 February 1999
3. G.V. Chitnis, President, All India Trade Union Congress, Maharashtra State Unit, Mumbai, 11 February 1999.
4. Govind D. Karatmol, General Secretary, Kamgar Audyogik Utpadak Sahakari Society, KTL, 17 February 1999.
5. P.R., Krishanan, Secretary, CITU, Maharashtra, State Unit, 14 February 1999.
6. Sudhakar Nalawade, General Secretary, KEU, Mumbai, 10 February 1999.
7. V. Shreedharan, Secretary, Kamani Employees Union (Representative of Kamani Tubes Limited), Mumbai, 8 September 2007 & 20 March 2008.
8. B.S. Survashe, Vice-President, Kamgar Ekta, Kamani Tubes Limited, 17 February 1999.
9. Hema Thakur, Deputy General Manager, IDBI, 24 February 1999.
10. D. Thankappan, Director, CWM, Delhi, and Working President of KEU, Mumbai, 14 February 1999 & 8 September 2007.

CHAPTER 15

Handloom Weavers' Struggles in the Context of Liberalization

K. SRINIVASULU

The handloom sector is the largest employer in India after agriculture, with around 16 million weavers estimated to be employed in this sector. Andhra Pradesh, after Tamil Nadu, has the second largest concentration of handlooms in the country. There are around 25 lakh weavers employed on 5.35 lakh handlooms in the state.

Recurrent crises, experienced since the 1980s, have brought about a perceptible decline in this sector. Though rise of input prices and intense competition from the powerloom sector were the immediate factors contributing to the crisis, the lackadaisical governmental response and the absence of proper implementation of policy safeguards meant for the protection of the handloom sector also weakened the sector and made it vulnerable. The liberalization process, with its rhetoric of market efficiency, competitiveness and viability as the criteria to judge the relevance of a sector of economy and community livelihoods and collective skills, has only underscored the changed role of the state in relation to traditional occupations and communities. The weak policy support to traditional occupational communities, in fact, perceptible withdrawal of state support to the socially and economically vulnerable people, has to be seen in the context of economic reforms and liberalization of economy. The result of this is the erosion of livelihoods and employment, decline of wages and increasing insecurity among the weavers. The number of suicides and starvation deaths among the weavers since the late 1980s is an indication of the intensity of the crisis.

In the context of the macro policy changes mentioned above, the grassroot mobilization and organization of the weaver community in Andhra Pradesh has to be analysed as a response to this crisis. It is important to note that it is because of the failure of the organized

Left to respond to the crisis, the mobilization largely took a spontaneous form and depended on local resources. The major achievement of these struggles lies in their successful dissemination of information and analysis of the impact of policy changes on the working population. This was achieved through the Telugu periodical *Netanna* (weaver) and through regular conferences and classes conducted with the help of civil society organizations and non-party, independent intellectuals. When the movement expanded and lasted, the political parties entered the scene and expressed their solidarity with the agitating weavers. Given these dynamics, this experiment assumes significance and deserves to be understood as an important aspect of the working class struggles in post-liberalization India.

This paper examines the policy, context and factors responsible for the crisis in the handloom sector. This highlights the historical significance of the handloom sector in the anti-colonial struggle as the symbol of Swadeshi movement and the experiences of its severe crises in the post-Independence period, in terms of employment. Given the continual significance, huge presence of workforce and the actual or potential value generation in this sector, its place in the political economy of India cannot be overlooked.

First, we examine the changes in the handloom industry after Independence and especially in the post-Green Revolution period. Then, the impact of policy changes related to the textile industry in general, and the handloom sector in particular is analysed. Afterwards this study deals with the specific policy initiatives visualized and sought to be implemented as part of the liberalization process to restructure the textile industry and, as part of this, the handloom sector. Finally, we analyse the weavers' grassroot mobilization against the crisis.

ORGANIZATIONAL STRUCTURE

The state of the handloom sector has to be seen in the overall perspective of the modernist development visualized and sought to be translated into reality by the political and policy elite in the post-Independence period. A significant step in this direction, especially in relation to the rural economy and life in the countryside, is the Green Revolution. It is fairly well-documented that the acceleration of the process of modernization and commercialization of agrarian economy, following the Green Revolution, has its drastic impact on rural farming and artisanal and other traditional occupational communities. The decline in and erosion of livelihood patterns of certain traditional occupation groups such as the traditional potter, blacksmith, etc., have been quite drastic. It is perhaps only the handloom weavers who have shown a greater degree of tenacity at survival through restructuring of the sector spatially and internally.

Within this broad socio-economic context, the handloom sector has undergone significant changes in the spheres of production, technology and marketing since the late 1960s in response to (besides the agrarian transformation induced by the green revolution) the changes in textile production and marketing, though with regional variations. This has its impact on the socio-economic conditions of the weaver communities and in shaping their survival responses.

The factor that contributed significantly to this change is the phenomenal growth of the powerlooms, which recorded an unprecedented increase from 1.5 lakh in 1963 to 3.09 lakh in 1975. The direct impact of the powerloom growth on handlooms can be gauged from the assessment of the high-powered committee of the Planning Commission, headed by Shivaraman (GoI 1974), according to which the addition of one powerloom resulted in displacement of six handlooms. The impact of the proliferation of powerlooms can clearly be seen in the gradual and visible displacement of the weavers, decline of their economic well-being and loss of their independence in the production process.

To appreciate the above processes it may be useful to examine the changes in the organizational structure and relations of production in the handloom industry. On the basis of this the handloom industry can be divided into (1) independent weaver sector, (2) cooperative weaver sector, and (3) master-weaver sector.

Independent Weaver Sector

Independent weavers are those who produce cloth on their own, i.e. they own the instruments of production, purchase raw materials from the market and make fabric with family labour and sell the products in the local market or to traders.

With the proliferation of powerlooms since the 1960s and low-priced powerloom products penetrating the market, especially in the countryside, handloom weavers had to face stiff competition. Further, the rising prices of cotton hank yarn and dyes made the handloom weavers vulnerable. The most affected were independent weavers and small master-weavers-cum-traders owning few looms and employing wage labourers. The displacement of independent weavers led to the growth of major urban powerloom and handloom centres under master-weavers: men weavers migrated there and women weavers shifted their job to beedi-making. In the urban areas, where alternative employment opportunities were relatively better, young weavers started to take up jobs like that of shop assistants, construction work, auto rickshaw driving, etc., as the skilled handloom weaving was found to be less attractive due to low wages and insecurity.

Cooperative Weaver Sector

The handloom cooperatives were a major segment accounting for a large proportion of weavers, next to the master-weaver segment. The cooperative movement, which was initiated with the objective of protecting the weavers from the dominant intermediaries like master-weavers and traders, made big achievements in certain states like Andhra Pradesh. The rise of vested interests and increased use of the handloom cooperatives as channels for political ascendancy by the community elite led to drifting of cooperatives away from their intended purpose. Increased political and governmental interference, development of bureaucratic tendencies and corruption hindered their autonomous functioning. Further, the ineffectiveness of the cooperatives in ensuring regular supply of raw materials and the inordinate delay in payment of wages, forced the average weaver to shift to the master-weaver system. Because of this, a number of cooperatives, once successful, were rendered non-functional. Bogus cooperatives, floated by influential master-weavers, traders and local politicians (as well as powerloom owners) to corner the subsidies and marketing facilities extended by the government and state apex handloom cooperative body, had restricted/denied genuine co-operatives' access to governmental support and robbed them of their due share. This has significantly contributed to the credibility crisis of the cooperative movement.

Master-Weaver Sector

The third system of production is the master-weaver system. The master-weaver system became well-entrenched and formidable over a period. With the marginalization of weavers' cooperatives and the decline of independent weavers, this system became dominant, accounting for three-fourths of the total handloom production in the state.

In this system, the master-weaver-cum-entrepreneur used to employ wage labour to produce cloth. The cloth thus produced was either directly marketed by him or supplied to traders. It had two kinds of practices, on the basis of conditions of work and nature and extent of dependence: put-out system and *kharkhana* system.

In the put-out system, the weaver used to get raw materials to his house, which was both his living and working place, prepared warp and spun cloth on his own loom as per the master weaver's specifications. All members of the weaver's family were involved in production process—with the adult members engaged in weaving and the aged and children helping in the preparation of accessories. Here the wages were paid per piece, in addition to a payment for the preparation of warp, bobbins and other accessories. Though this practice was generally on the decline, it could still be found in handloom centres like Pochampally (in Nalgonda) and Gadwal (in Mahabubnagar), where specialized tie and dye and *jarri* varieties are produced. For all practical purposes, the weaver here is a wage-labourer, yet his ownership of the loom and possibility of demonstrating his workmanship give him a sense of satisfaction and perceived independence.

In the *kharkhana* system, weavers worked on the looms provided by master-weavers under one roof. This system was prevalent in the handloom centres where migrant weavers were dominant like Mangalagiri in Guntur and Koyalagudem in Nalgonda in Andhra Pradesh. These homeless and loomless migrant weavers worked for the master weavers in their worksheds, each accommodating a dozen or so pitlooms. They lived in one-room tenements rented out by the latter. With the decline of independent weavers and the marginalization of the cooperative sector, the master-weaver sector acquired a major share in handloom production.

1985 TEXTILE POLICY AND CHANGES

The 1985 textile policy introduced by the government of Rajiv Gandhi has to be appreciated against this background. It made a decisive departure from the earlier policy regime by visualizing an entirely different textile scenario. While the earlier policy framework viewed the textile industry in terms of its employment potential, and therefore, accorded a prime place to handlooms *vis-à-vis* the other two sectors (i.e. powerlooms and mills), the 1985 policy marked a departure from this by emphasizing market-led productivity and efficiency as the chief objectives.

In accordance with the shift of emphasis from employment to productivity, the 1985 policy announced a shift from a sectoral view (the three sectors being handlooms, powerlooms and mills) to a process view (the important processes being spinning, weaving and product processing) of the textile industry. Considering, without much justification, the sectoral orientation of the textile industry as the leading cause of the 'structural rigidities' in the industry, in its place, it suggested prioritization of processes for a 'comprehensive view' of the industry, and thereby, to eliminate its rigidities. Accordingly, it promised 'fuller flexibility in the use of various fibres' and 'pragmatic policies regarding creation or contraction of capabilities by units to increase competition and promote healthy growth' (GoI 1985: 1-2).

Taking a view of textile industry based on the processes involved, it must be noted, by overlooking the specificities of each of the sectors in terms of raw materials and capital, labour conditions, production and marketing structure and consumer demand pattern, the relative strengths/weaknesses or advantages/disadvantages of the different sectors, the policy sought to treat all the sectors to be equal in their ability to compete in the market. Thus, by emphasizing productivity as the main objective and insisting on the process view of the industry, the 1985 policy sought to create a level playing field for all the three: handlooms, powerlooms and mills. This policy perspective, needless to say, was clearly to the disadvantage of the handloom sector as the crisis in the late 1980s and early 1990s amply demonstrated.

HANDLOOM (RESERVATION OF ARTICLES FOR PRODUCTION) ACT, 1985

In spite of changes, the 1985 policy continued to promise support to handlooms. A major move in this direction was the Handloom (Reservation of Articles for Production) Act, 1985, which reserved 22 varieties of articles for exclusive production in the handloom sector. Though it was promised that this Act 'shall be strictly enforced and the machinery for doing so shall be suitably strengthened' (GoI

1985: 4), it became clear soon that whatever limited legal safeguards the handloom weavers were promised had been diluted and rendered ineffective.

Challenged by the powerful powerloom and mill lobbies, the reservation Act remained subjudice for eight years until the Supreme Court upheld it in 1993. With whatever limited legal restrictions that were there rendered inoperative, the aggressive powerlooms proliferated, encroaching on handlooms' territory. It is important to note that subsequently, instead of creating the necessary institutional mechanism to implement the Act as the high-powered committee headed by Abid Hussain had also recommended, the government issued an order reducing the reserved items from 22 to mere 11.

HANK YARN OBLIGATION

The Hank Yarn Obligation, another protection measure provided by the Act, required the spinning mills to process 50 per cent of their production in hank form to meet the requirements of handlooms. However, making use of various exemptions, the mills never actually met the target. In fact, 'the actual deliveries of hank yarn generally averaged about 25 per cent of the total yarn output during the last decades'. Instead, the obligation was transferred to the public sector—the National Textiles Corporation (NTC) and the state government—and cooperative mills (World Bank 1999: 10-34).

If the 1985 policy could be seen as an important move towards the liberalization of the textile industry, then the macroeconomic reforms initiated in 1991 pushed it further. The most important and immediate consequence of this was the relaxation of export of yarn and dyes. As a result of trade liberalization, there was a sudden increase in export of yarn and hank yarn, especially in the counts of 1920s and 1940s used by a majority of handloom weavers (Srinivasulu 1996).

Critical to the crisis in the handloom industry was the rise in the prices of yarn and dyes. It is important to note that the Abid Hussain Committee, while reviewing the 1985 policy, emphasized the 'high and fluctuating prices of yarn' imposing great hardship on handloom weavers, especially on account of the violation of the Hank Yarn Obligation, which required spinning mills to produce 50 per cent of their output in hank yarn form (GoI 1990: 11).

Trade liberalization further compounded the problem by allowing exports. In 1991, as the experience of the weavers in Andhra Pradesh showed, with the master weavers disinclined to continue production, the weavers, finding themselves out of work, were pushed into starvation and suicides.

As a response to this crisis, government responded with two specific schemes: Mill Gate Price Scheme (MGPS) and Hank Yarn Price Subsidy Scheme (HYPSS). Though the per annum requirement of the hank yarn was assessed to be around 460-80 million kilos, the hank yarn target under MGPS was just 10 million kilos and under the HYPSS 20 million kilos (with a subsidy of Rs 15 per kilo) for weavers in the cooperative sector.

If the above schemes were inadequate to address the magnitude of the problem, then the introduction of the 'Loom to the Loomless Weavers' scheme in the midst of the crisis showed the callousness of the governmental response. This scheme, launched with a budget of Rs 523.20 crore (with one-fourth as subsidy component) and phased over three years from 1993-4, targeted distribution of 1.09 lakh looms per year (GoI 2005: 23-44). When the real problem facing the weavers was the unpredictable rise of hank yarn prices, it was shocking to note that the government came out with this scheme and allocated a whopping Rs 523.20 crore to it as against a mere Rs 30 crore to HYPSS. Further, when there were only weaverless looms on the ground, an imagined 'loomless' weaver was accorded priority.

As a matter of fact, the loomlessness and loom idleness are two aspects of the displacement and marginalization of handloom weavers: when a weaver gets displaced from work, he leaves his native village, he would become loomless and his loom would become idle. The migrant weaver working on a loom provided by the master weaver, in fact, does not need a loom as much as he needs yarn at a reasonable price to continue to be employed. This basic fact, which should be in the knowledge of the policy makers, has been ignored.

LIBERALIZATION AND THE SATYAM COMMITTEE REPORT

The National Textile Policy (2000) proposed a major shift for the textile industry comprising handlooms, powerlooms and mills. The need for a new textile policy was necessitated by the fact that the last policy came into effect a decade and a half back and a lot of changes had occurred since then. Significant among the policy changes were the reforms initiated in the Indian economy and the new world trade regime at the behest of the World Trade Organization (WTO). A textile policy suitable to meet the challenges and requirements of the changed environment was stated to be the need of the hour. In this section we examine the implications of this policy shift for handlooms.

What was crucial to the formulation of the 2000 textile policy was the report of the Satyam Committee, constituted by the Government of India in July 1998 specifically to make recommendations for this purpose. This confidential report visualized an entirely different scenario for the textile industry. Thus, the recommendations of the committee had far-reaching consequences for the handloom sector.

The principal objective of the policy was one of coping with competition in the international market. The handloom weavers, it stated, need market. While suggesting the government to support the weavers in this by devising special schemes, the committee did not hesitate to recommend the scrapping of the Reservation Act and Hank Yarn Obligation, which despite their ineffective implementation had been two crucial legal measures meant to protect the interests of handloom weavers.

Crucial to the understanding of the recommendations of the Satyam Committee pertaining to the handloom sector was the classification of handloom weavers. The panel sought to dismantle the categorization of weavers on the basis of organization—cooperative, master weaver and independent weaver—and differentiate them into three tiers on the basis of the 'quality' of cloth produced by them. In the first tier were grouped the weavers 'producing unique, exclusive, high value added items'; in the second tier were the producers of 'medium priced fabrics and made up articles from not-so-fine counts of yarn', and in the third tier were those producing 'plains and low-cost textile items'.

There is no evidence to believe that the committee made any attempt to justify why it had chosen to view the handloom industry in terms of product quality as against the systems of production. Nor had there been any attempt to estimate the proportion of weavers in each tier either in terms of production of fabric or the volume of employment. On the contrary, it was simply assumed that the third tier comprised the bulk of weavers producing coarse fabric and, by implication, the less skilled lot of the handloom weavers!

Thus, the most significant of the recommendations of the committee was to shift the weavers of the third tier to other tiers of handlooms, powerlooms and other occupations. For the 'least painful conversion', the first tier of powerloom and handloom sectors was identified as 'alternative avenues of livelihood'. The government was recommended to take steps in this direction by providing the weavers with semi-automatic looms and requisite training.

The poor and inadequate database on handlooms, which the committee acknowledged, had not deterred it from making far-reaching recommendations. Such a callous exercise, it was rightly argued, would prove to be disastrous to the vulnerable weavers who belong predominantly to the backward classes, Dalit, tribal and minority communities. For, the assumption was that not only were the weavers in the third tier not skilled, but also the cloth produced by them had no demand!

The issue that report clearly failed to address was the crisis in the handloom sector.[1] As suggested earlier, the handloom sector experienced severe crises in the post-Independence period, each leading to further marginalization and displacement of the weavers as well as their indebtedness. This caused starvation deaths and suicides. This was largely due to the liberalization process initiated by the 1985 Textile Policy and the structural adjustment programme taken up in 1991. The process of marginalization of the once fairly well-to-do handloom weaver community, which was slower earlier, had been hastened since the mid-1980s. At the root of the crisis was the sudden and unpredictable rise in hank yarn prices caused by the increase in exports. The failure or rather reluctance of the committee to note this significant macroeconomic policy shift obviously led to its failure to diagnose the nature and causes of the handloom weavers' crisis.

The major thrust of the government's neoliberal reforms has been on orienting the handloom sector to the globalization process as a principal strategy for its survival.[2] What was lost in the process was the strength of the handloom sector, which lies in the acceptance of and demand for its products in the local market. The specificity and speciality of handloom products have largely been determined by the local needs, governed by traditions and customs. The community skills and techniques involved in different stages of production were historically evolved and have been the property of the community, owned and imparted communally. For this reason, handloom production is characterized by its region-specific diversity. Thus, it cannot be understood only in terms of abstract demand and supply principle of the market.

The 'ability to commercially produce the goods in small volumes, quick switchover to new designs and creation of exquisite designs which cannot be made on the powerlooms' were seen by Mira Seth Committee as the strength of handlooms. For this reason, this committee recommended an export-led strategy for the sector's survival. When the strength of handlooms lies in their region-specific skills and designs, local initiative and product diversity, the path of development the pro-reform policy elite supports only leads to homogenization of handloom production as its future is oriented to the elite domestic and export market. Needless to say, the chief characteristic of globalization is centralization of decision-making and concentration of the conditions of production. When geared predominantly to the global market, due to the latter's extremely fickle nature and advertisement-induced behaviour, handloom production would not only go (has in fact increasingly gone) into the control of exporters (leading to further decline of the cooperative and even master weavers' initiative), but also prove to be suicidal to the weaver community. At the most a small section of the master weaver/trader segment may survive, perhaps may even prosper. With the World Trade Organization regime coming into full effect and the whatever limited protections to the handloom weavers as also to other artisanal communities phased out, they have been facing unrestricted competition from powerful players in the international market.

The illusion of export-oriented development would not only push millions of already impoverished weavers into further misery and destitution, but also transform handlooms, once the symbol of swadeshi, self-reliance and self-identity into *objet d'art* to be preserved in museums of national heritage and culture.

WEAVERS' STRUGGLES

In the last couple of decades the handloom sector has seen periodic crises, which are, in an immediate sense, a consequence of the unpredictable and sharp rise in prices of cotton yarn and chemical dyes. As analysed above, these crises are the result of the specific policies related to the handloom sector and policy processes initiated and pursued as part of the neoliberal economic reforms. Needless to say, the most visible victims of these policies are those sections of society which are disorganized and whose community support base is weak. The plight of handloom weavers is illustrative of the grim prospects for vulnerable communities in our society in the context of economic liberalization.

The handloom sector crisis has been endemic but manifested in phases in the 1980s and 1990s. The handloom weavers' movement in Andhra Pradesh since the 1980s has to be seen against this backdrop. Before we go into the dynamics of this movement, it is necessary to note that the handloom sector in the post-Independence period had not seen a strong and sustained movement and leadership except for issue-based struggles. Even when such a possibility emerged, the leadership came from the dominant party system and when the struggle sprang up from the community it was co-opted by the parties. The fragmentation of the weavers' communities had been such that in spite of being the victims of the greed of master weavers, traders and moneylenders and the apathy of the state, the weavers have remained mute spectators to the crisis they are in. Even when they had undertaken certain forms of collective action, sporadically and locally, the dominant interests in the handloom sector had broken their struggle.

It is pertinent to note that the Left, with its preoccupation with the working class in the organized sector, could not or rather did not make any serious attempt to influence and organize this significant traditional artisanal communities. Therefore, their weavers' fronts have remained mere showpieces. The crises in the handloom industry, springing up from the neo-liberal polices of the government, provide an opportunity to the political forces that claim to be fighting against the anti-people policies. For, this is the terrain where the struggles ought to be conducted.

It is against this background of the failure of the Left to articulate and give a politico-organizational expression to the anxieties of this sector that the spontaneous articulation from within the community of their own aspirations has to be understood.

The crisis in the handloom centres in coastal Andhra, like Chirala (in Prakasham district), Mangalagiri (in Guntur), led to a spate of starvation deaths and suicides in 1988. The crisis was the immediate fallout of cotton export, which was allowed in the face of a farm sector crisis and suicides by cotton farmers. As a result of exports, local production of cotton yarn was affected, leading to a hike in yarn prices. The master weavers, unable to meet the rising cost, especially in the absence of a corresponding rise in prices of their products, reduced and even stopped production on their looms. The conditions in the cooperative sector were no different. With the loss of employment and nothing to fall back upon, the vulnerable weavers resorted to the extreme step of taking away their lives.

This prompted the youth in these handloom centres to respond. With the traditional weavers' organizations affiliated to different political parties including the Left not rising up to the challenge, the youth from weaver families initiated collective protest actions. Chirala stands out as a leading example in this mobilization. The credit for this goes to Macharla Mohan Rao. Using his position and popularity as the sarpanch of local gram panchayat, he took a lead in mobilizing the weavers, especially the youth. The issues that were highlighted in this struggle, like control of yarn prices, supply of yarn at reasonable prices, lifting of stocks piled up with the master weavers, etc., being within the experience of different strata of weavers and master weavers, stirred up enthusiastic response. The methods of struggle like sitting on hunger strikes, *bandhs*, mass protests at the *mandal* revenue offices and collectorate, *rasta rokos* and *rail rokos* forged a new sense of identity and agency to the otherwise quiet weavers. This struggle attracted governmental response only in a contingent manner.

In this phase, the weavers were not only able to rally the different strata of handloom industry, but also gained popular sympathy and support from civil society organizations. The story of Chirala weavers' struggle in fact encouraged young weavers in other areas. Out of this experience emerged an autonomous weavers' organization, named, Cheneta Karmika Samakya (Handloom Weavers' Federation). It was visualized as a federation of weavers' organizations across the state. This initiative grew in stature in subsequent years and emerged as a state-level organization.

In this history, the handloom crisis of 1991, within months of the presentation of the 1991-2 Budget, as a direct consequence of the increase in the prices of 40-60-80 counts yarn from Rs 45 to 115 per bundle of 4.5 kg., occupies an important place. Finding it unprofitable to continue production due to the price increase, master weavers discontinued production, thus throwing workers out of employment and pushing them into starvation, disease and death. Within a span of three months, between September and November 1991, there were around 110 starvation deaths and suicides. The handloom centres of Mangalagiri and Battiprolu in Guntur district led the list with 40 deaths, followed by Epurupalem and Chirala in Prakasham district with 28 deaths. Throwing the principle of accountability to winds, the Congress state government kept denying that these deaths had anything to do with starvation, instead attributing them to old age and ill-health.

This gave rise to a militant struggle all along coastal Andhra. The connections established in the course of the earlier struggle and the work of Cheneta Karmika Samakya in the intervening period paved the way for a concerted campaign and common understanding of the handloom question and forms of struggle. Along with hunger strikes, *bandhs*, mass protests and *rasta rokos*, public rallies were also conducted. The fast-unto-death camps in different locations, despite their disruption by the police, became a major form of protest and attracted visits by prominent personalities, thereby gaining nationwide attention.

In this entire struggle, *rail roko* has a special place. As Chirala is located on the main railway line to Chennai, *rail roko* was found to be an effective mode of attracting national attention and communicating the seriousness of the issue. Thus, weavers in thousands thronged railway lines along the handloom clusters and stopped trains. This forced the government to respond to weavers' demands.

It is a testimony to the veracity of the struggle that Ashok Gehlot, the then Union minister for textiles, visited Chirala and interacted with the weavers to appreciate the ground realities. The struggle resulted in reduction of yarn prices, supply of yarn to weavers and procurement of cloth by the apex cooperative body.

Next important phase in this history is related to the Satyam Committee Report and the 2000 Textile Policy. As discussed in the previous section, the Satyam Committee Report made recommendations for the restructuring of the Indian textile industry with a view to tune it to global competition. The consequences were far-reaching for the handloom industry as well as weavers' livelihoods. This also led to mass protests in handloom centres. The major achievement of the *Cheneta Karmika Samakya* and its organ *Netanna* in the lead lies not only in the generation of a critical debate on the policy discourse implicit in the Satyam Committee Report, but also in advancing an alternative policy perspective on the issues raised by the report and endorsed by the official discourse. This struggle against the report in Andhra Pradesh, without exaggeration, demonstrated an unmatched ideological and political maturity in terms of policy critique.

The story of the handloom weavers' movement in Andhra Pradesh draws our attention to the fact that the struggle against imperialist globalization in our part of the world and the fight against anti-people policies that form part of the liberalization package, given the continuing relevance of the traditional community-based production systems and livelihood patterns, must articulate the anxieties of these communities. The history of working class struggles in post-liberalization India would be incomplete without a chapter on the struggles of the handloom weaver community in Andhra Pradesh.

NOTES

1. The anti-handloom dispensation of the policy makers becomes amply clear from the point of view that 'generally the handloom weavers remain tradition bound and are averse to change. . . . For more than five decades, the poor handloom weavers remained spoon-fed through Government Schemes and they continue to look up the Government for anything and everything'. This is the premise, though parades as a conclusion, which in fact, served as the basis of the Satyam Committee recommendations.
2. The earlier committee headed by Mira Seth, viewing globalization as inevitable, suggested, quite unmindful of the ground realities, policies and programmes like modernization of looms, establishment of Common Facility Centres with 'world standard' pre-loom and post-loom facilities, CAD and CCM, achievement of BIS-14000/ISO-9000 standards to tune this sector to the changing global market.

REFERENCES

GoI (1974): 'Report of the High Powered Study Team on the Problems of Handloom Industry', Ministry of Commerce, Government of India, July.

——— (1985): 'Statement on Textile Policy: June 1985', Ministry of Supply and Textiles, Department of Textiles, Government of India.

——— (1990): 'The Textile Industry in the 1990s: Restructuring with a Human Face', Report of the Committee to Review the Progress of Implementation of Textile Policy of June 1985, Government of India, January.

——— (2005): Compendium on Handloom Schemes: Compendium on Handloom Schemes, Development Commissioner for Handlooms, Ministry of Textiles, New Delhi.

Srinivasulu, K. (1996): '1985 Textile Policy and Handloom Industry: Policy, Promises and Performance', *Economic and Political Weekly*, 7 December.

World Bank (1999): 'India: Cotton and Textile Industries: Reforming to Compete', vol. II, Rural Development Sector Unit, South Asia Region, 14 January 1999, Report No. 18857–IN.

CHAPTER 16

Working Class Movements in Individual Sectors

P.N. SAMANT

The industrial history of India can be divided into three periods. The first is the pre-Independence period when the British rulers initiated industrialization in India, as a part of the industrial revolution. They promoted industries in India to get the raw materials for their own industrial development. The first industry in India was a textile mill, Bombay Spinning and Weaving Mills, which was started by Kawasji Nanabhai Davar in 1854 at Tardeo in Bombay (present Mumbai). Gradually, the number of textiles mills increased to 71 in 1896 with 78,455 workers.

Narayan Meghaji Lokhande who was working as a storekeeper in Madhav Mills started the first union of workers with the establishment of Bombay Mill Hands Association in 1884. The first demand of the workers' association was a weekly holiday on Sundays and it was granted on 10 June 1890. This was the first achievement of the working class movement in India. In 1881, the first Factories Act was enacted to safeguard the health and provide other safety measures for the industrial workers.

In 1852, the first railway was started from Mumbai to Thane and in 1855, the first jute mill was established in Calcutta. In 1897, a railway men's union by the name of Amalgamated Society of Railway Servants of India and Burma was formed.

In those days, the workers and their so-called associations or societies (the word trade union was not probably known) agitated to meet their small demands. The employers had to concede to the demands because otherwise, industrial workers were not easily available at that time. There was a plague epidemic in Bombay in the late nineteenth century and workers were not coming from villages to cities due to the fear of this disease.

One interesting event was the provision of electricity in Mumbai city in 1905. However, the textile workers agitated against this electrification of factories, because, they were forced to work in the mills for 24 hours including the night time. Earlier they were made to work from dawn to dark and the work was stopped only because there was no light. Before 1905 and 1908 there were several strikes for such demands. It was only after the provision made under the Factories Act for a 12-hours day and half an hour recess after six hours of work that these agitations were withdrawn, of course, with great success.

There was also a historic strike by the textile workers of Bombay when Lokmanya Bal Gangadhar Tilak, was sentenced for six years. On 22 July 1908, the workers observed a six-day strike in protest. Fifteen workers were killed and several got injured in police firing. However, this strike was the first major strike known worldwide. Comrade Lenin had sent a laudatory message to the Indian working class people on this occasion.

The textile workers of Ahmedabad had a number of successful strikes from 1917 onwards. Mahatma Gandhi went on a hunger strike for the demands of these workers. The mill owners of Ahmedabad locked out the mills. The workers got 35 per cent wage rise in this whole episode and the Textile Labour Association was formed which was one of the leading trade unions in the country. It was significant to note that Anusayaben Sarabhai, the sister of a mill magnate, Sarabhai was the founder of this Textile Labour Association.

On 16 July 1920, the first trade union All India Trade Union Congress (AITUC) was formed at Parel in Mumbai under the leadership of N.M. Joshi. The first president of this union was Lala Lajapat Rai, a prominent political leader of pre-Independent India. The Trade Unions Act, 1926 was passed in the central legislative assembly which legally provided registration of trade unions under this Act and for that minimum seven workers or employees were required. This figure of seven is now amended to 10.

The leading agitations and strikes in the country were the following:

A strike by 1,50,000 textile workers in Mumbai in 1919 for the demand of bonus and rise in wages.

- In 1920, another strike which demanded reduction in working hours and it was reduced from 12 to 10 hours. Moreover, achieved provisions for compensations on accidents while on duty, rise in wages and also fair price shops facilities in the industries.

- In 1928, the formation of Communist Party of India also commemorated with a five-month strike of Bombay textile workers. The recognition of committees and some other fringe demands were achieved by the workers.
- In 1930, the railwaymen went on strike under the leadership of All India Railwaymen's Federation.
- From 1927 to 1929 the steel workers of Jamshedpur went on strike and the Indian Congress leaders Rajendra Prasad, Jawaharlal Nehru, Subhas Chandra Bose, Chittaranjan Das, Govind Vallabh Pant took the leadership and achieved 40 per cent wage rise and provisions for provident fund, standing orders, etc., to these workers.
- In 1938 about 46,000 textile workers of Kanpur went on strike for 52 days. Govind Vallabh Pant took initiative in the settlement.
- The Bombay textile workers made an important demand of dearness allowance (DA) because of the rising prices of all commodities during the Second World War. It was for the first time decided that the prices for the month of August 1939, i.e. before the start of the World War, were considered as 100 and the DA was paid at 113 per cent in 1940, and so on. This system of variable DA was adopted later in the whole country.
- The textile workers of Bombay also struck work in support of the Indian Navy men who went on a revolt against the government in 1944. This was purely a political movement and considered as the most valid historical movement by the working class.
- There were strikes by coal mines workers in Bihar in 1944, a strike by 24,000 workers at Calcutta Municipal Corporation, etc.
- In 1946, the Post & Telegraph workers went on strike under the leadership of V.G. Dalvi, and the workers got substantial benefits.
- In January 1947 the workers in all the industries in Kanpur went on strike for the demand of privilege leave. The British government declared a 10-days leave in a year. However, the employers opposed it and there was violent agitation in which six workers were killed and many were jailed. Finally, the demands were conceded and all was well.

- In 1947, the workers of Buckingham Carnatic Mill went on strike and in 1948, 23,000 workers in the Komtur Textile Mill also went on a strike. The workers did get some benefits from these strikes.
- In 1950, there was a prolonged strike of textile workers in Bombay led by the Mill Mazdoor Sabha, under the leadership of Ashok Mehta for bonus. However, it was not successful. The workers had observed Mumbai Bandh for one day to support this strike.
- In 1952, there was a strike of defence employees under the banner of All India Defence Employees Federation. Aruna Asaf Ali, Jayaprakash Narayan, S.M. Joshi were their leaders. The strike was against the retrenchment of defence employees which was then deferred by the government.
- In 1958, there was a strike by 10,000 workers of Premier Automobiles, Bombay. This was supported by other workers belonging to Hind Mazdoor Sabha (HMS).
- There was an all-India strike of all central government employees including railways, post & telegraph, etc. It started on 11 July 1960 and was withdrawn after four days and was not successful. The central government promulgated an ordinance Essential Services Maintenance Act (ESMA) to curb this strike. However, the government also awakened and appointed the First Pay Commission to recommend the pay revision of government employees. After 1960, there has not been a major nationwide strike or agitation of central government employees. The government announced the five-year plans and invested huge funds in public sector industries where there was a good employment potential.
- In 1972, there was an agitation of Godrej & Boyce Co. workers at Vikhroli, Mumbai, in which one police inspector and a constable were killed. This caused police action on hundreds of workers and their leaders Datta Samant, Dina Bama Patil and others. Many were sentenced to jail for four months to one year.
- There was also a nationwide strike of railwaymen in 1972 led by George Fernandes. Although it paralysed the railways at many places in the country, it was withdrawn after a lot of victimization. When Madhu Dandavate became the railway minister in Janata Party government, he took back many of those victimized employees back in the railways.

There were various strikes, lockouts and agitations in a number of industries in Mumbai and other parts of Maharashtra under the leadership of Datta Samant, R.J. Mehta, AITUC, CITU and Sena Union. There were prolonged lockouts and strikes in NRC-Kalyan, Premier Automobiles, API–Aurangabad, Indian Tools–Nashik, Bombay Forging, Mukund Ltd., Hindustan Forodo, Asbestos Cement, Vidyut Metalik, Siemens, Hindustan Lever–Sewree, Firestone–Sewree, Standard Batteries, VIP Industries–Nashik, etc., during 1980-90. It may be significant to note that all these agitations had to withdraw without much gain for the working class.

MILL WORKER'S STRIKE IN 1982

Two and half lakh workers of 65 cotton textile mills in Mumbai went on an indefinite strike on 18 January 1982 under the leadership of Datta Samant. This strike was recorded in Guinness Book of Records as the biggest and longest strike. Here I present the brief history of that strike.

As per the Bombay Industrial Relations Act, 1946, the Bombay State government allowed one union in one industry in the prescribed local area. Thus in Bombay, all the cotton mill workers were united under one union Rashtriya Mill Mazdoor Sangh (RMMS). This union was affiliated to the Mill Owners' Association and supported by the Congress government and its labour union Indian National Trade Union Congress. There were thousands of *badli* (contract) workers in the mills who were exploited both by this union and the employers. In the Gold Mohar Mills, the management used to recruit *badli* workers everyday, they got works only for five days in a month. The RMMS office-bearers were regularly signing settlements in the mill matters, allowed retrenchment of a large number of workers, giving them only their legal dues and *badlis* were recruited *en mass* to man the machines. There was a regular practice of deduction of 3 to 5 per cent for the payment to RMMS. The RMMS was given the sole agency for so-called supply of rationed items like rice, wheat in the fair price shops of all the mills. They were paid a handsome amount as commissions out of these ration shops. Meanwhile, the average salary of a mill worker was Rs. 600-700 per month in 1981.

In the Empire Dying, a process house at Lower Parel, under the leadership of Datta Samant and his Maharashtra Girni Kamgar Union, a good wage settlement was signed which ignited a spark in the heads of the surrounding mill workers. During the Diwali festival of 1981, nine mills' workers (about 40,000) struck work over bonus issue and came to Samant to join his union on 18 October 1981. Samant held a meeting of the workers at Shriniwas Mill Gate. This meeting was attended not only by the workers of the nine striking mills, but also thousands of other mills workers. Then almost 90-5 per cent workers joined in Samant's union by December 1981. In order to assess the strength of workers, Samant announced a one-day strike on 6 January 1982 and it was a complete success.

On 10 January, 1982, the pay day, the workers of a number of mills refused to pay contribution of RMMS and there were many violent acts between the activities of two unions. The workers at a large number of mills struck work and waited for Samant to advise them. An emergency meeting was held at Bhoiwada Maidan where the workers compelled Samant to announce an indefinite strike. The strike started with a most jubilant and enthusiastic note and all the mills were closed. This continued for three to four months. The state government, police and political leaders were, however, opposing the strike and curbing the activities of workers. A large number of workers were arrested. The worst was that Arun Gawli, a gangster and his men who were in jail under the National Security Act, were released and were asked to provide workers who should be sent to the mills to break the strike. These elements frightened the workers who also had to go on work. The state and central governments moved political wheels to break the strike. They prevented the mill owners to hold any discussion with strikers or Samant to settle the demands. The mills were given full support to remove old machinery as the workers were already out. The RMMS signed several settlements to reduce the workforce of these departments, and thus, a large number of workers were not allowed to join duty because their machines were removed. This gave advantage to declare them as sick units to consolidate their working while the profit-making mills also rationalized the workers by settlements with RMMS and removed the strikers and their leaders.

The textile production, especially cotton textile, was also receding in textile market because of the high cost of cotton and there was a high demand for polyster and other man-made fibre. Also the powerloom sectors in Bhivandi, Ichalkaranji, Vapi, Daman, Tarapur, Surat, etc., were coming up fast and the Bombay textile strike gave it an advantage.

At the state government level, Vasantdada Patil, an experienced Congressman was brought back from Delhi to become the chief minister of Maharashtra. He was instrumental in moving the concerned parties to break the strike and run the mills whichever were to be run. Those who could not run were allowed to close.

In October 1982, the Congress party wanted to celebrate its centenary in Mumbai by holding a rally at Shivaji Park. Samant announced that the textile workers will demonstrate in front of Indira Gandhi with black flags. In order to avoid this demonstration, the government, nationalized 13 loss-making textile mills in Mumbai by an ordinance. This was just to show that the government wanted to help the workers but actually to prevent the black flags to be shown to Indira Gandhi. These 13 mills lost over Rs 1,000 crore in next few years and had to be closed down. The Congress party had more interest in its own status than the thousands of crores of rupees of the government invested in the sick mills. There was a serious discontent amongst the workers not only against their economic plight, but also against the RMMS. The workers announced in the press meetings that they were not demanding a wage rise, but they wanted to remove RMMS and its collection of money from their wages every month.

Now even after 28 years, journalists, politicians and trade unionists who belong to the next generation, believe that Samant ruined the textile mills in Bombay. They, however, ignore the fact that 75 mills in Ahmedabad were all closed even earlier than the closure of Bombay mills during these years. Same was the case of Kanpur and Indore mills. Also one dozen mills in various towns of Maharashtra were all closed. There was no strike at these places. It was a transition period for the textile business during that period of 1980 to 1990 that the composite mills were all closed. Because cotton fabrics had almost disappeared, the spinning departments were closed all over. The weaving, processing, packing, were decentralized into small units. Many were also connected with garment factories. Another important factor was the workers were totally unorganized and exploited as at Bhivandi, Surat, Tarapur, Vapi, etc. There were no unions and all were working on the contract system. The government made powerful hand-processing units completely free from excise duty while the composite mills had to pay quite a heavy excise duty. Even in 1982, some textile mill managements were getting their production from powerloom and hand-process and selling with their brand name, thus evading taxes but earning the same profits.

Justice Pratap of Bombay High Court in his judgement over the textile mill strike stated that although it was an illegal strike, it was a valid strike. Under the BIR Act, there was no legal strike, so any strike in a textile mill was illegal. It was, however, a valid strike for valid reasons and a justified mode of agitation under the circumstances of that time.

Moreover, Vasantdada Patil, who was instrumental in breaking the strike, also held meetings later with the mill owners and RMMS and gave a good wage rise to the mill workers. This shows that the demands of the workers were also justified.

In the Indian trade union history, the 2,50,000 textile workers, during this historic strike of 1982, had taken resort to all possible types of mass agitation. They courted mass arrests. Many thousand workers were arrested and sent to all the jails in Maharashtra for 14-days period. They were holding meetings, demonstrations, hunger fasts, court cases and also political battles. They contested in the election against Vasantdada Patil at Sangli, when all other political parties had decided not to contest against him. The mill workers' candidates scored 16,000 votes in Sangli against the 40,000 votes of Vasantdada Patil. The strike was supported by all other industrial workers in Bombay, by observing a one-day token strike. The striking workers were given monetary help also by various other unions. The farmers from Maharashtra from where the textile workers hailed sent 3,000 bags of rice and wheat to distribute among the striking mill workers.

Eight or nine workers who were observed breaking the strike, were killed by mobs of striking workers. Thousands of workers were arrested on various charges. Fortunately, not a single worker was sentenced on any of these charges including the murder charge. The union had provided legal aid in all courts including the criminal and labour courts for these workers. It is on record that not a single worker was sentenced. Also hundreds of innocent workers who were kept out, won their cases in the Labour Court and were taken back on duty. Many others, however, did not want to go back to their jobs because they were disappointed. There are still some workers who had gone to their native places but have not come back to collect their service dues.

From all the above events it can be surmised that the 1982 Bombay Textile Workers' Strike was not just a strike for a wage demand. It was a revolution and it cannot be considered as a failure. After 1982, there were overall better results and achievements of trade unions in Bombay and Maharashtra. In fact, the union leaders and workers were threatening the employers that they would go to Samant, if they did not get their demands and it had worked also. The employers were much more submissive and much of the exploitations of workers were stopped almost automatically. It was openly said that the working class had gained at the sacrifice of Bombay textile workers.

TRADE UNIONS' CONNECTION WITH POLITICAL PARTIES

The working class is organized by various trade unions, most of which are affiliated to the political parties. It is a point of debate whether the trade unions should be affiliated or have a direct connection with political leaders or political parties. But since the beginning, we can see the connection between political parties and trade unions.

While Jawaharlal Nehru was saying that workers and students should not take part in politics, it was the very opposite in practice in our country. In 1942, in the Quit India movement, a large number of students took a leading part in the movement. All political parties including the Congress party, had formed their trade unions to support the party. The following is the account of function of prominent trade unions in India *vis-à-vis* the political parties.

The first trade union was formed in 1920 namely, All India Trade Union Congress. While this union was formed by N.M. Joshi, its annual general meetings were presided by Lajpat Rai, Motilal Nehru, Annie Besant, Joseph Baptista, etc., who were all political leaders. These leaders were taking part in the trade union movement to settle the demands of the workers from time to time, without any political aims.

It was in 1928 when the Communist Party of India was formed that they took active part in the trade union work because of the slogan from Soviet Russia to bring workers' raj. They were depending entirely on workers and farmers. They, therefore, were dominated in AITUC functioning and attracted the workers from various sectors like textiles, defence, banks, insurance, steel, etc., S.A. Dange, S.S. Mirajkar, Joglekar, Nimbalkar, Ruikar were the prominent communist leaders who were closely associated with the AITUC unions in Bombay.

In 1929, almost all the communist leaders were arrested by the government when their party was banned. Dange and others were involved in the famous Meerut Riot case. This reduced the pressure of communists on the trade union movement. At the same time, the other labour leaders started opposing the militant policies of communists and in 1929 in the Annual Conference of AITUC at Nagpur, N.M. Joshi, Deewan Chamanlal and others opposed the union's domination by the communists and formed a new Indian Trade Union Federation.

From 1942 to 1947 intense political activities were taken place for Independence. It was just after 1947 that the Congress leaders found it necessary to have their own trade union and the Indian National Trade Union Congress was born in May 1947. Sureshchandra Banerjee was the first president and Khandubhai Desai was the general secretary of the first session of INTUC which was held at Delhi under the chairmanship of Sardar Vallabhbhai Patel.

In 1948, when the Congress Socialist Party was formed, HMS affiliated to the socialists, was also formed. Jayaprakash Narayan, Ashok Mehta, R.S. Ruikar were its founders.

Later, the socialists were divided into another group led by Rammanohar Lohia and formed their own union, namely, Hind Mazdoor Kisan Panchayat (HMKP). Later when, George Fernandes became a union leader, he joined HMKP and organized the Bombay Electric Supply and Transport Company (BEST) workers in Mumbai.

The AITUC also got divided into another union, the Centre of Indian Trade Unions (CITU) when the Communist Party of India was divided and the Communist Party of India (Marxist) (CPI-M) was formed in 1964. The other small factions of the communists like Forward Block, Radical Democratic Party, Royists, etc., also formed their own unions, namely, the United Trade Union Congress (UTUC), All India Railwaymen's Federation, etc. When Shiv Sena was formed in 1966, it started trade union activities to suppress the communist influence among the working class through their Bharatiya Kamgar Sena. Apart from these major trade unions, there are several individual unions also like the unions of the Congress leaders H.N. Trivedi, Dina Bama Patil, Sachin Ahir, Bhai Jagtap, Gulab Joshi, Vijay Kamble which are affiliated to INTUC, unions belonging to Madhukar Sarnaik and Ganesh Naik, the Shiv Sena leaders, etc. When Bharatiya Janata Party was formed in the late 1970s, it also formed a central trade union organization, Bharatiya Mazdoor Sangh (BMS), which is now spread all over India.

From the above historical data, it will be seen that almost every political party requires a trade union. There may be various reasons for this trend. However, one significant event noted during the strike of mill workers in 1982 was that despite the strong hold of Congress party, Communist Party of India and Shiv Sena, the 2,50,000 mill workers joined Datta Samant's union. In fact, these parties were against this strike and stood with the mill owners and the government. The owners of the mill used to fund their elections also. So Datta Samant's union and its powerful leadership was a blow to all these parties. Even though some mill owners wanted to settle the demands of strikers, it was the Congress government of state and central, which did not want to settle but to break the strike. Samant, therefore, made the workers aware of this political exploitation of workers and he announced a workers' political party Kamgar Aghadi. While all other political parties used to have their trade union wings, Kamgar Aghadi itself was a political party. This was quite appealing to the working class and in 1985 elections Kamgar Aghadi contested in four Lok Sabha seats. Samant also got elected. Also in the subsequent assembly elections, three contestants of Kamgar Aghadi were elected. It also had four municipal councillors.

While in 1984, Samant formed Kamgar Aghadi, the Congress government, postponed the corporation election of Mumbai under special powers vested in the government. This happened for first time in the city's 108 years history. This was because they feared that if elections were held a sizeable number of Kamgar Aghadi candidates in Giragaon and at other areas where Samant had unions would have been elected and the political map of Maharashtra would have changed. Kamgar Aghadi was like the British Labour Party. It is, however, observed that politics in India is in the hands of a few family hierarchies and the capitalists. The working class is definitely suffering because of this political phenomenon.

One glaring example was that of the owner of Simplex Mill in Mumbai. He was also having mills in Solapur. He was elected three times as the member of parliament (MP) from Solapur city with more than 60,000 mill workers' votes. As an MP, he never represented the mill workers nor was instrumental for giving better service conditions to his own workers of Simplex Mill at Mumbai and Solapur. The workers never realized that they were always loyal to him for giving votes and even working for him during the election without any gains. Samant and other union leaders held a public meeting in Solapur and openly spoke about this. Soon, all mills in Solapur were closed.

As against the above political trade unions, the individual trade unions like that of Datta Samant and R.J. Mehta succeeded because they were not politically inclined and had only the interest of the workers.

The policy towards workers adopted by a government, either state or centre, cannot be opposed by their affiliated trade union leaders. For example, when employees' pension scheme was announced in 1995, INTUC did not openly oppose it, but were only expecting some amendments to it, because the Congress government was in power at that time in the centre as well as in Maharashtra. It was opposed by all other unions and some of them filed writ petitions. The political leaders wanted the workers to work for their elections and also wanted favour from the employers in various manners. It was, therefore, clear that such leaders will not support the workers' movement or agitate against such owners.

The working class movement in India thus a major setback at the hands of political leaders who wanted workers as their vote bank. It will be significant to note that up to 1980s, all social organizations like cooperative banks, credit societies, gymnasiums, temple trusts, etc., in Girgaon were dominated by political parties, mainly by Congress and the Shiv Sena. There was not a single such institution run by workers or local citizens. This was done to keep in constant touch with textile workers who were predominantly staying at Girgaon.

LABOUR ACTS

The working class movement is also very much connected and dependent on the labour laws enacted from time to time. It will also be significant to note the time or the years in which the Acts were passed. Immediately after Independence, a number of important labour laws were passed which show that the ruling party leaders were aware of the fundamental needs of the working class. The Industrial Disputes Act, 1947, the Employees' State Insurance Act, 1948, the Factories Act, 1948, the Industrial Employment (Standing Order) Act, 1948 and the Minimum Wages Act, 1948 will show this phenomenon. The provident fund scheme was passed in 1952. This also shows the government's good intentions in passing various labour laws for the benefit and welfare of the working class in those early years. After a number of agitations adopted by Dange in Mumbai for the bonus to textile workers, the Payment of Bonus Act, 1965 was passed with Dange on the committee to recommend it. Then the Payment of Gratuity Act, 1972 was implemented.

After 1972, however, no significant labour law has been passed or substantially amended. The barometer of working class movement thus shows that after 1972, the workers who were divided into unions dominated by a large number of political parties, did not get any advantage of labour legislation power except an addition of Chapter V-B, i.e. the Sections 25-M, 25-M, 25-N and 25-O to the Industrial Disputes Act, which became an extreme necessity at that time.

After expanding industrialization in the country after Independence, there was a recession period. Also due to strong trade union movements in Bengal and other states, the industrialists started closing down the industries in such states and shifted to other states where union activities were nil. Some tax holidays were offered by the government to industries in backward areas. Mumbai city became a high wage island. Housing industry started prospering in cities like Mumbai, Thane and Pune. It was for this reason that Chapter V-B was added in the Industrial Disputes Act to enable the government to play the responsible role for giving permission for lay-offs, retrenchment or closure as a precondition. While in the initial years, the state government had laid down a policy of not giving permission for retrenchment or closure. Subsequently, the governments also conceded to the owners and started giving permissions almost regularly.

Then came the liberalization and globalization policy in 1991. This has changed the whole scenario of industries, industrial relations and trade union movement.

Earlier, if an employer wanted to retrench workers or close down his factory, it was vehemently opposed by the trade unions and also the government. This has now changed gradually and both the working class (or even trade unions) and the government, support the closures or retrenchment by way of Voluntary Retirement Scheme (VRS). The only struggle is how to get the maximum amounts of VRS for the working class. In Bayer (India) and Clariant (India) at Thane, the workers are paid up to Rs 28 lakh as VRS compensation in addition to the gratuity, PF and other legal dues. All the workers have now no participation in the union or even knowledge of the recognized union.

All the 50 textile mills in Mumbai city had been closed down and thousands of workers had gone voluntarily by taking VRS. They did not wait for an applicability of Section 25-O, i.e. taking prior permission from the government. The owners had, therefore, taken the advantage of selling their huge vacant land to builders for hundreds of crores of rupees, because there was no legal obstruction from workers. These workers and their unions are now keeping the iron hot by demanding houses for workers and employment for their children in the businesses which come up on the mill lands. Wonder whether this can be termed as working class movement at all!

MORAL SETBACK OF TRADE UNIONS

There is an important step in the direction of labour movement adopted by the trade unions in Mumbai and Maharashtra. In or about 1980, a joint trade union action committee was formed in which all the leading trade unions, AITUC, CITU, HMS, HMKP, UTUC, Samant's Kamgar Aghadi, state employees, central government employees in Maharashtra, employees of banks, Life Insurance Policy and General Insurance Policy, teachers unions, western and central railway unions, air corporation employees union, etc., were included. There are 31 major unions in this body who are representing the sizeable working class in this state on common programme. One important event held by this joint action was the mass agitation and Maharashtra Bandh observed on 25 April 2001 which was fully successful. It was to oppose the central government's proposal to amend the Sections 25-M, 25-N, 25-O and increase the statutory number of workers in these sections. Fortunately, the Shiv Sena, INTUC and Bharatiya Mazdoor Sangh also supported the bandh, and therefore, it was a big success.

Both the central and state government took due lessons from this unanimous protest of the working class and deffered their proposal for amendment. Since then, both the governments are trying to bring this amendment to encourage foreign industries. The Indian industrialists are also frequently pressing the government for the same. However, the government has not brought this amendment as yet. The Joint Trade Union Action Committee, is regularly keeping the working class abreast of the issues and taking meetings, conferences and also meeting both state and central governments to ventilate the grievances of the working class. A mass movement, conferences, demonstrations have been held in support of the unorganized labour by this action committee at various centres in Maharashtra and also in Delhi. The action committee even went one step further when BJP ruled. Five of their leaders met all the heads of political parties in Delhi including Sonia Gandhi, Sharad Pawar, Balasaheb Thackeray, etc., and gave a memorandum requesting that it should oppose the labour law amendment. Because of their concerted efforts, the BJP government did not bring the amendments in the Industrial Disputes Act in parliament and the workers also got aware about the issue.

The recession in the United States also has an impact on the working class since August 2008. A large number of export-oriented industries have suffered in India. Many have retrenched the workers. The garment, diamond, automobiles and construction industries have suffered the most. Unfortunately, most of these workers are unorganized and they never work on permanent basis. There is, therefore, no question of any working class movement for them. Since about 93 per cent of the working class in India is now in the unorganized sector, the whole labour movement is dependent on 7 per cent of labour force out of which nearly 40-50 per cent are government and semi-government employees. This makes a very poor picture of a working class in private, industrial sector who are organized. These workers have therefore to safeguard their own interest and the unions have also restricted their activities to these few, but they are a better paid and privileged class of workers. While this sector of organized workers is getting all the fruits of labour movement, it is these workers who have to support the unorganized workers and to the best possible extent. There are some strong unions of domestic workers, *anganwadi* women workers, loading and unloading of export goods at Nhava Sheva, Jawaharlal Nehru Port Trust, etc., who are actively agitating for their demands and are also getting fringe benefits with their agitations.

An entirely new department in the industries, the Human Resource (HR) Department, has completely bypassed the labour departments. The Factories Act provides for a labour welfare officer in every industry having more than 500 workers. The new HR experts have now captured the Labour Department and they are caring more for the officers and managers than the labour in every industry. They have many novel ideas to curb the working class industry. One important step is to recruit the workers with the designation of officers and executives. There are typists, peons who are designated as MC-I, MC-II (Management Cadres) or multi-skill employees, etc. These employees are working in the office on computers for a few hours and then take charge of a machine or a chemical plant in 2nd shift at 3 p.m. to 11 p.m., a blue collar job. They are called multi-skill executives and they are prohibited from becoming the members of any union. In some factories all such executives are working on machines while contract labour is used for cleaning, housekeeping and other jobs. So there are no trade unions in such units. Unfortunately, the government and the political unions are totally silent on this issue and there is no law to regulate this ever-increasing HR phenomenon. The worst is that these executives are not permanent workers and can be fired at any time.

There is yet another menace created by the BJP government of 2002. By introducing an amendment to Central Model Standing Order, they introduced the term 'Fixed Term Employee' in the definition of working class category. Then the public sector and even the private sector have started recruiting hundreds of employees on fixed terms of one to two years' terms. In Mazgaon Dock Ltd., a public sector undertaking, over 1,000 blue-collared workmen are recruited for a period of two years. Hundreds of them are getting simply terminated exactly after completion of two years, with PF and even gratuity for 2 years service. A fresh batch would be recruited at the same time on fixed term of employment and this process is continuous. About 75 per cent of the 6,000 permanent unionized category workers will be retiring in next five years. There will be no permanent workers except a few thousand contract labour and few thousand fixed term employees. If a PSU like this, manufacturing the most vital warships, submarines, etc., are having this type of HR policy, the private sector can be said to be better for workers and unions. It was surprising that the politicians and their trade unions have not raised this issue against this amendment to the Standing Orders Act in Lok Sabha and Rajya Sabha.

In a multi-state company, Crompton Greaves Ltd., all the clerical staffs are termed as executives and are kept away from union membership. Not necessary that their service conditions and even security of employment are better than the unionized workers.

When M/s. Aventis India Ltd., a multinational chemical company merged with Bayer India Ltd., another multinational company in India, they changed the designations of all the clerical staff and made them officers before the merger so that they were kept away from the Bayer Union.

The working class movement and their rights are also curbed by various courts and especially, the Supreme Court in last few years. The views of the Supreme Court about contract labour, salesmen, medical representatives, etc., have been totally contradicting their own earlier decisions. While a few thousand contract workers of Air Corporation of India, became permanent by a judgement of the Supreme Court, the same judgement was reversed by a larger bench, stipulating that no contract workers can be made permanent even after the abolition of contract labour system in that establishment. In case of *Secretary, the Government of Karnataka* vs *Umadevi and others*, the Supreme Court, reversed the order of regularizing a large number of contract workers of Karnataka government, who were working continuously for 10 years. In this judgement, the Supreme Court has admonished all the high court and has ordered that no high court should entertain any such cases for regularization of contract labour. Many seminars are held and articles are written on this judgement, criticizing the Supreme Court's order, of course, with careful words. It is, however, significant to note that no courts have taken any major decisions in the cases.

There is thus a moral setback to trade union movement from the above examples and events. However, it gives the trade union workers a challenge and they should accept the same and work with more vigour. After all, difficulties and challenges make a real leader.

CHAPTER 17

Municipal Working Class Movement in Andhra Pradesh

M.A. HUSSAIN AND C. NAGARAJA RAO

The municipal workers, who are hereditarily engaged in unclean occupations for several decades in Andhra Pradesh, had launched many struggles for the amelioration of their living conditions, but with little or partial success. They had been victims of local political bickering for several decades, and at the same time, they had been too weak to combat local political manoeuvres and eke out livelihood to lead a life with dignity and self-sufficiency. They had at last found solace in March 2009, when the Government of Andhra Pradesh headed by Y.S. Rajasekhara Reddy decided to pay their salary and allowances from the consolidated funds of the government every month.

The municipal workers have to perform three types of functions—sweeping of roads, cleaning of drains and manual scavenging. Several efforts were made and a variety of programmes were taken up to eradicate manual scavenging during the last three decades. Although open defecation continues in certain places in the state, the government could eliminate manual scavenging by constructing toilets under various schemes, thus, minimizing the most unclean work for scavengers. The government also demolished dry type latrines in all towns and constructed individual household toilets as well as community toilets. As individual household toilets need more space, community toilets were constructed when there was not enough space. However, the construction of toilets through the cities enabled the conversion of municipal scavengers into sweepers or drain cleaners.

DEBT TRAP OF MONEYLENDERS

The financial position of the municipalities was satisfactory till 1986 when they used to collect property tax regularly once in every five years. Besides the assessments were updated from time to time which kept the income of municipalities equal to expenditure. During this period the municipal staff did not face much financial difficulty since wages were paid regularly. Since 1986, the general revision of taxes was almost stopped on some pretext or other, and the increase of income of municipalities did not keep pace with the expenditure. While expenditure of the municipalities increased from time to time due to increase of wages or dearness allowances and maintenance charges, income remained the same. The municipality cleaners faced the hardest part of life besides the professional hazard. They did not get wage for several months, which inevitably forced them to borrow money from private moneylenders at an exorbitant rate of interest ranging from 10 to 25 per cent according to necessity. Thus, the municipal workers were very often caught in the debt trap of moneylenders with the result their lives remained most miserable in a poverty-stricken state.

Since the government, for several decades, totally neglected urban administration, the horrible condition of municipal workers remained unchanged and it was not a matter of concern for the government. In a disparate mood, the municipal employees went on an indefinite strike in November 1986, demanding the prompt payment of wages. The strike was called off on the promise which was not kept up fully. Thus, there was no improvement in their living conditions.

PROTEST AND AGITATIONS

The change of government in December 1989 did not bring any change in their conditions. The state of affairs of municipalities and the municipal workers remained unchanged. In certain municipalities, the income was much less than the expenditure. The workers had realized that agitations served no purpose. Hence, they continued to work under protest. After prolonged sufferings, the employees again went on indefinite fast in December 1991, demanding provincialization of municipal services. But the government had not accepted the demand, but released special grant to municipalities to pay wages up to date. This was, however, only a temporary solution and solace to workers.

The situation continued to be as bad as it has ever been after two years leaving no option for the workers except to go on strike again in October 1993, demanding provincialization of municipal services.

But government thought that provincialization would lead to a sense of irresponsibility on the part of employees towards work and supervision would be ineffective. Instead of provincialization, the government had taken stringent steps to increase municipal revenues and improve their financial position through cash flow scheme. The government had strictly implemented penal provisions for delayed payment of property tax by rate payers. This had improved the situation to some extent, but it was also a temporary solution.

The government appointed the pay revision commissions (PRC) five times during 1978-93 and implemented revised pay scales to all government employees including municipal workers as per the recommendations of the PRC. This had increased the salaries of the workers, and at the same time, increased heavy expenditure of the municipal treasury also. Thus, municipalities had gradually become totally bankrupt. This had naturally made the life of municipal workers most horrible and miserable due to inordinate delay in the payment of monthly salaries to the workers.

The municipal workers' unions are mainly affiliated to All India Trade Union Congress (AITUC), Centre for Indian Trade Unions (CITU) and Indian National Trade Union Congress (INTUC). They took indefinite fasts under the auspices of these organizations several times demanding an improvement in their living conditions, besides prompt payment of salaries. The Government of Andhra Pradesh at last issued orders for payment of salaries to the regular municipal workers from the consolidated funds of the state through government treasuries. Thus, a new era in the lives of regular municipal sanitary workers commenced, putting an end to their long-drawn struggle and agitation for ameliorating their living conditions.

OUTSOURCED WORKERS

While that was the case of regular workers, in order to reduce the cost of municipal services, the government stopped filling up of the vacancies that arise due to retirement or death of municipal public health workers, and instead, started to engage the services of workers through outsourcing/contracting. This has brought many other problems. The services of private workers were engaged through tender system. The agency which quoted the lowest rate was awarded the contract. In the process, the contractor or supplying agency took always about 50 per cent of the wage payable to the workers, and the workers received only 50 per cent of the wage that she/he was genuinely entitled for her/his work. Thus, the municipal contract workers continued to be exploited.

The contract municipal workers started agitations for payment of minimum wages prescribed by the government for unskilled labour, duly providing insurance coverage and deduction of provident fund. After prolonged agitation, the Government of Andhra Pradesh issued orders enabling all the urban local bodies to pay minimum wages to the outsourced municipal workers at the rate of Rs 3,900 duly incorporating the provision for provident fund and insurance. This was a great relief for the outsourced workers.

CHAPTER 18

Employment and Existence *vs* Ethics and Social Responsibility: A Case Study

P.C. RETHI THAMPATTY

Among the factors of production like land, labour, capital and organization, labour is the most important factor because it is not separable from the labourer. For a labourer, a day's loss is a loss forever. In India, more than 75 per cent of people live in rural areas or semi-urban towns with minimum amenities and standard of living. Most of them are landless and working under somebody like a factory owner or a landlord for minimum wages.

With the industrial revolution, the concept of working class emerged and since the birth of working class in 1830s, it has been evaluated as a social force. Indian working class people are facing two antagonist forces: imperialist political rule and economic exploitation by capitalists. All working class movements in India have always been influenced by social, economic and political processes. Even though workers had achieved many favourable laws like minimum wages, compensation for retrenchment and layoff, bonus, health, welfare and safety measures under the enactment of Factories Act, 1948, they still have to struggle to find out solutions for many problems like occupational health diseases and guarantee for employment to dependents, rights against unnecessary suspensions and dismissals, etc.

Even in this millennium, workers are cheated and exploited through many ways. They live without knowing their human rights and with the fear of job insecurity and poverty. By the means of political agony, they do not have unity among themselves. They do not have self-confidence and courage to struggle against big capitalists. So they need unity and support of the trade unions. Meanwhile, they are also being cheated by selfish and corrupt trade union leaders. However, it is the peak time to hold the responsibility of uniting and mobilizing workers against such exploitations and to safeguard workers' human rights. In the *Communist Manifesto*, the first step in the revolution is to raise the proletariat to the position of ruling class to win the battle for democracy.

OBJECTIVE OF THE STUDY

This paper is a postmortem study of a private factory, Grasim Industries, in Kozhikode district of Kerala. It finds out how the workers of this company have been cheated and exploited. The industrial house of Birla established Gwalior Rayons (later Grasim industries) in Mavoor, beside the river of Chaliyar in Kozhikode district in the 1960s. More than 3,000 people were working in the factory and Mavoor developed into a township soon.

When the factory started to produce pulp and fibre, simultaneously, it also started polluting the water of Chaliyar River. Dead fish started washing up ashore the river. The toxic effluents of the factory affected the health of villagers, cancer has become more common. The overexploitation of raw materials led to destruction of bamboo-rich forests of Kerala. Despite the repeated demand of many politicians, environmentalists, workers and government, the factory was not ready to clean the river and ultimately, shut it down by retrenching their own employees without their knowledge and agreement. The workers' struggle to re-open the factory witnessed even the suicide of 14 workers.

This study analyses the real situation from the beginning to the end of the struggle and the reasons for the closure of the factory. It also presents the issues among the working class, environmentalists and society. Also it is the objective of the study to know the aftermath of the struggle after the factory closure. Primary data of this study has been collected by survey and personal and telephonic interviews with the previous employees of the company, villagers and government agencies. The secondary data is collected from newspaper clippings and some publications. Only limited interviews were conducted with ex-employees due to lack of time and unavailability of them.

The people's struggle against the pollution of Chaliyar River caused by Grasim is the first environment movement in Kerala. The struggle began in 1962 and has not ended with the winding up of the factory in 2001. Grasim remains as a sad example of plundering of forest and water resources of a place by corporate management, with full consent of the government and the cooperation of trade unions.

THE GRASIM STORY

The Grasim story tells us how workers had ensured their salary and perks in hurry without considering the larger social and ecological responsibilities. Whenever there is a conflict between an opportunity for salaried jobs for a few and subsistence livelihoods for a large mass, the priority has to be given to the latter. Unfortunately, in the case of Grasim, trade unions joined hands with the management initially to ensure their salary, ignoring the large mass who protested to the corporate management in the name of environment. But later, they turned against the management when it was closed for ever. Highly regrettable was that the state government could not take any consoling measures for the labourers as well as any ardent measures against the company for environment pollution.

In 30 May 1958, when an agreement was signed by the Kerala government with the Birlas for setting up a pulp and fibre factory in Kozhikode, the government promised an annual supply of raw materials, i.e. bamboo at the rate of Re 1 per ton. This agreement was revised on 3 August 1962 by increasing the supply into double. In 1963, a pulp factory was also started at Mavoor in 250 acres of land purchased at the rate of Re 1 per one cent of land. The government thought by the establishment of these factories, unemployment problem could be solved up to an extent. On the very first day, the factory let out the untreated effluents into the nearby river Chaliyar at Kalpelly, 1.6-km downstream which started to pollute the river water. Under the leadership of Vazhayad Panchayat president K.A. Rahman, people launched the first agitation against the pollution of river. The management promised to discharge the effluents directly into the sea by installing a 20-km pipeline by 1966. It was a false promise, and in 1967 more protests were conducted by villagers. Instead of listening to the demands, in 1968 again the management started another fibre unit.

Due to local pressure by the environmentalists and journalists, the government appointed an expert committee to study and report environment pollution of the Chaliyar River and the role of the factory. Meanwhile, up to 1972, pollution continued and the committee took four years to recommend setting up an effluent treatment plant and entrusting the job with National Environment Engineering Research Institute. During 1973, there were more agitations. This time government appointed another committee to review the implementation of the earlier recommendations.

In 1974, the Indian parliament enacted the Water Act and in Kerala, the government set-up a state board for prevention and control of water pollution. On 10 July 1973, the company and the state government signed the second supplementary agreement with the promise to increase the supply the raw material (bamboo) four times than before since the sustained yield of bamboo in the contract area had depleted. At the same time, the production capacity of the company increased with huge profit. The agitation intensified. On 16 December 1974, the company and the government signed the Ramanilayam Agreement which recommended the shifting of the effluent discharge point to Chungapally, 7-km further downstream. Kerala Sasthra Sahithya Parishad observed it as the most unscientific and illogical solution for the problem of river water pollution. During 1977, the estimate committee of the Kerala assembly visited the factory and locals persuaded the committee members to visit the polluted areas. On 16 December 1978, thousands of people trooped to Elamaram and partly demolished the bund constructed by the company to prevent contaminated water reaching the water intake point of the factory. After the construction of the bund toxic effluents had stagnated in the river. In 1979, M.K. Raghavan, who was a minister then, visited the area and ordered the company to complete the effluent pipeline to Chungapally at the earliest. Instead of obeying the order, Grasim closed the factory for a few months citing labour problems as the reason.

The effluent pipeline was commissioned on 3 December 1980. On 13 January 1982, people of Chungapally damaged the pipeline and toxic effluents spread to paddy fields, water tanks and wells. So the company discharged the effluents through the old outlet at Kalpally. People prevented the company technicians from repairing the pipeline. Grasim demanded police protection. The district collector advised the company to stop discharging effluents to any other place where it would endanger the water supply to the city.

On 1 March 1982, the company filed a case in the high court seeking police protection for pipeline repairs. While allowing the plea for protection, Justice R.K. Narendran made a significant observation 'the banks of Chaliyar once, a health resort have virtually become a hell on earth. For the past one decade people there are suffering. If the state government and the Kerala State Board for Prevention and Control of Water Pollution had taken effective steps, this could have been prevented long ago'.

On 9 September 1982, the chief minister convened a conference at Ernakulam and recommended to reduce the pulp production. The conference also recommended a monitoring committee with people's participation. On 7 July 1985, the company stopped work followed by a labour strike. It was a relief for the protesters but the workers fell into misery. Fourteen workers committed suicide due to poverty and a massive protest built-up against Grasim demanding the reopening of the factory. A. Vasu started hunger strike and an agreement was signed for reopening the factory based on two norms—reduce raw materials and promise of non-strikes for next five years. Trade unions conceded the management's demand. During 1986 the Rajya Sabha Committee submitted its report on the basis of petitions submitted.

IMPACT ON HEALTH

In 1994, the Vazhakkad Panchayat conducted a health survey which revealed that in the five years prior to it, 199 persons had died of cancer, in addition to 58 by heart diseases, 176 by TB, 134 by asthma, 117 by ulcer, 50 by kidney diseases, 129 by epilepsy, 75 by mental diseases, 82 by skin diseases, 514 had eyesight problem and 244 had diabetic diseases.

In 1995, the State Pollution Control Board (SPCB) sent a telegram to stop effluent discharges through unauthorized outlets. During that period three Grasim workers died, while repairing a manhole in the effluent and the district collector ordered an inquiry into the incident. An expert team led by the joint director, Department of Factories and Boilers reported that the absence of safety measures and management was found responsible for the death of workers. SPCB collected more samples and filed a case against Grasim in the Kunnamangalam Judicial I Class Magistrate (JFCM) Court and obtained an interim injunction against discharging any effluent into the river until they had satisfied the prescribed standards. At that time, the Regional Cancer Centre, Thiruvananthapuram conducted a 'cancer detection camp' at Vazhakkad. PCB also sent a notice against the company effluents. After considering JFCM's absolute injunction and company's appeal to the session court, the session court allowed the company's revision petition, setting aside the Kunnamangalam JFCM's orders on the ground that only the pollution control board and not its chairman had powers to authorize the regional engineer to file a petition under Section 33 of Water Pollution Control Act.

At that time, a local leader K. Abdul Rahman also had become a cancer patient. Furious mass conducted a state level convention demanding the closing of the entire unit and demanded to pay compensations to workers and villagers. During this occasion, due to sulphur dioxide leak from the factory 10 workers were hospitalized.

SPCB ordered the closure of the unit and a Chaliyar Action Committee began an indefinite relay hunger strike in front of the factory. Company closed, machines stopped. Villagers were happy but the workers lost their job and salary. Their strike continued for many days. They had to sell all their assets, even sarees of their family members to buy food. After losing expectations of reopening the factory, some left for their native places, some entered into other jobs and some people had started small businesses in connection with tourism. After two years the company closed forever. Management left without giving any money as compensation to workers or villagers.

In the above story who all are guilty? Who are innocent? Who are clever? Is there any meaning in the term 'collective bargaining'? When and how working class are helpless between social responsibility and existence? Could the working class sacrifice something for the large common folk and warn the management in the very first stage? Why did the government and judiciary support the big capitalist? Who are ultimate losers?

After eight years Chaliyar now flows free from pollution of factory effluents, but fearing plastics pollution with the development of tourism.

My interpretations are:

- Social irresponsibility of trade unions is one of the major reasons for the failure in getting public support and in collective bargaining with management.
- Unemployment, poverty and fear of losing job and unawareness of self-employment and entrepreneurship are the main reasons for not showing social responsibility in some critical moments.

- Bureaucracy and judiciary are always with big capitals with the dream of giving employment to people.
- Big capitalists by offering employment (who knows the real situations of unemployed) bargain with government for further profits by means of reduced rate for raw materials, land and other means of production. Moreover, by harassing workers in the form of threatening, dismissals, suspensions, etc., they exploit labour and natural resources. They are not at all bothered about the societal health, safety and welfare.
- There are bogus people in the government and judiciary who argue for big capitalists, but remain unaware of the hopes and wishes of ordinary people.
- Capitalists and labourers are always in opposite and extreme poles.
- Even today the main weapons of the capitalist are dismissals of workers, divide and rule and ultimate closure of the factory only after earning several times more than investment.
- Capitalists always exploit innocent, poor and ignorant people by keeping in custody all the natural resources which have to be equally distributed among society. They are very careful for getting maximum labour power by paying minimum wages.
- Nobody is brave enough to question the big capitalists since all are afraid of the power of money.

CONCLUSION

Even in the twenty-first century, an average Indian worker lives in poverty or with bare minimum standard of living keeping so many dreams. As she/he fears capitalists and their money power, she/he does not go to bargain for her/his rights. If one labourer bargains for her/his right, suspension/dismissal or losing the job itself will be the result which leads to the utter poverty and curse of dependents.

Trade union leaders' ego clash, *status quo*, different opinion, non-unity, political rivalry, etc., add the strength of capitalists in divide and rule, which can lead to harmful decisions. Workers are persuaded to obey any condition to safeguard their employment. Both government and judiciary even today are the toys in the hands of capitalists and politicians. Government will wait to take decisions and make orders only when it has to face a working class movement in the forms of statements of leaders, procession, dharna, picketing, etc. Democracy is found only in the Constitution, but in reality practises the policy of survival of the fittest. The capitalist sows and takes the harvest using public resources and energy alone. The entire loss is for workers and common folk.

To solve the above situations, we need an enactment of new labour laws. More self-employment opportunities and entrepreneurship development programmes for common folk should be implemented. Universities and intellectuals have to approach common people to make them understand unprotected common man's problems like pollution and have to conduct more discussions, seminars, debates, symposiums, workshops, etc., on current social issues.

CHAPTER 19

Waiting for a Movement: The Plight of Banarasi Saree Weavers

RAKHI SINGH

Movements addressing the questions of working class population, grouped into several categories, have gone a long way and covered a large portion scattered throughout the country in organized as well as unorganized sectors. Peasants, industrial workers, employees of public and private sectors, small self-employed groups and other business class population have exerted pressure on policy making process and political leaders to consider their voice and provide relief. I do not claim that there has been equality in demand-fulfilment relations. Neither the pressure by all groups nor the responses to their demands have been equal. I do not take up this debate here and want to stop by saying that this inequality has been a function of availability of discretion and non-availability of system-individual coordination.

Still there are certain categories of workers who have never felt that anything like an organization is possible among them which can be helpful for them. There are groups of workers who are engaged in a particular work or related activities traditionally. They show all features of bonded labour and they work in an environment which does not have a basis of contract, rather projects the equations that indicate towards forced labour. The industries in which these workers are working are numerous and spread all over the country in different forms and dimensions. These industries do have an association but of employers and owners, not of workers. I hereby present such a traditional industry which reveals the plight of saree weavers in Varanasi district, Uttar Pradesh.

This paper is based on a study done by the author as a part of her research project to evaluate the social and political consciousness of the disadvantaged class of the population of Varanasi district. In fact, the main areas taken for study were Kotava and Lohata, the two main riot-prone villages where the communal antagonism is at the highest. But the economic activity of weaving the sarees stands at special status as it sometimes helps in bridging the gap that exists between the two communities at practical as well as psychological levels. The data collected are based on personal meetings and interviews. Thus, the analysis is based on the data collected from primary sources only.

BRIEF INTRODUCTION OF VARANASI

Varanasi, earlier known as Banaras, is in the eastern part of Uttar Pradesh. On the basis of 2001 Census report, the total population of Varanasi district is approximately 31,47,000, among them, rural population is 1,87,810 and the urban population is 1,26,057. There are 16,49,187 male and 14,89,484 female. The literacy is about 68 per cent. The city has been traditionally known as a seat of knowledge from ancient times. Situated on the bank of river Ganges, it occupies today a special status in the state and national politics. The rural areas form the majority part of the district. The employment opportunities are not much as there are no major industries in the area that can provide local unskilled employment. The result is that majority of the rural population depends on petty works owned by a few rich people. Saree production is such an economic activity that employs many rural people. Here I present certain facts regarding this industry and its employer-employee relation and an account of the working conditions and working terms of a huge workforce engaged in an industry having huge profit possibilities.

It is an eye-opening fact that in spite of the great efforts to prevent child labour and bonded labour, this group of workers is a challenge to the efforts of government. We must take note of following features about them: there are child labourers in this industry. These child labourers do not receive wage in their hand. Parents or other guardians might have taken advance money from their employers. So, their inability to repay the amount forces these children to work and not allow them to leave the job.

In Varanasi district, the urban saree industries are comparatively more mechanized. They use modern technologies and are professionally managed. They have auto looms and thus, have fewer weavers. Nevertheless, the industry needs many other workers for assistance;

and hence, the child labour is totally absent in urban areas. But the situation is very different in rural areas. In rural areas, the industry completely depends on weavers. The interesting point is that the maximum production centres of Banarasi Sarees are in rural areas. The saree production centres like the villages Kotava and Lohata are having huge Muslim populations. Kotava is only 10 km away from Varanasi Railway Station which has a Muslim population of about 25,000. One more village which is only 3 km away from Kotava is another centre for Banarasi saree production, which is a pocket of about 15,000 Muslim population. Lohata is only 4 km away from Kotava. The fact is that within a range of 15 km, 50,000 Muslim people are dependent only on the saree business.

In Kotava, about 8,000 weavers engaged in this industry are Muslims. This figure may be even high because the number of the persons engaged in weaving from the owner family is difficult to know. One noteworthy aspect of this workforce is that about 30 per cent of them are Muslims and are connected to the family of owners of the loom. In general sense of the term, they do not consider such people as workers but take pride in maintaining their status as employers.

Among 70 per cent of Hindu saree production workforce, the major constituents are Harijans and Yadavas. It is interesting to note that upper castes are generally absent in this workforce. It can be noted here that upper castes including Brahmins and Kshatriyas were doing this work earlier, but now they are totally absent from this industry.

SOCIAL AND ECONOMIC BACKGROUND OF SAREE WEAVERS

The workers of this industry are coming from different sections of society. Mostly they come from rural poor families. Traditionally speaking, those who work as saree weavers are called Butikarhawas. There were only two categories of children: those who go to school and those who go to work in saree industries. To send the child to schools needed economic capacity, but to send child to work is a source of income. Thus, the poor parents who could not afford to send their children to school force them to work. Among weavers, the majority are from the lower castes. Harijans are even today a staple for weavers. There seems to be a typical reason for it. It will not be correct to say that those who are going for weaving do not have any opportunity in agriculture or any other domestic work. Actually, they are interested in weaving sarees because of many reasons: they get cash wages, their parents force them to go for weaving, as the employer was a potential source of advance and they are not subjected to cultural subordination based on caste categorization.

The first two reasons are directly related to their economic background but the third one is bit complicated and has several dimensions to be looked at. It confirms to the same embedded experiences that provide basis for theorizing about religious conversions. The poor villagers who go for weaving experience a difference at the workplace. Those working for agriculture labour, paid by upper caste Hindus, are always forced to realize that they are subordinate, low caste, sudras or untouchables. But for those who go for weaving, are away from these psychological pains. As the owners of the industries are generally Muslims, the work place culture is good at least in one sense. As Muslims do not believe in untouchability, the workers can find a sense of pleasure of being equal in this particular respect.

CULTURAL BACKGROUND OF WEAVERS

This is particularly interesting to note that majority of the workers come from the Hindu community. They have a common belief in the way of life and common festivals to celebrate. There is hardly any difference on these grounds among workers. But the owners of the industries are of different cultural background which is not only different but antagonistic to the culture of workers. There is another important aspect to note that cultural diversity on the basis of caste and socio-economic status has not filtered down to the societal level. The way they worship, their belief, concept of *moksha* or the grounds of morality are same for lower and upper caste, for rich and poor and for educated and uneducated. I can conclude here by saying that culture is not at all an obstacle in the unification or organization of workers. Of course, there are some workers who are Muslims, thus, in a sense, saree industry provides a good field in which people of two different and even antagonistic cultures meet, interact and work together. The industry remains closed on both Hindu and Muslim festivals. In such a situation, the knowledge about festivals and celebrations of both cultural communities are exchanged between their followers. This may be taken as a step towards social cooperation and cultural recognition.

Here one point is worth noting. This particular case of cultural recognition prepares the grounds for the realization of the concept of multiculturalism. Multiculturalism believes in the negation of cultural relativism and neutrality of state in relation to culture. This example does not deal with the neutrality of state or equal protection of cultures but it certainly satisfies the condition of the requirement that a multiculturalist needs from society. Perhaps, this cultural mixing and participation in mutual cultural festivals and respecting them, and engaging into dialogue are assets for societal cooperation and mutual understanding.

Theoretically, the cultural contact between Hindu and Muslims appear to be sound enough to have some impact on reducing the cultural tension and religious antagonism. But the practical experiences do not confirm it. Kotawa and Lohata are most sensitive to communal conflicts. However, it is not correct to deal with a complicated issue in such a light way but this can be said for certain that the cultural mixing plays an important role in normalizing the situation after communal conflicts.

Now the condition in this area regarding the working class is that their life is miserable because their economic condition is poor, their educational status is low, their health condition is substandard and they are like bonded labourers who are forced to work with the master as their families have already taken financial advance from the employers. The poor conditions of this group of workers damage the society as a whole as they do not feel comfortable with the people who are not in their industries. They are stigmatized by other members who charge them as being impure because they work at a Muslim's place who are like untouchables for many Hindus.

The poor condition of this group of workers results into their self-alienation and they develop complex and a feeling of subordination and inability. It is a shame to society, to government and to the nation. They actually do not participate in political activities. Their votes are manipulated. Their participation capacity is not enhanced because of lack of education. Thus, in an area, the young people of this group are unable to protest against traditionalism through the use of power of human reason.

It is not out of place here to talk about how we see the world. John Locke says that we see the world through the experiences of society. The embedded experiences come to mind to pass through a process of synthesis. The mind accepts some and rejects the rest. What it accepts becomes our knowledge and we see the world through it. E. Kant says that the human mind has specific category. This category which is pre-existing influences the experiences. Thus, according to Kant, one sees the world as his mind shows the world. Contemporary philosopher F.A. Hayek adds to Kant and says that it is true that every human mind has particular category and that category influences the experiences. But this influence mechanism is not one sided. It is mutual. The human mind category influences the experiences and is also influenced by the experiences. And as such, one sees the world as circumstances show him. Now that is what is true for the working class group in consideration. These people have developed their own world which is of confinement, separation and isolation, resulting into non-participation in public life and no enthusiasm in political activities. This has formed a vicious circle in which these workers are trapped.

I request the academics and the activists to seriously think about their plight and plan to take them out of it. This will be an endeavour to liberate the subordinated and strengthen the democracy. It will be a real attempt towards establishing social justice.

PART IV

EMERGENCE AND STRUGGLE OF RURAL WORKING CLASS

CHAPTER 20

Sugar Industry and Working Masses: Prospects and Challenges

KUMAR SHIRALKAR AND UDAY NARKAR

An intense struggle has begun in the sugar industry of Maharashtra, in which capitalists, big traders on one hand, and the toiling masses on the other have been pitted against each other. While the former have monopolized the industry, the latter are the real producers. This struggle has to be seen as part of a class struggle which has commenced all over the world in the wake of globalization. If one were to thoroughly comprehend the depth and breadth of this conflict, it is necessary to identify historical events and the forces behind them in this industry.

In this paper we intend to pay a considerable attention to the period of imperialist globalization that began in the 1990s. We also compare briefly the movement in the Maharashtra sugar industry with that in the other states. We have pointed out certain significant factors in the world sugar industry and mentioned about the natural process of sugar production from sugar cane as well as man-made products of sugar and ethanol. However, we will begin with the more recent history of the sugar industry in Maharashtra.

The first factory to manufacture sugar from sugar cane was set-up in 1919 by a British company at Haregaon village in Ahmednagar district.[1] Then in 1930, Walchand Group set-up a factory at Walchandnagar in Pune district. Three more factories at Phaltan (Pune), Kolhapur and Ravalgaon (Nashik) were started in 1933. Again, three more factories were started at Belwandi, Malinagar and Tilaknagar in 1934. They were followed by factories at Sakharwadi and Shripur in 1939 and at Changdeonagar and Lakshmiwadi in 1941. All these twelve factories were privately owned.

A conference of farmers presided by Dhananjayrao Gadgil, who had irrigation facility, was organized in 1945. The conference unanimously passed a resolution to establish a cooperative sugar factory. Vitthalrao Vikhe-Patil took upon himself the responsibility to start this cooperative venture—the first of its kind. Thus, the Pravara Cooperative Sugar factory was set up at Loni in Ahmednagar district. It eventually proved to be an inspiring effort for other sustainable ventures in this sector. The cooperative sector went on developing steadily till 1953 and quite rapidly from 1961, i.e. after the formation of the Maharashtra state. The number of cooperative sugar factories jumped from one to 173 in a span of merely five decades! Not that all of them run successfully or equally so. However, about 140 factories can be safely said to be running to some level of satisfaction. Although the number of privately owned factories kept on reducing till the 1990s, it went up from 4 to 22 as a result of the new economic policy.

Since 1990 the area under sugar cane cultivation grew from 1.98 to 10.17 lakh ha and the production of sugar cane from 48.36 to 834.44 lakh tons. Consequently, the sugar production galloped from mere 5 to a whopping 90 lakh tons!

The production capacity of sugar factories in Maharashtra has grown quite considerably during the last five years or so. The investment in the industry has also grown significantly. Many factories have started making use of modern technology. The production capacity of the cooperative sugar factories grew 853.6 times during 1980-1 to 2006-7; while that of the private factories grew 1.97 times. It is thus obvious that the cooperative sector has grown quite impressively. These sugar factories from the cooperative sector have become an important vehicle of comprehensive and integrated development of rural Maharashtra. The sugar industry is an important industry in the organized sector which is actually based on the unorganized sector.

But this important industry is mired in all sorts of corrupt practices: selfishness, political opportunism, mismanagement, fraud and many other vices. This sector has actually witnessed a loss of the visionary leadership which was once given by the persons like Vikhe-Patil, Vasantdada Patil, Yashwantrao Chavan and Nagnathanna Naikwadi. The industry is now rampantly used for profiteering and factional politics. It has become a source of tremendous wealth for a few politically powerful houses. The rulers are involved in these practices of corruption and gross misuse of resources. That is why the ruling elite are blatantly incapable of forcing the sugar industry to run transparently and for the benefit of people. As a consequence of all these factors, the struggle between those who have monopolized this industry and toiling peasants and workers is becoming intense day by day.

SUGAR AND SUGAR CANE PRODUCTION IN MAHARASHTRA

One hectare of area yields about 90 tons of sugar cane in Maharashtra. The rate of sugar production in Maharashtra is 10.47 to 12.2 per cent, whereas the same is 10.2 to 10.6 per cent nationally. On an average 18 lakh tons of sugar can be produced per month in the state. During 2006-7, 90.947 lakh tons sugar was manufactured by crushing 798.49 lakh tons of sugar cane. The Maharashtra government paid Rs 131 crore to farmers as compensation for their uncrushed sugar cane. During the season of 2007-8, 90.976 lakh tons of sugar was produced from crushing 761.74 lakh tons of sugar cane. Rs 25 crore was paid as compensation to the farmers for uncrushed sugar cane. The sugar cane available in the year 2008-9 was 530 lakh tons. Sugar manufactured was 62.5 lakh tons.

In the season of 2009-10, sugar produced in one month spanning October-November was 9.24 lakh tons. The rate of sugar production per ton was a record-breaking 11.53 per cent. Sugar production in the state in the year 2009-10 was 70 lakh tons. It was 12 per cent higher than the same in previous year. The sugar production per ton was a record breaking 11.53 lakh tons. Sugar production in the state in the year 2009-10 was 70 lakh tons. It was 12 per cent higher than the same in previous year.[2] One hundred and forty-two factories were given licences to operate during the season of 2009-10. Of these, 112 were from the cooperative sector and 30 from the private sector. About 31 factories did not work. As a result 35 lakh tons of sugar cane was left uncrushed. The factories last year produced white sugar by processing raw sugar. Raw sugar was not processed in 2010. According to Prakash Naiknavare, the managing director of Maharashtra State Sugar Factories Confederation, 46 lakh tons of sugar was manufactured by crushing 400 lakh tons of sugar cane. This, however, needs to be confirmed.

The sugar cane yield is 15 per cent higher in 2011 as compared to 2010. The satellite survey estimates that the area under sugar cane cultivation in Maharashtra is 10 lakh ha in the current year (2010-

11). The cooperative minister of Maharashtra, Harshavardhan Patil claims that the state will produce about 75 lakh tons of sugar. However, according to Naiknavare, the area under sugar cane production in Maharashtra is only 7.70 ha. It is true that the state expects a record yield of sugar cane this year, about 8 crore tons. However, as a result of untimely rains, scarcity of labourers and agitations by farmers and sugar-cutting workers it appears highly improbable that the entire crop would be crushed. If at all the entire 8 crore tons of sugar cane is crushed, sugar production is expected to reach 90 lakh tons. Even though the season has formally begun from 1 October, the actual cutting, because of untimely rains and agitations, has been quite low. Some other organizations have estimated that about 95 lakh tons sugar will be produced in 2010-11. It has been decided that sugar factories will run for 170 days this season.

Of the 1.20 crore farmers in the state, 30 lakh are the sugar cane cultivators. Year 2009 figures tell us that out of the total 8 lakh ha under sugar cane in the state, 60 per cent fall in the western and central Maharashtra. Also, 70 per cent of the total 170 sugar factories are concentrated in this region. There is about 10 lakh ha area under sugar cane in the year 2010-11. Farmers have opted for the new variety called 9805 VSI, which matures early and it contains a high level of sucrose.

The white sugar produced from sugar cane in India does not have much demand in the international market. Several countries have their own refineries to process raw sugar which they import. We, therefore, have no easy access to the export market. The Maharashtra government had given export subsidy of Rs 1,000 per ton in 2008. This was over and above the subsidy of Rs 1,350 given by the central government. These subsidies were for exporting sugar to the tune of a million tons.

It is obvious that the policies of the government, both state and the centre, significantly impact the sugar industry. According to the policy announced on 1 November 1999, no new sugar factory is permitted unless it has a crushing capacity of 2,500 tons. Also, no permission is given to a new factory if it falls inside the circle of 15 km of an existing factory. Sugar factories grew 42 per cent from 1991 to 2007. This growth in the previous decade was merely 10.2 per cent. But, interestingly, the area under sugar cane cultivation did not register a comparable growth. It naturally had an adverse impact on the supply of the sugar cane to factories. The government gave permission to 26 new factories in the year 2000. However, only 88 per cent of these are working properly. The machinery of the remaining ones are virtually rusting. The Supreme Court has, by its order, validated the Sugarcane (Control) Amendment Order of 2006 which prohibits starting of a new sugar factory within a radius of 13 km of an old factory. The Maharashtra government does not take its own policy seriously when it comes to give licence to a new sugar factory.

SUGAR CANE AND SUGAR PRODUCTION IN INDIA

Sugar cane is cultivated in 1 lakh villages and towns of India. It means one in six villages/towns produces sugar cane in the country. Five crore farmers depend on it for their livelihood. A similar number of agricultural workers and sugar cutters depend on it. There are about 5 crore workers working in 571 sugar factories and allied industries. The sugar cane production in the country has fluctuated between 23.3 and 35.5 tons in the last decade. The period has also witnessed a low level of productivity: a meagre 40 tons per ha.

Sugar cane is one of the heaviest water-consuming crops. On an average 100 kilos of sugar cane requires 25,000 litres of water. Fifty-eight per cent of the total irrigated land in the country falls under bore well and other well irrigation. Of the remaining, 32 per cent is irrigated by canals, 5 per cent by water tanks and 5 per cent by other sources. Because of the water extraction from well and bore wells, underground water table goes on depleting. Although there is a dire need of using drip irrigation for proper water management, very few landowners have adequate capital. In the periods of drought sugar cane yield is adversely impacted. This, of course, goes on to similarly impact the sugar industry.

Three per cent of the total land cultivated in the country comes under sugar cane production. Sugar cane is an important cash crop and 7.5 per cent of the total agricultural gross value is provided by sugar cane alone. The central Planning Commission had estimated that the area under sugar cane cultivation would grow by about 6 lakh ha in the Tenth Plan period.

Post-Independence India experienced a geographical shift in the sugar industry. In about 1960-1, 60 per cent of sugar production came from Uttar Pradesh (UP) and Bihar. These states were later on overtaken by Maharashtra, Tamil Nadu and Karnataka. The rate of sugar percentage, efficiency of production is higher and the production cost is lower in these states. As of today the leading states in sugar cane productions are UP, Maharashtra and Karnataka. UP produces about 36-8 per cent sugar cane, whereas, Maharashtra about 17-25 per cent and Karnataka about 10-15 per cent.

The area under sugar cane production in 1950-1 was 17.1 lakh ha and sugar cane production was 570.5 lakh tons. It went on increasing, with very few exceptions, every year. The following Table 20.1 shows this growth in each decade and especially after globalization, post-1990.

Table 20.2 provides data which enables us to arrive at a comparative analysis of state-wise sugar cane production. The data are from the year 1997-8. UP was the highest with 19.6 lakh ha followed by Maharashtra (4.6 lakh ha), Tamil Nadu (3.2 lakh ha) and Karnataka

TABLE 20.1: ALL-INDIA PRODUCTION AND YIELD OF SUGAR CANE

Year	Area (million ha)	Production (million tons)	Yield (kg/ha)	Coverage under Irrigation (per cent)
1950-1	1.71	57.05	33,422	67.3
1960-1	2.42	110.00	45,549	69.3
1970-1	2.62	126.37	48,322	72.4
1980-1	2.67	154.25	57,844	81.2
1990-1	3.69	241.05	65,395	86.9
1991-2	3.84	254.00	66,069	88.0
1992-3	3.57	228.03	63,843	88.3
1993-4	3.42	229.66	67,120	89.0
1994-5	3.87	275.54	71,254	87.9
1995-6	4.15	281.10	67,787	88.5
1996-7	4.17	277.56	66,496	
1997-8	3.97	276.25	69,647	
1999-00	4.22	299.32	70,900	
2000-1	4.32	295.96	68,600	
2001-2	4.43	297.21	67,400	
2002-3	4.36	281.58	64,600	
2003-4	2.99	236.18	59,100	

Source: Agricultural Statistics at a Glance, Directorate of Economics and Statistics, Department of Agriculture and Cooperation, Ministry of Agriculture, Government of India.

TABLE 20.2: STATEWISE AREA, PRODUCTION AND YIELD OF SUGAR CANE 1997-8

State	Area (million ha)	Total Area (per cent)	Production (million tons)	Total Production (per cent)	Yield (kg/ha)	Percentage Coverage under Irrigation (1995-6)
Andhra Pradesh	0.19	4.8	13.73	5	72,263	95
Assam	0.03	0.8	1.29	0.5	43,000	–
Bihar	0.11	2.8	5.04	1.8	45,818	22.4
Gujarat	0.17	4.3	11.84	4.3	69,647	100
Haryana	0.14	3.5	7.55	2.7	53,929	97.2
Karnataka	0.31	7.8	28.33	10.3	91,387	100
Madhya Pradesh	0.06	1.5	2.11	0.8	35,167	97.3
Maharashtra	0.46	11.6	38.18	13.8	83,000	100
Orissa	0.02	0.5	1.14	0.4	57,000	100
Punjab	0.13	3.3	7.33	2.7	56,385	94.9
Rajasthan	0.02	0.5	1.16	0.4	58,000	96.4
Tamil Nadu	0.32	8.1	35.68	12.9	111,500	100
Uttar Pradesh	1.96	49.4	119.97	43.4	61,209	51.4
West Bengal	0.03	0.8	1.83	0.7	61,000	70.9
Others	0.02	0.5	1.07	0.4	–	–
All-India	3.97	100	276.25	100	69,647	88.5

Source: Indian-commodity.com

(3.1 lakh ha). But there is no correspondence between yield and area of cultivation. This happens because of the variation in the area under irrigation, soil quality, climate and inputs such as seeds-fertilizers, etc. The area under sugar cane in Andhra Pradesh and Gujarat, for example, was 1.9 and 1.7 lakh ha, respectively. The respective yield, however, was 137.3 and 118.4 lakh tons.

The Table 20.2 shows comparative data on area under sugar cane, total production and yield per ha in different states.

If we look at the Table 20.3, the area under sugar cane cultivation in Maharashtra appears to have grown considerably to reach 5.9 lakh ha in 1999-2000. We already have mentioned that, by 2010-11, it has touched a phenomenal figure of 10 lakh ha. One can see how

TABLE 20.3: AREAWISE SUGAR CANE CULTIVATION IN 1999-2000 AND 2003-4

States	1999-2000		2003-4	
	Area under Cultivation ('000 ha)	Production ('000 tons)	Area under Cultivation (ha)	Production ('000 tons)
Andhra Pradesh	231	18,508	203	14,616
Bihar	97	489	103	4,222
Gujarat	201	14,066	155	10,850
Haryana	137	7,640	161	9,340
Karnataka	373	37,567	237	15,800
Maharashtra	590	53,143	526	26,982
Punjab	108	6,770	123	7,870
Tamil Nadu	316	34,285	185	19,714
Uttar Pradesh	2,011	115,419	2,030	112,754
Others	11	482	11	401

Source: Food and Public Distribution Department, Government of India.

the policies of globalization and neoliberalization have helped the growth of sugar cane production than any other crop in the country. We can see, in Table 20.3, comparable figures of hectarage under sugar cane and its yield in some states.

Sugar cane production which was 10 lakh (1 million) tons in 1950 has now reached three crore tons! It is estimated that sugar be more than 2.55 crore tons in 2010-11. The domestic demand for sugar is 2.35 crore tons. The rate of growth in sugar consumption during the Tenth Plan period was projected to be 9 lakh tons per annum. However, the rate of consumption was actually slower than this. It grew by a mere 4 per cent between 2007 and 2009.

Maharashtra, UP, Karnataka, Tamil Nadu, Gujarat and Andhra Pradesh are the states which are at the forefront in sugar production in India. The sugar produced by these states together accounts for 92 per cent of the national production. In 2009, Maharashtra has come to the number one position with 91 lakh tons, followed by UP with 73 lakh tons. These two states have garnered between them a corpus of 62 per cent of the total national production. Although UP is the highest in sugar cane production its average sugar production is lowest in the country.

The Indian Sugar Industry Analysis Report notes that this industry has reached the sphere of great strength in the last 50 years of its development. Sugar production in 2006-7 reached 2.83 crore tons, the highest ever till then. The annual growth rate reached a phenomenal 46.6 per cent! The production lowered a little by 7.1 per cent in 2007-8 and registered a figure of 2.63 crore tons. The hectarage under sugar cane came down drastically in 2008-9 resulting in the lowest sugar production—1.47 tons. The sugar production in the season 2010-11 is again expected to reach 2.55 crore tons.

GUR (JAGGERY) AND KHANDSARI PRODUCTION

Sugar cane is cultivated in humid and hot climatic areas. In India, sugar cane is the main raw material used for making sweet products. Similarly, sugar is mainly manufactured from using sugar cane as raw material. About 80 per cent of the total production cost of sugar is spent on sugar cane. Sixty-five per cent of the total sugar produced in the country is used in processing eatables and drinks.

Two important rural cottage industries—gur and khandsari—consume 28-35 per cent sugar cane, producing 1 crore tons of goods. The states of UP, Andhra Pradesh, Tamil Nadu and Karnataka are the leading producers of gur and khandsari. Haryana and Punjab also produce a significant quantity.

Table 20.4 shows the quantity of sugar cane used for producing gur-khandsari in some of the states.

TABLE 20.4: STATEWISE QUANTITY OF SUGAR CANE USED FOR PRODUCING GUR AND KHANDSARI (PER CENT)

State	1998-9		1999-00		2000-1		2001-2	
	Sugar	Gur & Khand-sari	Sugar	Gur & Khand-sari	Sugar	Gur & Khand-sari	Sugar	Gur & Khand-sari
AP	69.5	22.8	63.3	29.0	55.8	36.6	57.9	34.5
Haryana	66.8	20.7	67.4	20.1	73.2	14.4	67.6	19.9
Karnataka	37.6	39.7	39.3	27.6	34.8	26.4	43.8	24.9
Punjab	59.8	27.7	68.3	19.2	65.8	21.7	67.9	19.6
Tamil Nadu	57.4	32.5	54.5	35.4	55.7	34.2	58.7	31.2
UP	35.4	50.8	42.3	43.5	43.2	43.0	46.8	39.4

Source: Department of Food and Public Distribution, Government of India.

Interestingly, it is observed that, in the year the yield of sugar cane is high, the quantity of sugar cane used for gur-khandsari decreases. Conversely, in the year the yield is low, the use of sugar cane in gur-khandsari industry goes up.

MOLASSES AND ALCOHOL

The production of molasses, which is a byproduct of sugar, has increased significantly in the country. Molasses and alcohol are required mainly for the chemical industry and producing liquor. The country produces sufficient quantity of the former for this purpose, over and above 50 crore litres required for producing ethanol.

The data on the quantity of molasses-produced, alcohol used in the alcohol-based industry, alcohol used for liquor, etc., are given in Table 20.5. How significantly has the production of molasses been raised along with the raise in sugar production is evident from the data.

Eleven factories in UP have started erecting facilities for producing 7.5 crore litre anhydrous alcohol. There already are many factories of anhydrous alcohol elsewhere—7 of 6.25 crore litre capacity in Tamil Nadu, 8 of 6.65 crore litre capacity in Karnataka and 4 of more than 4 crore litre capacity in Andhra Pradesh. Maharashtra and Punjab too are taking the same route.

It is true that ethanol can be produced from other agricultural raw material. Yet the use of molasses for producing ethanol is bound

TABLE 20.5: ALL-INDIA ALCOHOL PRODUCTION (1998-9 TO 2006-7)

(in million litres)

Alcohol Year	Molasses Produced	Production of Alcohol	Industrial Use	Potable Use	Other Uses	Surplus Availability
1998-9	7.00	1411.8	534.4	5840	55.2	238.2
1999-00	8.02	1654.0	518.9	622.7	576	455.8
2000-1	8.33	1685.9	529.3	635.1	588	462.7
2001-2	8.77	1775.2	5398	647.8	59.9	527.7
2002-3	9.23	1869.7	550.5	660.7	61.0	597.5
2003-4	9.73	1969.2	578.0	693.7	70.0	627.5
2004-5	10.24	2074.5	606.9	728.3	73.5	665.8
2005-6	10.79	2187.0	619.0	746.5	77.2	742.3
2006-7	11.36	2300.4	631.4	765.2	81.0	822.8

Source: http://www.ethanolindia.net

to rise. The sugar industry is therefore sure to hugely benefit from the ethanol industry.

ETHANOL FROM SUGAR CANE

Sugar, jaggery, molasses, alcohol, bagasse and ethanol are the most important products of sugar cane. Bagasse is used in sugar factories to provide energy. Besides, it is used as cattle feed, as raw material for paper and for electricity generation.

Crystal sugar is produced as a result of several mechanical and chemical processes. Even after extracting sucrose from sugar cane juice for sugar production, about 30 per cent sucrose and 25 per cent glucose and fructose remain in the molasses. Molasses is therefore used to make sweet syrups. One hundred and thirty-five kg of sucrose from 1 ton of sugar cane can be converted into 70 litres of ethanol. The combustion energy of this much ethanol is 1.7 GJ. Although theoretically it is possible to get 97 per cent ethanol from sucrose, in practice it reaches 76 per cent only.

A hectare of sugar cane can give 4,000 litres of ethanol. No extra energy is required for this since the bagasse obtained from sugar cane provides more energy than actually required for producing ethanol. This means that the transformation capacity, from solar energy to ethanol, is 0.13 per cent.

Ethanol is a byproduct of sugar production. It should actually be called a co-product of sugar. It is used as a biofuel, as an alternative of gasoline.

In Brazil, 45 per cent sugar cane is used for making sugar and the rest 55 per cent for ethanol. Forty per cent of sugar thus produced is exported. This explains why Brazil is able to produce sugar linking it to the demand and supply in the international market.

In Maharashtra, 23 sugar cooperative factories, after a gap of two years, have resumed the production of ethanol. Of the rest producing ethanol, eight are privately-owned sugar factories and one is a direct manufacturer of ethanol. Thus, there are 32 ethanol-producing factories in Maharashtra. Due to absence of consistency in policy only seven factories could produce ethanol in 2009-10.

According to A.V. Gade, Joint Director, Sugar Byproducts, in the past, 28 projects of ethanol were in operation in Maharashtra. However, owing to uncertainty in prices, only seven of them kept running. There are 77 distilleries in the state and 43 of them are having licences to produce ethanol. Several oil companies have received purchase orders. Many contracts, along with bank guarantees, have also been signed. Oil companies are likely to require 105 crore litre ethanol in 2010-11. Maharashtra will supply 14 crore litres.

The Union Ministry of Petroleum and Natural Gas has decided to mix 5 per cent ethanol in petrol. The central government is most likely to fix price for ethanol. The interim price fixed is Rs 27. As the production of ethanol goes up, the oil companies require to raise their demand for it. They have to create facilities necessary for mixing ethanol and petrol. The current sluggish demand for ethanol is not helping its production. Many countries have adopted the practice of mixing ethanol and petrol. India should raise the content of ethanol in petrol from the current 5 to 15 per cent. It is also argued that it might help in mitigating pollution.

The task force appointed for sugar industry during the Tenth Plan period has recommended a national policy of alternative fuel. Gasoline mixed with ethanol has been accepted by this policy. Brazil uses the mixture of 20-4 per cent ethanol with gasoline as fuel. In the United States, 10 per cent ethanol produced from maize is mixed with gasoline. The task force has recommended the use of ethanol mixed with gasoline as a useful automobile fuel.

The demand for gasoline in 2001-2 was 79 lakh tons. It touched a high point of 1.16 crore tons in 2006-7. The required 5 per cent ethanol jumped from 46.5 crore litres in 2001-2 to 68.2 crore litres in 2006-7.

If the ethanol molasses could fetch better price, it would help in effect farmers get more price for their sugar cane. The sugar cane crushing capacity of Indian sugar industry is actually more than required. More investment in sugar industry, therefore, does not look possible. Yet, there is scope for investment in other value-added products. Thus, more investment can be made in processing raw sugar, producing alcohol, ethanol and electricity.

Of course, the production of ethanol and mixing it with petrol, etc., can be thought of only after ensuring adequate supply of sugar to common people at affordable prices. Otherwise, the field will be open for rampant profiteering by sugar barons and oil companies. The activists resorting to class struggle on behalf of the toilers need to identify whose interests are being looked after in the policies such as making liquor from grains and ethanol from sugar cane. They need to firm up their positions only after such careful understanding.

WHY SUCH HASTE FOR SUGAR CANE-CUTTING MACHINES TODAY?

Sugar barons have been raising the bogey for the last 10 years that they are facing the scarcity of workers to cut sugar cane. They have imported machines to cut sugar cane from Germany and Australia. The Maharashtra Sugar cane Cutters' and Transport Workers' Union under the leadership of D.L. Karad and Subhash Jadhav vehemently resisted this attempt. It was also seen that these machines are not really useful in sugar cane fields of Maharashtra. Therefore, sugar cane had to be cut, with a few exceptions, by workers themselves. But the sugar barons did not care to pay them more than a pittance.

Over the years, the demand for workers cutting sugar cane kept up growing in the states of Gujarat, Karnataka, Tamil Nadu and Madhya Pradesh. The wage rate for cutting sugar cane in these states in 2009 was between Rs 170 and 230 per ton. In Maharashtra also it had reached Rs 180 per tons towards the end of the season. However, the Sugar Federation sided adamantly with the sugar barons and kept the rates as low as Rs 111 per ton. This resulted in the growing migration of workers to other states. They started migrating in thousands to as distant lands as Tamil Nadu. Workers resorted to constant and intense agitations. Recently a conference was organized in which the Shetkari Sanghatana led by Raghunathdada Patil, Sugarcane Cutters' and Transport Workers' Union, Maharashtra Kisan Sabha and representatives of sugar factory workers' unions participated. The conference gave a call for intense struggles. Enthusiastically responding to this call, workers organized a *rasta roko* at several places. The agitation was specially intense in Pune and Ahmednagar districts. As a result, the sugar factories announced a raise in the sugar cane prices. The farmers would now get a price anywhere between Rs 1,750 and 2,100 per ton. The sugar cane cutters themselves got a raise, Rs 137 per ton.

One has to see some of the official statements against this background. Prakash Naiknavare has stressed the need of using sugar-cutting machines. Sugar barons have always been actively canvassing for their use. Naiknavare's views need extensive quoting to understand his bias in favour of the sugar barons. He says,

> It is believed that the year 2010-11 is beneficial to farmers. We import sugar from Brazil and Thailand. The price of sugar today is Rs 2500 per quintal. It should in fact be Rs 3250. In the six month season that commences in

October-November nine lakh workers are required for cutting sugarcane from farms. But this year we are likely to get only 7.5 lakh workers. A year later on the figure of workers available will fall to 5 lakhs. Then there will be need for sugarcane cutting machines. We have about 100 machines in the state. But these are just a drop in the ocean! We have raised the wages of the workers too, from Rs 111 last season to Rs 137 per tons. Even so there will be a fall in the number of available workers. There has been a sixty year old practice of using migrated workers from Osmanabad and Beed districts of Marathwada. Cutting sugarcane is a specialized work and it requires skilled workers. But today the educated children of sugar cutting workers are reluctant to take to this profession. The practice in the states other than Maharashtra is different. There the farmers and their families themselves do the work of sugarcane cutting. The sugar industry in Maharashtra is linked to politics. The Maharashtrian farmers regard doing this work is below their dignity. This will result in further raising the wages to cutters which will, in effect, give more price to sugarcane. This will eventually lead the sugar industry to suffer huge loss, thus the farmers will not get money.[3]

Naiknavare has owned four 'truths' though inadvertently. First, the work of sugar-cutting is a skilled work; second, these workers in Maharashtra are not treated with 'dignity'; third, the profiteers are in dire need of cutting machines; and fourth, the farmers will not get money!

A different opinion has been expressed by Vijay Joshi, the managing director, Godavari Biorefineries, a privately owned sugar factory. The area under sugar cane cultivation, according to him, is parcelled in small plots of land. The small farmers, therefore, will not be able to afford the use of machines. In the current year, according to Joshi, much of standing sugar cane will be left uncrushed.

It is no doubt true that the use of machines for cutting sugar cane is growing all over the world. In spite of this, the proportion of the sugar cane cut manually, i.e. by the sickle-wielding labourers, is more than half. In a developing country like India, sugar cane is mostly cut by using human resource of labourers. In Brazil, the sugar cane is first burnt and then manually cut. The ash of burnt leaves is used as manure. This fire, however, does not affect the stem or roots. The sugar cane is cut a few inches above the ground thus keeping the rootstock intact for renewed growth. A skilled worker in Brazil cuts about 500 kg sugar cane in a hour!

Austoft 7000 is the first modern sugar-cutting machine. Many more modifications and improvements are regularly made to it. This machine cuts about 100 tons of sugar cane in one hour. Austoft 4000, a smaller version is made to work in farms where the cane is planted in rows 4 feet apart. This machine is so small that it does not harm the roots of standing cane when it cuts the cane in one row. This machine is meant to be used in the small and medium sugar cane fields of India, Africa and South-East Asia. This machine with 170 HP engine can cut 60 tons of sugar cane in one hour.

How does it compare with manual work? While a skilled worker cuts 4 tons of sugar cane in eight hours, this machine cuts 800 tons in eight hours! Thus, one machine unemploys 200 workers! But this figure pertains to Brazil. An average worker in Maharashtra cuts three-fourths tons (750 kg) of sugar cane in eight hours. In Maharashtra, therefore, one machine will snatch the employment of 533 workers!

Whether machines should be used for cutting sugar cane or not is a crucial question for the class struggle in this industry. The sugar cane-cutting worker is in need of employment. This hereditary occupation has made these workers skilled in it and they can bear tremendous hardship involved in migration and similar conditions. They will, of course, willingly accept a better and alternative employment, if offered. But there is no such possibility in these times of capitalist-neoliberal globalization. This is why they are vehemently against the use of sugar cane-cutting machines. Otherwise, there was no need for them and their organization to oppose their entry in the sugar cane fields. Opposition to these machines is in the class interest of these workers.

Contrary to this, all those who do not care for the workers' interests, gang up to wholeheartedly welcome these machines. Their only aim and objective is to garner super profit even if it means pauperizing the workers. Naiknavare is not alone in declaring at the top of their voice that Maharashtra will face a scarcity of workers and that it surely will keep on growing. His masters have become adept at rubbing shoulders with the vested interests of international capital and finance capital.

HEAVYWEIGHTS OF SUGAR INDUSTRY

Sharad Pawar and Gopinath Munde are perceived to be the people who have had a firm grip over this industry. Vijay Mallya holds a powerful sway over the alcohol industry which uses molasses as its raw material. It is not enough to look at the immediate owners. The sugar industry is in fact organically bound with national and international capital. Similarly, the fate of all products and byproducts of the industry is firmly tied to the vagaries of international market. The industry is today trapped in the whirlwind of imperialist globalization and it surely is not likely to come out of it. In these conditions the conflict between, on one hand, producer farmer, sugar-cutting workers, sugar factory workers, other toilers associated with this industry and those who stand to protect the interests of the common consumer and profiteers on the other, is bound to be intensified. That the fire will not be confined to a localized space is quite evident. One can understand the meaning hidden behind the declarations and pronouncements. Added to this will be the policies of both state and central governments, which are aimed at strengthening the neoliberal ethos.

In fact, Brazil is the country which can single-handedly satisfy the growing demand for sugar in the world. However, drought has played havoc with the sugar industry there. China and Russia too are facing the dire prospects of low production due to inclement weather conditions. The unprecedented floods in Australia and Pakistan will reduce sugar production a great deal. All this will result in the growth in demand for sugar, raising sugar prices on an unprecedented scale. As of today itself they have reached the highest point in the last 30 years. The sugar price has gone up by 67 per cent.

Between 2008 and 2009 there was a big fall in sugar production. The prices therefore rose by 50 per cent. The sugar industry made hay as the sun shone very brightly!

Nirmal Shah, an analyst of Alchemy Share and Stock Brokers, has cautioned that purchasers of Indian sugar will have to wait for it as the crushing season has got delayed. He said, Yatin Wadhwa, the managing director of Sukden India, has predicted that India will export 20 lakh tons of sugar in 2010-11.

Bajaj Hindustan Ltd. (BHL) is the largest sugar producing company in India. In 2010, the company raised its sales by a whopping 71 per cent to reach Rs 6,200 crore! Its rate profit went up from 9 to 23 per cent. The company has shown a loss of Rs 56 crore in 2010. Well, it is nothing but eyewash!

Renuka Sugars Ltd. acquired V.D.I. Sugar Factory of Brazil in 2010. Renuka Sugars purchases raw sugar paying American dollars and sells it in the Indian market for rupee. This company leads in processing raw sugar into white and other byproducts and sell them on the market. The company had garnered a huge profit of Rs 900 crore after paying taxes. The profits of this company are so huge as to acquire a Brazilian company. After acquiring this company, the Renuka Sugars will be further emboldened to look for greener pastures.

IMPORT-EXPORT POLICIES AND SUGAR-SUGAR CANE PRICES

Sharad Pawar explained the government's sugar export policy in the recently held general meeting of the Vasantdada Sugar Institute, the body that looks after the interests of all the stockholders of the industry. To begin with 5 lakh tons of sugar is being exported, he told the gathering. He also stated that sugar prices go up if we import sugar and they fall if we start exporting it. The rates of levy sugar have been raised to Rs 89.

According to an official, the ministry has decided to purchase sugar by raising the purchase price by 5.7 per cent. This has resulted in raising the market price by Rs 75-100 in the span of a week only. Total sugar production in the country this year is expected to be about 2.50 crore tons. This is in addition to the 54 tons surplus of the last year. The total sugar available will then be 3 crore tons. The need of the entire country is 2.20 crore tons. Forty lakh tons will have to be reserved for the year 2010-11. There is an option of exporting the surplus 40 lakh tons. Therefore, 5 lakh tons is being exported, to begin with. After a regular review monthly quota for exporting will be fixed.

Alagh Committee has recommended that expenses on cutting, transporting, marketing charges and insurance premium should be taken into account to fix the sugar cane price. Farmers' organizations have demanded that this recommendation should be considered for determining the statutory minimum price (SMP) for the year 2010-11. They have also demanded to accept the many other recommendations of the Mahajan Committee, Bhargav Committee and Tuleja Committee.

Although some of the recommendations by these committees are in favour of the farmers to an extent, many of them, especially those of Samir Somaiya, the president of Indian Sugar Mills' Association, are supportive of the forces of privatization and globalization. These recommendations are not in favour of the interest of the toiling sections—sugar cane producing farmers, sugar workers, sugar cane cutters and transport workers. Transforming small landholdings, where sugar cane is cultivated, into large ones and corporatization of the sugar industry are two crucial recommendations. This is done under the pretext that corporates possess adequate financial capital required for the production of alcohol, paper, ethanol and electricity. It is also claimed that only corporates will be in a position to maintain the high quality of sugar required for exporting. False claims about the possibility of giving high price to producers are also made.

There are some suggestions about exporting raw sugar too. The countries of the European Union are not willing to accept the white sugar, which is inferior in quality. They want to import raw sugar so that they can process it in their own refineries. All this amounts to transforming the entire sugar industry as an exporting industry. There are also vociferous demands for decontrolling sugar. There are government controls which regulate the quantum of sugar to be brought into the market every month. There is a cry that this authority should be vested with the factories themselves. This is in consonance with the spirit of neoliberalism. The factories are required to supply 10 per cent of sugar to distribute it among the below poverty line (BPL) families. There is no such condition imposed on any other kind of factory. So there is a hoarse demand to remove this condition.

The central government introduced a Bill that nullified the Ordinance of 21 October 2010. Sharad Pawar declared that the Bill fixing the fair and remunerative price (FRP) will be brought in the parliament to replace the existing statutory minimum price.[4] Thus the FRP Bill was passed in the Lok Sabha. The Rajya Sabha followed the suit by passing Essential Commodities (Amendment) Bill. The state governments strongly opposed to give the difference that resulted from the variance between the prices announced by the central government and those by the states. As per the earlier SMP Act, it was incumbent upon the sugar factories to disburse 50 per cent of the income derived from the sale of the byproducts. Clause 5A of this Act (which was recommended by the Bhargav Committee) benefitting the farmers was dropped. Thus, the central government has played a dirty game of filling the coffers of the sugar barons and worsening the lot of the real producers.

The government permitted to import the tax free raw sugar from

21 September 2004. Taking advantage of the government's 'Advance Permit Plan', the Indian sugar factories had imported 20.70 lakh tons of tax-free raw sugar between 21 September 2004 and 15 April 2008. The government had imposed the condition on these factories that they should export as much finished sugar as they had imported the raw sugar. The government communiqué on 29 December 2010 mentions that Indian sugar factories will export sugar to the tune of 9.67 lakh tons by 31 March 2011. It does not at all mean that all the factories will be in a position to take advantage of selling their sugar at high prices in the international market and pass on the profits thus acquired to sugar cane producers. The blind demand, the ban on sugar export, be revoked, that is not at all in the interests of farmers, workers and cutters.

One of the most anti-people policies of the government, in the times of neoliberalism, is removing controls over futures trading of essential commodities. As a result, the grain prices shot up incredibly. As the hue and cry, inside the parliament and outside, made government uneasy, controls were reintroduced. However, the government has recently decontrolled wheat and the government has no consistent policy about sugar, though it is an essential commodity. As the sugar price touched Rs 45 a kg, the government put a ban on futures trading from 1 May 2009. The ban came to end in September 2010. The sugar barons had been pressing the government hard to once again resume the operations of futures trading. They have seen the advantages of this trade for their own profits.

The National Sugar Federation—the Indian Sugar Manufacturing Association (ISMA) had been after the government to allow futures trading. The government has honoured their wish and the futures trade in sugar has started from 27 December 2010. As a result of this development, the already high price of sugar is bound to go still higher. The skyrocketing prices do not automatically translate into a better deal to farmers and workers. The sugar barons have already shown their true colour by defrauding workers of their provident fund. They will be too pleased with the prospect of collecting as much profit as they can through futures trading. It is therefore essential to understand that those who back open market and futures trading do so for the benefit of obscenely rich barons and not the peasants and workers.

The hidden meaning of the triad of globalization-liberalization-privatization is nothing but uncontrolled market in the shameless service of finance capital. Those who are sympathetic to the interests of the toiling sections associated with the sugar industry should uncompromisingly oppose these gamblers of the open market. It is necessary to understand that the struggle for liberation of the toiling masses can be taken ahead only if the struggle underlines the true interests of the working masses. It is to the credit of the organizations of farmers and sugar-cutting workers and other associated sections in Maharashtra that they have shown a firm belief in this understanding. Of course, the struggle has just begun. There is an open field ahead. We face the challenge of steeling our organizations to conquer that field. We need to take up this challenge.

NOTES

1. Kumbhar Vijay, 'Crisis in Sugar Cooperatives in Maharashtra, India', http://www.articlesbase.com/industrial--articles/crisis-in-sugar-cooperatives-in-maharashtra-1230287.html
2. Hrishikesh Joshi, 'Sugar Output Up by 15% in Maharashtra this Year', *Business Standard*, 4 May 2010.
3. Kripa Raman, 'Maharashtra May Not Have Enough Hands to Harvest Canes Crops This Time', *Business Line*, Mumbai, 24 November 2010.
4. Commodity Online, New Delhi.

CHAPTER 21

A Brief History of Dalit Agricultural Labourers' Resistance in Kerala

R. RAMAKUMAR

> In the actual social conditions of Kerala, the development of the democratic movement is bound to be linked with the organised struggle against caste-Hindu domination.
>
> (NAMBOODIRIPAD: 1981)

> A study of the tortuous and deep road to abolition of their bonded labour, of the winds of modern change which swept over Kerala, the upsurge for human rights and the success in securing a new deal for the Pulayas, has a national importance in the perspective of the civil revolution in our country.
>
> (IYER 1981)

The defining feature of the developmental process of Kerala in the twentieth century is the decisive advancement of socio-economic freedom of the people belonging to the lower rungs of the society. In this historical context, the changes in the socio-economic structure[1] of Dalits in Kerala demands serious academic attention from social scientists. In this short paper, I review the processes that have led to changes in the socio-economic freedom of the most oppressed category within Dalits in the state's history: the Dalit agricultural labourers.

The standard of living of Dalit agricultural labourers in Kerala is significantly better than that of Dalit agricultural labourers in other Indian states. Dalit agricultural labourers in Kerala own at least a plot of homestead of their own. The conditions of education and health of Dalit agricultural labourers in Kerala are more advanced than in other states. They enjoy higher wages and better conditions of employment than their counterparts in other states. They also enjoy access to agricultural labour pensions of the state government every month, as well as medical allowances from the labour welfare funds. These achievements, clearly, are the results of public action—from above and below—in the state, beginning from the early part of the twentieth century.

I argue that the lesson from the historical experience of Kerala is that any meaningful change in the socio-economic conditions of Dalits involves appreciation of the links between individual freedom and agrarian structure. In Kerala, the process of expansion of individual freedom of Dalits would not have been possible without weakening the material basis of caste discrimination through changes in land relations. In other words, the struggles of Dalits in Kerala—through the peasant movement and the agricultural labour movement—involved militant struggles against big landlordism and for land reforms.

In any discussion of the history of agricultural labourers and their struggles in Kerala, it is very important to highlight the regional differences in agrarian relations. When the princely States of Travancore and Cochin and the British Indian district of Malabar (which was a part of the Madras Presidency) were brought together to form the State of Kerala in 1957, there were distinct differences in the state of agrarian relations in the three regions. Capitalist forms of agriculture were advanced in most of the princely states, particularly in Travancore. However, Malabar was where the most backward form of landlordism persisted, and where the agrarian structure was characterized by complex forms of sub-infeudation of holdings, rack-renting and bonded labour.

AGRICULTURAL LABOURERS IN COLONIAL MALABAR

Let us take the region of Malabar. It was known to have had one of the most oppressive agrarian regimes in colonial India. On the one hand, the monopoly of land and big landlordism was the chief characteristics of the agrarian scene in Malabar (Panikkar 1978: 880). The landlords (*janmi*) owned all the agricultural land, forest land and cultivable wasteland in the district. All other categories of the agrarian population—*kanakkarans* (superior tenants), *verumpattakkarans* (inferior tenants) and landless labourers—did not generally own land

(Ramachandran 1996: 205-356). The members of Dalit households, particularly, who were almost totally landless agricultural labourers, were denied ownership rights to land.

An important feature of the agrarian regime of Malabar in the early nineteenth century was the presence of slavery among the Pulaya, Paraya and Cherumar caste groups. While mostly slaves were attached to arable lands and transferred along with the land, others were treated as chattels too, i.e. movable personal properties. The writings of many travellers as well as the British administrators are evidence to the nature of exploitation that they faced. For instance, Abbe J. Dubois, who was a missionary in Malabar between 1792 and 1823, noted that the conditions of the Parayas and their state of bondage were:

> . . . at its worst. . . . All children born to Parayas were serfs by birth, just as [their] parents were. . . . If one of these Parayas escapes and takes services under another, the master can recover him as his own property. . . . It is by no means uncommon to see a debtor who is unable to pay his debts in . . . cash satisfy his creditors by handing over to them a number of Paraya slaves. (cited in Nair 1986)

In 1843, under pressure from the movements for slavery abolition in Britain, the colonial state abolished slavery. Yet, for many reasons, the practice of slavery continued to exist. The local administrative mechanism in Malabar was filled with people of the upper castes, who themselves were slave owners and did their best to sabotage the law.

Thus, despite slavery abolition, traditional forms of bondage for the backward castes in Malabar survived till the middle of the twentieth century. New, particularly monetized, forms of bondage emerged. Debt bondage became more common. The burden of debt forced many workers of the traditional slave castes to attach themselves to their old landlords. E.J. Edona, a missionary in Kannur district in the early twentieth century, noted that even after the abolition of slavery, 'social disabilities and economic bondage have fettered their freedom', and that 'the perpetual burden of debt binds them with an iron chain to their masters' (Edona 1940). Debt-bonded workers could not usually work for any landlord other than their creditor, and were to present themselves for any kind of work at the landlords' call.

The practice of untouchability was a characteristic feature of social life in Malabar. Untouchability in Malabar was, in practice, a detailed system of distance pollution. Adrian Mayer has described the different gradations of distance pollution prescribed for different caste groups in Malabar (Mayer 1952). A Nair could not touch a Namboodiri (Brahmin), a Tiyya had to keep at least 32 feet from him, and a Cheruman or Pulaya had to keep at least 64 feet. Further, a Cheruman or Pulaya had to keep 32 feet away from a Tiyya.

In addition to untouchability, there were detailed norms on speech usages and behavioural codes for Dalits. A Pulaya worker had to stand in front of the *janmi* with his back bent forward and hands clasped in front, or else he would be severely punished. Pulayas could not wear a *mundu* beyond knee length, had no right to wrap towels around their forehead and had no right to wear *chappals*.

Landlords had resisted the education of Dalit children in the nineteenth and the early twentieth century. While there were efforts by the state and Christian missionary groups to improve access to school education for oppressed castes, landlords effectively undermined most of these efforts. In his autobiography, E.K. Nayanar, a leader of the Communist Party of India (Marxist), has described cases where Dalit students who came to enrol at schools in the 1930s were beaten up and thrown out of the school compound by the henchmen of landlords (Nayanar 1982). Mass literacy among the Dalits of Malabar did not become a reality till the second half of the twentieth century (Ramachandran 1996).

In sum, caste-based discrimination and oppression in Malabar were rooted in the nature of agrarian relations. First, the conditions of bondage in the life of Dalits were directly related to the existence of upper-caste landlordism. Second, upper-caste landlordism helped sustain a highly oppressive system of untouchability in everyday life. Third, upper-caste landlordism also frustrated all attempts on the part of Dalits to improve their conditions through education. These inter-linkages between caste and land are analysed in detail in the writings of the Communist leader E.M.S. Namboodiripad on Kerala's history; he has argued that

> . . . the institution of caste in India concealed the essence of class division in society. . . . It would therefore be unrealistic to pose the problem as if it is either class struggle or caste conflict. The fact is that there is a certain interpenetration of class and caste. . . . In the actual social conditions of Kerala, . . . the origin and development of the janmi domination is . . . inseparably connected with the existence and development of the caste hierarchy. (Namboodiripad 1981)

PEASANT MOVEMENT IN MALABAR

From the 1930s to 1950s, there was a peasant movement that gave leadership to the struggles of peasants and agricultural labourers in Malabar. It was as a part of the struggle by *verumpattakkarans* that the organized peasant movement emerged in Malabar, inspired by, and in close association with, the socialist group of the Indian National Congress (Karat 1976; and 1977: 3). Both *verumpattakkarans* and agricultural labourers faced the common threat of eviction from landlords. The slogan of 'land to the tenant and homestead land for landless workers' of the peasant movement brought peasants and agricultural labourers of Malabar together. In 1937, the All Malabar Karshaka Sangham (AMKS) was formed. The AMKS organized agitations by *verumpattakkarans* and agricultural labourers, demanding security of rights for tenants and agricultural labourers on land, estimation of fair rent, use of standard measures for measuring rent (in kind), and abolition of non-rent extractions under different names (George 1992).

Struggles undertaken by the AMKS were important moments in the history of agrarian relations in Malabar. Peasants and agricultural labourers clashed with the British police in villages like Morazha, Kayyur, Karivelloor and Kavumbai. Many activists were killed in police firings, jailed in fabricated cases and beaten up in jails.

In the 1940s and 1950s, the AMKS led agitations for better conditions of work for agricultural labourers across Malabar. Although the AMKS was an organization of peasants, it demanded that landlords raise wages for agricultural labourers, prohibit children up to 15 years of age from working in the field with parents and institute two months of maternity leave with full pay for female agricultural labourers. In his famous Minute of Dissent to the Malabar Tenancy Committee of 1940, E.M.S. Namboodiripad pointed out that its recommendations had totally ignored the demands of agricultural labourers and Dalits (Namboodiripad 1940).

While the AMKS focused its energies on attacking *janmi* landlordism, it also gave leadership to agitations against caste discrimination. The first meeting of the Malabar Karshaka Sangham, held in Parassinikkadavu in 1936, passed two resolutions: first, it demanded the abolition of traditions and customs regarding the manners of speech and use of phrases to be followed by members of backward castes; second, it demanded that all illegal levies charged by *janmis* on tenants be stopped immediately (Vishnubharateeyam 1980). The Sangham frequently organized anti-untouchability days in districts; in an article announcing one such agitation in Kannur, P. Krishna Pillai—the founding member of the Communist Party in Kerala—demanded an ordinance to make untouchability illegal.[2] Significantly, he also noted that efforts to prohibit untouchability were an important part of anti-imperialist struggles.

Following up on the mass mobilization of agricultural labourers under the AMKS, agricultural labourers formed the Palakkad Taluk Agricultural Labourers Union (PTALU) in 1954 (Vishnubharateeyam 1980). The PTALU was the first agricultural labourers' union in Malabar. In Palakkad, members of the freed slave castes and other agricultural labourers were under annual debt-based contracts with their employers. Unpaid labour services were freely extracted from this group of workers. For instance, labourers employed by a landlord to harvest the first crop were not paid any additional harvest wage for ploughing and planting the second crop in the same field. The PTALU pressed the demands for separate harvest wages, security of work, standardization of wages-in-kind and removal of caste-based discrimination against workers. The landlords were forced to accept many of the above demands after the agitation. Similar struggles of agricultural labourers took place in different parts of Malabar.

Until land reforms were implemented after 1957, the pressure built-up by the peasant movement and the agricultural labour movement was crucial in freeing the agricultural labourers from different kinds of bonded labour relations and improving their working conditions.

AGRICULTURAL LABOUR IN TRAVANCORE

Contrary to the experiences of Malabar, the princely State of Travancore had the advantage of considerable tenurial reforms in the nineteenth century itself. Tenurial reforms in the nineteenth century Travancore were a part of the struggle between the monarchy on one side and local chiefs on the other. Pro-tenant regulations were enacted in 1829 and these legislations considerably weakened the *kanakkarans*. As a result, all land came to be owned by the monarchy and all cultivators became tenants of the state, with permanent occupancy rights and fair rents. In 1865, the Travancore monarchy conferred the ownership rights over these lands to the tenants, thus creating a 'peasant-proprietorship' system, unlike in Malabar (George 1992).

However, these changes in tenancy relations and the subsequent growth of capitalist agriculture in Travancore did not end slavery and bonded labour. The institution of slavery weathered many of these initial progressive changes.

The activities of Christian missionaries in the eighteenth and nineteenth centuries influenced a number of changes in the institution of slavery. Missionaries protested against slavery, converted a number of Pulayas and Parayas into Christianity and provided them with modern education. In 1815, owing to pressure from the missionaries, slavery was declared illegal, except in agricultural activities. In 1853, a royal proclamation prohibited all forms of slavery in Travancore. According to this proclamation, all children of state-employed slaves born after that date were declared free. In 1855, another proclamation declared all existing slaves under the state also to be free, thus strengthening the provisions of the 1853 Act.

Though these Acts did have a *de jure* effect, it did not mean a *de facto* freedom for the slaves. The abolition of slavery did not lead to the emergence of a 'free' labour force in Travancore. What emerged was a system of 'attached labour', especially in the areas of Kuttanad in Alappuzha district. Attached labour system in Kuttanad was a relationship hinged on debt bondage. These workers were called as Onapanikkar. In his book, veteran agricultural labour union leader N. Kamalasanan explains the nature of this relationship succinctly as follows (Kamalasanan 1993):

> . . . In advance of the cropping season, the Pulaya family approaches the landlord at his house. . . . The landlord lends to him 15 paras of paddy and Rs 10 or 20 paras of paddy and Rs 15 to the Pulaya, called as velakkadam. This is a contract that prohibits the Pulaya or his family members from working for any other landlord in the following year. He should be available on call anytime in the day and is supposed to do any kind of work that is demanded. . . . By dawn, the Pulaya should reach the landlord's house. He should milk the cows and do a variety of domestic works till around 9 to 10 a.m. His wife also assists him in these works. Then, he goes off to the farm, where his work extends till around 10 p.m. This cycle continues till the time of harvest of the crop. Even for a small mistake that he may make, the punishment may be severe; often he is tied to a coconut tree and beaten up till he faints. Many times, his hut is destroyed by the landlord's goons.

AGRICULTURAL LABOUR MOVEMENT IN TRAVANCORE

The unfreedom among Pulayas and Parayas persisted in Travancore until their organized struggles overthrew it in the 1940s. Agricultural labour movement in Travancore was born under the influence of social reform movements led by reformers like Sree Narayana Guru. Inspired by the ideals of the Guru, the Sree Narayana Dharma Paripalana Yogam (SNDP) had been formed in 1903. Under its control, splinter organizations already existed in Kuttanad like the Sree Narayana Seva Samithi and Sree Narayana Prakasini. These splinter groups started organizing agricultural labourers and protesting against atrocities committed against them.

The successes of the SNDP inspired the organization and struggle of Dalits in Travancore under leaders like Ayyankali and Vellikkara Choti, and in Cochin under leaders like K.P. Vallone (Saradamoni 1981). In particular, two struggles led by Ayyankali served as important rallying points for larger struggles against caste discrimination in Travancore and Cochin. In 1893, Ayyankali challenged upper caste groups by violating rules that disallowed Pulayas to walk on the public roads in Balaramapuram in Trivandrum. His act of defiance included travelling on a bullock cart (called a *villu vandi*) on the road, dressed like an upper caste Nair.[3] In 1915, Ayyankali led a successful strike of Dalit agricultural workers in Neyyattinkara in Trivandrum protesting the denial of entry to a Pulaya girl in a local school.[4] In 1916, Ayyankali led another successful struggle in central Travancore for the rights of Pulaya women to wear bead necklaces (*kallu maala*) and cover their breasts with cloth. Both these struggles had involved physical clashes with upper caste landowners.

The 1915 strike organized by Ayyankali was one of the first strike actions of agricultural labourers in Kerala. Ayyankali attempted to gain admission for a Pulaya girl in a government school in Ooroottambalam village in Neyyatinkara near Trivandrum. The people of the upper castes of the area began a campaign of violence against the Pulayas for this act and, after violent clashes, burned the school down. Ayyankali organized a strike of agricultural labourers, and work stopped in the fields of the upper castes. Government intervened, and after a magistrate's inquiry, the strike ended in favour of the workers.

In the meantime, inspired by the activities of the SNDP, the coir workers in Alappuzha had formed the Travancore Labour Association (TLA) in 1922. The news of struggles of the TLA and their achievements reached Kuttanad soon and these inspiring stories led agricultural labourers to form the Thiruvithamkoor Karshaka Thozhilali Union (TAWU) in 1939 at a meeting in Pallathuruthy village (Kamalasanan 1993). The landlords and the state government tried their best to destroy the union in various ways. Following the historic Punnapra-Vayalar agitation in 1946, the TAWU was banned and its leaders operated their organization from underground. The ban was finally lifted in 1951 and the union was affiliated to the All India Trade Union Congress (AITUC) in 1953.

The consistent struggles waged by the TAWU broke the back of the attached labour system in the 1940s itself. In 1951, the union submitted a charter of 44 demands to the government, of which an increase in the harvest wages in kind from one-twelfth to one-tenth of produce was the most important. As these demands were not met, the union organized a protest strike during the harvest period of 1953. The peculiar conditions of Kuttanad demanded that harvest be completed within a short time span after the crop became ripe. Forced to budge, the Labour Commissioner thrashed out a compromise between the adamant workers and the landlords, which raised the wages of women workers, fixed working time as seven hours in *kayal* lands (paddy land) and eight hours for *kari* (charcoal) lands, both with a 30-minute lunch break.

Demand for *theerpu* wages was another major demand of agricultural labourers. *Theerpu* referred to the advance payment in kind of paddy sheaves (unthreshed) to the workers immediately after harvest, but before threshing. After threshing, the remaining payment was made in kind as paddy—called *pattam*—after deducting the *theerpu*. The union waged a long drawn battle against the landlords, who strongly opposed this. But the landlords had to accept it at the end, and from then on, payment of *theerpu* became a custom in Kuttanad (George 1992).

Such struggles meant that by 1957, when the first communist ministry came to power in Kerala, agricultural labour relations in Travancore had been transformed greatly; capitalist production had advanced and most importantly, oppressive forms of attached labour had been eliminated; Dalit workers were free to choose their employers.

LAND REFORMS

In 1956, the State of Kerala was formed by bringing together all the Malayalam-speaking regions of the Malabar district of the Madras Presidency and the erstwhile Travancore and Cochin States. In the elections to the first assembly held in 1957, the Communist Party of India came to power with E.M.S. Namboodiripad as the chief minister. In its first week in power, the new government set in motion the process of land reform that was to profoundly alter agrarian relations in the state. Land reforms in Kerala were the result of many years of struggle by peasants and agricultural workers. As Richard Franke put it, 'Kerala's land reform law was the outcome of more than a century of spontaneous rebellion, organizing, petition signing, marching, meetings, strikes, battles with police and landlord goon squads, election campaigns, and parliamentary debates' (Franke 1993).

Kerala's land reforms had three basic components (Ramachandran 1996). First, security of tenure was provided to the tenants and all evictions undertaken after the formation of the state were held illegal. The government took ownership of all tenanted land and the payment of rent on that land was stopped. Second, ceilings were set on ownership holdings of land. The holding of a family with five members could not exceed 15 acres of double-cropped paddy land or its equivalent. In the case of larger families, the ceiling was raised at the rate of one acre per additional member, with a maximum ownership limit of 25 acres. Ceiling-surplus land was to be taken over by the state and redistributed. Third, landless agricultural workers were given ownership rights over homestead plots.

There is a general consensus among scholars that land reform in Kerala was successful with respect to tenancy abolition and the distribution of homestead lands. In the period after 1957, more than 2.8 million tenants were conferred ownership rights (or had their rights protected) and more than 0.6 million hectares of land accrued to them. Between 1957 and 1996, about 528,000 agricultural labour households were issued homestead ownership certificates. The allotment of homestead plots gave agricultural labourers an owned space for housing, which greatly reduced their dependence on the landlord. However, Kerala's land reform was not successful with respect to acquiring and distributing ceiling-surplus land to the landless (mostly Dalits). Only 1.47 per cent of the total operated area had been redistributed between 1957 and 1993. As a result, the component of land reform that directly benefited landless Dalit agricultural workers was the distribution of homestead land (Ramakumar 2005).

The failure in successfully distributing ceiling-surplus land to the landless was mainly due to the significant opposition that the communist ministries faced from the central government, from the judiciary and from landlord-supported political parties in the state. A detailed review is required to understand the fierceness of this opposition and the struggles of the Left movement to overcome them.

IMPLEMENTATION OF LAND REFORMS IN KERALA

The provisions of the land reform policy of the first Communist Party ministry were set out as an Ordinance in 1957, and later incorporated into the Kerala Agrarian Relations Bill (KARB) of 1959. Soon after the state assembly passed the Bill, non-communist political formations, initiated a violent campaign of social disturbance in Kerala, supported by landed interests, led by the Congress party and upper caste organizations. The campaign finally led to the dismissal of the state government by a hostile union government in 1959.

The Congress government that came to power in 1960 was unable to ignore the powerful mass support for the KARB. A greatly diluted version of the KARB was presented to the state assembly for passing. The modified version of the Bill was passed in 1960 and came to be known as The Kerala Agrarian Relations Act (KARA), 1960 (Raj and Tharakan 1983: 31-90). Landlords moved against the KARA, 1960; the Act was challenged in the courts, citing the fundamental rights to property, equality and freedom guaranteed in the Indian Constitution as an argument against confiscatory land reforms. The judiciary stood in favour of the petitioners against land reform, and judged the KARA *ultra vires* of the Indian Constitution. As a result, the government passed another Bill in the assembly in 1964, which came to be known as the Kerala Land Reforms Act (KLRA), 1964. KLRA, 1964 was placed in the Ninth Schedule of the Constitution, so that it could not be challenged in any court.

The Congress government's KLRA of 1964 was weaker on four major counts compared to the KARB, 1959 (Raj and Tharakan 1983). First, the clause that prohibited all evictions that had occurred after the formation of the State in 1956 (in anticipation of land reforms) was removed. Second, the maximum ceiling on landownership was raised to 36 acres (from 25 acres). Third, exemptions were further extended by excluding the following types of land from the purview of the Act: cashew estates of more than 10 acres in size, mono-cropped pepper and coconut gardens larger than five acres and wetlands reclaimed from the backwaters in the Kuttanad region. Fourth, the definition of 'small owners' was modified to include landowners owning up to 24 acres, up from the earlier limit of five acres. These modifications left out large areas of land from the purview of land reforms and seriously affected the availability of surplus land for redistribution.

In the meanwhile, landlords resorted to massive land transfers through changes in ownership and possession. The following quote from a report of the Centre for Development Studies that cites data from the Land Reforms Survey, 1966 brings out the extent to which landlords exploited loopholes in the Act (CDS 1975):

> . . . over the decade 1957-66, ownership was transferred on about 0.22 million acres of land (two-thirds by sale and the rest by partition and gift), about one quarter of which was land already leased out. During the same period, transfer of possession was effected on about 0.19 million acres of land, nearly 85 per cent of which was through transfer of lease rights; such transfer of lease rights was effected either through surrender of leased-in land to landlords or by transfer of these rights from one tenant to another through the 'machinations of landlords'.

In 1967, a ministry led by the CPI(M) returned to power, with E.M.S. Namboodiripad himself as the chief minister. One of the first actions by this ministry was to make two amendments to the KLRA, 1964 (Raj and Tharakan 1983). They were the restoration of security of tenure for tenants evicted after 1956 and the addition of a provision to give landless agricultural workers (mostly Dalits) in homestead lands not only the option of fixity of tenure, but also the right to purchase up to 10 cents of land at a nominal price.

This ministry was instrumental in passing the Kerala Land Reforms (Amendment) Act, 1970. Exemptions provided by the KLRA, 1964 were cancelled and the maximum ceiling on landownership was brought down to 20 acres. The provisions regarding house sites were of special importance for Dalit agricultural labourers. The Act gave landless agricultural labourers the option of purchasing 10 cents of land in panchayats or townships, for which they were required to pay only 25 per cent of the market value in normal cases and 12.5 per cent of the market value if the landowner possessed land above the ceiling. Fifty per cent of the amount finally payable was subsidized by the state with the remaining 50 per cent to be paid in 12 annual instalments (which was never paid).

However, the exit of the CPI(M) government in 1969 created new hurdles in the implementation of the land reform laws. Sensing the revisionist-led government's inaction on land reform, the Kerala Agricultural Workers Union newly formed under the CPI(M) in 1968 unleashed a massive 'surplus land agitation' (*miccha bhoomi samaram*) across Kerala in 1970 (Radhakrishnan 1989). This agitation was concerned with identifying surplus land across the state and bringing it to the notice of the state government. The agitators entered such plots forcefully and occupied them temporarily. The agitation was greatly successful in mobilizing people to push forward the agenda of land reform. The then state government, led by C. Achutha Menon, went ahead with the distribution of surplus land as homesteads only after this agitation became widespread.

Even after KLRA 1970 came into being, the right-wing governments introduced amendments at various points of time, which diluted the various provisions in the Act. One such amendment was in 1979, which came to be popularly known as the Gift Deeds Act. This Act validated all 'gift' transfers from landlords with ceiling surplus lands to their family members between 1970 and 1974, and considered such lands as already alienated from their holdings. According to one estimate, the extent of area that was made unavailable as a result of this amendment was about 14,000 acres. Till 1970, 74,757 households had received ownership rights to redistributed land, at the rate of 0.63 acres per household. At the same rate, about 22,000 potential beneficiary households were denied ownership rights to redistributed land due to the Gift Deeds Act (Tharakan 1982).

As a result of the Gift Deeds Act and other evasions, the surplus land declared by the government in 1980 was 44,000 ha, which accounted for only 6 per cent of the land notified as surplus in 1957. According to P. Radhakrishnan, a sociologist who has studied land reforms in Kerala, the sole losers as a result of the amendment were the 'thousands of landless labourers, especially the Harijans and persons from other socially and economically backward sections of the society', who could have been provided with agricultural land (Radhakrishnan 1989).

IMPACT OF LAND REFORMS

Yet, Kerala's land reforms had impacts that go beyond the simple statistics of redistributed land. As V.K. Ramachandran has argued, land reforms in Kerala were important, both intrinsically and instrumentally (Ramachandran 1996). Intrinsically, land reform was important as it weakened the foundations of an oppressive agrarian regime and freed workers from different forms of non-freedom. Land reforms were instrumentally important, as the post-land reform society that emerged was favourable to advances in the social and economic conditions of the poorer sections. The movement for land reforms in Kerala brought within its ambit a host of social issues that concerned the standard of living of the poor. These issues included access to education, public health systems and food distribution networks and better working conditions.

Traditional forms of servitude and various forms of caste discrimination such as untouchability have ceased to be the dominant features of post-land reform Kerala society. The *janmi* system or landlordism was the base on which forms of discrimination like untouchability survived. Land reforms did not just undermine feudal landlordism, but also the material base of upper caste domination. Kathleen Gough noted in her study of Palakkara village in Cochin between 1949 and 1964 that there was 'greater social equality for [Dalits], who in 1964 walked freely in the streets, ate in the tea shops, and no longer observed distance-pollution in relation to the higher castes' (Gough 1970: 129-64). Among agricultural labourers in Palakkad and Kuttanad areas after land reforms, Joan Mencher noted that 'there is certainly a sense of freedom and human dignity that almost all our sample households talked about' (Mencher 1980: 1781-2).

The instrumental importance of land reforms becomes most evident from the advances in the field of schooling. Historically in Malabar, educational achievements were determined by the person's caste status, which was closely associated with one's status in the agrarian economy. While members of the Brahmin and upper caste households were the most educated, Dalits and adivasis were the least educated among all. In contemporary Malabar, the correlation between achievements in education and one's position in the agrarian economy has been considerably weakened by land reforms and the spread of public schools. Without land reforms, it would have been impossible to imagine the universal spread of literacy and mass schooling in Malabar.

According to Michael Tharakan, many scholars have failed to understand the significance of the allotment of homestead land to Dalits in the state. Tharakan notes that:

> This provision guaranteed a residential plot to landless agricultural labour households who mainly belonged to the scheduled castes (Dalits) and had been systematically denied access to land by the rules of the caste system. With this gain, however, even landless agricultural labourers were able to bargain better for wages, for a better public distribution system, and better school education and health care. As a result of this provision, the lowest in the caste and agrarian hierarchies gained access to rudimentary social progress, just as the middle-level communities had through the social and ritual reform movements. (Tharakan 2002)

Further, as a result of the electoral victories of political parties involved in the mass movements for land reform and against social discrimination, a number of social security issues have been brought into the legislative agenda of the state (Ramakumar 2005). Kerala is the state in which the government has most effectively intervened for social security for the rural poor, especially agricultural workers. Kerala was the first, and the only, state in India to attempt to bring agricultural workers out of the informal sector by actually legislating with respect to the conditions of employment of different sections of rural workers. The Kerala Agricultural Workers' Act (KAWA) of 1974 was India's first comprehensive legislation for agricultural workers. It sought to give statutory sanction to minimum wages, to regulate working hours and working conditions and to establish tripartite mechanisms to settle labour disputes. In 1980, the Act was amended by a CPI(M) ministry to include a scheme to pay pensions to retired agricultural labourers over the age of 60 years. Yet another important social security measure is the Public Distribution System (PDS), which provides food grains at subsidised prices for the poor. Kerala has the best PDS among Indian states, and it has been a major factor in providing nutrition to the income-poor.

CONTEMPORARY CHALLENGES

The transformation in the conditions of life and work of Dalit agricultural labourers in Kerala was brought about through a long period of consistent and militant struggles around the question of land reform and wages. It is significant to note here that the long struggle for land reform in Kerala was an integrated one: a struggle where there was a convergence of resistance against different forms of class- caste- and gender-based discriminations. This is indeed the lesson from Kerala's history for the rest of India. This historic struggle was inherited to, and later, led by the communist movement.

However, the list of achievements of Dalit agricultural labourers in Kerala noted here has to be considered as modest. While in comparison to most Indian states, the conditions of Dalit agricultural labourers in Kerala are superior, internal inequalities across caste groups persist in Kerala. Recent studies show that while economic growth in Kerala has accelerated, levels of income inequalities have risen (Ramakumar 2005). In this process of growth, it is the Dalits labouring households that have been gradually sidelined. It is suspected that landlessness among Dalits is rising; they are alienated from their house sites lured by the real estate offers of high land prices. Also, the vast majority of Dalits is still trapped in low-income manual labour activities in rural areas, which reveals the weak economic basis on which social welfare gains have been made.

The new developments that have followed growth acceleration in Kerala underline the need for targeted attention to be paid to Dalits in public programmes. Welfare programmes need to consolidate the little gains made by Dalits over a period and prepare them to participate equally in the search for new opportunities. In the distribution of surplus land to the landless, Dalits have to be given priority. Social security systems need to be upgraded and a wider variety of benefits, such as in employment and health care, need introduction. Greater attention has to be paid to improve the occupational mobility of Dalits through skill upgradation. All of these require public action, from above and below, of a new type: one that learns from Kerala's history, and yet is forward-looking.

NOTES

1. I shall, for the purpose of illustration, cite one indicator here. In the 1960s and 1970s, the share of income-poor (the headcount ratio; the HCR) among Dalit households in Kerala was significantly higher than in India as a whole. However, in 2004-5, the HCR among Dalits in Kerala was 21.6 per cent, while that in India was 36.8 per cent (see http://tribal.nic.in/writereaddata/mainlinkfile/File890.pdf).

2. *Deshabhimani*, 7 August 1947.
3. As Sanal Mohan points out, 'the mode of dressing is capable of emitting messages of dominance and subordination. In the caste hierarchy, it is very obvious that the mode of dressing and caste had an inverse relationship. With a single act of conducting a journey in a *villu vandi*, Ayyankali could subvert the symbolic world of *jati maryada*' (see Mohan 1999: 1-24).
4. Alex George's research suggests that a strike of Pulaya agricultural workers in 1907 also had school entry as one of its demands (see C.P. Chandrasekhar, V.K. Ramachandran and R. Ramakumar, (2001), "Issues in School Education in Contemporary Kerala", A report prepared for UNICEF, New Delhi).

REFERENCES

Chandrasekhar, C.P., V.K. Ramachandran and R. Ramakumar (2001): 'Issues in School Education in Contemporary Kerala', A report prepared for UNICEF, New Delhi.

CDS (1975): *Poverty, Unemployment and Development Policy: A Case Study of Selected Issues with Reference to Kerala*, Centre for Development Studies (Chennai: Orient Longman).

Dreze, Jean and Amartya Sen (eds.), *Indian Development: Selected Regional Perspectives* (New Delhi: Oxford University Press).

Edona, E.J. (1940): *The Economic Condition of the Protestant Christians in Malabar with Special Reference to the Basel Mission Church* (Calicut: Empire Press).

Franke, Richard W. (1993): *Life is a Little Better: Redistribution as a Development Strategy in Nadur Village, Kerala: Conflict and Social Change Series* (Boulder, Colorado: Westview Press).

George, Jose (1992): *Unionisation and Politicisation of Peasants and Agricultural Labourers in India (With Special Reference to Kerala)* (New Delhi: Commonwealth Publishers).

Gough, Kathleen (1970): 'Palakkara: Social and Religious Change in Central Kerala', in K. Ishwaran (ed.),.*Change and Continuity in India's Villages*, (New York: Columbia University Press).

Iyer, V.R. Krishna (1981): 'Foreword', in K. Saradamoni, *Divided Poor: Study of a Kerala Village* (New Delhi: Ajanta Publications).

Mayer, Adrian (1952): *Land and Society in Malabar* (London: Oxford University Press).

Kamalasanan, N.K. (1993): *Kuttanad and the Agricultural Labourers Movement* (Trivandrum: Chinta Publishers).

Karat, Prakash (1976): 'The Peasant Movement in Malabar, 1930-40', *Social Scientist*, 5 (3), September.

——— (1977): 'Organised Struggles of the Malabar Peasantry, 1934-40', *Social Scientist*, 5 (6-7), March.

Mencher, Joan (1980): 'The Lessons and Non-Lessons of Kerala: Agricultural Labourers and Poverty', *Economic and Political Weekly*, 15 (41-3), pp. 1781-1802.

Mohan, Sanal (1999): 'Dalit Discourse and the Evolving New Self: Contest and Strategies', *Review of Development and Change*, 4 (1), pp. 1-24).

Namboodiripad, E.M.S. (1940): *Dissenting Note in Report of the Malabar Tenancy Committee—1940, Government of Madras, Madras, reprinted in Selected Writings*, vol. 2 (Calcutta: National Book Agency).

——— (1981): 'Once Again on Castes and Classes', *Social Scientist*, 9 (12), pp. 12-25.

Nayanar, E.K. (1982): *My Struggles: An Autobiography* (New Delhi: Vikas).

Panikkar, K.N. (1978): 'Agrarian Legislation and Social Classes: A Case Study of Malabar', *Economic and Political Weekly*, 13 (21), p. 880.

Radhakrishnan, P. (1989): *Peasant Struggles, Land Reforms and Social Change: Malabar 1836-1982* (New Delhi: Sage).

Ramachandran, V. K. (1996): 'On Kerala's Development Achievements', in Jean Nair, K.K. Ramachandran Adoor (1986): *Slavery in Kerala* (New Delhi: Mittal Publications).

Ramakumar, R. (2005): 'Socio-economic Characteristics of Agricultural Workers: A Case Study in the Malabar Region of Kerala', Ph. D. thesis submitted to the Indian Statistical Institute, Kolkata.

Raj, K.N. and P.K. Michael Tharakan (1983): 'Agrarian Reform in Kerala and its Impact on the Rural Economy: A Preliminary Assessment', in Ajit Kumar Ghose (ed.), *Agrarian Reform in Contemporary Developing Countries* (London, New York: Croom Helm and St. Martin's Press).

Saradamoni, K. (1981): *Divided Poor: Study of a Kerala Village* (New Delhi: Ajanta Publications).

Tharakan, P.K. Michael (1982): 'The Kerala Land Reforms (Amendment) Bill, 1979: A Note', in Sheo Kumar Lal (ed.), *Sociological Perspectives of Land Reforms* (New Delhi: Agricole Public Academy).

——— (2002): 'Land Relations in Kerala', in V.K. Ramachandran and Madhura Swaminathan (eds.), *Agrarian Studies: Essays on Agrarian Relations in Less-Developed Countries* (New Delhi: Tulika Books).

Vishnubharateeyan (1980): *Adimakalengane Udamakalaayi? (How did the Slaves Become Owners?*) (Trivandrum: Chinta Publishers).

CHAPTER 22

The Radicalism in Agrarian Structure for Social Transformation: The Case of Bihar

MANOJ KUMAR

Bihar[1] has been one of the states in India where radical agrarian movements have been active under the leadership of communist ideology, in particular, the Maoist philosophy of social change.

Bihar is considered as being the most condemned, ridiculed, hated and feared state of the country because of its deplorable socio-economic and political situation, abysmally low human development parameters, widespread lawlessness, corruption, caste-class violence and oppressive feudal tendencies (Das 1992: 72-4). The mention of the word, Bihar, itself evokes a feeling of aversion and hatred in the minds of fellow countrymen, and probably, even among people of other countries so much that many men and women from Bihar, residing out of the state for reasons of their own, either try to hide their identity as being *Biharis* or feel shame and guilt while mentioning their antecedents to the state. Such people, irrespective of their caste and class, do this to escape the pangs of low self-image and suspicion by others.

The people of this state belonging to various castes and classes migrate to other areas for reasons of their own; the poor in search of means of survival and also for better social dignity, while the better-off Biharis move to other states mostly for better education and career opportunities as well as in quest of more peaceful and harmonious social environment with better law and order situation.

The state which is privileged to have a glorious ancient history is suffering from many ailments mostly related to the socio-economic evils that have caused widespread violence in the rural agrarian structure, especially since the late 1960s, for equitable social transformation. The nature and magnitude of the problem necessitate a deeper and analytical understanding of the causes of agrarian conflict and suggestions for a suitable way out with a view to ensure peace and harmony in society on the basis of distributive justice and human dignity. This paper examines the causes of the underdevelopment of this state with special reference to caste-class contradictions and anti-feudal struggle for radical changes in the basic socio-economic and political order under the guidance of communist ideology in general, and Maoist thought and strategy in particular. The paper also assesses effectiveness and achievements of the Maoist movement and its aim, the agrarian revolution for success of the people's democratic revolution. The radical movement of poor and marginalized peasantry belonging mostly to the lower caste/class is being bracketed with that of communal or secessionist terrorists, anti-national and anti-social elements posing threat to the internal security of India. This study helps understand the causes, nature, scope and aims of this agrarian radicalism of peasantry class and also suggests some solutions.

This analytical and descriptive qualitative research work is based on the secondary and primary data collected by making use of the published/unpublished literature and the tools and techniques of questionnaire schedule and extensive interview method. The term 'Naxalite movement', 'radical peasant struggle', 'armed agrarian movement' or revolution, 'radical peasant movement', and armed agrarian revolution or resistance have been used synonymously to avoid repetition. Similarly, the terms such as, 'open fronts', 'open mass fronts' and 'mass fronts' have been used interchangeably with the same view.

Bihar played a prominent role in the first Indian struggle for Independence in 1857, under the leadership of Kunvar Singh of Shahabad (presently comprising the districts of Bhojpur, Rohtas, Buxar, Kaimur—active regions of the Naxalite movement). Orissa was separated from Bihar in 1936. Once again, Bihar was bifurcated with 37 districts and a separate state, Jharkhand, was carved out on 15 November 2000. The areas having mineral resources went to the newly-formed state of Jharkhand, while Bihar retained a share of land without irrigation, floods during the rainy season affecting *kharif* crops, and droughts during the *rabi* season (Prasad 2000: 1-6).

AGRARIAN SOCIAL SITUATION

Bihar is a landlocked state. The present state is divided into two distinct parts; the north Gangetic plain (north Bihar plain) and the south Gangetic plain (south Bihar). The areas of north Bihar plain have fertile land and many rivers such as, Kosi, Gandak, Ghagra and

Bagmati. This region is densely populated and largely rural and gets affected almost every year by heavy floods causing huge loss to life and property. The infrastructural facilities in this region are in a very bad shape and this part of the state is known for poverty, backwardness and unemployment. A large number of labourers of north Bihar migrate to other parts of the country, like, Punjab, Assam, Delhi, Mumbai, for economic and social reasons.[2] The river Kosi is infamous as 'a curse for north Bihar' for causing devastating floods. The land in Purnea district is infertile due to the sand deposited by this river while the paddy crop of this area is constantly destroyed by the erratic flow of this river (Singh 2001: 230). The farming in north Bihar is considered as a gamble because of the uncertainty of the monsoons and the devastating effects of rivers during summer and rainy seasons. The southern part of the state is relatively better in terms of infrastructural facilities, agricultural productivity and urbanization.

Bihar is predominantly agricultural and industrially underdeveloped. It is the third most populous state, after Uttar Pradesh and Maharashtra. The literacy rate is 47.53 per cent (60.32 per cent in case of male and 33.57 per cent in the case of female) [Census of India (Bihar) 2001a: 11]. The percentage of the decadal growth rate of population is 28.43 per cent against India's 21.34 per cent. The population density of Bihar is 880 per sq km as against India's 324 [Census of India (Bihar) 2001a: 12]. The 89 per cent of the state population resides in rural areas. The urban population in the state is 10.47 per cent as against 27.78 per cent of India [Census of India (Bihar) 2001b: 125-6]. The poverty level at the state level is 42.60 per cent (Government of India 2002: 239). A major portion of the workers' population is that of the non-workers which is reflected in the following table on the distribution of workers.

DISTRIBUTION OF WORKERS' POPULATION

(*in percentage*)

Total Workers	Main workers	25.40
	Marginal workers	08.48
	Non-workers	66.12
	Total	100.00
Category of Workers	Cultivators	29.17
	Agricultural labourers	48.18
	Workers in household industries	03.87
	Other workers	18.78
	Total	100.00

Source: Census of India (Bihar) 2001c: ix-x.

Agriculture is the source of livelihood for more than 80 per cent of the state population. The growth rate in the state has been very slow. The country's growth rate was faster in the 1990s compared to the 1980s, but Bihar is the only state which had not made any significant progress during the 1990s. It was one of the most depressing phases for Bihar with almost all socio-economic indicators at the bottom such as, health, education, literacy and per capita consumption expenditure and gender equality (*The Indian Express* 2002). Children from poor families were not able to continue their school education as they had to go to work to support their parents. The ratio of teacher to pupil was low and the cases of teachers not attending schools in the rural regions were high. Health care, sanitation, welfare of children and disabled were not taken care of properly by the state. As a consequence of extremely bad condition of public health care system, a large number of private health care clinics came up, which were costly, and therefore, unaffordable for the poor. The social security measures and the old-age pension schemes were also in bad shape (Sharma et al. 1999: 51). Poverty, stagnation in agricultural and industrial growth, rising population pressure and the increasing caste class contradictions forced the people to either migrate or take up arms against the oppressive and exploitative system. The rural areas of Bihar still have been under the grip of unrest and violence due to social and economic evils.

CAUSES OF SOCIO-ECONOMIC BACKWARDNESS

The factors of caste rigidity and the system of permanent land settlement or *zamindari* system have been the most responsible causes for the socio-economic deterioration of society of Bihar. They have widened the social and economic disparities leading to violent clashes between the dominant upper caste and the oppressed section under the leadership of radical communist movement. The oppressive system of *zamindari* made the life of peasantry class miserable and even after the enactment of land reform legislations (in the post-Independent India) to abolish this tyrannical system and ensure distributive justice.

While in the other regions of the country, especially where the cities are located near the sea, such as Kolkata, Mumbai and Chennai, development occurred immediately when they emerged as centres of trade and business. Modern scientific education and the growth of metropolitan culture led them in their social, economical and cultural spheres. As a result, social evils and feudal tendencies weakened in those areas. In Bihar, it did not happen. The landlocked Bihar remains under the strong influence of caste bigotry and *zamindari* attitude still now (Das 1992: 26).

The state has been industrially backward as the people of Bihar are keen on government jobs or professional occupations rather than investing money in setting up industrial units. The possession of land is considered as a symbol of social status. Earlier zamindars did not take any interest in the development of industries. For them the *zamindari* income was more secured than the risky returns from the industrial investment (Das 1992: 31). In the decade of 1950s, Bihar was economically better-off in terms of energy, irrigation and industrial aspects and growth rates compared to the average national growth rate (Prasad 2000: 1). In the subsequent years, the state kept going down as no attention was paid to the agricultural sector which was the backbone of its economy. The lack of infrastructural facilities such as irrigation, electricity, roads for transportation, capital investment, agricultural marketing and high quality seeds and fertilizers were the main reasons for the poor economy. Moreover, high population rate as well as the traditional methods of farming sans scientific approach also deteriorated the economic condition.

Besides the above factors, other reasons for economic backwardness of Bihar were the lawlessness, lumpenization and widespread anti-social violent activities. Violence by anti-social criminals, shoot-outs for taking tenders of contracts for constructing roads and bridges, violence in buses and streets and between various castes and classes, the incidents of kidnappings and the practice of *rangadari* tax or illegal exactions by criminal elements were routine occurrences.

Corruption was rampant in government offices, banks and in various institutions. It was difficult for the common people to get a loan from the bank without paying a certain amount of commission as a bribe to please bank officials and clerks. Those problems are still continuing all over the state.

The caste-class conflict in Bihar can be said to have originated from the inhuman treatment meted out to lower caste tenants during the *zamindari* system which has been continued by the dominant landlords even after the abolition of this system. The underprivileged poor peasantry mostly belonged to the lower castes. The powerful landlords behave like the erstwhile zamindars. The poor peasants had high hopes of owning land by the implementation of the land reform measures. But the non-disclosure of land reform legislations by dominant landholders forced a large number of poor and landless people either to migrate to other areas in search of *roti* and *izzat* (food and dignity) or to take arms and join radical peasant movement (Das 1992: 79). The main social composition of radical agrarian movement in Bihar is poor toiling masses, mainly belonging to lower caste classes.

CASTE/CLASS CONTRADICTIONS IN AGRARIAN BIHAR

The caste rigidity and feudal oppressions are special features in the society of Bihar. The caste system which is based on the *varna* ideology, has conditioned the consciousness of the lower castes and they accept their inferior status in the caste hierarchy as being a divine will and this system has been prevailing for over 3,000 years (Akalank 1991: 19). This exploitative system was evolved by Brahminical ideology with the help of scriptures and rituals to perpetuate their supremacy and to keep the lower castes in bondage for ages (ibid.: 66). The lower castes have always suffered discrimination in all walks of life. Caste plays an important role at every level of social life in Bihar even today, right from the allotment of party tickets and the formation of state ministries to appointments to numerous boards, committees and commissions and this seems to be accepted as something legitimate by a large number of people (Karanth 1996: 107). In almost all castes, powerful caste leaders have provided tacit support and protection to the criminals of their castes. Decisions even regarding educational posts like the appointment of principals and vice-chancellors are made usually on the basis of the caste dominance of the appointees (Tripathi et al. 1999: 142). The influence of caste runs deep in almost all walks of life in the rural as well as the urban areas. Even a criminal is not considered a criminal but a saviour of the caste to which he belongs (Pandey 1985: 83).

The social hierarchy on the basis of caste can be broadly categorized into three broad sections; forward or upper castes, middle castes or backward castes and lower castes. The forward or upper castes comprise the Brahmins, Bhumihars, Rajputs and Kayasthas. The middle caste is also described as the intermediate castes. It comprises the upper and lower backward castes. Dominant among the upper section of backward castes are the Yadavs, Kurmis and Koeris, who have emerged as the neo-dominant rural powers and they are also politically powerful. A large number of them are middle peasants and tenants. The depressed backward castes are mostly agricultural labourers. The lower castes are generally landless and poor peasants, especially among Harijans, almost all are agricultural labourers. Upper castes are the privileged sections of society in Bihar to which most of the big landlords belong. The poor among them engage physically in agricultural activities, but they support their castes at the time of clashes with the other lower/ backward castes or on the issue of caste oppression.

Upper middle castes are largely agriculturists. Among them there are sharecroppers as well as landlords. They are economically and politically strong and purchase land from the upper caste landowners who are now shifting to non-farming sectors. They are the neo-dominants in rural areas and dominate in the political scene of Bihar. The lower Sudras are backward class in almost all fields.

The Scheduled Castes and Scheduled Tribes are largely poor and landless peasants who earn their livelihood by working in the fields of others or are engaged in other works as labourers. They suffer discrimination in almost every aspect of their life. The Doms and Halalkhors are in the worst conditions and live generally at one end or outer parts of their villages having poor access to water and roads. Their entry into temples and direct access to wells for drinking water are prohibited even today in rural areas. They are at the lowest rung of the social ladder and have joined the radical agrarian movement in large numbers. They are the main revolutionary forces of the movement. They are actively involved in the Naxalite movement, fighting against the socio-economical exploitation by a dominant landlord class. With the development of consciousness among the lower castes, the conflicts began between the privileged sections (upper castes) and underprivileged lower castes, which is a natural outcome, because of the inherent unjust inequalities of the caste system.

The significant economic and political rise of the upper section of the backward castes, especially, Yadavs, Kurmis and Koeris, was clearly noticeable in the 1967 elections when they entered into the Bihar legislative assembly in large numbers. Then the conflicts emerged at two levels; the upper caste *versus* upper backward castes (and also with lower castes as the political consciousness had developed among them as well) and the upper middle castes *versus* the lower castes, especially Dalits. These neo-emergent dominant upper intermediary castes had started organizing themselves in the early twentieth century for social reform within their castes and improved their social position. In the early 1930s, they joined together and formed the Triveni Sangh to fight against social oppression by the upper castes and to make improvements in their social, economical and political life (Choudhary and Srikant 2001: 69-83).

The Yadavs, especially because of their numerical superiority and muscle power, have emerged as the new rich powerful peasants, in rural areas and have grabbed lucrative construction contracts and various dealership licences. A large number of them joined with the Scheduled Castes and Scheduled Tribes to fight against their common enemy, upper castes, especially in the areas where they (Yadavs) have suffered oppression by the latter, for examples, in the regions of Aurangabad and Palamu. A bulk of the poor and agricultural labourers belonging to the Yadav caste have joined the Naxalite movement (Gupta 1992: 1304-6). The regions of south Bihar, where economic conditions and consciousness among the backward castes and the lower castes were relatively better and higher, became the battleground for socio-economic and political transformation.

One of the major problems or the causes of caste-class conflict in Bihar was deprivation of social dignity to the lower caste men and women. The issue of sexual exploitation of women belonging to the lower castes by the dominant landlords and their henchmen belonging mostly to the upper castes became one of the main issues of the radical peasant movement. The lower castes were not allowed to sit on a cot in front of their own house and defiance to it invited a severe punishment including death (Louis 2002: 90). The upper section of the backward castes, especially Yadavs and Kurmis became new perpetrators of the lower castes. The attacks on poor and landless lower castes by the dominant upper and middle caste landlords increased in those areas where the former had started organizing themselves to resist the oppression by the latter often led to violent incidents and mass killings (Urmilesh 1999: 96-7). These socially and economically oppressed lower castes and Dalits were mobilized by the Maoist organizations in the late 1960s.

The focus of the peasant movements in the 1930s and 1940s was mainly on the problems of tenants and had demanded abolition of the *zamindari* system as this system was considered as the root cause of all socio-economic evils in the life of peasants. But since the late

1960, the Maoist organizations had taken those issues of poor and landless peasants belonging mostly to the lower castes which were not attended properly either by the peasant movement organizers or by the communists. The peasant masses, under the guidance of Maoist thought, have struggled on the issues of land, wage and social dignity or *izzat*, which are enshrined in the Constitution of India but not implemented or ensured by the state government; thus the toiling peasants are compelled to resort to radicalism to assert their constitutional fundamental rights.

RADICAL AGRARIAN MOVEMENT

The underprivileged frustrated sections of Indian society belonging mostly to the lower castes, especially Scheduled Castes (most of them are agricultural labourers and a few of them the marginal farmers) formed the core social base of the radical agrarian movement and have effectively challenged the traditional dominance of the upper castes and classes and questioned the authority and legitimacy of the existing political system. These deprived peasants, who have been forced by the existing social situation to adopt even extra-constitutional means to assert their rights to livelihood and social dignity, guaranteed by the Constitution, are described by the government-media-capitalist-bureaucrats interest groups and some sections of intelligentsia as being the anti-national and the single biggest threat to the internal security of the country.

There are historical records of upsurges and insurrections by the suffering peasants in the country during the British rule against the exploitation and oppression of zamindars (Banerjee 1980: 23). The peasant movements of Telangana, Tebhaga and Punnappra in the 1940s were led by the communist leaders to achieve humanist goals. In 1967, radical members of the Communist Party of India (Marxist) [CPI(M)] began mobilizing the Indian peasantry under the guidance of Maoist thoughts and found the strategy of Chinese communist revolution suitable in Indian situation as they considered the social environment similar to that of pre-liberated China.

NAXALITE MOVEMENT AND ITS IDEOLOGY

In May 1967, a radical agrarian movement emerged in Naxalbari region of West Bengal under the leadership of the Maoist faction of the CPI(M). Later this movement was spread rapidly to different parts of the country and came to be known as the Naxalite movement.

According to Naxalites (also known as the Maoists), the proletarian revolution is applicable to Western countries where industrial means of production determines classes in society but in an agricultural country like India, the radical agrarian movement is the only suitable option, as the most oppressed and exploited poor and landless peasantry are the main revolutionary forces in the Indian situation. The Maoist strategy in China has been adopted for the success of Indian revolution on the basis of the assumption of a similar Indian situation prevailing at that time to that of the pre-liberated China.

In Bihar, social issues have been dominant in the areas of people's struggle for social change besides the issues of wages, and surplus land. The people belonging to poor lower castes have been fighting for their human dignity or *izzat* under the leadership of Naxalite organizations more than their struggle for economic gains. It is because of the dominance of the issue of struggle for social dignity which has earned the name for the radical peasants' movement as being an *izzat ki ladai*.[3] Violent clashes between radical peasants and the private armies of landlords have led to a number of massacres, especially after 1980. In Bihar, the Naxalite movement became active in 1968 in Mushahari block of Muzaffarpur district under the local leadership of Raj Kishore Singh and Satyanarayan Singh, a state leader of All India Coordination Committee of Communist Revolutionaries (AICCCR), Bihar unit, which was later reconstituted as the Communist Party of India (Marxist-Leninist) in May 1969. The movement spread rapidly into many villages of Mushahari block and to other districts of Bihar. Many landlords and moneylenders were killed at different places and many left their villages out of fear. In the early 1970s, however, the movement declined because of severe state repression and internal bickering. When it was fading away everywhere, the Ekbari village of the Bhojpur district in central Bihar (united) became the main centre of the agrarian conflict and spread to many blocks of the district. The movement faced severe state repression during the emergency in the mid-1970s and almost vanished from the scene (see Mukherjee and Yadav 1980). But towards the late 1970s, it not only re-appeared with a new vigour after the decline of the Bihar movement (also known as 'total revolution' led by a veteran socialist leader, Jayaprakash Narayan) and formation of Janata government at the centre, but also spread very rapidly to many districts of central Bihar. This radical peasant struggle grew intensely in the 1980s under the leadership of various Naxalite organizations pursuing the line of armed agrarian revolution. The violent actions carried out by the Naxalite factions, such as, the Maoist Communist Centre (MCC), the Communist Party of India Marxist-Leninist Liberation [CPI (ML)], the CPI(ML) Party Unity and private *senas* (caste-based private armies of landlords of upper and upper-backward castes to suppress Naxalite movement) like Kunwar Sena, Bhoomi Sena, Lorik Sena, Brahmarishi Sena, etc., turned Bihar into 'flaming fields' causing frequent violent clashes between the dominant landed class and underprivileged sections of poor and landless peasants.

Usually, the peasant agitations emerge in socio-economically backward and underdeveloped areas but in case of Bihar, the relatively better-off part of the state, the south central region became the main battleground between dominant feudal forces and poor masses. The region has fertile agricultural land with higher productivity, and an affinity for land is relatively more in this region because of the land value. One of the main causes of the growth of the radical agrarian movement in this part of the state is the change in agricultural situation and the relation between the landowners and labourers after the construction of Sone Canal. The availability of irrigation facility increased the productivity of land, making the cultivation profitable as a result of which, the landowners, who used to lease out their lands to tenants, engaged themselves in agricultural activities. The production increased but not wages which strained the traditional organic relationship between the landowners and agricultural labourers belonging mostly to lower castes, resulting in sharpening of caste-class contradiction and migration of landless and poor peasants to non-farm sectors (Das 1983: 245-6). The polarization of privileged sections and underprivileged sections along the lines of caste and classes led to violent conflicts between them.

The grip of Brahminical ideology was not as strong in this region as was in northern Bihar and the lower castes too had access to education creating in them the feeling of self-dignity and general awareness. The people belonging to middle castes followed Kabirpanthi, Nanakshahi and Dasnami that preached against unjust nature of caste system (Prasad 2002: 195-9). The teachings of these sects contain the seeds of resistance. The areas of Magadh (in central Bihar) have a history of more exposure to war and violence compared to other regions of the state. Militant nature of the people of this region could be seen in the light of its historical background.

This region was under the influence of the peasant movement of 1930s, involving the districts of Gaya (divided into the districts of Aurangabad, Jahanabad and Arwal which were later created), Patna, and old Shahabad (this district was later divided into new districts like, Bhojpur, Rohtas, Kaimur and Buxar) and had generated consciousness among people residing in these areas. The participation of agricultural labourers and poor peasants in this movement was nominal as their issues were not taken up seriously by the Bihar Provincial Kisan Sabha (BPKS). These poor masses belonging mostly to the lower castes joined the radical peasant movement in the late 1960s led by the Maoist organizations (see Prasad 1994: 175-90).

In 1933, the Yadavs, Kurmis and Koeris joined together and formed an organization, the Triveni Sangh in Shahabad district to create awareness for socio-cultural reforms within these castes and to oppose the oppressive upper caste-feudal elements which developed consciousness among them regarding their socio-economic and political condition. The Sangh was active in the areas of central Bihar and created consciousness among the backward castes regarding their socio-economic condition imbibing in them the spirit of resistance. The lower castes (or classes) were comparatively better-off in this part than their counterparts in north Bihar. They were capable of managing their living without the support of the landlords, unlike their counterparts in northern region of the state, who were mostly dependent for their livelihoods on the landlord class (Singh 1995: 95-6). Their relatively better-off economic conditions helped them oppose the exploitation and oppression by the upper caste landlords.

The landlords of this region were more notorious for socio-economic oppression and exploitation compared to other parts of the state. The poor and landless lower castes were badly treated by the powerful landlords and their women often sexually exploited. Rape was so widespread in the Nema village of Patna district that it was a difficult task to marry off girls in this area (Das 1983: 241). The big landowners of this region behaved as those of old zamindars and perpetrated excesses on poor lower castes, thus creating a situation for agrarian clashes. The restoration of dignity to lower caste women became one of the main issues of the Naxalite movement.

The disappointment and disillusionment of the aspirants of the radical socio-economic change due to failure of the Bihar movement and the collapse of the Janata Party government at the centre, including the failure of the land reform measures encouraged and accelerated the Naxalite movement in Bihar. Mainly, the caste/class contradiction and failure of the reform measures as well as the administrative apathy to the needs and problems of the poor became rallying points for mobilization of the underprivileged sections under the leadership of Naxalite organizations. Many ex-activists of the Bihar movement found the path of Naxalite movement as the only one suitable option.

RADICAL PEASANT ORGANIZATIONS AND THEIR STRUGGLE

Many Naxalite groups operate in Bihar. Except the Maoist Communist Centre (MCC), most of them are splinter factions of the CPI(ML) which emerged after the decline of the movement in the mid-1970s. The main among them are; the CPI(ML) Liberation, the (MCC) and the CPI(ML) Party Unity (the latter merged with People's War Group (PWG) of Andhra Pradesh and formed the CPI(ML)PW in January 1998).[4] The MCC is considered as an ultra left group for its belief and practice of violent means, while the CPI(ML) Liberation has been described as being Sarkari Naxalites for its shift towards parliamentary path of electoral politics since 1985. All of these groups have formed their open mass fronts while keeping their underground activities alive. Main areas of their activities were Bhojpur, Patna, Jehanabad, Aurangabad, Gaya, Rohtas, Nalanda, Nawada, Palamu, Hazaribagh, Garhwa, Chatra, Giridih, Ranchi (latter six districts are in the Jharkhand), etc.

By the end of 1970s and the early 1980s, almost all factions of the Naxalite organizations began reviewing strategic and tactical policies as a result of which, an open mass movement was considered as a necessity along with the underground activities for progress of the people's democratic movement. In accordance with the changed policies, the formation of open fronts was emphasized to create awareness and mobilize the masses which would be subordinate to the underground organization. This resulted in intense agrarian conflicts between the 'haves' and 'have nots'. The underground factions such as, the MCC and the Party Unity, faced severe state repression in 1980s, as they had rejected the constitutional path and adopted the means of armed resistance. These parties focused on the need of combination and consolidation of secret activities, mass fronts and armed actions in order to effectively respond to the state oppression and protect the gains made by the movement (Sanjiv 1996: 52-3).

The activists of the AICCCR assembled at a secret place in Calcutta and formed the CPI(ML) in May 1969 to lead the revolutionary peasant movement. The party assessed Indian society as being semi-feudal and semi-colonial, dominated by the oppressive feudal forces and comprador bureaucratic capitalists. The contradiction between the feudalism and toiling masses was viewed as being the principal one and the agrarian revolution was made the basis of the people's democratic revolution in India. The rural areas became the centre of the peasants' radicalism where oppression and exploitation by the feudal elements were believed to be at its peak. The analysis of the Indian situation and the strategy adopted by the party was greatly influenced by the Chinese communist revolution and its leaders, including the media. The movement under its leadership spread into many parts of India by the end of the 1969 but declined in the early 1970s due to intra-party differences and state oppression leading to the split of this party into many groups. The peasant radicalism and revolutionary violence in the villages of the Mushahari block almost faded away but the villages of Bhojpur district became the new areas of agrarian unrest and violence. The CPI(ML)-Charu Mazumdar Group-anti-Lin Piao faction[5] became active in Bhojpur district which was later renamed as the CPI(ML) Liberation.[6] The liberation group mobilized a large number of poor and landless peasants, especially, the Scheduled Castes or Dalits, and effectively challenged the hegemonic position of oppressive landlords belonging mostly to the upper castes.

The CPI(ML) Liberation reviewed its strategy and adopted the tactics of developing people's mass movement using the legal and constitutional means while keeping the underground activities intact. The party formed the BPKS, a peasants' open front in the early 1981 to take up the issues related to the poor and landless peasants and mobilize them for a people's democratic revolution. A political mass front, the Indian People's Front (IPF) was also formed in the 1982, in which many revolutionary and people's organizations were merged. These open fronts helped the party in establishing contacts and interact with various democratic and progressive forces at the national level. The party decided to participate in electoral politics through the IPF and began contesting elections since mid-1980s while giving priority to the underground party activities. Both of these fronts (BPKS and IPF) helped the party expand its areas of influence to many districts of central Bihar and the socio-political dominance of powerful landlords was challenged. By 1987, the movement spread to 27 districts of Bihar (Urmilesh 1999: 75). The radical peasants fought against feudal landlords and their protectors, criminal gangs, private armies and politicians. A number of landlords and criminals were killed and large tracts of land illegally occupied by the powerful landlords were confiscated which was distributed among the poor and the landless. In retaliation, severe repression campaign was launched by the state and poor peasants were also killed in the name of being Naxalites or their supporters.

The Maoist Communist Centre (MCC) came into existence in 1969 and remained an independent party until its merger with other Naxalite groups and formation of the CPI(Maoist). The MCC did not join the CPI(ML) as the former held the view that the situation was not ripe for formation of the third revolutionary communist party because a clear demarcation was not made between the revisionist and the revolutionary line through ideological and revolutionary class struggle, and the formation of the People's Army (AIRSF 1996: 23-4). The MCC became active in south Bihar in the late 1960s and began mobilizing peasants. Despite the severe state repression, the party remained active, particularly, in Gaya and Hazaribagh districts. The party launched an annihilation campaign in January 1973, by killing an oppressive and infamous landlord, in Kasma panchayat of Gaya district. The MCC formed its open fronts in various sections of society, such as, the Krantikari Kisan Sabha (KKC), the Krantikari Buddhijivi Sangh (KBS), the Jan Pratirodh Sangharsh Manch (JPSM), etc., and expanded its base since the early 1980s (Louis 2002: 6). The MCC was considered the most dreaded of all Naxalite factions because of its violent activities.

The armed activists of the party attacked landlords and police at many places and killed many of them. More than 40 peasants belonging to the Rajput caste were killed by the armed members of the MCC in 1987 in the twin-village Dalelchak-Baghaura. The MCC also lost many of its active members in fake encounters that were a part of the repressive campaign launched by the state in the name of various operations like, the 'Operation Flash' and 'Operation Lalkhand', etc. (Sanjiv 1996: 54; *The Hindustan Times* 1996). At many places, the party confiscated lands and crops of dominant landlords for distribution among poor and landless. The MCC punished the anti-social elements in a cruel manner, for example, chopping off their nose, ears, hands, etc., even for trivial acts of theft. The party launched rectification campaign to review and rectify its past mistakes and methods of work, and also emphasized the need of consolidating unity within the party and also with other revolutionary communist groups for success of the armed agrarian movement. This self-critical and correcting method helped develop the strength of the party and widen its areas of operation.

The CPI(ML) Party Unity was formed in the early 1980s, by the Naxalites who were released from jails in the post-nationwide emergency period after formation of the Janata Party government at the centre. The party began mobilizing peasants in Bhawanichack-Sikaria region of Gaya district and from there its activities spread to other areas of the state. The Party Unity formed its mass front, the Mazdur Kisan Sangram Samiti (MKSS) to develop revolutionary consciousness among the peasants for social transformation. The front was banned after the Arwal massacre in which 23 poor peasants, presumably, the supporters of the MKSS, were killed in police firing after they had assembled for a meeting in the compound of the library in Arwal block of Jehanabad district (AIRSF 1996: 57, 64-5). The incident was described as being similar to that of Jallianwala Bagh (Amritsar, Punjab) massacre in April 1919.

The armed squads of the Party Unity began selective annihilation of the Bhoomi Sena leaders and imposed economic blockade on them. A large area of land belonging to the Sena leaders remained uncultivated. The crops of the Sena leaders were burnt which terrified the Sena leaders, who, then, surrendered and accepted the conditions laid down by the party. The ultimate aim of the party was to capture state power through prolonged class struggle to build a socialist society (Louis 2002: 183). It focused mainly on the issues of fishing rights, protection of dignity of women belonging especially to lower castes, and elimination of anti-social activities. The party protested against the police repression in which it received the support of the IPF. Many of its members and supporters were killed in police repression and attacks by the private armed gangs of landlords. The armed members of the party attacked police camps and looted their arms, cartridges and police uniforms. The firearms of landlords were also snatched away and a campaign was launched to punish criminals and corrupt politicians (*The Times of India* 1996). The party withstood joint repression by the landlord-police combine, captured land illegally held by landlords which was distributed among poor and landless. The wage rate was enhanced and the dignity of women restored, especially in areas of its influence. In 1998, the CPI(ML) Party Unity merged with the People's War Group (PWG) of Andhra Pradesh and a new party, the CPI(ML) People's War (PW), was formed. This new party later joined with the MCC and formed the CPI(Maoist) in September 2004. The new party is active in many states of India.

The armed peasant guerrillas are also known as the Lal Sena (Red Army). It is considered by the poor people as their own army. Almost all Naxalite groups formed their own armed squads to fight against oppressive police and landlord forces to protect and promote the interests of the toiling masses. The Lal Sena fights against the reactionary forces and also safeguards the gains made by the toiling peasantry. The armed guerrillas of Lal Sena killed many infamous feudal landlords and notorious anti-social elements, including armed goons of private armies. The MCC is widely known for its 'blood for blood' policy, particularly due to massacres of upper caste men in the cruellest way by slitting their throats. The armed guerrilla of this party killed 42 Rajputs in Dhalechak-Bhagaura village of Aurangabad district in the 1987, 37 Bhumihars in Bara (Gaya) in the 1992, and 34 Bhumihars in Senari village of Jehanabad in 1999 (Singh 2006: 29-30). The thieves and anti-social elements were punished cruelly even for their trivial crimes or thefts, in the name of eliminating social evils.

The armed actions and violence were accorded priority over the socio-economic programme by these groups. The CPI(ML) Liberation reviewed its strategical-tactical policy and adopted a line of development of the mass movement and selective annihilation. This faction resorted to violence only when it became a necessity at certain stage as a result of people's upsurge against the class enemy.[7] The armed squads of the CPI(ML) Liberation annihilated many members of the Ranvir Sena in areas of Bhojpur district in retaliation to the mass killing of poor and landless lower castes carried out by the Sena men. Armed peasant guerrillas belonging to various groups attacked the police stations and camps and took away rifles, carbines, cartridges, police uniforms, torches, helmets and chest belts (Urmilesh 1999: 136; *The*

Times of India (Patna) 16 June 1996; *The Hindustan Times* (Patna) 10 October 1997; *The Times of India* (Patna) 11 November 1997). The radical peasants had effectively challenged the hegemonic position of the powerful landlords bringing about significant changes in spheres of social, economical and political fields. They struggled on the vital issues of social dignity, seizure of surplus lands and crops of feudal landlords, elimination of anti-social elements with a final aim of capturing state power and build an exploitation free society.

The repressive violent acts carried out by the private goons of powerful landlords in connivance with state administration and the radical assertion of peasants on the issues of land, wages and social dignity or *izzat* had led to a number of violent clashes and carnages such as, the Rupaspur-Chandwa massacre in the 1971, the Belchi massacre in the 1977, the Arwal massacre in 1986, and the Bara massacre in 1992, etc. Despite their repression by the private armies of landlords and the state police, the radical peasants under the leadership of open fronts of the Maoist factions confiscated lands which were in excess of ceiling limits and distributed them among the poor and landless. The wage rate in areas under the influence of Naxalites was increased from approximately 800 grams to 2.5-3.0 kg, and the equality in wages between male and female workers restored (see Louis 2002: 211-13; Bhatia 2005: 1542-3). The wage rate had been kept flexible considering affordability of the poor, small and middle peasants, and also the paying-capacity of rich peasants and landlords. One of the causes of Bathani Tola massacre (Bhojpur) in 1996, in which 21 agricultural labourers belonging to Dalits and Muslims communities were killed, was the dispute over wage rate. Though wage rates were enhanced in areas of intense movement but overemphasis on wage rate kept the small peasants away from the Naxalite movement as they were not in position to afford the enhanced rates of wages.

One of the core issues of the radical agrarian movement was the issue of restoration of human and social dignity to lower castes men and women. Because of the dominance of this issue in the movement, the anti-feudal struggle of peasants had been described as being the *izzat ki ladai* (struggle for dignity). Besides this, the peasants had also struggled for elimination of social evils, thefts and crimes, by mobilizing poor peasants, small traders and businessmen as they often suffered because of these anti-social activities (see Louis 2002: 222-4). The movement achieved reasonable success in restoring the social dignity of lower caste women and men as well as in eliminating the anti-social elements to certain extent.

The radical agrarian movement grew intense in the 1980s causing violent conflicts between the deprived sections of poor peasants and reactionary forces of feudal landlords which were projected as a caste war and the problem of law and order by the state government and the media. These conflicts were treated as an issue of law and order and not as a manifestation of socio-economic problems. The massacres of Kansara, Parasdiha, Darmia, Dhalechak-Bhagaura, Chhotaki-Chhechhani, Bara, Sankarbigha, Senari, Miyanpur, and several others were carried out in a sequence of violence and counter-violence between the dominant caste-classes and the underprivileged caste-classes. Besides the violent clashes between the radical peasants and private armies of landlords, the inter-factional conflicts among Naxalite factions too led to a number of killings in which the poor peasants, supporters of the agrarian revolution were killed.

The radical resistance of oppressed castes/classes made the villages of central Bihar a war field and led to indiscriminate killings. The radical peasants confiscated the lands illegally held by the landlords and forced the latter to enhance wage rates and restore the dignity of lower caste men and women. The factors of caste, religion, have been impeding the progress of the movement. However, the killings of upper caste-poor and marginal farmers by armed squads of the Naxalite factions are against their own advocated revolutionary, democratic and humanist principles of the class struggle.

CHALLENGES AND PROSPECTS

The tendency of governments to bracket Naxalites with those of other categories of terrorists and the state's 'security-centric' approach is problematic for both. The identification of Naxalites with terrorists is a part of official tactics to defame and malign the Naxalite movement on one hand; while on the other, the state's approach of looking at the struggle of poor peasantry from the law and order perspectives prevents it from recognizing and understanding various socio-economic problems faced by the marginalized sections of society. The report of the Expert Committee (EC), constituted in 2006, by the Planning Commission, recognized the Naxalite movement as a political movement with strong base among the landless and poor peasantry and tribals. The committee considered the movement as a struggle for social justice, equality, protection and development (*EPW* 2008: 5). The expert group, while identifying causes of the emergence and growth of Naxalism in the country, which included landlessness, the failure of land reforms, non-payment of a minimum wage, control of the powerful and dominant class on the community property resources, concentration of wealth in the hands of a few causing sufferings to others, the denial of justice and human dignity to deprived sections, particularly, Scheduled Castes and Scheduled Tribes, as well as their increasing marginalization and alienation, because of denial to their basic human rights, including large-scale displacement and the ineffectiveness of resettlement and rehabilitation policy, made suggestion to adopt a multi-pronged approach. It recommended measures to improve the socio-economic conditions and also protect the interests of the marginalized sections by implementing the provisions of legislations enacted for their protection and development. Though the report suggested strengthening of the police force to effectively counter the Naxal extremism, the emphasis was laid on the redressal and development measures than the repressive tactics.

The question which arises is: whether the central and state governments are going to respond positively to these suggestions and accord priority to development and redressal issues over the repressive measures, unlike the previous trends? It seems unlikely, as the nature of the governments seem deep rooted in law and order perspectives. One of the instances of the governments' obsession with security approach is reflected in the speech delivered by the Prime Minister Manmohan Singh, during the chief ministers' conference on the issue of internal security in December 2007, in which he described the Naxalites as being the single biggest security challenge, a virus, which had to be crippled and crushed. State support to private armies in Bihar and Salwa Judum in Chhattisgarh, including the stand taken by big political parties like the Congress and Bharatiya Janata Party reflect a repressive attitude of the state and central governments as well as the existing political party culture. The state is becoming more aggressive and repressive which could be noticed in its tendency to arm police force with draconian powers by enacting various legislations in the name of providing safety measures to the citizens of the country. Simultaneously, it launches a number of welfare and anti-poverty programmes claiming to represent people and promote their interests but, in true sense, it serves the interests of bourgeois class more while creating illusion of benevolence among the poor.

The state, conventionally, particularly in a democratic set up, has been playing balancing roles between various contesting groups (and stakeholders, such as, big capitalists, civil society and toiling masses) functioning along different ideologies and programmes by adopting measures in pursuant to the nature and provisions of existing socio-political order, within which it works. In the post-1990s period of globalization, liberal policies and privatization, the capitalist forces have pumped huge amount of money as capital investment in various sectors in the name of development, while the civil society organizations, particularly, the NGOs have been spreading their wings of influence and power which has been made possible due to the 'blessings' of state and its growing tendency to share power with the former. The rise in power of civil society, the huge capital investment of big bourgeois in various sectors, emerging dominance of market-based economy, growing economic gap between the rural and urban regions, the decline of feudal forces in rural areas and the emergence of new form of aggressive-exploitative and oppressive capitalist forces in urban locations, including increase in the feeling of relative deprivations among people, especially marginalized sections, necessitate a rethinking for a new approach to analyse the changed social situation so as to identify the main contradictions in Indian society and adopt a compatible strategy for transformation of existing socio-economic order.

Now the other question arises as to how is the Naxalite movement going to cope with this situation? Will the movement survive the onslaught of new form and methods of market-based capitalist economy (which are provided with tacit support of the state) or fizzle out in the days to come under the pressure of combined repressive forces of state and capitalists, including the vacillating character of the civil society organizations? Will the movement collapse as it happened in the early 1970s? What is the nature of the movement? The movement active in different parts of the country is rural-based armed struggle, whereas the capitalist elements are growing more powerful in urban areas. Are the Naxalites capable of countering the state repression, facing a strong military equipped with modern weaponry and technology at its disposal? What is the fate of this movement? Is armed struggle a viable option at this juncture? Is the strategy adopted by the Maoists compatible to the concrete situation of the country? Will the traditional approach to the class analysis of society and adoption of strategy and tactics lead to victory of the movement with its weak mass support, killer image, and strategy of armed struggle with the help of smaller number of ill-equipped Liberation Army, compared to that of the state with its sustained popular image? What is in store for the movement? How are they going to achieve their goal of creating a humanist egalitarian society with the help of an armed class struggle? Will the movement succeed and achieve the objective of transforming Indian society along radical socialist lines or is it destined to collapse and become, at the most, a reformist movement, instead of a revolutionary one? It is difficult to answer these questions at this moment but one thing seems almost clear that the possibility of a revolutionary success with the help of strategy of armed struggle in the existing situation, keeping in view the national and international scenario, appears to be far and distant. The image of the movement created among the public is that of more terrorist than revolutionary, because of its overemphasis on the armed actions. The boycott of elections (including disrupting voting process through the use of violent means observed during general elections, particularly, elections held in April 2009) and other constitutional means having potentials to help in development of a mass movement, empower people and cause decline in the dominant political position of the bourgeois class, add to the problems and constraints that the movement is already facing. The Maoists need to introspect and rethink on the issues relating to their analysis of Indian situation, the ideological-strategic, including tactical policies so as to advance the movement to a higher stage, leading to a substantial success by effectively taking on the exploitative and oppressive imperialistic-capitalistic forces.

CONCLUSION

The failure of the land reform measures due to lack of strong political will, insincerity of government officials and manipulations by landed gentry have been the factors responsible (to the great extent) for the spread of Naxal-related violence. The socio-economic objectives of the land reform legislations could not be achieved, as a result of which, large numbers of frustrated and disappointed poor masses belonging mostly to the lower castes joined the Naxalites-led agrarian movement.

Various Naxalite factions, mainly the MCC, CPI(ML) Liberation and Party Unity mobilized the poor and landless peasants and helped them challenge the hegemonic position of traditionally dominant feudal landlords. The peasants fought on the core issues of social dignity, land and wages. The radical resistance of poor against the feudal and state repression invited more repression, making rural areas of Bihar a killing ground in which persons belonging to both sides were killed.

Despite the attacks by private armies of the feudal landlords and state police, the movement has been expanding to new areas. The radical agrarian movement or the Naxalite movement is a socio-economic conflict, and therefore, should not be treated merely as a law and order problem or caste conflict. The poor and landless peasants belonging mostly to the lower caste-classes, especially the Harijans, have been its main social base and have participated in the movement in large numbers on the core issues of land, wage and social dignity. Unless the government adopts and implements a suitable socio-economic programme with sincerity and ensures improvement in the life of a suffering poor peasantry, mere use of repressive methods and illusory reform tactics are unlikely to check the Naxalite-related problems.

The situation may improve if the state government implements land reform legislations effectively, and ensure the protection of poor tenants and sharecroppers. The fake encounters, harassment to the poor and innocents and violation of civil rights must be stopped. The surplus land must be acquired by the government and distributed among the poor and landless. The provision of infrastructural facilities and supply of agricultural inputs, such as, credit loan, high quality seeds, fertilizers, including the provisions of transportation, agricultural marketing and protection of remunerative prices will certainly reduce the pain and suffering of the poor peasants, improve their living standards and thus wean them away from indulging in violent activities. Besides this, provisions for education, health care, employment, house for the poor, special protection to the marginalized social groups, development of backward regions and other measures for development of agro-economy and overall economy of the state will prove effective in containing the violent agrarian radicalism and in restoring peace and harmony in the society.

The measures to improve socio-cultural life of the untouchables (Dalits) and ensure their right to social dignity (by uprooting the practices of untouchability) must be undertaken. Official corruption and nepotism that cause frustrations among the deprived sections must be curbed. The disputed cases related to surplus land and the non-compliance of tenancy act must be disposed of speedily in the interest of deprived castes-classes. Besides these, the provisions for social security and medical assistance to the marginalized sections will improve the social situation. Unless the distributive justice is ensured and socio-economic life of deprived people is improved, it seems difficult for the state to contain the Naxal violence, merely, by launching a repressive campaign against the agitating radical peasants.

NOTES

1. Bihar was divided and a new state Jharkhand was formed on 15 November 2000. This study is mainly focused on the current phase of the Naxalite movement after the nation-wide emergency period of 1975-7 and the formation of the Janata Party government at the centre when a large number of Naxalites were released from jails and the ban on their organizations was lifted. The Naxalite movement gained strength and momentum, especially when a number of ex-JP movement (Jayaprakash Narayan had provided leadership to students agitation during emergency period and added socialist content to it and described it as 'Total Revolution') activists joined the Naxalite organizations providing them with a new lease of life and vigour to the anti-feudal movement. The study covers the areas of both the states (united Bihar) under the influence of Naxalism.
2. Informal interviews with cross sections of migrant labourers belonging to different regions and various caste-classes at various occasions. Poor belonging to the upper castes migrate for economic reasons while people belonging to lower castes move out to other regions within the state or outside of it for both; survival and self-respect. The substantial positive change in terms of social dignity to poor belonging to lower castes has been observed, particularly in the post-1990s period. However, the urban areas provide better social environment compared to rural areas in terms of caste rigidity and resultant oppression of lower castes by upper caste dominant sections obsessed with feudal mindset.
3. The issue of caste-based oppression and exploitation became one of the major factors for mobilization of toiling masses belonging mostly to the lower caste-classes. The radical peasants had to use their firearms to ensure their social dignity. Interviews with K.D. Yadav, Central Committee Member and senior leader, CPI(ML) Liberation, Patna, 12 December 2002, and also with other activists.
4. In September 2004, the MCC and CPI(ML) PW merged together and formed a new party, the CPI (Maoist). The new party is active in more than nine states of India, especially in Chhattisgargh, Andhra Pradesh,

Bihar, Orissa, Jharkhand, Maharashtra, Madhya Pradesh, Uttar Pradesh and West Bengal.

5. Lin Piao, an important leader of the Chinese communist revolution, the next prospective Chairman of the Communist Party of China, after Mao Zedong, was killed in 1971, in a conspiratorial manner, by his rivals. The announcement of his death was officially made by the party after two years and he was denigrated as being a traitor, which resulted in confusion and factionalism in the CPI(ML) in pro- and anti-Lin Piao groups. See Chakrabarty: 1990: 118-22, for details.
6. Many Naxalite factions emerged by the mid-1970s when the movement suffered massive setbacks due to many reasons, such as, dissention within CPI(ML) on the Bangladesh issue and characterizations of Indo-Pak War of 1971, annihilation campaign, disclosure of the report on the visit of Naxalite leaders to China and comments made by the Chinese leaders on the strategy and tactics adopted by Indian Maoists or the Naxalites, excessive influence of Chinese revolution on the Naxalite movement, controversial death of Lin Piao, severe state repression, etc. Anti-Lin Piao Mazumdar group emerged stronger and led the movement in Bhojpur areas which expanded to other parts of the state. Interview with Prabhat Choudhary, Central Committee Member, CPI(ML) Liberation, Patna, 12 December 2002.
7. The CPI (ML) Liberation, in theory, believes in utilization of constitutional and extra-constitutional means and methods for success of the 'New Democratic Revolution' to facilitate transformation of society. Interview with K.D. Yadav, a senior leader, CPI (ML) Liberation, Patna, 13 December 2002. However, in practice, its emphasis on electoral politics has made other ultra left factions describe it as being revisionist.

REFERENCES

AIRSF (1996): *Naxalbari is Not Just the Name of a Village! (Twenty Five Years of the Naxalite Movement)*, Published by Chandan Roy (Calcutta: All India Revolutionary Students Federation Publication, Calcutta).

Akalank (1991): *Reservations for Backward Classes: Mandal Commission Report of the Backward Classes Commission, 1980* (New Delhi: Akalank Publications).

Banerjee, Sumanta (1980): *In the Wake of Naxalbari: A History of the Naxalite Movement* (Calcutta: Subarnarekha).

Bhatia, Bela (2005): 'The Naxalite Movement in Central Bihar', *Economic and Political Weekly*, 40 (15): 1536-49.

Census of India (2001a): *Census of India (Bihar), Series 11, Provisional Population Totals, Paper I of 2001* (Patna, Bihar: Director of Census Operations).

——— (2001b): *Census of India (Bihar), Series 11, Paper II of 2001, Provisional Population Totals, Rural-Urban Population Totals* (Patna: Director of Census Operations).

——— (2001c): *Census of India, 2001, Bihar, Series 11, Paper III of 2001, Provisional Population Totals, Distribution of Workers and Non-Workers* (Patna: Director of Census Operations).

Choudhary, Prasanna Kumar and Srikant (2001): *Bihar Mein Samajik Parivartan Ke Kuchh Ayam* (in Hindi)(New Delhi: Vani Prakashan).

Das, Arvind N. (1983): *Agrarian Unrest and Socio-Economic Change in Bihar: 1900-1980* (New Delhi: Manohar).

——— (1992): *The Republic of Bihar* (New Delhi: Penguin Books).

EPW (2008): 'Widening Debate on the Naxalite Movement', *Economic and Political Weekly*, 43 (19): 5-6.

GoI (2002): *Economic Survey 2001-2002*, Ministry of Finance, Economic Division (New Delhi: Government of India).

Gupta, Tilak D. (1992): 'Yadav Ascendancy in Bihar Politics', *Economic and Political Weekly*, 27 (26): 1304-6.

The Hindustan Times (1996): '7 MCC men gunned down in Aurangabad', Patna edition, 23 January.

——— (1996): 'Naxalites were Killed after They Surrendered: PUCL', 2 July

——— (1997): 'PU Activists Attack Jehanabad Outpost', 10 October.

The Indian Express (2002): 'Most States Move Forward, Bihar Slips Out of Growth Radar' 24 April, Mumbai.

Karanth, G.K. (1996): 'Caste in Contemporary Rural India', in M.N. Srinivas (ed.): *Caste: Its Twentieth Century Avatar* (87-109) (New Delhi: Penguin Books).

Louis, Prakash (2002): *People's Power: The Naxalite Movement in Central Bihar* (New Delhi: Wordsmith).

Mukherjee, K. and R.S. Yadav (1980): *Bhojpur: Naxalism in the Plains of Bihar* (New Delhi: Radhakrishna).

Pandey, Sachchidanand (1985): *Naxal Violence: A Socio-Political Study* (New Delhi: Chanakya Publications).

Prasad, B.N. (2002): *Radicalism and Violence in Agrarian Structure: The Maoist Movement in Bihar* (New Delhi: Manak Publications).

Prasad, Jagdish (2000): *Nav Bihar: Ek Bhavishya Nirupam* (in Hindi) (Patna: Patel Foundation).

Prasad, Pradhan H. (1994): 'Poor Peasant Movement in Central Bihar', in K.K. Sharma (ed.): *Peasant Struggles in Bihar: 1931-1992: Spontaneity to Organisation* (175-90) (Patna: Centre for Peasant Studies).

Sanjiv(1996): 'Naxalbari Ki Raah Par', *Samakalin Bahas* (in Hindi), an irregular journal (Patna: Rashtriya Press), November: 47-56.

Sharma, A.N. (1999) (ed.): *Dynamics of Employment, Poverty and Human Development in Bihar* (New Delhi: Institute for Human Development).

Singh, D.K. (1995): *Agrarian Transformation* (Jaipur: Rawat).
Singh, Joginder (2006): 'CRPF is Raising Crack Force Against Naxals', *South Asia Politics*, 4 (12): 29-30.
Singh, Rajendra (2001): *Social Movements: Old and New, A Post Modernist Critique* (New Delhi: Sage).
Sinha, Arun (1997): 'Class War, Not Atrocities Against Harijans', *Economic and Political Weekly*, 12 (50): 2037-40.
The Times of India (1996): 'Three BMP Jawans Killed in Naxal Attack', (Patna), 16 June.
——— (1996): 'Naxalites blow up Bihar MLA's House', 16 June.
——— (1997): 'Three BMP Jawans, ASI killed in MCC Attack', 11 November.
Tripathi, H.C (1999): 'Bihar: A Geo-Political Spectrum', *Journal of Social and Economic Studies*, vol. 14, combined Issue, 1997, New Series, Published in 1999 (Patna: AN Sinha Institute for Social Studies), 130-46.
Urmilesh (1999): *Bihar Ka Sach: Krishi-Sankat Aur Khetihar Sangharsh* (in Hindi) (New Delhi: Prakashan Sansthan), 3rd edn.

PART V

WORKING CLASS IN THE ERA OF LIBERALIZATION, GLOBALIZATION AND PRIVATIZATION

CHAPTER 23

Laying the Foundations of Rights: The Role of ILO in Evolving Rights of Working Class

ABDULRAHIM P. VIJAPUR

Although it is generally believed that human rights have become a universally agreed concept since the adoption of the United Nations (UN) Charter in 1945 and the subsequent adoption of the International Bill of Rights and many other human rights instruments, its origin, at least in social and economic dimensions, can be traced with the establishment of the International Labour Organization (ILO) in 1919. Both the Constitution and the ILO Conventions and recommendations have assigned a large place to human rights and have been a principal inspiration of the universal and regional texts/documents relating to economic and social rights. In the course of its 90 years of existence, the ILO has adopted 184 Conventions and 192 recommendations on different subjects concerning the rights of the workers up to the end of the 2001 session of the International Labour Conference (Swepston 2003: 92; ILO 1996 and 2003; ILR 2006: 197-290; Jenks 1960 and 1972; de la Cruz et al. 1996; Leary 1996, 2006 and 1979). These Conventions are widely ratified—over 7,000 ratifications in all, with most of the fundamental human rights Conventions in the ILO system having well over 150 ratifications—they, thus, provide a significant international human rights coverage around the world (Swepston 2005: 205). Thus, the ILO has become the most active standard-setting body in the UN system. It has also developed several human rights monitoring procedures that have since served as a model for the UN, the Council of Europe and other international organizations. The ILO was awarded the Nobel Peace Prize in 1969, on the occasion of its 50th anniversary, for its work in promoting peace and justice throughout the world.

PLACE OF HUMAN RIGHTS IN ILO CONSTITUTION

The initial text of the ILO Constitution formed Part XIII of the Treaty of Versailles of 1919 and it was amended and expanded in 1946. It not only contained provisions relating to the ILO's procedure, but it also established certain general principles with regard to which Rene Cassin has written that 'the notion of international common law regarding essential individual liberties was provided with a basis in treaty form in . . . the Treaty of Versailles, which constitutes the Charter of the ILO'. Cassin further writes that, it 'constitutes a genuine declaration of the worker's rights' (Valticos 1982: 363 and 1979: 679-97).

In accordance with the ILO Constitution of 1919, the ILO was established as an autonomous permanent intergovernmental organization mandated to promote worldwide programmes to achieve (1) full employment and the raising of standards of living; (2) the employment of workers in occupations in which they can have the satisfaction of giving the fullest measure of their skill and attainments and can make their contributions to the common well-being; (3) the provision, as a means to attaining this end, and under adequate guarantees for all concerned, of facilities for training and the transfer of labour, including migration for employment and settlement; (4) policies in regard to wages and earnings, hours and other conditions of work, calculated to insure a just share of the fruits of progress to all, and a minimum living wage to all employed and in need of such protection; (5) the effective recognition of the right of collective bargaining, the cooperation of management and labour in the continuous improvement of productive efficiency, and the collaboration of workers in the preparation and application of social and economic measures; (6) the extension of social security measures to provide a basic income to all in need of such protection and comprehensive medical care; (7) adequate protection for the life and health of workers in all occupations; (8) provision of child welfare and maternity protection; (9) the provision of adequate nutrition, housing, and facilities for recreation and culture; and (10) the assurance of equality of educational and vocational opportunity.

It is worth recalling here that the Article 427 of the Treaty of Versailles (1919) contained certain 'General Principles', popularly known as 'the Labour Charter', which the signatories thereto accepted to ameliorate the conditions of labour. These were:

1. Labour should not be regarded merely as a commodity or an article of commerce,
2. The right of association for all lawful purposes by the employed as well as the employers should be recognized,
3. The payment to the employed of a wage adequate to maintain a reasonable standard of life, as this was understood in their time and country should be guaranteed,
4. An 8-hour day or a 48-hour week should be the standard to be aimed at where it had not already been allowed,
5. A weekly rest of at least 24 hours, which was to include Sunday wherever practicable, should be provided,
6. Child labour should be abolished,
7. The principle that men and women should receive equal remuneration for work of equal value should be enforced,
8. Each state should make provision for a system of inspection in order to ensure the enforcement of the laws and regulations for the protection of the employed, and
9. Workers should be protected against disease and injury arising out of his employment.

The ILO survived the demise of the League of Nations to become the first specialized agency of the UN. Fundamental principles of the ILO are also contained in the 'Declaration concerning the Aims and Purposes of the ILO' adopted by the International Labour Conference at Philadelphia in 1944 and incorporated in the ILO Constitution in 1946. The Declaration states *inter alia*:

I

The conference reaffirms the fundamental principles on which the Organization is based and in particular, that–

Labour is not a commodity;

Freedom of expression and association are essential to sustained progress;

Poverty anywhere constitutes a danger to prosperity everywhere; . . .

II

All human beings, irrespective of race, creed or sex, have the right to pursue both their material well-being and their spiritual development in conditions of freedom and dignity, of economic security and equal opportunity.

The Constitution of ILO is unique as it provides a mechanism of monitoring human rights obligations contained in the Constitution, Conventions and recommendations adopted by it. Earl Warren, the former Chief Justice of the United States Supreme Court, while inaugurating the Abidjan World Peace through Law Conference in 1973 had rightly emphasized the importance of the machinery of ILO in the implementation of human rights.

> Standing before us also is the basic fact that a body of international law on human rights now exists. And because it exists we can now turn our attention to the means by which it can be implemented. . . . For the past three years, I have had the good fortune to be associated with a judicial review panel of the ILO. I have been impressed at the extent to which the basic features of effective implementation are built into the constitutional structure of the ILO—fact-finding, exposure, conciliation and adjudication. The handling of complaints, which is the heart of meaningful enforcement of human rights, has been carefully structured in a precise procedural manner. What is more important, there is a record demonstrating that these arrangements have produced concrete results. . . . The ILO experience can be applied to the entire range of human rights concerns. (Wolf 1984: 275; and 1975: 599-625)

TRIPARTISM: A FUNDAMENTAL CONCEPT

The great strength of the ILO, and the characteristic which distinguishes it from all other international organizations, is that it is tripartite. This means that decisions in the ILO are not made by governments alone, but by representatives of workers and employers as well. Each Member State of the ILO (currently has 183 members) is required to send to the annual conference a tripartite delegation, consisting of two government delegates and one delegate each from the most representative organizations of employers and of workers in that country.

The ILO's organs are thus composed of all three partners. In the conference, there are four votes for each Member State, two from the government and one each from the employers and workers. In conference committees, the system of tripartism goes even further, and the groups comprising the government, employers and workers each has one-third of the votes.

The governing body of ILO is also tripartite, with 28 government members, 14 employers and 14 workers.

The tripartite concept thus extends to the adoption and supervision of standards, to the taking of all fundamental decisions on the ILO's programme and to the day-to-day supervision of its work through the governing body. In the Member States it means that all decisions relating to the ILO and its standards should be taken on a tripartite basis. Many of the standards explicitly require the involvement of representatives of employers and workers in their implementation, and this is implicit even where it is not contained in the text of the relevant Convention.

HUMAN RIGHTS AND THE CONVENTIONS AND RECOMMENDATIONS OF THE ILO

As noted earlier, between 1919 and 2001 the ILO has adopted 184 Conventions and 192 recommendations on various aspects of human rights of workers. Each Convention is a formal legal instrument, adopted by the General Conference, regulating some aspect of labour administration, social welfare, or human rights and is binding upon all States that have ratified or acceded to it. Recommendations are adopted to provide guidelines for national practice. They are not binding, but apply equally to all Member States. The ILO recommendations are akin to general comments expressed by the committees of various treaty bodies (Mertus 2005: 149-50). It is not possible or desirable to give a detailed account here of the content of these various Conventions and recommendations which are often described as the 'International Labour Code'. Our purpose here is to provide a general outline of this code.

At the outset it may be said that practically all the ILO Conventions and recommendations deal with the promotion and protection of human rights in the broad sense, since even the most technical of them relate to concrete aspects of the right to just and favourable working conditions provided for in Article 7 of the International Covenant on Economic, Social and Cultural Rights (ICESCR). In fact, Articles 6 to 12 of the ICESCR contains those rights which are normally the subject of the ILO Conventions and recommendations, such as, right to work (Article 6), the right to just and favourable conditions of work including fair wages, equal pay for equal work and holiday with pay (Article 7), the right to form and join trade unions, including the right to strike (Article 8), the right to social security (Article 9), protection of the family, including special assistance for mothers and children (Article 10), the right to an adequate standard of living, including adequate food, clothing and housing and the continuous improvement of living conditions (Article 11), and the right to the highest attainable standards of physical and mental health (Article 12). Thus, it needs to be highlighted here that there are by now more than 75 ILO Conventions covering and developing the various concepts laid down in brief statements of principle in ICESCR. All the specialized agencies of the UN participate, including the ILO, in the implementation mechanisms/ procedures of ICESCR. Articles 16 and 18 of the ICESCR provide that the specialized agencies shall receive copies of the reports of States bearing on questions within their competence and that arrangements may be concluded in order for these agencies to submit reports bearing *inter alia* on the decisions of their competent bodies concerning the implementation of the provisions of the covenant falling within the scope of their activities. The specialized agencies may also submit observations on any recommendation made by the Commission on Human Rights (now Human Rights Council) (Article 20). Since the great majority of the provisions of ICESCR concern questions on which the ILO has adopted numerous detailed Conventions, the ILO's supervisory bodies may play a considerable role in the effective implementation of this covenant. Participation by the specialized agencies is also provided for, though in less precise terms, by the ICCPR (Article 40, para 3). Thus, it is not wrong to state that many of the rights enshrined in the early ILO Conventions provided language for the ICESCR and ICCPR, and the later the UN Conventions have likewise been elaborated upon through the recent ILO Conventions (Mertus 2005: 142).

Fundamental ILO Conventions (core agreements) are based on four basic principles of the ILO: Freedom of Association and Right to Tariff Negotiations, Abolition of Child Labour and Prohibition of Discrimination in Employment and Occupations. Many Conventions have been conducted and furthered the development of international minimum standards for economic and social rights. Such standards include the right to work and protection from discrimination in occupation, the right to strike, the right to form trade unions, the right to collective bargaining, the right to social security, as well as the prohibition of forced and child labour, the elimination of discrimination against women and the rights of indigenous peoples. Let us briefly elaborate some of the important ILO Conventions under the following headings.

FREEDOM OF ASSOCIATION AND RIGHT TO ORGANIZE CONVENTION

Two of the best ILO Conventions develop the principles of freedom of association (Haas 1970): the Freedom of Association and Protection of the Right to Organize Convention, 1948 (No. 87), and the Right to Organize and Collective Bargaining Convention, 1949 (No. 98). Convention No. 87 provides the right of workers and employers, without any distinction whatsoever, to establish and join organizations of their own choosing with a view to furthering and defending their interests. These organizations have the rights to run their affairs, to establish and join federations and confederations which shall enjoy the same rights and guarantees, and to affiliate with international organizations, Convention No. 98 goes on to provide protection for workers when they are exercising the right to organize; lays down the principle of non-interference between workers' and employers' organizations; and promotes voluntary collective bargaining.

Collective Bargaining Convention, 1981 (No. 154), complements and updates the provisions of earlier Conventions (Nos. 87 and 98) concerning collective bargaining between employers and employees. It provides that measures adapted to national conditions shall be taken to promote collective bargaining after prior consultations between organizations of employers and employees, and that provision for such measures should be incorporated in national laws or regulations.

RIGHT TO BE FREE FROM DISCRIMINATION IN EMPLOYMENT AND OCCUPATION

Most ILO Conventions apply without distinction to all persons in the workplace, with the exception of those intended to protect special categories of persons (women, children, etc). The ILO also has the mission to promote equality of opportunity and treatment in respect of employment and occupation more generally.

The Discrimination (Employment and Occupation) Convention, 1958 (No. 111) requires ratifying States to promote equality of opportunity and treatment through a national policy aimed at eliminating all forms of discrimination in respect of employment and occupation. Discrimination is defined as any distinction, exclusion or preference based on race, colour, sex, religion, political opinion, national extraction or social origin. The State concerned may also designate other grounds on which it undertakes to apply the Convention. The Convention covers access to vocational training, access to employment and to particular occupations, and terms and conditions of employment. The Convention also provides that special measures of protection and assistance provided for in other ILO Conventions and recommendations shall not be deemed to be discrimination; nor shall any distinction, exclusion or preference in respect of a particular job based on the inherent requirements thereof.

The implementation of the Convention is to a large extent successful. Most countries of the world have provisions in their labour legislation which prohibits discrimination in employment, and mostly modelled on Convention No. 111 or takes account of it. An increasing number of countries have established machinery to combat discrimination in employment, and significant differences can be discerned in recent years in many of them in the treatment of various minority or other disadvantaged groups. Nevertheless, in its 1988 general survey on the application of Convention No. 111, the Committee of Experts on the Application of Conventions and Recommendations, the role of which will be discussed in the subsequent section, noted that equality in employment could not be fully realized in a general context of inequality. Inequality in social status leads inevitably to inequality of treatment, and above all to inequality of opportunity in employment. It has been noticed that there is, in fact, no country in the world in which the problem of discrimination does not exist.

PROTECTION OF WOMEN AND THE ELIMINATION OF DISCRIMINATION

The ILO has adopted many Conventions and recommendations to protect the interests of women workers (Symonides and Volodin 1999). Most of these Conventions provide protection for women in employment, especially in relation to the conditions of work which may entail risks for maternity. A large number of ILO Conventions provide special condition for women when they would be endangered by exposure to particular substances or situations in the workplace; and others provide social security protection for women in pregnancy and child-bearing. Let us spell out briefly the content/provisions of some of the important Conventions and recommendations.

The general conference of ILO adopted Recommendation (No. 4) concerning the Protection of Women and Children against Lead Poisoning on 28 November 1919. In view of the danger involved in maternity and the physical development of children, the ILO members were requested to exclude women and young persons under the age of 18 years, from the employment in the following processes: (a) in furnace work in the reduction of zinc or lead ores; (b) in the manipulation, treatment, or reduction of ashes containing lead, and the desilvering of lead; (c) in the manufacture of solder or alloys containing more than 10 per cent of lead; (d) in melting lead or old zinc on a large scale; (e) in the manufacture of various kinds of lead or sulphate, etc.; (f) in mixing and pasting in the manufacture or repair of electric accumulators; and (g) in the cleaning of workrooms where the above processes are carried on.

The Recommendation (No. 13) concerning night work of women in agriculture was adopted on 15 November 1921. This recommendation requires that each Member State should take steps to regulate the employment of women wage-earners in agricultural undertakings during the night in such a way as to ensure them a period of rest compatible with their physical necessities and containing of not less than nine hours.

The Convention (No. 45) concerning the Employment of Women on Underground Work in Mines, 1935, provides that no female, whatever her age, shall be employed on underground work in any mine. This prohibition exempts females holding positions of management who do not perform manual work or those who belong to health and welfare services, or those who are conducting studies during the period of training.

The ILO Night Work (Women) Convention (No. 89), revised in 1948, states that women without distinction of age shall not be employed during the night in any public or private industrial undertakings such as mines, quarries and other works for the extraction of minerals from the earth. This prohibition is extended to other undertakings in which articles are manufactured, altered, cleaned, repaired and ornamented. The list of undertakings also includes those concerned with building and civil engineering work, including constructional, repair, maintenance, alteration and demolition work. According to the Convention the term 'night' signifies a period of at least 11 consecutive hours, including an interval period, falling between 10 o'clock in the evening and 7 o'clock in the morning.

This Convention (89) was revised through the 1990 Protocol. This protocol states that the national laws and regulations should be adopted after consulting the representative organizations of employers and workers concerning night work. The main feature of the protocol is that it prohibits applying the variations and exemptions allowed in the Convention to women workers during a period before and after childbirth of at least 16 weeks, of which at least eight weeks shall be before the expected date of childbirth. This prohibition can be lifted at the request of the woman worker concerned on condition that neither her health nor that of her child will be endangered.

This prohibition shall also apply to additional periods in respect of which a medical certificate is produced stating that this is necessary for the health of the mother or child during pregnancy or during a specified time prolonging the period after childbirth. Moreover, during this period a woman worker shall not be dismissed/terminated, except for justifiable reasons not concerned with pregnancy or childbirth. Also, the income of a woman worker concerned shall be maintained at a level sufficient for the upkeep of herself and her child in accordance with a suitable standard of living. This income maintenance may be ensured through an assignment to day work, extended maternity leave, social security benefits or any other appropriate measure.

The 1952 (Revised) Maternity Protection Convention (No. 103) stated that a woman worker in both industrial and non-industrial occupations should be entitled for a maternity leave of at least 12 weeks on the production of a medical certificate. National laws should prescribe the period of compulsory leave after confinement. In case of illness, medically certified, arising out of pregnancy, further appropriate leave may be granted which may be fixed by the competent authority. While absent from work on maternity leave, the women shall be entitled to receive cash and medical benefits. National laws should fix the amount of cash and medical benefits. There should be a compulsory social insurance scheme providing maternity benefits. An interruption of work for the purpose of nursing the child is to be counted as working hour and remunerated accordingly. During maternity leave no employer can dismiss the worker and give notice. Though the Convention is generally applicable to women workers of both industrial and non-industrial sectors, it allows State parties to exempt certain categories of non-industrial occupations from the application of the Convention such as agricultural undertakings, domestic work for wages in private households, wage earners working at home, etc., this can be done by filing declarations (reservations).

The Equal Remuneration Convention, 1951 (No. 100) provides equal remuneration for men and women for the work of equal value. This Convention is supplemented by the Equal Remuneration Recommendation, 1951 (No. 90). The principle may be applied by means of national laws or regulations, legal machinery for wage determination, collective agreements or a combination of these means, including the objective appraisal of jobs.

On 23 June 1981, the International Labour Conference adopted the ILO Workers with Family Responsibilities Convention, 1981 (No. 156). This Convention, which entered into force on 11 August 1983, applies to men and women workers with responsibilities in relation to their dependent children, where such responsibilities restrict their possibilities of preparing for, entering, participating in or advancing in economic activity. Children need parental care and support. It prohibits discriminating between men and women workers in extending rights under the Convention. Following rights are provided:

(1) With a view to creating effective equality of opportunity and treatment for men and women workers, all measures compatible with national conditions and possibilities shall be taken to enable workers with family responsibilities to exercise their right to free choice of employment; and to take account of their needs in terms and conditions of employment and in social security.
(2) All measures compatible with national conditions and possibilities shall be taken to account of the needs of workers with family responsibilities in community planning and to develop or promote community services, public or private, such as child-care and family services and facilities.
(3) The competent authorities and bodies in each country shall take appropriate measures to promote information and education which engender broader public understanding of the principle of equality of opportunity and treatment for men and women workers and of the problems of workers with family responsibilities, as well as a climate of opinion conducive to overcoming these problems.
(4) All measures shall be taken for these workers in the field of vocational guidance and training.
(5) Family responsibilities shall not constitute a valid reason for termination of employment.

This Convention may be applied by laws or regulations, collective arrangements, work rules, arbitration awards, court decisions or a combination of these methods. Each Member State ratifying the Convention shall submit, under Article 22 of the Constitution of ILO, reports the extent to which effect has been given or is proposed to be given to the Convention. Employers' and workers' organizations shall have the right to participate in devising and applying measures designed to give effect to the provisions of the Convention.

The Recommendation (No. 165), concerning Equal Opportunities and Equal Treatment for Men and Women Workers with Family Responsibilities was adopted by the general conference of the ILO on the same day when the Convention on the same topic was adopted. Compared to the Convention No. 156, the recommendation is very elaborate and detailed concerning the rights. It elaborates the national policy, training and employment, terms and conditions of employment, child care and family services and facilities and social security.

The Workers with Family Responsibilities Convention, 1981 (No. 156) requires the States parties to create an effective equality of opportunity and treatment for men and women workers with family responsibilities. It applies to both men and women workers with responsibilities for their dependent children or other members of their immediate families where such responsibilities restrict their possibilities of participating in economic activity.

RIGHTS OF MIGRANT WORKERS

Three Conventions on the rights of migrant workers have been adopted. The Convention No. 97 (adopted in 1947) on the subject requires ratifying States to establish services to assist and protect migrants for employment and their families, and to provide equality of treatment with its own nationals for migrants lawfully in the country. Ratifying States should conclude agreements with other States from which significant numbers of migrants come. The Convention No. 143 (adopted in 1975) aims at suppressing illegal migration for employment, and provides additional measures to assure equality of treatment for migrant workers. The Convention No. 118, 1962 provides equal treatment of migrant workers in terms of social security, on a reciprocal basis with other countries which have ratified the same Convention.

The UN adopted, in 1990, an International Convention on the

Rights of all Migrant Workers and Members of their Families (Rehman 2008: 429-59). The ILO took an active part in the deliberations leading to its adoption. This Convention entered into force in 2003 and the ILO is expected to participate actively in its implementation.

DISABLED WORKERS

In accordance with international labour standards, workers enjoy social protection in the event of disability, the principal aim being to ensure that disabled workers should have equitable access to employment and income from work. The underlying concept is that disabled workers, who are job-ready, after a process of rehabilitation, are not unjustifiably barred from access to jobs and are not denied the opportunity to choose their employment freely. The ILO's Vocational Rehabilitation and Employment (Disability Persons) Convention, 1983 (No. 159) reaffirms the right of disabled people to equal treatment in training and employment, and calls on governments and on employers' and workers' organizations to ensure that policies are pursued which protect disabled people's right to secure, retain and advance in employment.

INDIGENOUS AND TRIBAL PEOPLES

The ILO Conventions No. 107 of 1957 and No. 160 of 1989 are the only two international legal instruments adopted specifically on the subject by the international community. The UN has so far not adopted any treaty on the indigenous people. It was only in 2007 that the UN General Assembly adopted the Declaration on the Rights of Indigenous Peoples which was approved by the UN Sub-Commission on Human Rights in 1994 as a Draft Declaration on the subject (Crawford 1991: 235-65). The Convention No. 107 was the only Convention on this subject for 32 years. Adopted by the ILO with the full cooperation and collaboration of a number of other organizations in the UN system, it covers a wide number of issues, ranging from the working and labour conditions, and recruitment of indigenous and tribal peoples, to land rights, health and education.

During the last part of the 1970s and throughout the 1980s, some indigenous organizations, and a number of intergovernmental agencies and governments, started expressing disagreement with the philosophy and approach of the Convention No. 107, since it was perceived as having an 'integrationist' orientation. In June 1989, the International Labour Conference adopted the Convention No. 169 on Indigenous and Tribal Peoples, which took a very different approach.

It is encouraging to note that Norway, which is a party to the Convention No. 169, created a Sami (which is an indigenous group) parliament some time ago and this parliament has gradually assumed a greater role in managing the internal autonomy of the Sami people. Based on a suggestion made in the 'Report Form' on the Convention No. 169 (on each Convention, the ILO governing body adopts a report form, which is designed to help governments make their periodic reports. These forms contain questions to illustrate the kind of information desired under various articles, as well as more general guidelines on reporting on each Convention), the Norwegian government has begun to send its reports on the Convention to the Sami parliament for comment and transmits the parliament's comments to the ILO as part of its own report. The government has also asked the ILO to open a parallel dialogue with the parliament, giving the representatives of the Sami people a formal part to play in the supervisory process. While no exactly similar arrangement has emerged in any other country, the ILO Committee of Experts has been urging governments for some years to consult their indigenous peoples in drawing up their reports, and to state what these consultations have yielded (Swepston 2003: 105; Landy 1966 and 1970: 555-604; Rossilion 1974: 40-9; Joyce 1980).

OTHER IMPORTANT CONVENTIONS ON WORKERS' RIGHTS

The ILO has adopted many Conventions to protect and provide many social and economic rights. In this regard following Conventions may be noted.

(1) Social Security (Minimum Standards) Convention (No. 102), 1952, deals with nine main branches of social security—medical care, sickness benefit, unemployment benefit, old-age benefit, employment injury benefit, family benefit, maternity benefit, invalidity benefit, and survivor's benefit—and establishes the minimum standards for such benefits.
(2) Equality of Treatment (Social Security) Convention (No. 118),

1962, provides that nationals and non-nationals shall be treated equally in all matters of social security.

(3) The basic aim of Social Policy (Basic Aims and Standards), Convention (No. 117), 1962, is to improve standards of living in such fields as public health, housing, nutrition, education, the welfare of children, the status of women, conditions of employment, the remuneration of wage earners and independent producers, the protection of migrant workers, social security, standards of public services and general production, primarily by steps taken at the appropriate international, regional and national levels.

(4) Recognizing that employment is normally the first concern of every worker, Employment Policy Convention (No. 122), 1964, provides that each contracting State undertake to pursue, as a major goal, an active policy designed to promote full, productive and freely chosen employment.

(5) Medical Care and Sickness Benefits Convention (No. 130), 1969, provides regulation by the contracting States of the scope and character of State medical care and of sickness benefits with a view to ensuring that such care and benefits are made available to all persons on a basis of equality and without discrimination.

(6) Holidays with Pay Convention (No. 132), Revised, 1970, provides that all employed persons in a contracting State—seafarers are the only exception specifically mentioned—are entitled to annual paid holidays of not less than three working weeks for one year of service. Public or customary holidays are not counted as part of the minimum annual holiday, and a worker on holiday must be paid at least his normal or average remuneration.

(7) Paid Educational Leave Convention (No. 140), 1974, defines 'paid educational leave' as the leave granted to workers for educational purposes for a specified period during working hours, with adequate financial entitlements; and provides that States parties should grant such leave as necessary for (a) training at any level, (b) general, social, and civic education, and (c) trade union education.

(8) In 1999, the ILO adopted Elimination of the Worst Forms of Child Labour Convention (No. 182). This Convention defines the worst forms of child labour to include forced labour, such as forced recruitment of child soldiers; prostitution; drug trafficking; and employment hazardous to the development of the child. Enforcement of the Convention involves monitoring, prevention, enforcement and punishment of crimes.

DECLARATION OF FUNDAMENTAL RIGHTS AND PRINCIPLES AT WORK, 1998

In 1998, the ILO adopted a new kind of instrument. The Declaration of Fundamental Rights and Principles at Work codifies the ILO's long understanding of the fundamental human rights contained in its Constitution and standards as comprising freedom of association and the right to bargain collectively, freedom from forced labour, freedom from child labour and freedom from discrimination. It provides that all States, even if they have not been able to ratify the Conventions which embody these principles, have 'an obligation, arising from the very fact of membership in the organisation, to respect, to promote and to realise, in good faith and in accordance with the Constitution, the fundamental rights which are the subjects of the . . . ILO Conventions'. Global reports are prepared under the declaration, each focusing on one of the four subjects covered, examining its application around the world and giving rise to a plan of action for technical assistance. All of this work is done in a promotional framework.

Besides evolving norms and standards of human rights in its Conventions and recommendations, the ILO sometimes adopts less formal documents. For example, these include, the Tripartite Declaration of Principles concerning Multinational Enterprises and Social Policy, adopted by the governing body in 1976 and updated in 2000, and conference resolutions on such questions as the independence of the trade union movement and the relation of trade union rights and civil liberties. Based primarily on initiatives from the United States and the international trade union movement, there has been an effort to include, in international trade agreements, a 'social clause' to link 'basic workers' rights' or 'internationally recognized workers' rights' to trading privileges. The ILO has also adopted a number of codes of conduct and guidelines illustrating best practice in various respects, such as the Code of Practice on HIV/AIDS adopted by the ILO governing body in June 2001.

It is important to note that of the 182 Conventions that the ILO has adopted so far, eight have been designated by ILO as 'core Conventions'. These are: Conventions No. 29 (Forced Labour Convention, 1930), No. 87 (Freedom of Association and Protection of the Right to Organize Convention, 1948), No. 98 (The Right to Organize and Collective Bargaining Convention, 1949), No. 100 (Equal Remuneration Convention, 1951), No. 105 (Abolition of

Forced Labour Convention, 1957), No. 111 (Discrimination (Employment and Occupation) Convention, 1958, No. 138 (Minimum Age Convention, 1973) and No. 182 (Elimination of the Worst Forms of Child Labour, 1999).

ILO MACHINERY/PROCEDURES FOR IMPLEMENTATION OF HUMAN RIGHTS NORMS

The most remarkable thing about the ILO and human rights is the supervision of implementation of ILO standards. A report submitted to the United States House of Representatives Committee on Foreign Affairs by its sub-committee on International Organizations and Movements notes that 'the ILO procedures for inquiring into alleged breaches of their Conventions are probably the most sophisticated and most effective in the international sphere', and that the methods of the ILO 'for the protection of human rights should be emulated by other international organisations' (Wolf 1984: 276).

The ILO has the most comprehensive and sophisticated supervisory system in international law although many in the field of human rights are unaware of this, as most of the ILO Conventions focus on labour matters—an aspect of international human rights law that has been till recently largely neglected. The system of monitoring first developed between 1919 and 1927 was radical in some ways; it is even more so now (Swepston 2003: 95-6). The following pages provide a discussion on various methods and procedures of the ILO to implement international human rights obligations.

REPORTING PROCEDURES

The ILO Constitution establishes reporting procedures of two kinds on the Conventions and recommendations. (1) Article 19 of the Constitution requires Member States to bring any Convention or recommendation adopted by the International Labour Conference before the competent authority—in most cases the national parliament—for the enactment of legislation or other action. It further states that the submission to the competent authority should generally be made within one year and in no case later than 18 months from the date of their adoption. If any State fails to do so, the matter can be reported to the governing body by any other member. (2) All

States ratifying the ILO Conventions have to submit reports at regular intervals of between one and five years (Article 22 of the Constitution). At the same time, they are required (Article 23 of the Constitution) to send copies of these reports to workers' and employers' organizations. These organizations have the right to comment on these reports—they may state that the government is misrepresenting the situation or has not provided full information or even that they agree with the government's report. Such comments must be communicated to the ILO by governments, which may also attach their own comments. These reports must be drafted on the basis of detailed forms established by the governing body of the ILO; for non-ratified Conventions and recommendations, reports at intervals requested by the governing body, concerning the national law and practice, showing the extent to which the State concerned has given effect or proposes to give effect to those texts, and stating the difficulties which prevent or delay the ratification of the Convention concerned or the application of the recommendation in question. A total of some 2,000 reports are submitted each year by governments.

Two bodies are entrusted with the examination of these reports: an independent body, the Committee of Experts on the Application of Conventions and Recommendations (hereafter the Committee of Experts); and a body composed of nearly 100 representatives of governments, employers and workers, the Committee on the Application of Conventions and Recommendations of the International Labour Conference (hereafter the Conference Committee).

THE COMMITTEE OF EXPERTS

These reports are examined by the Committee of Experts, which was established in 1927. The committee is composed of persons of recognized competence who are completely independent of governments. This independence is marked by the fact that its members are appointed by the ILO governing body on the recommendation of the director general and not of the governments of the countries of which they are citizens. They are chosen from the highly qualified persons in the legal and social fields, principally in the judiciary (several have been chief justices of supreme courts), education (professors of international law, labour law, etc.), or from among the former statesmen. It has 20 members and meets annually. It is not a court, but its function is of a judicial character in that it is required to assess the extent to which national law and practice are in conformity with the provisions of the ILO Constitution or Conventions.

The committee examines nearly 2,000 reports annually—a massive workload. It makes any comments it feels are necessary—asking questions about application, or indicating that the national law and practice are not in conformity and requesting changes. This is done in two ways: (i) Direct requests are not published and consist of less serious or more preliminary points. It requests further information or ask for minor adjustments. (ii) Observations are published comments which appear in the annual reports of the Committee of Experts and are submitted to the International Labour Conference for possible discussion. They deal with more serious matters than do direct requests. It is gratifying to note that the committee's comments and findings on lack of conformity with a ratified Convention have led to positive results. For example, between 1964 and 1982, over 1,400 discrepancies have been rectified by governments as a result of observations and direct requests made by the Committee of Experts, with many of these related to Conventions on the basic human rights (Wolf 1984: 283).

THE CONFERENCE COMMITTEE

The report of the Committee of Experts is a powerful tool for those who want to compare their country's performance with its international obligations. This report is further examined by the Conference Committee, which is established by the International Labour Conference. This committee is composed of around 100 representatives from governments, employers and workers. It will usually decide to discuss, in public session, about 30 cases of the several hundred published in the report of the Committee of Experts. The Conference Committee invites the representative of the government concerned to appear before it and explain the reasons for the problem in question. This representative then takes part in a dialogue with the committee, usually led by the employers' and workers' own representatives. Statements clarifying the position are sought from government representative and she/he is asked to indicate a timetable for the implementation of measures requested by the Committee of Experts. Or the representative is asked to commit the government to inviting the International Labour office to carry out 'direct contacts' or technical assistance to resolve the problems. These sessions can be very difficult for government representatives, but often result in promises of improved performance.

CONTENTIOUS PROCEDURES: REPRESENTATIONS AND COMPLAINTS

There are two main complaints procedures in the ILO supervisory mechanism: (1) representation against members, (2) complaint against members.

Under Article 24 of the Constitution, a representation may be filed by any workers' or employers' organization, alleging violation of a ratified Convention. This results in the appointment of a tripartite governing body committee, which discusses the case, usually on the basis of an exchange of correspondence; it is thus particularly used in cases where the facts are not in doubt. Fewer than 100 representations have been submitted since 1919, but the increase in recourse to this procedure in recent times appears to reflect growing difficulties in numerous countries in securing observance of ratified Conventions (Swepston 2005: 200). Under Article 26 of the ILO Constitution, any government which has ratified the same Convention, any delegate to the International Labour Conference or the governing body of the ILO can file a complaint alleging the violation of a Convention by a country which has ratified it. This result in the establishment of a Commission of Inquiry which holds hearings in Geneva, visits the country concerned, and makes findings as to whether the Convention is being violated.

THE COMMITTEE ON FREEDOM OF ASSOCIATION

This committee was created in 1951 by an agreement with the Economic and Social Council of the UN. This committee, which has acquired world renown, is appointed by the governing body. It consists of nine members (three government, three employers and three workers). Its first chairman was Paul Ramadier, former prime minister of France, who continued in office for 10 years. It receives complaints of violations of freedom of association. These complaints may be filed by the organizations of employers and workers, regardless of whether the country concerned has ratified the ILO Conventions on the subject. It meets three times a year, and has dealt with more than 2000 cases. Its recommendations and decisions are mostly accepted by governments, and have led over the years to innumerable cases of freeing trade unionists from prison or facilitating their return from exile, as well as reforms in labour law and industrial relations, and many other improvements in various situations.

THE FACT-FINDING AND CONCILIATION COMMISSION ON FREEDOM OF ASSOCIATION

The Fact-Finding and Conciliation Commission is a much more formal procedure. Under this procedure a panel of three persons may investigate a case by visiting the country and making detailed recommendations. In principle, a case can be referred to the commission only with the consent of the government concerned. In the initial years many governments refused to give consent. In later years, many States found it difficult to refuse giving their consent. In 1991, the commission went to South Africa with the government's permission, and made detailed recommendations concerning the changes which would have to be made in the country's industrial relations system with the approaching end of apartheid. This illustrates that this procedure may also be used even in cases in which the country concerned is not a member of the ILO (South Africa was not at that time). In all cases, the approval of the government concerned is required before this procedure can be instituted—the only one of the ILO's procedures requiring consent. Thus, it can be said that the ILO was probably the most effective of all the international organizations in fighting apartheid in South Africa through persistent and detailed criticism combined with practical help to workers' organizations and since the installation of the new multiracial government of Nelson Mandela in 1992, to employers' organizations as well.

Julie A. Mertus opines that these complaint mechanisms underutilized (Mertus 2005:154) have great potential to raise labour standards, yet they remain.

IMPACT OF ILO'S WORK ON HUMAN RIGHTS: CONCLUDING OBSERVATIONS

Though it is often difficult to quantify the influence of ILO standards, it is certainly possible to conclude that its impact on human rights in Member States is remarkable. There has been ample evidence of the direct influence of these standards at the national level. The ILO standards are the basis for labour legislation adopted around the world, especially for countries which have recently attained independence or are undergoing democratization. Furthermore, the ILO's regular work includes helping countries to rewrite labour and human rights legislation on the basis of its standards.

It is true that the ILO's elaborate system of monitoring human rights standards has served as a model to the UN, the Council of Europe and other international organizations. Eminent jurists, such as Georges Scelle, Lord McNair (former president of International Court of Justice), and Earl Warren (former chief justice of the United States), who, were the members of the Committee of Experts, used to raise always a question as to what extent the ILO procedures might also be used in the framework of other international organizations. Professor Roberto Ago raised the question whether these procedures might not be extended to Conventions adopted under the auspices of the UN, or in relation to procedures for the protection of freedom of association (Valticos 1982: 394). Certain treaties of regional institutions, like the Council of Europe, provide measures of co-ordination. The European Social Charter, which was adopted in 1961 with the technical assistance and on the basis of the ILO standards, thus provides participation in consultative capacity by an ILO representative in the deliberations of the Committee of Independent Experts responsible for supervising its application.

The ILO's system for the protection of human rights is among the most advanced and effective mechanisms in the world. Since its creation in 1919, its Conventions and recommendations together with its supervisory mechanism have produced tangible results, improving the lives and working conditions of people all over the world.

REFERENCES

Crawford, Catherine (1991): 'The Status of the Rights of Indigenous Peoples in International Law and the Prospects for the Future', in Abdulrahim P. Vijapur (ed.): *Essays on International Human Rights* (New Delhi: South Asian Publishers; Absecon Highlands, NJ: International Book Company).

Haas, Ernest (1970): *Human Rights and International Action: The Case of Freedom of Association* (Stanford, California: Stanford University Press).

Hector, Bartolomei de la Cruz, Geraldo von Potobsky and Lee Swepston

(1996): *The International Labour Organisation: The International Standards System and Basic Human Rights* (Boulder: Westview Press).

ILO (1996): *International Labour Conventions and Recommendations 1919-1995* (3 vols.), International Labour Organization (Geneva: ILO).

——— (2003): *Fundamental Rights at Work and International Labour Standards*, International Labour Organization (Geneva: ILO).

ILR (2006): *International Labour Review*, Special Issue: Labour Rights, Human Rights, vol. 137, no 2.

Jenks, Wilfred C. (1960): *Human Rights and International Labour Standards* (London: Stevens and Sons).

——— (1970): *Social Justice in the Law of Nations: The ILO Impact after Fifty Years* (Oxford: Oxford University Press).

——— (1996): 'The Paradox of Worker's Rights as Human Rights', in Lance A. Compa and Stephen F. Diamond (eds.): *Human Rights: Labour Rights and International Trade* (Pennsylvania: Pennsylvania University Press).

Landy, E.A. (1966): *The Effectiveness of International Supervision: Thirty Years of ILO Experience* (London: Stevens and Sons).

——— (1970): 'The Influence of International Standards: Possibilities and Performance', *International Labour Review*, vol. 101, no. 6, June.

Leary, Virginia A. (2006): 'Lessons from the Experience of the International Labour Organisation', in Philip Alston (ed.): *United Nations and Human Rights*, 2nd edn. (Oxford: Oxford University Press).

——— (1979): 'The Role of the ILO: Present Action and Future Perspectives', in B.G. Ramcharan (ed.): *Human Rights: Thirty Years after the Universal Declaration* (The Hague: Martinus Nijhoff Publishers).

Mertus, Julia A. (2005): *The United Nations and Human Rights: A Guide for a New Era* (London: Routledge).

Rehman, Anisur (2008): 'Migrant Workers and Human Rights: A Study of the Gulf Region', in Abdulrahim P. Vijapur (ed.): *Implementing Human Rights in the Third World : Essays on Human Rights, Dalits and Minorities* (New Delhi: Manak Publications).

Rossilion, C. (1974): 'ILO Examination of Human Rights Situation', *Review, International Commission of Jurists*, vol. 40, no. 12, June.

Joyce, James A. (1980): *World Labour Rights and their Protection* (London: Croom Helm).

Swepston, Lee (2003): 'The International Labour Organisation's System of Human Rights Protection', in Janusz Symonides (ed.): *Human Rights: International Protection, Monitoring, Enforcement* (Paris: UNESCO Publishing).

——— (2005): 'The International Labour Organisation', in Rhona K.M. Smith and Christien van den Anker (ed.): *The Essentials of Human Rights* (London: Hodder Arnold).

Symonides, Janusz and Vladimir Volodin (1999): *Human Rights of Women: A Collection of International and Regional Normative Instruments* (Paris: UNESCO).

Valticos, Nicolas (1982): 'The International Labour Organisation (ILO)', in Karl Vasak (ed.), *The International Dimension of Human Rights* (Paris: UNESCO, Westport, Connecticut: Greenwood Press).

——— (1979a): *International Labour Law* (Deventer: Netherlands: Kluwer).

——— (1979b): 'The Future Prospects for International Labour Standards', *International Labour Review*, vol. 110.

Wolf, Francis (1975): 'ILO Experience in the Implementation of Human Rights', *Journal of International Law and Economics*, vol. 10.

——— (1984): 'Human Rights and the International Labour Organisation', in Theodor Meron (ed.): *Human Rights in International Law: Legal and Policy Issues* (Oxford: Clarendon Press).

CHAPTER 24

Impact of Globalization on Trade Union Movements

B.N. MEHRISH

This paper analyses the impact of globalization on the trade union movement in India and explains how globalization has affected the rights of workers and its linkages with political activities.

GLOBALIZATION DEBATE

As we all know, there are plenty of reasons to criticize globalization. Same of these are very familiar—often straightforward critiques of global capitalism, which emphasize the political-economic unevenness of the process. Equally familiar are those critiques that portray globalization as the latest phase in the long story of an expanding Western cultural hegemony. Globalization is identified as 'a cultural homogenization' by its Marxist critics. According to them there is a significant link between culture and economy.

Many researchers of development studies have specified inequality in the developing world. In the 1990s, the belief in progress was translated into the growth. On the one hand, there are various versions of post-modern (non-)development thinking, and on the other hand, the versions of the idea of global risk in the society. In the 1980s, development pessimism had set in with the realization of the ever-widening gap between poor and rich countries. Where economic growth had occurred, we can see a catastrophic impact on the environment and the end of existing socialism had removed socialist-inspired development trajectories from the academic and political agendas.

NARAYAN LOKHANDE: THE FOUNDER OF THE INDIAN LABOUR MOVEMENT

On 24 April 1980, the Race Course Ground in Bombay (Mumbai) witnessed a massive public meeting of more than 10,000 workers organized by Narayan Meghaji Lokhande, considered 'the father of Indian trade union movement'.[1] Lokhande established the Bombay Mill Hands Association (BMHA)—the first labour organization in the country in 1884.

Born in 1848 in Thane, Narayan Lokhande started his career with the railways and the postal department. Afterwards, he joined the Mandavi Temple Textile Mills as a store keeper in 1870. This mill life provided him ample first hand exposure to the exploitative nature of factory work, and the miserable living conditions of the mill workers, which prompted him to organize them for their basic rights.

Till the enactment of Factory Act in 1881, no legislation was there to protect workers, who toiled in appalling conditions in Indian factories. Workers were allowed hardly any rest. The workplaces were unhygienic, ill-ventilated and without proper sanitation facilities. The temperature in the factories was excruciating due to the constant running of machines. As per the census report of 1881, the share of both female and child labourers (below 15 years) stood at around 23 per cent each in Bombay textile workers, and the working time ranged from 10 to 14 hours.[2]

The growing concern about this exploitative nature of work in factories impelled the government to enact the Factory Act of 1881, despite the organized resistance from the mill owners. Lokhande viewed the appointment of Factory Commission as an opportunity to formally place the grievances of the workers before the government. His petition to the Factory Commission as the president of BMHA is considered 'prophetic', as many of the concepts in contemporary labour welfare legislation such as accident relief and compensation, death gratuity and family pension seem to have been envisioned by the leaders of labour unions.

In 1890, BMHA started an agitation against the arbitrary decision of the mill owners to close down the mills. When the Factory Labour Commission was constituted by the government of India in 1890, Lokhande was included as an associated member for the Bombay presidency. He made trade unionism a means for addressing social issues and injustice.

As an ardent follower of Mahatma Jyotirao Phule, Lokhande was highly influenced by the activities of Satyashodhak Samaj and devoted his life in fighting against social evils and for improving the status of the downtrodden people. Lokhande was instrumental for labour mobilization for social action. He also organized different occupational groups and marginalized segments such as labours, rickshaw pullers, women workers, and so on. The first protest of women workers in India was organized at the erstwhile Jacob Mills in Bombay on 25 March 1895 for equal wages for equal work, paid weekly holidays and an eight hour working day. Despite all these, the contributions of Lokhande remain largely overlooked and unsung.

ROLE OF TRADE UNIONS

Trade unions occupied an important place in the economic and social framework of industrialized countries, particularly those in which the incidence of unemployment was comparatively low. They functioned as an organized force in the economic field and constituted an important source of political strength for those who led them. Leaders of unions could negotiate and bargain with employers from a position of strength, particularly when they were backed and supported by a highly skilled labour force that was not easily replaceable. In the United States 'the labour unions became organizations that selected and formed leaders who, upon becoming successful, took their place alongside politicians in both major parties and the national power elite' (Wright 1959).

In the less developed countries, organized workers constituted a small percentage of the economically active standpoint, unions frequently constituted a group equipped with means through which they presented, and occasionally imposed their views upon the larger society.

POLITICAL UNIONISM

In the specific context of India, the role of trade unions has been closely related to the history of the national freedom struggle. The struggle needed the support of mass industrial workers to fight against the British domination. Hence, there was a national interaction between trade union movement and freedom struggle in India. Although unions were not formally affiliated to any political party during the freedom struggle but many important political leaders were openly associated with the labour movements. Thus, the trade union movement in India reflected a cross-section of the prevailing political ideologies.

According to some scholars, the working class were mobilized by its leaders not for class-based economic gains, but the professional middle class participated in this movement as an integral part of the nationalist effort to weaken the British hold in the country. The working class developed no autonomous structures and remained dependent on the political movement. This type of association had been described by Stanley Kochanek, Van Kennedy and Michael Bogaert as 'political unionism' (Giri 1969). Political unionism covers a diversity of relationships ranging from ideological sharing of views or policies to explicit cooperation and shared leadership.

An explanation of the phenomenon of political unionism in India in the specific historical context of the emergence of the trade union movement has been attempted by Rajni Palme Dutt and Sukomal Sen (Sood 2007). There was no political movement inspired by the socialist ideology till the 1920s and the concept of class struggle did not figure in the political movement.

In the pre-Independence period, almost all socialist and communist leaders worked under one umbrella of the Indian National Congress. Under a system of dual membership, an affiliation to their separate political organization was allowed. In the trade union field there existed, however, a common affiliating organization—All India Trade Union Congress (AITUC). As a result of differing perceptions of communist and non-communist leadership on support to the war effort after Hitler's invasion of the Soviet, Union, there occurred a major split in the AITUC. In 1947, the non-communist leadership organised the Indian National Trade Congress (INTUC) as a rival to AITUC.

After 1947, other political parties set up their own organizations to capture the allegiance of the industrial proletariat. The AITUC became the exclusive preserve of the Communist Party of India. The INTUC was controlled by the Congress party. The erstwhile Socialist Party set-up the Hind Mazdoor Sabha (HMS).

Trade union movement in India has been analysed by various scholars from different perspectives. In the context of curtailed civil liberties during the British rule, trade union movement in India developed certain special characteristics. These were reinforced by plentiful supply of unskilled labour coupled with scarcity of skilled labour. There were also structural and behavioural determinants, such as, the operational style of the leadership and the membership of the trade unions.

GLOBALIZATION IMPACT

Globalization has weakened the trade union movement in India. Trade unions had become an inevitable concomitant of industrialization. After Independence, the involvement of trade unions in the politics of India has been increased. Trade unions and their leaders are now concerned more with political issues because many problems that affect labour can only be solved by the government. On many labour issues, a union leader may find himself alongside an aligned politician taking a similar stand.

In the post-Independence period, the union leadership was split between two extremes. The Left was keen to transform the successful anti-colonial struggle into a new struggle for eventual socialism. The Right had used the working class primarily as an instrument of trans-class national protest.

Several new major trade union organizations were set-up gradually; the Bharatiya Mazdoor Sangh (BMS) came up in 1955 and was linked with RSS/Jan Sangh (present Bharatiya Janata Party). The Centre of Indian Trade Unions (CITU) was formed in 1970, linked with CPI(M). Even the Akali Dal organized its own trade union, viz., Punjab Mazdoor Dal. Many other organizations came into existence as the result of factional splits or on minor ideological grounds. These include the Hind Mazdoor Panchayat, the All India Red Trade Union Congress, the National Labour Organization and the National Federation of Indian Trade Unions. A few of these organizations wield a little local influence in some states.

It is obvious that the aims of the trade union movements have not been confined only to the achievement of immediate economic goals. The policies of the trade union leaderships have been largely conditioned by the association of unions with political parties committed to diverse ideologies. There have been leaders who broadened their aim to include the goal of national independence, leaders who conceive their purpose to regulate the free market economy and leaders for whom the purpose of unionism is co-terminous with radical politics aimed at a peaceful transformation of capitalist economy and multinational corporations. The Marxists advocate the elimination of capitalism and the need for the control of industry by workers. Meanwhile, the non-Marxists reject the basic proposition that capitalism deserves to be abolished or maintained. Its abolition is a political concept which has little to do with genuine trade union activity. In both cases, they oppose the induction of politics into trade unions except in so far as the role of unions as pressure groups working for their members may be termed as political. The *sine qua non* of trade union actively is an immediate concern with the problems of wages, hours and conditions of employment and other similar issues of immediate economic welfare. Workers' sympathy can be alienated if their needs are subordinated to political objectives. Under such circumstances, workers begin to seek unofficial leaders to champion their most immediate needs (Sood 2007).

Among various issues that related to the trade union movement, there is none that is more controversial than the question of the goals of the movement. Karl Marx visualized the overthrow of capitalism as a historic task of the working class.[3] Lenin argued that the very fact of existence of working class led to the spontaneous rise of trade unionism.

In the 1950s the Congress party and INTUC had progressively defined India's national goal as a socialist pattern of society. Now they aim for liberalization and globalization. Many leaders of the United Progressive Alliance government suggested that the proper role of trade unions in India includes persuading workers to forgo immediate demands and urged restraint, discipline in order to increase the rate of economic growth and check inflationary pressures. Only the INTUC leadership has remained aloof from political agitations. In effect, unions 'are utilised by parties to nurture new political activist' (Sood 2007). In operational terms, most of the trade union leaders tend to apprehend the role of the organs of the state power as the role of the government.

The union leaders in India face imprisonment for an allegedly 'political offence' for going on an 'illegal' strike. Occasionally, union leaders get arrested on the eve of a proposed agitation or a strike or would be sacked by the management. The police arrest the union activists under the Sections 107 and 151 of the Indian Penal Code (relating to peace).

To sum up, it is clear from the above analysis that linkages between unions and political organizations do exist.

NOTES

1. Labour File (New Delhi), March-June 2008, p. 51.
2. Ibid.
3. According to the Marxist ideology, the capitalist state is an instrument of the bourgeoisie, with the police and judiciary among its instruments of oppression.

REFERENCES

Wright, L.C. (1959): *The Power Elite* (New York: Oxford University Press).

Giri, V.V. (1969): *Labour Problems in Indian Industry* (Bombay: Asia Publishing House).

Sood, Santosh (2007): 'Trade Unions and Political Parties in Punjab', in Harish K. Puri and Paramjit S. Judge, *Social and Political Movements* (Jaipur and New Delhi: Rawat).

NOTES

1. [illegible] March [illegible] 2003 [illegible]
2. [illegible] to the Marxist ideology, the capitalist [illegible] ruthless [illegible] [illegible] with the [illegible] among [illegible] of [illegible]

CHAPTER 25

Working Class Movement: Modern Economic System, Social Structure and Power Conflict

SANGEETA N. PAWAR

India's inherent strength and comparative advantage lie in the presence of entrepreneurial acumen of the highest quality, established scientific and industrial base, cheap, skilled English-speaking workforce and a large domestic market. The contribution of industry to gross domestic product (GDP) is an important indicator of nation's progress in the process of structural transformation from a rural agricultural society to a more urban industrialized one. Further, an increase in the per capita income is associated with a rise in the share of industry along with a fall in the share of agriculture in national income.

In the early stages of industrialization, when the per capita income was very low, the primary sector occupied a dominant position in the economic structure. As capital and skills accumulate, both productivity and per capita income increase. A highly competitive environment is rapidly emerging, driven by rising economic and social aspirations on one hand and external conditions like market forces on the other hand.

POWER CONFLICT

It is necessary to view the movement of the working class and the industrial sector of our society in terms of power struggle in the era of liberalization, privatization and globalization (LPG). First it should be noted that our society itself is clearly caught up in the play of power. Innumerable groups and organizations are relying on the exercise of power in seeking to maintain positions, achieve goals and to ward off threats. The interest groups arise whenever individuals become organized or united in pursuit of some actual or imagined common interest and seek to forge in a line of action on behalf of that interest. Our democratic society gives an extensive freedom to people everywhere to organize. Our national life consists of acts of such groups like the local clubs, chambers of commerce, business groups, teacher's organizations, political clubs, trade associations, medical associations, labour unions, educational societies, industrial corporations and a variety of other organizations which seek to realize the special interests of their own. This proliferation of interest groups imparts a vital power dimension to our national life. As these groups seek to sustain or protect their respective interests, they are thrown in to conflict with each other at innumerable points. At these points power relations emerge and develop as a result of efforts to use strategic position, strength, influence and skill to achieve or protect interest that are threatened, hindered, or blocked by opposing interests. The conditions in our industrial life are peculiarly conducive to the emergence of power relations (Mazumdar 2008).

The extension and integration of the economic market bring a large number of economic-interest groups and increase the chances of conflict between their lines of interest. The dynamic changes in our economy open new areas for exploitation, and thus, for increased encroachment of groups on groups. The growth of huge organizations increases the inner conflict and struggle for control, and with the increasing unionization of industries workers mount pressure on the unions. As a result of conditions and influences, our industrial society is subjected to power actions among trade associations, business corporations, labour unions and managements, etc.

Most power relations in our society are localized and restricted and the preponderant portion of them scarcely affects the welfare of the community life. Power actions come to its purest form in the case of big power groups. In the economic system like mixed economy, there are drawbacks which can cause hindrances to the national economic growth. But the basic characteristics of the mixed economic system will remain unchanged: like the basic and heavy industries will be run under government control and the consumer-based and public utility industries will be run both by the private persons and the government. And moreover, some industries and activities will be completely left for the private sector.

THE LPG EFFECT

Earlier, trade, commerce and other business activities were carried out under the control of the state through registration, etc., which had caused several hurdles to the entrepreneurs. Nevertheless, liberalization has provided them much freedom and encouraged entrepreneurs to set-up new industries and businesses. Liberalization was the end of licence raj. The capital market has been opened to private enterprises. The liberalization policy permits any new company to float by issuing the shares/debentures, etc., without seeking permission of the government. After lifting government control in the name of liberalization, many companies thus started to loot innocent people in the name of public issue.

Privatization means an emphasis on private sector. First, out of 17 industries reserved for the public sector, 11 have been opened for the private sector. Thus, six industries are still under the control of state/central government. However, even in such reserved sectors of the government, the private sector has been given permission which means that there will be a tough competition between public and private sectors in these six areas. Second, the government is also privatizing the public sector undertakings under the disinvestment scheme. Further, the central government offered greater opportunities of investment to foreign private investors to extend the scheme of privatization of Indian economy (Narain 2005: 289-15 and 316-53; Samujh 2005: 358-66).

Now due to revolution in the field of communications and transportation facilities, the world has become a 'global village'. Now no country can grow without keeping proper coordination between domestic and world markets, i.e., there is an integration of domestic economy and the world economy. In the name of globalization of economy, the rupee has been made fully convertible in current accounts in the balance of payments. The relaxation in import laws has enabled the importers to deal with foreign goods easily.

In fact, the new economic policy in the name of LPG had opened the movement of exchange rate, foreign exchange, imports, exports and foreign direct investments (FDI) in the country. However, this is not relevant to discuss the success or failure of new economic policy applied during 1991, but it is necessary to analyse its impact on the creation of jobs available to the public and also its impact on the reservation policy.

SHORTAGE OF JOBS IN PUBLIC SECTOR

The apprehension that the application of the LPG policy will be dominated in private sectors and the number of public sector employment will be reduced is proving true day by day. In central government, employment was growing from 1987 to 1992 and in 1994 and 1995, but after the implementation of LPG policy in 1991, the employment opportunities in central government have been badly affected. There was a minus growth in 1993, 1996 and 1997. There was little increase in employment in the state government since 1991, and moreover, a sharp decrease in employment had been reported in local bodies. Although there was an increase in employment registered in the private sector after 1991, it was not to the extent as was expected.

No doubt, the country was struggling with unemployment problems even before the initiation of LPG policy, yet the new economic policy has aggravated this problem. In this high-tech and multinational companies-dominated economy, all unemployed youth have not got job opportunities as they are vanishing day by day, and particularly, the job opportunities for the Scheduled Castes and Scheduled Tribes based on the reservation policy.

In the beginning of LPG, it was expected that foreign investors would come and open heavy and high-tech industries in the country which would create greater job opportunities enabling the economy of the country to flourish. In fact, the multinational corporations (MNCs) do not want any gestation period which is generally required in a heavy industry. Their motive is to earn profit from the date of establishment of the business and not to provide jobs to the Indians, let alone the implementation of reservation policy. Thus, the MNCs have not only failed in creating the new and sufficient number of jobs, but they have also damaged the cottage industries of the country.

The LPG policy is not favourable for reservation in the private sector. The jobs for the Scheduled Castes and Scheduled Tribes as well as the other backward castes are limited to unskilled jobs or lower stage of supervisory jobs.

The expression of 'socialist' was introduced in the Constitution with an objective to incorporate the philosophy of socialism. The principal aim of a socialistic state is to eliminate inequality in income and status of standards of life. The basic framework of socialism is to provide a decent standard of living to the working people, especially to provide security from cradle to grave. It also envisages economic equality and equal distribution of income. Despite having noble objective, the reservation policy has always been controversial since its inception. Since ancient days, we are following an unscientific division of labour which denies proper opportunity to the large number of population. This has become detrimental to the nation. Although an equalitarian justice ensures freedom to all, its pre-conditions, existence of homogeneous society and equality of status are not yet achieved.

Two approaches can be examined which promote employment and social security for the labour force in India: (1) Through public works programme; and (2) by an initiative to provide social security for the workers. In India, private sector employers achieve flexibility by following labour practices such as casualization, feminization, use of contract labour, job contracting, relocation of production, deskilling of labour, substitution of individual for collective bargaining, etc. A loose labour market characterized by high and increasing unemployment helps employers adopt flexible labour practices bypassing labour laws.

Industrialization was one of the main objectives of planning in India. It was expected to spur the process of withdrawal of disguised unemployed from agriculture and their absorption in high wage industrial employment. It is alleged that though the labour market is not deregulated in theory, it is deregulated in practice.

In the federal set-up such as in India, some states are identified as socially more progressive and administratively more efficient than the others. The impact of recent economic changes due to reforms on the labour market reveals a mixed picture, while the pace of employment generation picked up after the initial years of reform, the recent years have witnessed a reduction in employment growth. It is also observed that the quality of employment has generally deteriorated. This is because most of the employment opportunities are being created in the informal sector where practically there is no provision for insurance and social security. The labour market has witnessed a significant change in its nature and character. The trend towards casualization, sub-contracting and flexibility has increased (Deshpande et al. 2004). Although the process of feminization has simultaneously occurred, it is mostly in the case of flexible categories of labour. Industrial restructuring has reduced significantly in the organized sector, especially in the bargainable or unionized categories. Meanwhile, there is an increase in the non-bargainable category which means development has led to weakening of the power of trade unions.

JOB SECURITY

Job security is a major concern for a worker. There is no social security in the unorganized sectors. In any industrial establishment the workforce is divided into distinctive groups. It is attached with the labels of status such as permanent, temporary, casual and contract. The work status carries different incomes and different levels of security. The share of permanent workers in employment declined over the years of liberalization. Among the non-permanent workers, the share of casual workers has shown a steeper growth. This growth of non-permanent workers varies with the size of the firms. The larger the firm, the higher is the share of the non-permanent labour. It is generally believed that in the formal sector the earnings of the worker consist of a basic wage, dearness allowance and a bonus. But many firms pay a consolidated wage (GoI 2007: 381-401).

CONCLUSION

There are inter-state variations in minimum wages. Presently, there is a significant variation even in the wages for the same occupation. To prevent exploitation of workers in the unorganized sector, awareness generation may be stepped up in collaboration with voluntary organizations, trade unions and other committed individuals. To reach out to the entire labour force employed many of the existing institutional laws and programmes have to be restructured, pertaining to reform of vocational training system, occupational safety and health, labour regulation and social security of workers. Unions are not as ubiquitous as their critics make them out to be. They are found in larger numbers in cotton textiles, basic metals and alloys industries. Bigger firms are more likely to be unionized than smaller firms. They are more widespread in West Bengal and Kerala and moderately so in Maharashtra. The share of firms reporting the presence of more than one union is very small, but it is much higher in bigger firms employing 200 or more workers each. Kerala leads in the multiplicity of unions which is followed by Tamil Nadu, Andhra Pradesh and

West Bengal. The growth of employment and high labour flexibility do not go well with union presence. Union activities restrain the freedom of employers to employ flexible workers. Ideology counts. The states ruled by communists had a restrained growth of flexibility, but at the cost of industrial unrest. The liberal states such as Tamil Nadu, Gujarat and Madhya Pradesh show a very high degree of flexibility with lower incidence of unions and industrial unrest. Union is both an economic and a political institution. Its impact depends on many things such as its quantitative and qualitative strength and its leadership.

REFERENCES

Deshpande, Lalit K. and Alakh N. Sharma (2004): *Liberalisation and Labour Flexibility in Indian Manufacturing* (New Delhi: Institute for Human Development).

GoI (2007): *Sectoral Policies and Programmes Tenth Five-Year Plan*, vol. II, Planning Commission (New Delhi: Government of India).

Mazumdar, Dipak and Sandip Sarkar (2008): *Globalisation, Labour Markets and Inequality in India* (London: Routledge).

Narain, Laxmi (2005): *Public Enterprise Management and Privatisation* (New Delhi: S. Chand and Company Ltd.).

Samujh, Ram (2005): *Reservation Policy: Its Relevance in Modern India* (Mumbai: Samrudh Bharat Publications), February.

CHAPTER 26

Trade Unionism at Crossroads: Impact of Liberalization Reforms in Kerala

B. VENUGOPAL

Sixty years ago, India accepted the concept of mixed economy by rejecting the two extreme systems, namely, capitalism and socialism after a long debate. Under this system, respective roles were assigned to both public and private sectors. This system worked for a long time within its own weaknesses and strengths till the downfall of the erstwhile Soviet Union. Though India recognized the socialistic pattern of society by assigning a dominant role to the public sector, the basic character of the Indian economy remained capitalist in nature during this period. In the early 1980s, India started opening up its economy to foreign capital, which led India to an economic crisis towards the end of the decade. By the end of June 1991, the foreign exchange reserves declined to bare 1.1 billion dollars, just sufficient to finance two weeks requirements only (Sidhu and Cheema 1999). This situation was further aggravated partly by an exogenous event—the Gulf crisis—and partly by the wrong decision taken by the Government of India to import oil in excess of the prevailing high international price. But the major causes of the sharp erosion in the foreign exchange reserves were identified as the fall in exports, increase in imports, insufficient growth in invisible foreign exchange earnings and increased flow on account of external debt servicing.

To put the economy in the path of sustained growth with low inflation, the challenge was to restore the macroeconomic balance and to remove those policy-induced distortions, which had an adverse impact on productivity. For this, India adopted a new economic policy in July 1991, comprising a wide range of economic reforms using trade, fiscal and monetary instruments. This was in accordance with the advice given by the World Bank, which believed that a structural adjustment programme is necessary to achieve higher rates of economic growth. Thus, in short, structural adjustment or liberalization symbolizes measures to stimulate economic growth by reorganizing production and focusing on shifting the emphasis from state to the market and forging a closer interaction between the national and global economy. The structural reform measures undertaken along with the process of liberalization include a number of areas like industrial policy, exchange and trade regimes, tax structure, foreign investment policy and finance sector reforms.

These economic reforms have brought significant changes in the organization of work, labour markets, employment relations and workplace practices as well as re-evaluation of the social worth, public status and discursive meanings of various forms of work and labour. As is well known, the legitimacy of labour rights and of working class political activism has yielded to the perceived compulsion to augment efficiency, international competitiveness and private importance. The economic importance of manual work has been devalued and the role of the labour has also been undermined as a constituency in democratic, party politics or as a major presence on leftwing politics (Gooptu 2007).

At the political point of view, the impact of economic liberalism on the state power and authority has twofold implications. First, it entails transfer of substantial economic and political power of the state to dominant powers at the global level. Second, it involves a transfer of considerable social responsibility to the non-governmental agencies, powerful donor groups and nations. More importantly, the liberalization policies made a shift of focus in the mindset of the state in its relationship with the labour. The role of the public and services sectors in the nation-building processes has been undervalued, while the private sector is encouraged at the maximum possible level. Retrenchment of workers has become a common feature and ultimately it causes the growth of the jobless population and other social problems. The workers' unions are forced to concede to the retrenchments and the reduction in wages. Collective bargaining is practically limited only to the wages, but not to the labourers' rights. The concept of collective bargaining, thus, has been conveniently converted into concession bargaining like wages, dearness allowances, incentives, etc. The attitude of the management also has undergone great changes. Managements have become more authoritative, aggressive and militant. The labour laws are amended conveniently in favour of the managers of the industry, overriding the old concept of welfare of the workers. It is more visible that the state comes to the rescue of the employers rather than the labourers through legislation and policy formulation.

The International Labour Organization (ILO) points out that in the changed circumstances, especially in the climate of tough competition, monetary discipline, privatization of utilities and public enterprises and deregulation of labour markets, the government feels less need to consider the views of the trade unions. There is a decline in the organized workforce, trade unions are becoming weak and their political leverage is also declining (Reddy 2003). The World Labour Report 1997-8 has also observed: '. . . it is generally agreed that the trade union movement has fallen on hard times. . . . Workers' organisations are losing members. Some even have doubts about their future'.

Will the unions survive into the next century? Thomas Henk cautions that the trade unions are currently in danger of being eliminated as a significant social institution. A combination of social control, institutional structure and government ideology has made it almost impossible for workers to organize in defence of their interests. Even the so-called socialist China considers an industrial action as a threat to social stability and economic development.

TRADE UNIONS IN KERALA

The first trade union in India—All India Trade Union Congress (AITUC)—was set-up in 1920.The purpose of its formation was 'to co-ordinate the activities of all labour organizations of trade centres through out India and to promote the Indian labourers in their socio-political and economic interests' (Giri 1958). The period between 1920 and 1935 was one of intense industrial strife in India. During this period, the Communist Party began to extend its influence over the Indian labour force. A number of historic struggles like the general strike of Bombay textile mills, general strike of Bengal jute mills and the railway strike were launched and waged under the patronage of the communist leadership. It was during this period that efforts began in Kerala also in the direction of organizing labour forces and making trade unions. In 1922 April, the first labour association was formed among the coir workers in Alappuzha. This organization played a crucial role in spreading the philosophy of trade unionism all over the erstwhile Travancore state and getting the cadres trained for the cause of trade unionism and revolutionary movement.

The trade union movement in Kerala was not only confined to the larger sections of the working class such as agricultural and industrial workers, but the movement also penetrated into the smaller sectors like toddy tappers, coconut climbers, carpenters, oil mill workers, fishermen, beedi workers, scavengers, etc. By the end of the 1940s, there was no section of working class left without an organization. No wonder, the labour force and unionism had become a common feature in Kerala among all the sectors, including government servants, independent professionals and the beauracrats from top to bottom.

Political involvement of the trade unions all along remains an undisputed fact in Kerala politics. Political involvement of trade union leaders and vice versa cannot be seen at a narrow view. In Kerala, the trade union movement and activism are being initiated and handled by two types of leaders, that is, the leaders who are primarily concerned with the workers' welfare and those concerned with their politics. But as every route of social and economic activities in the state are clearly politicized, it is very difficult to find out the leader of the first type here. Almost all the union leaders in Kerala have apparently strong political convictions. They have a strong political identification and also are deeply involved with the political processes, decision-making and the power games. It is very hard to draw a line between the union interests/activities and the political interests/activities. This is evident from the fact that since the first general elections onwards a good number of trade union leaders and activists find their convenient places in the law-making bodies. This trade union-political interaction has an adverse impact on the industrial development of the state. Lokanathan, in his report on the techno-economic survey of Kerala has remarked: trade unionism prevails in the state, which is always mixed with political parties, has been responsible for retarding progress of investment in Kerala by the potential investors from outside the state (quoted in Sankaranarayanan and Karunakaran 1985). In the words of P.A. Sangma, 'the small pace of industrial growth and mounting unemployment in Kerala is the consequence of the Malayalee's trade unionism, which has been deliberately fed to the gullible sector of workforce by self styled politicians . . . for their own self interest' (*The Indian Express*, 20 July 1981).

The labour movement or trade unionism in Kerala stemmed from the lower and downtrodden class of people, who were basically agricultural workers. Unlike other parts of India, trade unionism in Kerala was based on the social system at the rural villages and not at the technologically developed or urban centres. On structural basis the workers' unions were characterized with (1) well-organized system; (2) party support; (3) high bargaining power; (4) good wage rate; (5) a higher degree of political and social consciousness; and (6) high literacy rate and a higher regard for rights and duties. But contemporary workers' unions or trade unions in Kerala are different from what it had been in the 1930s, 1940s or 1950s.

In the present stage of economic and structural transformation, trade unions are facing increasing difficulties in defending and extending their organizational base. Trade union movements have lost their vision and objectives. They are seen to be the organizations for just protecting the rights of the workers and improving their wages and living conditions, forgetting their historic social responsibilities. Even in the highly industrialized countries like the Unites States, the influence of organized labour force has been reduced very much during the last two decades. A large number of workers are conveniently forced to keep away from the unions.

RESTRICTION ON TRADE UNIONS

Along with the union government and other states in India, legislations were made in Kerala also, to restrict union movements in industries. These legislations provide (1) restrictions on registration of new unions; (2) limitations on collective bargaining, particularly in public sector; (3) restrictions on the freedom to organize and prohibition to do so in special economic zones (SEZs) and free trade zones; and (4) legislations that facilitate dismissal and reduce the period of advance dismissal notification.

Like the trade unions of the developed countries and the other developed states in India, the trade union movement in Kerala is also facing multidimensional challenges from the industrial sector, like: (1) technological changes; (2) emergence of private sector enterprises; and (3) increase in the number of women workers and the casual temporary workers.

The process of industrial restructure which took place in the light of the economic reforms during the 1990s and 2000s had a negative impact on the workers, particularly at two levels, reduction in employment and the minimum role of the labour unions. While the managers had significant roles, they began to adopt new measures in the industrial sector like reduction of permanent workforce, utilization of ancillary units, recruitment of unprotected labourers, migration of production units to other states where labour was cheap and non-unionized and signing of agreements with individual workers neglecting the unions, etc. This ultimately resulted in the decline of trade union membership and the increase of casualization and feminization of wage labourers. Moreover, the emergence of white collar unions, managerial unions, weak power structure, uncommitted membership, emergence of industry level unions, intra- and inter-union rivalry, interests of affiliated political parties, ineffective state strategies, inconsistent policies and programmes, concentration of union power in a few hands resulting in delayed and inconsistent reaction, politically inclined motives, rampant corruption among leaders and the rapid growth of unorganized sector had highly intensified the problem. In one way or other, these factors greatly contributed to the decline of the trade union strength and activism.

From 1980 onwards, the trade union movement in Kerala has undergone remarkable changes. The process of liberalization has its impact on Kerala too, even though the state is very weak in the industrial sector. Certain new measures have been introduced in the industrial sector in the light of the new economic policy such as reducing the number of permanent workforce, creating ancillary units of production purposes, etc. All these have created an anti-union atmosphere in Kerala.

NEW ECONOMIC POLICY

The new economic policy was introduced in the state without considering the industrial situations and the circumstances prevailed in the state. Though the government claimed that the reforms would bring drastic changes in the industrial sector, what happened was the rise of a serious crisis. Policies like import liberalization, tariff reduction and removal of subsidies had affected even the traditional and small-scale industries in the state leading to de-industrialization. Almost all the public sector units were on the verge of disinvestments and closure. And many of these public undertakings were already on a loss, so, there arose the possibility of privatization. A large number of industrial units were growing sick and could not even pay the minimum wages to the workers.

The liberalization policies of the government and the impact of these policies have brought drastic changes in the industrial organization and management, with severe consequences for the working class. As governments increasingly compete for footloose enterprises and capital, the interests of workers are relegated to the second place.

An important feature of the present-day trade unionism in Kerala is that it has lost its earlier militancy of which Kerala unions were famous. It is argued that the industrial stagnation in Kerala has been mainly due to the high pick trade unionism, trade union militancy and a typically negative work culture encouraged by unions. The trend, however, had been changed towards the end of the twentieth century. The hitherto labour militancy declined and in their place the managers of industries assumed the position. The employer-employee relations had been turned into a new direction, widening the way for the master-slave discipline instead of the old practices like cooperation and negotiations. The bargaining capacity of the workers through the democratic weapons like strike became practically ineffective and meaningless, and in turn, the managers had become militant. This is evident from the statistics regarding the strikes and lockouts during the last decade, i.e. 1990-2000. The number of strikes launched by the trade unions had decreased from 104 in 1983 to 10 in 2000, while the number of lockouts had increased from 15 in 1990 to 30 in 2000. Among the recorded strikes (455) that happened in Kerala between 1983 and 2000, more than half took place between 1983 and 1990, while 72 per cent of the lockouts had taken place since 1991. This proves that along with the decline of trade union membership, the number of strikes too has decreased. Another important point to be noted here is that the very existence or functioning of a trade union in many industrial units have become at the mercy of the industrial management. Unlike the past, now, the trade unions are not allowed to function freely. Many industrialists have sought the intervention of the courts to restrict the working of the trade unions. In an important judgement, the High Court of Kerala declared that the trade unions have no right to erect a flag post in the premises of the industrial units. The court is of the view that peace in the industries is to be maintained not at the expenses of the management. The court rejected the argument of the unions in favour of their rights to function in the premises of the industry (*The Hindu*, 8 January 2009).

All these highlight the point that the militancy and the bargaining capacity of the industrial workers are declining. Increasing feminization of employment also has resulted in weakening trade unions. There has been an increase of women's employment in manufacturing industries. With the coming of SEZs and export processing zones for textiles, garments, electronics, etc., the female share of employment has increased in Kerala also. The managers, government and the non-governmental organizations (NGOs) encourage the growth of feminized employment that is low paid and insecure part-time contract work. Organizational changes in the form of sub-contracting and home-based production have further driven women into low-end jobs. Economic liberalization has also altered the nature of women's jobs. There is an increase of the services sector where women have been able to compete effectively with men (Misra 2004).

It is thus clear that the liberalization policies have made a more severe impact on the Kerala society. The effects of liberalization policies such as casualization, rapid turnover of jobs, unemployment, declining standards and downward social and economic mobility of the labouring poor, compounded by urban social and spatial polarization, retreat of the state, lack of state protection, growing physical insecurity and lawlessness have not only led to the decline of class-based action, but also fragmented the working class, fuelled ethnic or religious tensions and identity politics, generated political unrest and protests and turned urban areas into sites of political instability, conflict vigilantism, crime, drug-trafficking and violence, We have to note that what Jan Breman said about Gujarat is equally valid for Kerala also. He examined the impact of industrial decline in Ahmedabad and concluded that with the decline of the textile mills economy, the erstwhile political tradition of the working class collective action gave way to narrow sectarian identities and religious mobilization, within a wider context of the rise of fundamentalism, caste conflict and communal tensions (Breman 2002).

Like other states of India, Kerala is also witnessing the development of the informal sector. It is an economic space in which workers engage in economic activities that are different from the capitalist organization of production. In particular, the prevalent form of labour in the informal sector is self-employment, which is different from the usual wage-based employment resting on the alienation of labour from capital.

The forces of globalization have created conditions for informalization in the following ways:

1. Faced with competition at the global level, firms in the formal sector of developing economies are engaged in a battle of cost-cutting. They are increasingly relying on outsourcing of production processes to informal units, where the wage costs and costs associated with complying with labour and environmental standards are considerably lower.
2. The inflow of cheaper imports has caused a contraction of import-competing industries in the formal sector, but the expansion of export sector has failed to generate sufficient employment to compensate for the loss. Moreover, global competition has forced domestic private as well as state enterprises to raise labour productivity and adopt lean production methods involving large-scale retrenchment of workers. Further, the neoliberal focus on fiscal discipline and inflation targeting has eroded the power of the state to otherwise create employment. In other words, job destruction has outpaced job creation in the formal sector, forcing those thrown out of employment to eke out a living in the informal sector.

There was another development also. The public sector employment has steadily declined over the period 1999-2005. Private enterprises in the formal sector have generated additional employment entirely in the category of unprotected regular, casual or contract wageworkers, which constitutes informal employment within the formal sector.

The changed role of the government, disinvestment policies, voluntary retirement schemes and above all the new forms of politicking have jointly increased the ineffectiveness of traditional unions, which in turn, resulted in their declining membership. The declining industries have also led to the decline in membership of the unions, especially the left unions in the state. And many of the employers have taken measures aimed at taking over the functions of the trade unions so that there is no need for these unions for the workers. On the other hand, the traditional manner of union functioning is considered as futile in the emerging industrial environment. Resultantly, unions have not only witnessed a decline in their membership, but also are facing competition from non-affiliated or independent trade unions.

In his article on the membership of trade unions in India, Ruddar Datt gives the details of declining membership of the unions at all-India level. The data provided by him has relevance in the case of Kerala as well. He says that, at all-India level, the Bharatiya Mazdoor Sangh (BMS) has become the first union in India with regard to membership. In some states like Tamil Nadu and Gujarat, independent unions have surpassed all affiliated unions. The Centre of Indian Trade Unions (CITU), the Communist Party of India (Marxist)-led union, is losing its grip in a few places and has been pushed off to fifth place as against the third in 1989. It is still enjoying first place in West Bengal and Kerala, but the declining membership is evident everywhere else (Datt 2009). Kerala is not an exception to this all-India situation. The Ministry of Labour and Employment Notification 2008 stated that in Kerala also, BMS has increased its membership compared to the Indian National Trade Union Congress (INTUC), CITU and all-India Trade Union Congress (AITUC). BMS has doubled its membership in the state, while INTUC is declining and other trade unions are stagnant (*The Indian Express*, 19 January 2008).

The decline in the membership of INTUC may be attributed to its own internal problems like the split in the parent organization, the Indian National Congress, group rivalries and open street fights on behalf the groups. But CITU and AITUC are not suffering from such problems and the stagnation must be because of other reasons. The main reason may be the dissatisfaction of the working class towards their worn-out statistics and the duplicity in the functioning. But the most important point we have to recognize is that it is the BMS that has gained in the present situation. BMS is generally regarded as a child of the Sangh Parivar and Kerala is a state where it cannot have a strong foothold. So sure, it is not politics that attracts the working class towards the BMS. It seems that the BMS is the only organization now that can claim to be free from party influences or control. It is assumed that the BMS, though a member of Hindutwa family, is largely free from the political control of the Bharatiya Janata Party.

Ruddar Datt is of the view that CITU should do some introspection and look whether the working class is fed up with its duplicity on labour issues—to have a belligerent attitude in states ruled by other parties, but very docile in the Left-ruled states. Moreover, the working class people are fed up with their style of functioning, especially calling a hartal or an all-India strike or a bandh for silly reasons (Datt op. cit.). This is also applicable to all unions in Kerala, where now people are looking at the unions with hatred and suspicion.

The trade union leaders in Kerala draw much of their support from their association with apolitical party of their affiliation. As such, now CITU or AITUC is better placed to get benefits from workers. But CITU has become ineffective and inefficient and the corrupt leadership is not in a position to draw a new support base. The new situation is not at all suitable for the traditional trade unions to function effectively. Their age-old methods like hartals, bandhs or strikes draw no attention from the working class. There is a general disgust from the part of the people towards these methods. Changing equations amongst political parties have led to a further marginalization of the trade unions as well as their leaders. Intra- and inter-trade union rivalry, conflicting interests of political party's affiliations, negative and stale strategies, inconsistent policies and programmes, concentration of power on the top leadership resulting in delayed and inconsistent reactions, politically biased motives, etc., have jointly led to the declining powers of trade unions, which in turn, resulted in distrust. The employers and government are finding it too easy to sidetrack unions in the trade union environment of the state.

The immense changes posed by the liberal restructuring of the economy have provided some impetus for the strategic reorientations in the attitudes of the trade unions towards the society, social movements and social struggles. In the past, in Kerala, all the social struggles had the support of the trade unions, be it for land, food or educational rights. The trade unions were in the forefront of all struggles for social justice and social reformation. And the trade unions were rightly regarded as the vehicles of social change and transformation. The trade unions regarded the link with social movements as a matter of pride. But now this entire stand has been changed. A hostile relationship now can be seen between the trade unions and the social movements. The social movements and NGOs are looked at as something coming up for destroying the rights and life of the working class by posing against the developmental activities. The workers are worried over their families, future and job security only. They are not at all concerned with their surroundings or society. They do not care what happens to the society or their comrades. They want only one thing to make secure their lives and jobs (Murali 2003).

The relationship between the social movements, NGOs and the

unions is of prime importance as the liberalization of the economy has caused the rise in the number of new social movements, which can effectively take over the role of the state. It is quite evident that the trade unions fear the social movements. This fear may be due to a variety of reasons. The first concern is that these new movements are emerging from the changed objectives of rolling back all forms of direct state intervention and the promotion of entrepreneurial activity and market-based solution to social problems and developmental goals. Again, the trade unions, especially the Left ones, consider the NGOs with caution. Parties and trade unions affiliated to them tend to reflect suspicion as to the motives of the NGOs. This is often related to the sources of NGO-funding and their rapid growth, and generally depoliticizing effect of their activities. More important, many NGOs are seen as working to displace the influence and the role of trade unions themselves. Such fears of competition from the NGOs are particularly evident with respect to workers in the unorganized sectors.

Sadly the competitive spirit between social movements and trade unions are going from bad to worse in Kerala. The recent trend is physical combats between the two. When the landless communities started an agitation in Chengara for land rights, it was the trade unions irrespective of their political affiliations which came out to oppose the move. The trade unions were even ready to declare social blockade against the agitators, claiming that the agitation is causing loss of jobs for the workers. This blockade went to the extent of denying food and medicines for the agitators and led to the death of a few. The same was happened in the case of hill tribals of Kerala who were fighting for their land rights. At present, when the poor displaced people of Vallarpadam and Moolamppilly fight against their forceful evacuation from their land, the trade unions are coming up against these people and arguing for the government that the eviction is necessary for the development of the state. All these to prove that the trade unions of Kerala, which were once so famous for their social consciousness and social responsibility have become more and more self-centred and isolated in their goals and social objectives.

CONCLUSION

The erosion of the influence of the union movement in the context of liberalization can be seen as a result of a combination of external pressures and internal problems. The external pressures derive from a perception of the union as a distortionist institution that needs to be minimized to facilitate fully the globalization process. The internal problems are the creation of the union movement itself and are a major threat to the survival of the labour movement in the present context. As seen earlier, the problems are over-centralization and bureaucratization of leadership, power seeking, opportunistic political alliances and rent-seeking leadership, the inability to reach out to the small-scale and unorganized sectors, to women and casual labourers, etc. This has become worse by informalization and technology-driven structural changes in employment, both are the creation of the present liberalization policies.

Liberalization policies of the government is a testing period for all the social partners, even more so for the trade unions since the burden of this transitory period falls mainly on workers' shoulders. The unions, therefore, would have to take a comprehensive approach in meeting the ensuing challenges.

The trade union movement in Kerala has a responsibility to ensure the application of trade union rights, irrespective of organized or inorganized sector. The unions should do away with their habit of living on the past glories and must have a futuristic vision. The worker today wants concrete results and is not satisfied, if after a prolonged struggle, she/he is left high and dry. Some trade unions, especially the independent and specific industry-based ones have recognized this reality and have modified their attitude and strategy, while others, especially the Left-oriented ones, stick to the old idioms and continue with confrontation without achieving any concrete results. There is no alternative to a systematic and professional management of the affairs of the unions. Unions are expected to strive continuously for a better deal for employees in respect of monetary rewards, working conditions and control over the work situations. The involvement of trade unions in the affairs of the larger community and social and economic policies at various levels is also important in the present situation.

REFERENCES

Breman, Jan (2002): 'Communal Upheaval as Resurgence of Social Darwinism', *Economic and Political Weekly*, 20 April.

Datt, Ruddar (2009): 'Spread of Indian Trade Unions', *Mainstream*, 2 May.

Giri, V.V. (1958): *Labour Problem in Indian Industry* (Bombay: Asian Publishing House).

Sankaranarayanan, K.C. and V. Karunakaran (1985): *Kerala Economy* (New Delhi: IBH).

Gooptu, Nandini (2007): 'Economic Liberalisation, Work and Democracy', *Economic and Political Weekly*, 21 May.

Misra, Swetha (2004): 'Globalisation and Gender Issues in India', in Govind Prasad and Anil Datta Misra (ed.): *Globalisation: Myth and Reality* (New Delhi: Concept).

Murali (2003): *Thozhilinte Maranam* (*Death of Job*) (Thiruvananthapuram: Melin Books).

Reddy, Narasimha D. (2003): 'Economic Globalisation, Past and Present', in K.S. Jomo and Khoo Khay Jin (eds.): *Globalisation and its Discontents, Revisited* (New Delhi: Tulika).

Sidhu, A.S. and C.S. Cheema (1999): 'Economic Reforms in India: An Evaluation', in P.P. Arya and B.B. Tandon (eds.): *Multinationals vs Swadeshi Today* (New Delhi: Deep and Deep).

Bibliography

Ackroyd, S, G. Burrell, M. Hugh and A. Whitaker (1998): 'The Japanization of the British Industry', *Industrial Relations Journal*, 19 (1).

AIRSF (1996): *Naxalbari is Not Just the Name of a Village! (Twenty Five Years of the Naxalite Movement)* (Calcutta: An AIRSF Publication, Published by Chandan Roy).

Akalank Publications (1991): *Reservations for Backward Classes: Mandal Commission Report of the Backward Classes Commission, 1980* (New Delhi: Akalank Publications).

Alam, Mohammad J. (1996): *Bihar Ka Aarthik Vikas: Samasya Aur Samadhan* (in Hindi) (Patna: Bihar State Council, Communist Party of India).

Alexander, K.C. (1972): *Participative Management: The Indian Experience* (New Delhi: Shri Ram Centre for Industrial Relations and Human Resources).

Anjaria, J.S. (2006): 'Street Hawkers and Public Space in Mumbai', *Economic and Political Weekly*, 41 (21): 2140-6.

Antony, Francis Cyril (ed.) (1982): *Gazetteer of India: Union Territory of Pondicherry*, vol. 1, Pondicherry.

Appeal Against BIFR's order dated 21-3-2006 in Case no. 218/87, Appeal nos. 103/06, 125/06, 154/06 & 157/06 addressed to AAIFR (KEU *vs.* BIFR & Ors).

Appellate Authority for Industrial & Financial Reconstruction (AAIFR) (2006): New Delhi, Order no. 18906 dated 18- 9-2006 on appeal nos. 103/2006, 154/2006 & 157/ 2006 (KEU *vs.* BIFR & Ors)

Baker, K. and K. Christensen (1998): *Contingent Work: American Employment Relations in Transition* (New York: Cornell University Press).

Banerjee, Anjana (2010): *Working Class Movement* (Delhi: Global Vision Publishing House).

Banerjee, Sumanta (1980): *In the Wake of Naxalbari: A History of the Naxalite Movement* (Calcutta: Subarnarekha).

———(1984): *India's Simmering Revolution: The Naxalite Uprising* (London: Zed Books).

Baumohl, Bernard (1993): 'When Downsizing Becomes Dumb Sizing', *Time Magazine*, 15 March 1993.

Beck, U. (1992): *Risk Society: Towards a New Modernity* (London: Sage).

Bhatia, Bela (2005): 'The Naxalite Movement in Central Bihar', *Economic and Political Weekly*, 40 (15): 1536-49.

Best, M. (1990): *The New Competition* (Cambridge: Harvard University Press).

Best, Michael H. (1990): *The New Competition: Institutions of Industrial Restructuring* (Oxford: Polity Press).

Beynan, H. (1973): *Working for Ford* (Harmondsworth: Penguin).

——— (1997): 'The Changing Practices of Work', in R.K. Brown (ed.): *The Changing Shape of Work* (Basingstoke: Macmillan).

Bhowmik, S.K. and N. More (2001): 'Coping with Urban Poverty', *Economic and Political Weekly*, 37(35): 4822-7.

Blanchard, Gordon and Rizwanul Islam (2001): *East Asia Labour Markets* (Geneva: ILO).

Blanchard, K., J.P. Carlos and A. Randolph (1999): *The Three Keys to Empowerment* (San Francisco: Berret-Koehler).

Boal, A. (1979): *Theatre of the Oppressed* (London: Pluto).

Bootle, R. (1996): *The Death of Inflation* (London: Nicholas Brealey).

——— (2001): *Money for Nothing* (London: Oxford University Press).

Boquérat, Gilles (2004): 'France's Political Interaction with India through the *Quai d'Orsay* Archives 1947-1972', in Max-Jean Zins and Gilles Boquérat (eds.), *India in the Mirror of Foreign Diplomatic Archives* (New Delhi: Manohar).

Bound, J. and G. Johnson (1992): 'Changes in the Structure of Wages in the 1980s: An Evaluation of Alternative Explanation', *American Economic Review* 82: 371-92.

Board for Industrial and Financial Reconstruction (BIFR) (1988): *Sanctioned Scheme: Kamani Tubes Limited*: no. 218/1987, Kurla, 1988.

——— (2006) Case no. 218/87: Kamani Tubes Limited, Bench-1, *Summary Records of the Proceedings of the Hearing Held on 21-3-2006 Before S/ Shri Ravindra Gupta, Chairman and A.K. Goswami, Member,* Reference no. 02/8/87-Bench-II, dated 31-3-2006.

——— Corrigendum dated 16 October 2007 on Case no. 218/1987.

Breman, Jan (1996): *Footloose Labour in India's Informal Economy* (Cambridge University Press).

——— (2002): 'Communal Upheaval as Resurgence of Social Darwinism' *Economic and Political Weekly,* April 20.

Broadbent, J. et al. (1998): 'The End of Profession?', in J. Broadbent, M. Dietrich and J. Robert (eds), *The End of Profession?: The Restructuring of Professional Work* (London: Routledge).

Brown, C. et al. (1993): 'Becoming a High Performance Work Organization: The Role of Security, Employee Involvement and Training', *International Journal of Human Resource Management*, 4, 2: 247-5.

Brown, Philip, Andy Green and Hugh Lauder (2001): *High Skills* (New York: Oxford University Press).

Brown, R.K. (1997): 'Flexibility and Security: Contradictions in the

Contemporary Labour Market', in Brown (ed.), *The Changing Shape of Work* (Basingstoke: Macmillan).

Burke, R.J. and C.L. Cooper (2000): *The Organization in Crisis: Downsizing, Restructuring and Privatization* (Oxford: Blackwell Publishers).

Burgess, S. and H. Rees (1996): 'Job Tenure in Britain 1975-92', *The Economic Journal*, 106: 334-44.

Cadene, Philippe and Mark Holmstrom (1998): *Decentralized Production in India* (New Delhi: Sage).

Caplinsky, R. (1993): 'Is Flexible Production Relevant to Less Developed Countries', *OECD Development Center Working Paper* (Paris: OECD)

Cappelli, P. et al. (1997): *Change at Work* (New York: Oxford University Press).

Cappelli, P. (1995): 'Rethinking Employment', *British Journal of Industrial Relations*, 33, 34: 563-602.

Castells, Manuel & Alejandro Portes (1989): 'World Underneath: The Origins, Dynamics and Effects of the Informal Economy', in Alejandro Portes et al. (eds.), *In the Informal Economy: Studies in Advanced and Less Developed Countries* (Baltimore: John Hopkins University Press).

Census of India (Bihar) (2001a): *Census of India (Bihar), Paper-I of 2001, Series-11, Provisional Population Totals* (Bihar: Director of Census Operations).

——— (2001b): *Census of India (Bihar), Paper-II of 2001, Series-11, Provisional Population Totals, Rural-Urban Population Totals* (Bihar: Director of Census Operations).

——— (2001c): *Census of India, 2001, Bihar, Paper-III of 2001, Series-11, Provisional Population Totals, Distribution of Workers and Non-Workers* (Bihar: Director of Census Operations).

Centre for Development Studies (1975): *Poverty, Unemployment and Development Policy: A Case Study of Selected Issues with Reference to Kerala* (Chennai: Orient Longman).

Chakrabarty, Sreemati (1990): *China and Naxalites* (New Delhi: Radiant).

Chandra, Jagdish (2003): 'The Return of the Working Class', *Socialism Today*, no. 76, July-August, London.

Chandrasekhar, C.P., V.K. Ramachandran and R. Ramakumar (2001), 'Issues in School Education in Contemporary Kerala', A report prepared for UNICEF, New Delhi.

Chatrath, K.J.S. (1994): *India in the Debates of French Parliament* (Delhi: Indian Publishers Distributors).

Chetty, Y. Narayana (2004): *Dynamics of Trade Unionism in India: Sociological Approach* (New Delhi: Anmol).

Choudhary, Prasanna Kumar and Srikant (2001): *Bihar Mein Samajik Parivartan Ke Kuchh Ayam* (in Hindi), 1st edn. (New Delhi: Vani).

Christopherson, Susan (1987): 'Workforce Flexibility: Implications for Women Workers', *ISSR Working Paper* 3 (2).

Clarke, J. and J. Newman (1997): *The Managerial State* (London: Sage).

Cohen, Jean L. (1985): 'Strategy or Identity: New Theoretical Paradigms and Contemporary Social Movements', *Social Research*, 52 (4).

Collinson, D. and M. Collinson (1995): 'Corporate Liposuction and the Re-Masculinisation of Management', Keynote address at *Gender and Life in Organizations Conference*, University of Portsmouth.

Confederation of British Industry (1996): *Flexible Labour Markets* (London: CBI).

Conrow, T. and L. Delp (1999): 'Teaching Organising through Workers' Experiences', *Labor Studies Journal*, 24(1): 42-57.

Cooper, C.L. and R.J. Burke (2002): 'Introduction: The New World of Work', in Cooper and Burke (ed.): *The New World of Work* (Oxford: Blackwell).

Cooper, R. (1995): *When Lean Enterprises Collide* (Boston: Harvard Business School Press).

Crouch, C. (1997): 'Skill Based Full Employment: the Latest Philosopher's Stone', *The British Journal of Industrial Relations*, 35, 3: 367-84.

CWM (1999): *Potential for Workers Cooperatives as a Tool for Revival of Sick Industries: An Analytical Study of Kamani Tubes Limited and KMA Limited* (Monograph), (New Delhi: Centre for Workers Management January).

Danford, Andy (1999): *Management Techniques and British Workers* (London: Mansell).

Das, Arvind N. (1983): *Agrarian Unrest and Socio-Economic Change in Bihar: 1900-1980* (New Delhi: Manohar).

——— (1992): *The Republic of Bihar* (Delhi: Penguin Books).

——— (1997): 'Bihar: A Worms Eye View', paper presented at the International Conference on 'Bihar in the World and the World in Bihar', An Interdisciplinary Workshop on and in Bihar, 16-19 December, Patna, organized by the Asian Development Research Institute (ADRI), Patna, and the European Science Foundation, France.

Das, K. and Panayiotopoulos (1996): 'Flexible Specialization: New Paradigm for Industrialization for Developing Countries', *Economic and Political Weekly*, 31 (52): 57-61, 28 December.

Datt, Ruddar (2008): 'Emergin Trends in Trade Union Movement' , *Mainstream*, 46(20), 3 May.

——— (2009): 'Spread of Indian Trade Unions', *Mainstream*, 47(20), 7-11, 33, 2 May.

Davis, M. (2000): *Magical Urbanism: Latinos Reinvent the US Big City* (London: Verso).

Derrick, P. and Phipps, J.F. (1969): *Co-Ownership, Co-Operation and Control: An Industrial Objective* (London: Longmans).

Deshpande, Sudha, Guy Standing and Lalit Deshpande (1998): *Labour Flexibility in a Third World Metropolis: A Case Study of Bombay* (New Delhi: Commonwealth Publishers).

Deshpande, Sudha and L.K. Deshpande (2002): 'Reform and Labour Market in India', *Reform and Employment* (New Delhi: Concept).

Deshpande, Lalit et al. (2004): *Liberalization and Labour: Labour Flexibility in Manufacturing* (New Delhi: Institute for Human Development).

de Vriese, M. (2006): *Refugee Livelihoods: A Review of the Evidence* (Geneva: United Nations High Commissioner for Refugees).

Dex, S. and McCulloch (1997): *Flexible Employment* (Basingstoke: Macmillan).

du Gay, P. (1996): *Consumption and Identity at Work* (London: Sage).

Dickinson, James (1986): *From Poor Law to Social Insurance: The Periodisation of State Intervention in the Reproduction Process* (London: Routledge).

Diwan, Ritu (2004): 'Captive Workers in Captive Small Scale Factories', *Indian Journal of Labour Economics*, vol. 47, no. 4: 1039-52.

Dua, Aarti (1993): 'A Management Guru for the Workers', *The Hindu*, 19 October.

Dutta, Kanika (1993): 'A Break with Tradition', *Business Standard*, 6 January.

Economic and Political Weekly (2008): 'Widening Debate on the Naxalite Movement', 43(19): 5-6.

The Economist (2005): 'The Great Job Switch', 1-7 October.

Edona, E.J. (1940): *The Economic Condition of the Protestant Christians in Malabar with Special Reference to the Basel Mission Church* (Calicut: Empire Press).

Edwards, P., M. Collinson and C. Reese (1998): 'The Determinants of Employee Responses to Total Quality Management: Six Case Studies', *Organization Studies*, Cochan and Osterman, pp. 449-75.

Elliot, L. and D. Atkinson (1998): *The Age of Insecurity* (London: Verso).

Engberg, E. (1993): 'Union Responses to the Contingent Work Force', in D.S. Cobble (ed.): *Women in Union: Forging a Partnership* (Ithaca, New York: ILR Press).

Faber, H. (1993): 'The Incidence and the Cost of Job Loss 1982-91', Bookings Papers on Economic Activity, *Microeconomics*, pp. 73-132.

Fallon, P. and R. Lucas (1991): 'Impact of Changes in Job Security Regulation in India and Zimbawe', *World Bank Economic Review*, vol. 5, no. 3: 121-34.

Felstead, A. et al. (1998): 'Insecurity at Work: Is Job Insecurity Really Much Worse than Before', *New Economy*-5: 180-4.

Forrester, P. (1994): 'Flexibility, Politics and Strategy: In Defence of the Model of the Flexible Firm', *Work Employment and Society*, vol. 8, no. 2: 221-42.

Frank, Thomas (2004): *What's the Matter with Kansas?* (New York: Metropolitan Owl).

Franke, Richard W. (1993): *Life is a Little Better: Redistribution as a Development Strategy in Nadur Village, Kerala*, Conflict and Social Change Series (Boulder and Oxford: Westview Press).

Freire, P. (1970): *Pedagogy of the Oppressed* (R.M.B. Ramos) (New York: Continuum).

Gallie, D. and M. White et al. (1998): *Restructuring the Employment Relationship* (New York: Oxford University Press).

Gandhi, Mahatma (1983): *The Collected Works of Mahatma Gandhi, LXXXIX (August 1, 1947-November 10, 1947)* (Delhi: Publication Division, Government of India).

Garrhan, P. and T. Stewart (1992): *The Nissan Enigma: Flexibility at Work in Local Economy* (London: Mansell).

George, Jose (1984): *Politicisation of Agricultural Workers in Kerala* (Calcutta: K.P. Bagchi & Company).

——— (1992): *Unionisation and Politicisation of Peasants and Agricultural Labourers in India (With Special Reference to Kerala)* (New Delhi: Commonwealth).

George, Jose, Manoj Kumar and Avinash Khandare (eds.) (2009): *Rethinking Radicalism in Indian Society: Bhagat Singh and Beyond* (Jaipur: Rawat).

Ghanashyam Shah (2004): *Social Movements in India* (New Delhi: Sage).

Ghosh, Sankar (1974): *The Naxalite Movement: A Maoist Experiment* (Calcutta: Firma KL Mukhopadhyay).

Giri, V.V. (1969): *Labour Problems in Indian Industry* (Bombay: Asia Publishing House).

Giriappa, S. (1987): *Beedi Rolling in Rural Development* (Delhi: Dayal Publishing House).

Goddard, J. (1998): 'Review of Change at Work', *British Journal of Industrial Relations*, 36, 3: 501-3.

Gokak, A.V. (1998): *Industrial Sickness* (Delhi: BRPC).

Gooptu, Nandini (2007): 'Economic Liberalisation: Work and Democracy', *Economic and Political Weekly*, 21 May.

Gopal, Vishnu (1984): *Industrial Democracy in India (A Sociological Study of Workers' Participation in Management)* (New Delhi: Chugh Publications).

Gough, Kathleen (1970): 'Palakkara: Social and Religious Change in Central Kerala', in K. Ishwaran (ed.), *Change and Continuity in India's Villages* (New York: Columbia University Press).

Government of Bihar, *Bihar: 1959-60: Facts and Figures*, Published by the Department of Public Relations.

Government of India, *Economic Survey 2001-2002*, Ministry of Finance, Economic Division.

Gray, J. (1995): 'The Undoing of Conservatism', in J. Gray (ed.): *Enlightenment Wake: Politics and Culture at the end of the Modern Age* (London: Routledge).

Guardialo-Rivera, O. (2010): 'What Comes after Sovereignty?', *Law, Culture and the Humanities*, 6(2): 185-207.

Guest, David (1997): 'Towards Jobs and Justice in Europe: A Research Agenda', *Industrial Relations Journal*, 28, 4: 344-52.

——— (2000): 'Management and the Insecure Workforce', in Edmund Heery and John Salmon (eds.): *The Insecure Workforce* (London: Routledge).

Gupta, B.D. (1974): *The Naxalite Movement* (New Delhi, Allied).

Gupta, Tilak D. (1992): 'Yadav Ascendancy in Bihar Politics', *Economic and Political Weekly*, 27 (26), 1304-6.

Habib, S.I. (2010): *To Make the Deaf Hear: Ideology and Programme of Bhagat Singh and his Comrades* (New Delhi: Three Essays Collective).

Hargreaves, P. and Peter Jarvis (1998): *The Human Resource Development Handbook* (London: Kogan Page).

Harvey, David (1993): 'Class Relations, Social Justice and Politics of Difference', in Michael and Pile (eds.): *Place and Politics of Identity* (London: Routledge).

Harris, N (1995): 'The Reproduction of Labour Force', in N. Harris (ed.): *The New Untouchables: Immigration and the new World Worker* (London: Tauris Publishers).

Heery, Edmund and John Salmon (2000): 'The Insecurity Thesis', in Heery Edmund and Salmon John (eds), *The Insecure Workforce* (London: Routledge).

Heery, Edmund and Brian Abbott (2000): 'Trade Unions and the Insecure Workforce', in Edmund and John (eds.): *The Insecure Workforce.*

High Court, Delhi, Order Number 706 dated 4 July 2006.

The Hindustan Times (1996: '7 MCC Men Gunned Down in Aurangabad', Patna edition 23 January).

——— (1996): 'Naxalites were Killed After They Surrendered: PUCL', 2 July.

——— (1997): 'PU Activists Attack Jehanabad Outpost', 10 October.

Holmstrom, B.R. and J. Tirole (1989): 'The Theory of the Firm', in R. Schmalensee and R.D. Willig (eds.): *Handbook of Industrial Organization* (Amsterdam: North Holland).

Horst, C. (2001): 'Vital Links in Social Security: Somali Refugees in the Dadaab Camps, Kenya', *New Issues in Refugee Research, Working Paper No. 38* (Geneva: United Nations High Commissioner for Refugees).

Hutton, W. (1995): *The State We're In* (London: Johnathan Cape).

Hyman, Jeff and Bob Mason (1994): *Managing Employee Involvement and Participation* (London: Sage).

Hyman, R. (1972): *Strikes* (Glasgow: Fontana).

ILO–FAAT (1996): *Indian Economic Reforms and Labour Policy* (New Delhi: ILO-FAAT).

ILO (2005): *World Employment Report 2004-05* (Geneva: ILO).

The Indian Express (Mumbai) (2002): 'Most States Move Forward, Bihar Slips Out of Growth Radar', 24 April.

Isaac, T.M. Thomas (1983): *Class Struggle and Transition to Specifically Capitalist Form of Production: Some Conclusions of a Study of Coir industry in Kerala,* Social Scientist, Issue no. 127.

Issac, T.M. Thomas, Richard W. Franke, Pyaralal Raghavan (1998): *Democracy at Work in an Indian Industrial Cooperative: The Story of Kerala Dinesh Beedi* (London: Cornell University Press).

Isaac, Thomas T.M. and R. Ramakumar (2011): 'Kerala: An Agenda for Sustainable, Equitable and Rapid Growth', in T. M. Thomas Isaac (ed.): *Kerala: Towards a Development Agenda* (New Delhi: Sage).

Iyer, V.R. Krishna (1981): 'Foreword' in K. Saradamoni: *Divided Poor: Study of a Kerala Village* (New Delhi: Ajanta).

Jacobs, J. (1961): *The Death and Life of Great American Cities* (New York: Vintage).

Jarvis, Peter (2000): 'The Age of Learning', in Peter Jarvis (ed.): *Continuing Education at the University of Surrey* (London: Oxford University Press)..

Jawaid, Sohail (1979): *The Naxalite Movement in India: Origin and Failure of the Maoist Revolutionary Strategy in West Bengal 1967-1971* (New Delhi: Associated Publishing House).

J. Burrange Publications (2001): *Freedom Movement in French India: The Mahe Revolt of 1948,* (Tellicherry: IRISH).

Jennings, Kent M. (1964): *Community Influential* (London: Oxford University Press).

John Tomilson (2002): 'Vicious and Benign Universalism', in Frans J. Schurman (ed.), *Globalisation and Development Studies: Challenges for the 21st Century* (New Delhi: Vistaar).

Johri, J.C. (1972): *Naxalite Politics in India* (Delhi: Indian Institute of Constitutional and Parliamentary Studies).

Jose, A.V. (ed.) (2002), *Organised Labour in the 21st Century* (Geneva: International Institute of Labour Studies)

Kalhan, A. (2004): 'Life Long Learning for What?', in *Teachers of the World*, July-September, vol. 5, no. 7.

Kamalasanan, N.K. (1993): *Kuttanad and the Agricultural Labourers Movement* (in Malayalam), (Trivandrum: Chinta Publishers).

Kannan, C. (1993): *Beedi Industry in Kerala and Benefits Achieved by the Beedi Workers* (Kannur: Cooperative Press).

Karanth, G.K. (1996): 'Caste in Contemporary Rural India', in M.N. Srinivas (ed.): *Caste: Its Twentieth Century Avatar* (New Delhi: Penguin Books).

Karat, Prakash (1976): 'The Peasant Movement in Malabar, 1930-40', *Social Scientist*, 5 (3), September.

——— (1977): 'Organised Struggles of the Malabar Peasantry, 1934-40', *Social Scientist*, 5 (6-7), March.

Kelly, J. (1997), 'Industrial Relation: Looking to the Future', *British Journal of Industrial Relations*, 33, 3: 393-8.

Kenny, M. and T. Florida (1993): *Beyond Mass Production the Japanese System and its Transfer to the USA* (New York: Oxford University Press).

Kolko, Joyce (2000): 'Restructuring the Working Classes', in Harry Dahms (ed.): *Transformations of Capitalism* (London: Macmillan Press).

Krishnamurthy, B. (ed.) (2006): *India and France—Past, Present and Future*, (Pondicherry: Centre for Nehru Studies, Pondicherry University).

——— (1991): *Frenchindia Vidhthalai Porattam* (*Freedom Movement in French India* (in Tamil)) (Pondicherry).

Kundu, A. (1993): 'Urban Informal Sector: An Overview of Macro Dimensions, Socio-Economic Correlates and Policy Perspectives in India', in H. Nagamine (ed.): *Urban Informal Sector Employment: A Cross National Comparison Study* (Nagoya, Japan: Institute for Regional Planning and Development).

——— (1993): 'Trends and Patterns of Female Employment in India: A Case of Organized Informalization', *Indian Journal of Labour Economics*, vol. 40, no. 3, July-September: 1785-93.

Lane, C. (1990): 'Vocational Training, Employment Training and New Production Concepts: Some Lessons for Britain', *International Review Journal*, 21, 4: 247-59.

Legge, K. (1998): 'Flexibility: The Gift-wrapping of Employment, Degradation', in P. Sparrow and M. Marchington (eds.): *Human Resource Management: The New Agenda* (London: Pitman Publishing).

Leisink, P. (1997): 'New Union Constituency Call for Differentiated Agenda and Democratic Participation', *Transfer*, 3: 534-50.

Louis, Prakash (2002): *People's Power: The Naxalite Movement in Central Bihar* (Delhi: Wordsmith).

Luttwak, E. (1994): 'Why Fascism is the Wave of the Future', *London Review of Book*, 7 April: 3, 6.

Latack, J.C. and R.B. Dozier (1986): 'After the Axe Falls: Job Loss as a Career Transition', *Academy of Management Review*, 11: 375-92.

Machiavello, M. (2003): 'Forced Migrants as an Under-utilised Asset: Refugee Skills, Livelihoods and Achievements in Kampala, Uganda', *New Issues in Refugee Research*, Working Paper No. 95 (Geneva: United Nations High Commissioner for Refugees).

Mannan, M.A. (1987): *Workers' Participation in Managerial Decision-Making (A Study in a Developing Country)* (New Delhi: Daya Publishing House).

Martin, Carnoy (1999): 'The Family, Flexible Work and Social Cohesion at Risk', *International Labour Review*, vol. 138, no. 4: 411-29.

Masilamani, S. (1993): 'Trade Unions on Defensive', *Sunday Observer*, 21 April.

Mayer, Adrian (1952): *Land and Society in Malabar* (London: Oxford University Press).

Meisiek, S. and D. Barry (2007): 'Through the Looking Glass of Organisational Theatre: Analogically Mediated Inquiry in Organisations', *Organisation Studies*, 28(12): 1805-27.

Melucci, Alberto (1989): *Nomads of the Present: Social Movements and Individual Needs in Contemporary Society* (London: Temple University Press).

Mencher, Joan (1980): 'The Lessons and Non-Lessons of Kerala: Agricultural Labourers and Poverty', *Economic and Political Weekly*, 15 (41-43): 1781-1802.

Mhaskar, Sumeet Ramdas (2006): 'Labour Movement in the Context of Liberalisation: A Case Study of Mumbai Textile Industry', M.Phil. dissertation submitted to the Centre for Political Studies, School of Social Sciences, Jawaharlal Nehru University.

Mirza, Masood A. (1982): *Workers Participation in Management in India and Abroad* (Aligarh: Printwell).

Misra, Swetha (2004): 'Globalisation and Gender Issues in India', in Govind Prasad and Anil Datta Misra (ed.): *Globalisation: Myth and Reality* (New Delhi: Concept).

Mitchell, M.F. (2005): 'Specialisation and the Skill Premium in the 20th Century', *International Economic Review*, vol. 46, August: 935-55.

Mohan, Sanal (1999): 'Dalit Discourse and the Evolving New Self: Contest and Strategies', *Review of Development and Change*, 4 (1): 1-24.

Mohanty, Manoranjan (1977): *Revolutionary Violence: A Study of the Maoist Movement in India* (New Delhi: Sterling).

Mukherjee (2004): 'Informal Manufacturing Sector in India: Pre- and Post-Reform Growth Dynamics', *Indian Journal of Labour Economics*, vol. 47, no. 2: 293-310.

Mukherjee, K. and R.S. Yadav, (1980): *Bhojpur: Naxalism in the Plains of Bihar* (Delhi: Radhakrishna).

Munck, Ronald (2002): *Globalization and Labour* (New Delhi: Madhyam Books).

Murali (2003): *Thozhilinte Maranam* (*Death of Job*) (Thiruvananthapuram: Melin Books).

Nagamine, H. (1993): *Urban Informal Sector Employment: A Cross National Comparative Study* (Nagoya: Research Institute for Planning and Development).

——— (2004): *Urban Informal Sector Employment: A Cross National*

Comparative Study (Nagoya: Research Institute for Regional Planning and Development).

Nagraj, R. (1994): 'Employment and Wages in Manufacturing Industry: Trends, Hypothesis and Evidence', *Economic and Political Weekly*, vol. 29, no. 4, 22 January: 177-86.

——— (2004): 'Fall in the Organized Employment a Brief Note', *Economic and Political Weekly*, 24 July: 3387-90.

Nair, Adoor, K.K. Ramachandran (1986): *Slavery in Kerala* (New Delhi: Mittal).

Nair, K. Ramachandran (2006): *The History of Trade Union Movement in Kerala* (Delhi: Manak).

Namboodiripad, E.M.S. (1940): Dissenting Note in *Report of the Malabar Tenancy Committee-1940*, Government of Madras, Madras, reprinted in *Selected Writings*, vol. 2 (Calcutta: National Book Agency).

——— (1981): 'Once Again on Castes and Classes', *Social Scientist*, 9 (12): 12-25.

Nandwani, Deepali and Anamika Rath (1991): 'No Longer a Workforce to Reckon with?', *Sunday Observer*, 16 February.

Narayan, Laxmi (1984): *Worker's Participation in Public Enterprises (A Macro and Micro-Level Survey and Report of a National Seminar)* (Bombay: Himalaya Publishing House).

Narasimha Reddy, D. (2003): 'Economic Globalisation, Past and Present' in K.S. Jomo and Khoo Khay Jin (ed.): *Globalisation and its Discontents, Revisited* (New Delhi: Tulika).

National Archives of India (NAI): 463-X/Secret/1936 and NAI.313-X/ Secret/36, Government of India—Foreign and Political Department.

Nayanar, E.K. (1982): *My Struggles: An Autobiography* (New Delhi: Vikas).

Nehru, Jawaharlal (1983): *India's Foreign Policy Selected Speeches, September 1946–April 1961*, 2nd rpt. (New Delhi: The Publication Division, Ministry of Information and Broadcasting, Government of India).

Neogy, Ajit K. (1997): Decolonisation of French India: Liberation Movement and Indo-French Relations 1947-1954 (Pondicherry: Institut Françaife de Pondichéry).

Nickell, Stephen, Patricia Jones and Leanda Quintini (2002): 'Picture of Job Insecurity Facing British Men', *The Economic Journal of Royal Economic Society*, vol. 112, no. 476: 542-55.

Nolan, J.P., I.C. Wichert and B.J. Burchell (2000): 'Job Insecurity, Psychological Well-Being and Family Life', in Heery and John (eds.), *Insecure Work Force*.

Nossiter, T.J. (1982): *Communism in Kerala* (New Delhi: Oxford University Press).

NTUI (n.d.): *Worker Cooperatives: A Force Resisting Industrial Closure: A*

Case Study of Kamani Tubes Ltd., and KMA Ltd. (New Delhi: New Trade Union Initiative).

OECD (1997): *Employment Outlook* (Paris: Organization for Economic Cooperation and Development).

Oliver, N. and B. Wilkinson (1992): *The Japanization of British Industry* (Oxford: Blackwell).

Ozaki, Muneto (1999): *Negotiating Flexibility: The Role of the Social Partner and the State* (Geneva: ILO).

Palande, P.S. (1991): *Revival of Kamani Tubes Limited* (a report) (Pune: Indian School of Political Economy).

Pandey, Sachchidanand (1985): *Naxal Violence: A Socio-Political Study* (Delhi: Chanakya).

Pandhe, M.K. (2006): 'Judicial Despotism and the Working Class', *People's Democracy,* 30(36), 3 September.

Panickar, G.K. (1974): *The Story of Kerala Dinesh Beedi: A Thrilling Experience* (Canannore: Kerala Dinesh Beedi).

——— (1988): *Dinesh Beedi, Sanghengalude Valarchayila Durgada Gathangalum, Vidhinirnaya Sambavangalum* (in Malyalam) (Kannur: Kerala Dinesh Beedi Society Publications).

Panikkar, K.N. (1978): 'Agrarian Legislation and Social Classes: A Case Study of Malabar', *Economic and Political Weekly,* 13 (21).

Parayil, Govindan (ed.) (2000): *Kerala Development Experience: Reflections on Sustainability and Replicability* (London: Zed Books).

Piore, N. and C. Sable (1984): *The Second Industrial Divide* (New York: Basic Books).

Polanyi, Karl (1957): *The Great Transformation* (Boston: Beacon Press).

Popali, S.L. (ed.) (1959): *Selected Documents on Asian Affairs: India 1947-1950,* vol. II (Bombay: Oxford University Press).

Prasad, B.N. (2002): *Radicalism and Violence in Agrarian Structure: The Maoist Movement in Bihar* (New Delhi: Manak).

Prasad, Ch. S. Durga (1995): *Workers' Participation in Management* (New Delhi: Discovery Publishing House).

Prasad, Jagdish (2000): *Nav Bihar: Ek Bhavishya Nirupam* (in Hindi) (Patna: Patel Foundation).

Prasad, Pradhan H. (1994): 'Poor Peasant Movement in Central Bihar', in K.K. Sharma et al. (eds.): *Peasant Struggles in Bihar: 1931-1992: Spontaneity to Organisation* (Patna: Centre for Peasant Studies).

Pratt, G. and C. Johnston (2007): 'Turning Theatre into Law and Other Spaces of Politics', *Cultural Geographies,* 14 (1): 92-113.

Radhakrishnan, P. (1989): *Peasant Struggles, Land Reforms, and Social Change: Malabar 1836-1982* (New Delhi: Sage).

Raj, K.N. and P.K. Micheal Tharakan (1983): 'Agrarian Reform in Kerala and its Impact on the Rural Economy: A Preliminary Assessment', in Ajit Kumar Ghose (ed.): *Agrarian Reform in Contemporary Developing*

Countries (London and New York: Croom Helm and St. Martin's Press).

Raj Kumar, N.V. (1951): *The Problem of French India* (New Delhi: Novin Press).

——— (ed.) (1952): *Background of India's Foreign Policy* (New Delhi: All India Congress Committee).

Ramasamy A. (1987): *History of Pondicherry* (New Delhi: Sterling Publishers).

Ramaswamy, E.A. (1992): 'Can Workers be Owners?', *Business India*, 30 March-12 April: 106.

——— (1993), 'A Glimmer of Hope', *Business India*, 27 September-10 October: 115-16.

——— (1998), 'Worker Cooperative in India: Lessons from Kamani', paper presented at the workshop held at the ICSSR, Vidyanagari, University of Mumbai, Mumbai, on 28 and 29 December on A Critical Analysis of Kamani Tubes Limited and KMA Limited.

Ramaswamy, K.V. (1999): 'The Search for Flexibility in Indian Manufacturing', *Economic and Political Weekly*, 34 (30), 6 February: 363-8.

Ramasrinivasan, R. (1998): *Karaikal in Freedom Struggle* (New York: PrintsAsia.com).

Ramachandran, V. K. (1996): 'On Kerala's Development Achievements', in Jean Dreze and Amartya Sen (eds.): *Indian Development: Selected Regional Perspectives* (New Delhi: Oxford University Press).

Ramakumar, R. (2005): 'Socioeconomic Characteristics of Agricultural Workers: A Case Study in the Malabar Region of Kerala', Ph.D. thesis submitted to the Indian Statistical Institute, Kolkata.

Ram, Mohan (1971): *Maoism in India* (Delhi: Vikas).

Ranjan, Sudhansu (1997): 'A Mystery Called Bihar', paper presented at the International Conference on 'Bihar in the World and the World in Bihar', An Interdisciplinary Workshop on and in Bihar, 16-19 December, organized by the Asian Development Research Institute (ADRI), Patna, and European Science Foundation, France.

Rao, Purnima and S.T. Sawant (eds.) (1993): *New Economic Policy: Problems and Alternatives* (New Delhi: Friedrich Ebert Stiftung).

Ratnam, C.S. Venkata (2006): *Industrial Relations* (New Delhi: Oxford University Press).

Ratnam, Venkata, Gerd Batterwack and Pravin Sinha (eds.) (1994): *Labour and Unions in a Period of Transition* (New Delhi: Friedrich Ebert Stiftung).

Ray R. and M. Fainsod (ed.) (2005): *Social Movement in India: Poverty Power and Politics* (New York: Oxford University Press).

Reddy, K. Venugopal (2006): 'Against the Colonial State: Working Class in India's Struggle for Freedom, 1939-1941', *The Indian Historical Review*, 33 (2), July: 112-33.

——— (2010): 'Working Class in "Quit India" Movement: Madras Presidency, 1942', *The Indian Historical Review*, 37 (2), December: 275-89.

Rehman, M.M. (2007): *Operation of Welfare Fund for Beedi Workers in Madhya Pradesh: Profile, Problems and Prospects* (Noida: V.V. Giri National Labour Institute).

Robinson, P. (2000): 'Insecurity and the Flexible Workforce: Measuring the Ill Defined', in Heery and John (eds.): *The Insecure Workforce.*

Rogers, K.K. (1995): 'Experience and Structure of Alienation in Temporary Clerical Employment', *Work and Occupations* 22(2): 137-66.

Roy, Sudita (1998): 'Lags in Employment Adjustment and Inter-industry Differential. . . . an Analysis Using Dynamic Inter-related Factor Demand Function', Discussion Paper no. 199, IGIDR, Bombay.

Rousseau, D.M. (1996): 'Changing the Deal while Keeping the People', *Academy of Management Executive*, vol. 10: 50-61.

Sahu, Bhabatosh (1985): *Dynamics of Participatory Management: Indian Experiences* (Bombay: Himalaya Publishing House).

Sanjiv (1996): 'Naxalbari Ki Raah Par', *Samakalin Bahas* (in Hindi), an Irregular Journal (Patna: Rashtriya Press): 47-56.

Sankaranarayanan, K.C. and V. Karunakaran (1985): *Kerala Economy* (New Delhi: IBH).

Saradamoni, K. (1981): *Divided Poor: Study of a Kerala Village* (New Delhi: Ajanta).

Saroja Sundararajan (1985): *Glimpses of the History of Karaikal* (Madras: Lalitha).

Schmitz, H. (1989): 'Flexible Specialization: A New Paradigm of Small Scale Industrialization', *Institute of Development Studies*, Paper no. 324: 27-33.

Seabrook, Jeremy (1992): 'Kamani Tubes: A Hope for Workers', 1 June, NFS India.

Secombe, W. (1986): 'Marxism and Demography, Family, Economy and State: The Social Reproduction Process under Capitalism', in J. Dickinson and Bob Russell (eds.): *Social Welfare* (London: Routledge).

Sen, S. et al. (eds.) (1978): *Naxalbari and After: A Frontier Anthology*, vols. I & II (Calcutta: Kathashilp).

Sen, S.P. (1958): *The French in India 1763-1816* (Calcutta: K.L. Mukhopadhyay).

Seth, P.D. (1997): 'Revival of Sick Public Sector Undertakings and Board for Industrial and Financial Reconstruction: An Empirical Study' (an unpublished M.Phil. Dissertation), Indian Institute of Public Administration, New Delhi.

Shaikh, Juned (2005): 'Worker Politics, Trade Unions and the Shiv Sena's Rise in Central Bombay', *Economic and Political Weekly*, 30 April-6 May, vol. 40, no. 18: 1893-1900.

Sharan, Shankar S. (2005): 'A Prescription for Bihar's Rapid Development', *Mainstream*, 43 (6): 15-20.

Sharma, Alakh and S.K. Sasikumar (1996): *Structural Adjustments and Labour* (Noida: VV Giri National Labour Institute) (mimeo).

Sharma, A.N. et al. (eds) (1999): *Dynamics of Employment, Poverty and Human Development in Bihar* (New Delhi: Institute for Human Development).

Sharma, K.L. (1986): *Caste, Class and Social Movements* (Jaipur: Rawat).

Sharma, Pamela Smith (2000): *India: Globalization and Change* (London: Arnold, co-published by Oxford University Press, New York).

Shyam Sundar, K.R. (2003): 'Flexibility and Rigidity in Labour Market: Towards Balanced Prospective', *Journal of Indian School of Political Economy*, vol. 15.3: 679-88.

——— (2005): 'Labour Flexibility Debate in India', *Economic and Political Weekly*, vol. XL, no. 22, 23 May: 4-10.

Sidhu, A.S. and C.S. Cheema (1999): 'Economic Reforms in India: An Evaluation', in P.P. Arya and B.B. Tandon (ed.): *Multinationals* vs *Swadeshi Today* (New Delhi: Deep and Deep).

Silver, B.J. (2003): *Forces of Labour: Cambridge Studies in Comparative Politics* (Cambridge: Cambridge University Press).

Singh, D.K. (1995): *Agrarian Transformation* (Jaipur: Rawat).

Singh, Joginder (2006): 'CRPF's Raising Crack Force Against Naxals', *South Asia Politics*, 4 (12): 29-30.

Singh, Kulbir (1990), 'Workers Participation: Welcome After Ground is Prepared', *Hindu*, 26 September.

Singh, Rajendra (2001): *Social Movements: Old and New, A Post Modernist Critique* (New Delhi: Sage).

Sinha, Arun (1997): 'Class War, Not Atrocities Against Harijans', *Economic and Political Weekly*, 12 (50): 2037-40.

Smith, D. (1997): *Job Insecurity versus Labour Market Flexibility* (London: Social Market Foundation).

Sood, Sabtosh (2007): 'Trade Unions and Political Parties in Punjab', in Harish K. Puri and Paramjit S. Judge, *Social and Political Movements* (Jaipur and New Delhi: Rawat).

Srinivas, Botlaguduru (1987): 'Deccan Textiles: A Case Study in Industrial Sickness', an unpublished M.Phil. Dissertation, Hyderabad, Department of Sociology and Anthropology, School of Social Sciences, University of Hyderabad.

Srinivas, B. (1993): *Worker Takeover in Industry: the Kamani Tubes Experiment* (New Delhi: Sage).

Srinivas, Ravi K. (1992): 'Underclass, Hi-Technology and Los Angeles Uprising', *Economic and Political Weekly*, 24-31 October: 2388.

Standing, Guy (1997): 'Globalization, Labour Flexibility and Insecurity: The

Era of Market Regulation', *European Journal of Industrial Relations*, 3, 1: 7-37.

——— (1999): *Global Labour Flexibility: Thinking Distributive Justice*, (London: Macmillan Press).

Stiglitz, J.E. (2002): 'Employment, Social Justice and Societal Well-being', *International Labour Review*, vol. 141, nos. 1-2: 9-29.

Stone, D. and M. de Vriese (2004): *Refugee Livelihoods: Livelihood Strategies and Options for Congolese Refugees in Gabon* (Geneva: United Nations High Commissioner for Refugees).

Stredwick, J. and Steve Ellis (1998): *Flexible Working Practices-Techniques and Innovations* (London: Institute of Personnel and Development).

Streeck, W. (1989): 'Skills and the Limits of Neo Liberalism: Enterprise of the Future as a Place of Learning', *Work Employment and Society* 3, 1: 89-104.

Subbaiah, V. (1990): *Saga of Freedom of French India* (*Testament of My Life*), (Madras: New Century Book House).

The Supreme Court order on BIFR Sanctioned Scheme Regarding Revival of Kamani Tubes Limited: A Synopsis, New Delhi, 1988.

Tabak, F. and M.A. Crichlow (2000): *Normalization: Process and Structure* (Baltimore and London: John Hopkins University Press).

Thankappan, D. (1992), 'Against All Odds', *Business Standard* (Calcutta edn.), 2 September.

Tharakan, P. K. Michael (1982): 'The Kerala Land Reforms (Amendment) Bill, 1979: A Note', in Sheo Kumar Lall (ed.), *Sociological Perspective of Land Reforms* (New Delhi: Agricole Publishers).

——— (2002): 'Land Relations in Kerala', in V.K. Ramachandran and Madhura Swaminathan (eds.): *Agrarian Studies: Essays on Agrarian Relations in Less-Developed Countries* (New Delhi: Tulika).

Thomas, C.P. (1995): 'We need a uniform floor wage', *The Economic Times*, 15 August.

Thomas, R. and A. Davies (2005): 'Theorising the Micro-politics of Resistance: New Public Management and Managerial Identities in the UK Public Services', *Organisation Studies*, 26 (5): 683-706.

Thompson, P. and S. Ackroyd (1995): 'All Quiet on the Workplace Front? A Critique of Recent Trends in British Industrial Sociology', *Sociology*, 29 (4): 615-33.

The Times of India (1996): 'Three BMP Jawans Killed in Naxal Attack', Patna edn., 16 June.

——— (1996): 'Naxalites Blow up Bihar MLA's House', 17 October.

——— (1997): 'Three BMP Jawans, ASI Killed in MCC Attack', 11 November.

Tripathi, et al. (1999): 'Bihar: A Geo-Political Spectrum', *Journal of Social and Economic Studies*, 14 (Combined Issue, 1997, New Series, Published in 1999 by A.N. Sinha Institute for Social Studies, Patna: 130-46.

UNHCR (2002): *A Human Rights Approach to Poverty Reduction Strategies* (Geneva: United Nations High Commissioner of Refugees).

Urmilesh (1999): *Bihar Ka Sach: Krishi-Sankat Aur Khetihar Sangharsh* (in Hindi), 3rd edn. (New Delhi: Prakashan Sansthan).

Vanek, Jan (1972): *The Economics of Workers Management: A Yugoslav Case Study* (London: George Allen & Unwin).

Varghese, Sheela (2003): *Employment of Women in Manufacturing Sector* (Jaipur: University Book House).

Varandani, Gursharan (n.d.): *Workers' Participation in Management: With Special Reference to India* (New Delhi: Deep and Deep).

Varma, Udayakumar, and M.M. Rehman (2005): *Tobacco Tendu Leaf and Beedi Workers in India: Problems and Prospects* (Noida: V.V. Giri National Labour Institute).

Venkatraman, C.S. (2004): *Negotiated Change, Collective Bargaining, Liberalization and Restructuring In India* (New Delhi/London: Response Books, Sage).

Virmani, B.R. (ed.) (1972): *Workers' Participation in Management (Proceedings of the Indo-German Seminar)* (Hyderabad: Administrative Staff College of India, and New Delhi: Embassy of Federal Republic of Germany).

Vishnubharateeyan (1980): *Adimakalengane Udamakalaayi* (*How did the Slaves Become Owners* (in Malyalam), (Trivandrum: Chinta Publishers).

Vision Mumbai (2003): 'Transforming Mumbai into a World-Class City: A Summary of Recommendations' (Mumbai: Bombay First and McKinsey & Company).

Vuuren, T.B. Klandermans et al. (1991): 'Employee Reactions to Job Insecurity', in J. Hartley, Jacobson et al. (eds.): *Job Insecurity: Coping With Jobs At Risk* (London: Sage).

Wayne, J. (1986): 'Function of Social Welfare in a Capitalist Economy', in Dickinson and Russell (eds.): *Social Welfare* (Routledge).

Wever, K. (1998): 'International Labour Revitalization: Enlarging the Playing Field', *Industrial Relations*, 37, 3: 388-407.

Wickham, J. (1997): 'Part-time Work in Ireland and Europe', *Work: Employment and Society*, 11, 1: 133-51.

Womack, J.P., D.T. Jone and D. Roos (1990): *The Machine that Changed the World: The Triumph of Lean Production* (New York: Dawson Mcmillan).

Wright, L.C. (1959): *The Power Elite* (New York: Oxford University Press).

Wright, Martin (2000): *Managing Competitive Prices* (Cambridge: Cambridge University Press).

Writ Petition Number of 2007 (KTL/syn2) in the High Court of Judicature at Bombay in its Ordinary Original Civil Jurisdiction (KEU *vs* AAIFR & Ors) under Article 226 of the Constitution of India.

Writ Petition no. 278 of 2007, High Court Bombay (KEU *vs.* AAIFR & Ors)

Yash, Chauhan (2001): *History of the Struggle of Beedi Workers in India* (New Delhi: N.M. Joshi Institute).

INTERNET SOURCES

Solow, Robert M. (2005): *What is Labour Market Flexibility?: What is it Good for?* Internet site www://. Britac.uk/pubs/src/keynes97/text.html.

Index